BACKLASH 9/11

# Backlash 9/11

Middle Eastern and Muslim Americans Respond

Anny Bakalian and Mehdi Bozorgmehr

**UNIVERSITY OF CALIFORNIA PRESS**  Berkeley  Los Angeles  London

University of California Press, one of the most distinguished university presses in the United States, enriches
lives around the world by advancing scholarship in the
humanities, social sciences, and natural sciences. Its
activities are supported by the UC Press Foundation
and by philanthropic contributions from individuals
and institutions. For more information, visit
www.ucpress.edu.

An earlier version of chapter 2 was published as
Mehdi Bozorgmehr and Anny Bakalian, "Post-9/11
Government Initiatives in Comparative and Historical
Perspectives," in From Arrival to Incorporation:
Migrants to the U.S. in a Global Era, ed. Elliot R.
Barkan, Hasia Diner, and Alan M. Kraut (New York:
New York University Press, 2008), 246–66.
    A very early version of parts of chapters 7 and 8
was published as Anny Bakalian and Mehdi
Bozorgmehr, "Muslim American Mobilization,"
Diaspora: A Journal of Transnational Studies 14, no. 1
(2005): 7–43.

University of California Press
Berkeley and Los Angeles, California

University of California Press, Ltd.
London, England

Library of Congress Cataloging-in-Publication Data

Bakalian, Anny P.
    Backlash 9/11 : Middle Eastern and Muslim
Americans Respond / Anny Bakalian and Mehdi
Bozorgmehr.
        p.    cm.
    Includes bibliographical references and index.
    ISBN 978-0-520-25734-4 (cloth : alk. paper)
    ISBN 978-0-520-25735-1 (pbk. : alk. paper)
    1. War on Terrorism, 2001—Moral and ethical
aspects.    2. September 11 Terrorist Attacks,
2001—Influence.    3. Hate crimes—United States.
4. Muslims—United States.    5. Arab Americans—
Crimes against—United States.    I. Bozorgmehr,
Mehdi.    II. Title.

HV6431.B3348    2009
973.931—dc22        2008013570

Manufactured in the United States of America

18   17   16   15   14   13   12   11   10   09
10   9   8   7   6   5   4   3   2   1

This book is printed on Natures Book, which contains
50% post-consumer waste and meets the minimum
requirements of ANSI/NISO Z39.48–1992 (R 1997)
(Permanence of Paper).

To the memory of my mother, who did not live to see the end
of this project
    —A.B.


To my father and mother
    —M.B.

# Contents

# Figures and Tables

# Abbreviations

| | |
|---|---|
| AAI | Arab American Institute |
| ACCESS | Arab Community Center for Economic and Social Services |
| ACLU | American Civil Liberties Union |
| ADC | American Arab Anti-Discrimination Committee |
| ADL | Anti-Defamation League |
| AMC | American Muslim Council |
| BRIDGES | Building Respect in Diverse Groups to Enhance Sensitivity |
| CAIR | Council on American-Islamic Relations |
| CAPPS | Computer-Assisted Passenger Prescreening System |
| CBO | community-based organization |
| DAAS | Detroit Arab American Survey |
| DHS | Department of Homeland Security |
| EEOC | Equal Employment Opportunity Commission |
| HELP | Human Rights Education Law Project |
| IAPAC | Iranian American Political Action Committee |
| INS | Immigration and Naturalization Service |
| JACL | Japanese American Citizens League |
| MAPS | Muslims in the American Public Square |
| MEMEAC | Middle East and Middle Eastern American Center |
| MPAC | Muslim Public Affairs Council |
| NAAP | Network of Arab American Professionals |
| NNAAC | National Network for Arab American Communities |
| NSEERS | National Security Entry-Exit Registration System |
| NSF | National Science Foundation |
| SAALT | South Asian American Leaders of Tomorrow |
| SALDEF | Sikh American Legal Defense and Education Fund |
| SMART | Sikh Mediawatch and Resource Task Force |

TIPS         Terrorism Information and Prevention System
TRIP         Traveler Redress Inquiry Program
TSA          Transportation Security Administration
USA PATRIOT Act
             Uniting and Strengthening America by Providing Appropriate
             Tools Required to Intercept and Obstruct Terrorism Act

# Acknowledgments

In the course of our research for this book, which began with a grant from the National Science Foundation (NSF) in October 2001, we have accrued many debts. Sociology Program Officers Reeve Vanneman (University of Maryland) and Patricia White were very encouraging and helpful in expediting the application process. The late Georges Sabagh of UCLA contributed to drafting the proposal. He passed away long before seeing this project to fruition. We miss his continuous support, encouragement, and friendship. Without the initial support we received from the NSF (SGER 014027), our project would have not materialized. Later, Mehdi Bozorgmehr received several supplemental small grants from the Professional Staff Congress of the City University of New York (PSC-CUNY).

We are most obliged to the generosity of the seventy-five leaders we interviewed across the country. These interviews make up the bulk of the evidence in our study. In spite of the overwhelming demands of their jobs in the aftermath of 9/11, they spoke to us at length. We hope they find our analysis of their collective experiences meaningful.

The Graduate Center of the City University of New York has offered us a stimulating and congenial scholarly atmosphere. The PhD program in sociology was a source of excellent research assistants over the years. Ronald Nerio assisted with transcriptions and Salvador Vidal Ortiz, with coding. Elizabeth Miller and Daniel Douglas assisted with the copyediting. Colleen Eren was helpful in reviewing the literature on mobilization and editing an early draft. Jessica Sperling was a meticulous and exceptionally competent graduate assistant who was indispensable as we finalized the manuscript. When we initiated our backlash research, Mehmet Kucukozer was a first-year graduate student at CUNY. He has contributed to our work ever since, interviewing, coding, collecting statistics from immigration yearbooks, and commenting on our ideas. We acknowledge them all and hope that they learned more than the tedious aspects of research. We also recognize the input of CUNY undergraduate research assistants Nyla Azam, Daniella Blanco, Marissa Joy Polnerow, and Inna Kitaychik over the years.

We are appreciative of colleagues whose input improved our data collection and writing. Helen Samhan of the Arab American Institute has been an important resource throughout our research, particularly in referring us to national organizations and commenting on the final manuscript. Louise Cainkar identified Middle Eastern and Muslim American leaders in Chicago and offered us a tour of the Arab suburbs. Michael Lichter invited us to Buffalo and set up several interviews for us with local Muslims. Rosa Haritos introduced us to N-Vivo, the qualitative software for data analysis, and coached us in its use.

We also owe thanks to Lara Rabiee, who competently assisted on some of the interviews and transcriptions, and Yasmine Ahmed, who worked diligently on citations and references. We are especially thankful for the support we have received from our friend Terese Lyons throughout the years. She used her language skills to transcribe some of the heavily accented interviews with a high level of accuracy and copyedited an early version of some of the chapters.

We are particularly grateful to the reviewers of our manuscript for the University of California Press. Steven J. Gold reviewed an early draft of the manuscript; we are extremely appreciative of his suggestions and positive comments. Roger Waldinger's repeated reviews of our manuscript were invaluable in shaping the book. His critical reading, pertinent questions, and insightful suggestions were instrumental in our multiple revisions. He alerted us to the fact that our book was about not only the backlash but also the response to it. His critique encouraged us to incorporate mobilization in our theoretical model. To the very end, his demand that we trim our copious quotes, reduce redundant explanations, and ensure that each quote accurately corresponded to our argument contributed to making the last draft far shorter yet superior than the original. Needless to say, we take full responsibility for the end product.

Muzaffar Chishti, who was engaged in documenting the backlash against Arabs and Muslims after September 11 with the Migration

Population Institute team, graciously introduced us to individuals who were in the thick of the action and invited us to forums where representatives from the affected communities met with immigration lawyers and other officials. As an immigration lawyer, he also carefully read the segments of the manuscript that dealt with legal matters and corrected our shortcomings.

We are indebted to Michael Mann for reading the comparative historical section and challenging our omissions. William G. Roy commented on mobilization. Joseph Jewells supplied us with extensive notes and references on the complex racialization thesis. We are also grateful to Helen Marrow and to our friend Claudia Der-Martirossian for their remarks on the use of the census data. Benjamin F. Alexander provided historical data. Our colleagues at CUNY—Pyong Gap Min, Philip Kasinitz, Maritsa Poros, and Maîvan Lam—read different sections of our manuscript and posed relevant questions that improved the argument.

When fellow researchers learned that Naomi Schneider was our editor at the University of California Press, they reassured us that we were in the hands of one of the most capable sociology editors in the business. Indeed, that has been our experience from the moment we approached Naomi to ask if she was interested in our book up until the finish. She handled the process with professionalism and kindness.

# 1

# Backlash against Middle Eastern and Muslim Americans

Tuesday, September 11, 2001, stands as one of the darkest days in modern U.S. history. It will long be remembered by the millions of Americans who witnessed the collapse of the Twin Towers over and over on their television screens. For Middle Eastern and Muslim Americans, "9/11" likewise signifies a shocking and sad day, but it also marks the beginning of a new era in which they became the victims of backlash. For many, the tragic events ushered in a period of hate crimes, profiling, and discrimination. Though stereotypes and discriminatory actions were not new to these minorities, the post-9/11 backlash was overwhelming and relentless.

Immediately after the attacks, individuals who appeared Middle Eastern or had Arabic- or Islamic-sounding names became the scapegoats of Americans' anger and vengeance. Balbir Singh Sodhi was the first murder victim of the backlash because his traditional Sikh looks—*dastaar* (turban) and *kesh* (unshorn hair)—were confused with Osama Bin Laden's *kaffiyeh* (male headdress) and beard. Ironically, Sikhs are neither Arab nor Muslim.[1] Hate crimes and bias incidents spiked immediately. According to the organization South Asian American Leaders of Tomorrow (SAALT 2001), 645 bias incidents were reported in metropolitan newspapers across the country in the week after 9/11. The *New*

*York Times* put it most succinctly: "Since the attacks, people who look Middle Eastern and Muslim, whatever their religion or nation of origin, have been singled out for harassment, threats and assaults."[2]

More seriously, a few weeks after 9/11, the U.S. government generated a series of initiatives and policies that targeted Middle Eastern and Muslim immigrant populations, especially men. Ostensibly, these decrees, administrative rule changes, executive orders, and laws aimed to stop terrorism; however, they legitimized the backlash in the eyes of the American public. From the perspective of Middle Eastern and Muslim Americans, it seemed as if the government was condoning stereotyping and scapegoating.

Given the enormity of the 9/11 backlash, one would assume that the targeted populations would go into hiding. Instead, Middle Eastern and Muslim American advocacy organizations representing these populations urged their constituents to claim their rights as Americans, to raise their voices, and to fight back against hate crimes, bias incidents, prejudice and discrimination, and governmental abuses of power. They responded in typical American fashion—through political activism and legal challenges. Their ultimate goal was civic engagement and political integration into the mainstream of American society. However, the relatively rapid mobilization of the affected groups was unusual from a historical perspective. Several Muslim American organizations shepherded a campaign to make Islam one of the core religions in America. The push to change the characterization of America's religious heritage from "Judeo-Christian" to "Abrahamic faiths" illustrates their seriousness and determination to sink deep roots in America.[3]

The populations affected by the post-9/11 backlash trace their ancestry to the Middle East, North Africa, and South Asia. The pioneers immigrated at the turn of the twentieth century from present-day Syria and Lebanon. Mostly Christian, they intermarried and assimilated within a couple of generations. A new wave of immigrants coincided with the repeal of restrictive immigration laws in 1965 and social and political turmoil in the Middle East. This time around, the newcomers were overwhelmingly Muslim; many came to pursue university educations and stayed. In the final decades of the twentieth century, immigration from Afghanistan, Pakistan, and Bangladesh has increased.

In the days immediately after 9/11, there were four confirmed cases of hate-motivated murders. On September 15, 2001, Balbir Singh Sodhi, a Sikh, was shot in Mesa, Arizona, at the gas station he owned. Also on September 15, 2001, Waqar Hasan, a Pakistani, was shot dead in his grocery store by Mark Anthony Stroman, a white supremacist in Dallas, Texas. On September 19, 2001, a U.S. citizen of Yemeni descent, Ali Almansoop, was shot in the back while escaping from his attacker, who had broken into his home in Lincoln Park, Michigan. Finally, on October 4, 2001, Vasudev Patel, a gas station owner from India, was killed during an armed robbery in Mesquite, Texas. This was Mark Anthony Stroman's second homicide in less than a month. Another seven murder cases are suspected to be motivated by hate (see Ibish 2003, 69–70).

Here, we offer a sample of hate crimes.

- In the days following September 11, 2001, many Arab and Muslim American organizations received threatening phone calls and slanderous e-mails. The American Arab Anti-Discrimination Committee (ADC) has published some of these messages: "I now enjoy watching Arabs and Muslims die"; "You F****** ARABS go to hell. You will pay"; "You should start acting like Americans and not terrorists"; "MAY YOU BURN IN HELL" (Ibish 2003, 85).

- On September 21, 2001, three Arab Americans were not allowed to board a Northwest Airlines plane in Riverside, California. They were told that passengers were not comfortable traveling with Middle Eastern men (Council on American-Islamic Relations [CAIR] 2002b, 18).

- Around Thanksgiving 2001 a Muslim man's gas station in Pennsylvania was shot at by a Caucasian male who shouted, "Towel heads!" The bullet shattered glass that went into the man's face and eyes (CAIR 2002b, 25).

- In Sunrise, Florida, on December 26, 2001, an "Arab American applied for a mortgage through a real estate company. After-wards, his real estate agent informed him that his home loan application had been rejected, disclosing that the reason for the rejection was an allegation coming from the company's under-writing manager that the Arab American applicant was a 'terror-ist.' . . . [He] had previously applied for a loan from the company and it had been approved" (Ibish 2003, 91).

- In its first anniversary issue (July 10–July 25, 2003), *Aramica,* an Arab American bimonthly newspaper serving New York, New Jersey, and Connecticut, reported virulent anti-Arab sentiments on a Web site in Bay Ridge. This Brooklyn neighborhood, which has been home to a large and complex Arab American community for several generations and which weathered the post-911 backlash without any major incidents, ironically became home to a hate-monger's Web site (www.bayridge.com). It posted the following message: "There are too many Arabs in Bay Ridge. . . . Our beautiful neighborhood has changed dramatically. . . . Instead of making 5th a one way street I would just firebomb the entire thing because of its grotesque nature. That would be a good way to get rid of most of the filthy Arabs who stink up our neighborhood." Eventually, *Aramica*'s publisher solicited the cooperation of leaders, politicians, and the local police, and the Web site was shut down.[4]

Immediately following the terrorist attacks, the government initiatives, a component of the "War on Terror," set the standard for the treatment, or rather the mistreatment, of Middle Eastern and Muslim Americans. These policies have been criticized for disregarding civil rights. Some scholars have gone so far as to call them "state-sponsored terrorism" (Minnite 2005, 182). The targeted immigrants hail from countries where the government is not to be trusted. Instead of earning the confidence of these new Americans, policies ended up crystallizing their views. To identify and capture homegrown terrorists one needs the cooperation of the targeted communities, a commitment that the community leaders have expressed repeatedly. The Migration Policy Institute's report concurs: "The U.S. government's harsh measures against immigrants since September 11 have failed to make us safer, have violated our fundamental civil liberties, and have undermined national unity" (Chishti et al. 2003, 7).

The Appendix lists in chronological order the government initiatives enacted to fight terrorism and strengthen the security of the United States in the aftermath of the terrorist attacks. Their frequency and intensity increased immediately after 9/11 but subsided after 2003. While the federal government mandated most of these policies, state and local governments also engaged in targeting. The policies have particularly affected men from Arab and Muslim countries who were in violation of their nonimmigrant visas. The Appendix also includes a sample of actions by the government, such as the Census Bureau's sharing of aggregated population statistics on Arab Americans with the Department of Homeland Security (DHS), and the State Department's denial of a visa to a prominent Swiss-born Islamic theology scholar, preventing him from assuming an academic position at the University of Notre Dame in 2004. Though strictly speaking these actions cannot be classified as initiatives, the affected populations experienced them as a continuation of the backlash.

Concurrently with federal policies, President George W. Bush condemned all vigilante acts of revenge and retribution. Visiting a mosque in Washington, D.C., on September 17, he proclaimed, "The face of terror is not the true faith of Islam. That's not what Islam is all about. Islam is peace. These terrorists don't represent peace. They represent evil and war."[5] Initially, the government's actions supported the affected communities. The U.S. Department of Justice's Civil Rights Division was vigilant in its prosecution of the perpetrators of hate crimes and discrimination. A five-member jury in Mesa, Arizona, convicted Frank Roque in October 1, 2003, for the murder of the first 9/11 hate crime victim.[6] The government ordered the Civil Rights Division and the FBI to prosecute vigilantism. In June 2002 Ari Fleischer, a White House spokesman, reiterated President Bush's belief that the U.S.-led battle against terrorism was not a war against Muslims: "Islam is a religion of peace. And that's what the president believes."[7]

Airline profiling of Middle Eastern and Muslim American passengers has led to the settling of discrimination suits. In June 2004, upon allegations that Delta Air Lines had discriminated against travelers appearing to be of Middle Eastern, Arab, or South Asian descent, the airline opted for a settlement. This agreement stipulates that the airline must spend at least $900,000 on civil rights training for flight attendants, pilots, and passenger service agents. The Delta negotiations represented the fourth discrimination-centered settlement against airlines since 9/11, with earlier settlements having even higher monetary settlement values. As the *Wall Street Journal* reported about a suit against American Airlines, "In February 2004, the airline, while denying guilt, settled the action for $1.5 million, to be spent on yet more 'sensitivity training.'"[8]

Nonetheless, the impact of the USA PATRIOT Act (Uniting and Strengthening America by Providing Appropriate Tools Required to Intercept and Obstruct Terrorism Act) and post-9/11 policies dominated the public discourse and muffled the occasional goodwill proclamations of the president and other high-ranking officials. Although Arab and Muslim American communities appreciated the initial outreach by the government, they felt that not enough had been done. Many observed that after the initial mosque visit the White

House was almost silent. There was surely a contradiction in the government's messages.

## RESEARCH ON 9/11

Americans have begun to mark time with reference to the terrorist attacks. They talk of "pre-9/11" and "post-9/11." Understandably, these events have garnered a lot of research attention, and no doubt more will follow. Publications cover a wide range of topics, genres, and authors—established and new scholars—from many disciplines, ideologies, and perspectives.[9] *The 9/11 Commission Report* (National Commission on Terrorist Attacks upon the United States 2004) stands in a class by itself. Within the social sciences, for example, sociologists have contributed to knowledge on urban settings (Sorkin and Zukin 2002), gender and terrorism (Kimmel 2003), the PATRIOT Act (Etzioni 2004), and the response of Muslim college students to 9/11 (Peek 2002, 2003). *Sociological Theory* published a symposium entitled "Theories of Terrorism" (Senechal de la Roche 2004). The *American Anthropologist* devoted an entire volume to 9/11 (Mascia-Lees and Lees 2002).[10] Psychologists have examined the impact of terror on individuals (Pyszczynski, Greenberg, and Solomon 2003), and those working in the field of disaster research have mostly addressed psychological trauma and individual recovery.[11] Sociologists of disaster have addressed risk perception and communication, the effectiveness of new technologies in management, and the effect of disasters on businesses.[12] Neil Smelser acknowledges that 9/11 was a typical case of cultural trauma: shock, numbing, mourning, the recognition that the event could not and should not be forgotten, and conscious efforts to commemorate the event (2007, 158).

Surprisingly, the interest of social scientists in the post-9/11 backlash against Middle Eastern and Muslim American communities has been rather limited. The edited volume by Elaine Hagopian (2004) and Louise Cainkar's chapter (2004a) on the impact of the government initiatives on Arabs and Muslims were the first scholarly publications. Hagopian's book includes eight essays on post-9/11 legislation, the demonization of Arabs and Muslims, and their criminalization. Cainkar's piece provides an overview of "special registration," reduction in nonimmigrant visas to Arab nationals, anti-Arab/Muslim stereotypes in the media, and their impact on the Arab and Muslim communities. She concurs with our findings that civic and political participation increased after 9/11 in the affected communities (see also Cainkar and Maira 2005). Tram Nguyen (2005), editor of *Colorlines* magazine, has published a collection of vignettes depicting the lives of individuals and their families caught in the dragnet of government initiatives. In *Mecca and Main Street: Muslim Life in America after 9/11*, journalist Geneive Abdo argues that after the terrorist attacks many "moderate" Muslims "felt an urgent need to embrace their beliefs and establish Islamic identity as a unified community" (2006, 3).

The Russell Sage Foundation has published three edited volumes on the economic, political, and social impact of 9/11 on New York City, out of which three chapters deal with the backlash. Jennifer Bryan (2005) conducted an ethnographic study of the Muslim immigrant enclave in Jersey City. Monisha Das Gupta (2005) surveyed taxi drivers, whose ranks contain a large proportion of Muslims from Pakistan, Bangladesh, and Egypt, and Lorraine Minnite (2005) analyzed the political incorporation of New York's new immigrants, including Middle Easterners. A handful of research projects funded by the Russell Sage Foundation (e.g., Cainkar 2008; Read and Oselin 2008), and analyses of data from the Detroit Arab American Survey (DAAS), conducted in 2003 (e.g., Jamal 2008; Shryock 2008), have been published.[13]

Legal scholars have been comparatively more prolific. David Cole (Cole 2003; Cole and Dempsey 2002; Cole and Lobel 2007) has been most prominent, but others (e.g., Akram and Johnson 2004; Akram and Karmely 2005; Brown 2003; Motomura 2006; Volpp 2002) have also contributed to the raging legal debates over security and civil rights after 9/11. Additionally, various civil liberties organizations, government agencies, and policy think tanks have issued reports on the post-9/11 backlash. To date, over forty reports have been issued, including about a dozen by Middle Eastern and Muslim American advocacy groups.

Yet since the "Attack on America" there has been no systematic analysis of the impact of the events on the targeted populations or their responses. Our book is an attempt to fill this significant gap. We have been following the post-9/11 backlash since that tragic morning in September 2001. Our analysis concerns Middle Eastern and Muslim American organizations that play a critical role in mediating between their constituents and the larger society. Our nationwide study is based on seventy-five in-depth interviews conducted with leaders and officials of organizations representing the affected populations, as well as civil liberties agencies and government institutions, and on analysis of their Web sites and listserv messages.

While legal scholars have been the most vocal in critiquing the various government initiatives, they generally do not study the affected populations. The scope and methods of our discipline, sociology, are ideally suited to the study of ethnic/religious communities. We have attempted to contribute to sociological theory by conceptualizing backlash for the first time and connecting the study of social movements with the study of immigration and with ethnic and racial studies. This book should be of interest not only to scholars but also to advocates in the fields of immigration and civil rights/liberties by providing a historically grounded context. We hope that Middle Eastern and Muslim Americans will find our study helpful in making sense of their individual and collective travails and experiences. It should provide them with the bigger picture and allow them to make educated choices about their future in America. Given the dearth of publications on Middle Eastern and Muslim Americans, even after 2001, it is our wish that this book will become a resource for those who want to learn more about these populations.[14] Finally, we hope that this book will bring to the attention of the American public the neglected perspective of the victimized Middle Eastern and Muslim communities.

It is necessary to state a couple of caveats here. First, as groups, African American Muslims and other converts have not been targets of government initiatives; thus they do not fall within the purview of our study. Second, our treatment of Sikhs is limited. Sikhs suffered inordinately from the hate crimes that followed the terrorist attacks because of mistaken identity. Hate-mongers tend to be not only violent and cruel but also ignorant. Sikhs were likewise victimized after the Iranian Revolution and the Iranian Hostage Crisis, since they were confused with the turbaned images of Ayatollah Khomeini shown on television. Nonetheless, Sikhs were not the targets of the post-9/11 government initiatives. They had mobilized before 9/11 to combat stereotypes and discrimination, and they stepped up their advocacy afterwards. They have been working through the courts and Congress to gain accommodations such as the right to wear the turban at work and to carry the ceremonial *kirpan* (ceremonial dagger) on an airplane. Although they are a newly prominent religious group in the United States fighting discrimination, there is no political agenda against them. Therefore, Sikhs are included in this volume only in relation to hate crimes and their visible presence in civil rights coalitions.

## THE STATE OF KNOWLEDGE ON BACKLASH AND MOBILIZATION

The literatures on social movements, immigration, and ethnic and racial studies are most relevant to this book. Social movement scholars in the United States have overlooked ethnicity and religion as the bases of collective action, and immigration and ethnic and racial studies scholars have paid little attention to mobilization. The social movement literature offers more detailed theoretical explication of the concept (e.g., components of claims making). Little effort has been made to merge these two fields (for exceptions, see Koopmans et al. 2005 and Okamoto 2003). At the end of this section we introduce our model, which connects backlash to mobilization and claims making.

First, however, we review the traditional literatures in sociology on intergroup conflict and solidarity and the more recent competitive ethnic relations model and middleman minority theory. We intentionally do not use the term *ethnic* in conjunction with *mobilization* because the post-9/11 response entailed more than one national-origin group (Arabs from the Middle East and North Africa) as well as a religious group (Muslims from the Middle East and South Asia). Therefore, we problematize the ethnic dimension of ethnic mobilization by reexamining the essence of ethnic groups via a brief review of the reemerging relational theory of ethnicity. Along these lines, we review pan-ethnicity and pan-ethnic mobilization as they relate to supranational categories of Arab, Middle Eastern, and Muslim.

### THEORIES OF INTERGROUP CONFLICT, HOST HOSTILITY, AND GROUP SOLIDARITY

Analyzing the post-9/11 backlash against Middle Eastern and Muslim Americans continues a long sociological tradition. Since the turn of the twentieth century, when the United States was trying to integrate the large numbers of immigrants that had arrived from eastern and southern Europe and the Levant,[15] American sociologists have been advancing theories on intergroup relations and conflict. Robert Park, Everett Hughes, and Louis Wirth focused on the natural laboratory of Chicago to study how the immigrant masses were assimilating. In his classic race relations cycle theory, Park (1950) postulated a four-step process between groups—contact, competition, accommodation, and assimilation. Competition was emphasized as the cause of conflict and violence and therefore was a fundamental component of intergroup relations. Writing in 1932, Donald Young likewise noted: "Group antagonisms seem to be inevitable when two people in contact with each other may be distinguished by differentiating characteristics, either inborn or cultural, and are actual or potential competitors" (1932, 586). Half a century later, Stephen Steinberg reiterated: "If there is an iron law of ethnicity, it is that when ethnic groups are found in a hierarchy of power, wealth, and status, then conflict is inescapable" (1989, 170). Yet conflict is not constant; it can be subtle or controlled for long periods (e.g., Redfield 1939).

It has been established that intergroup "clashes" are positively correlated with increases in ethnic solidarity. Georg Simmel (1955) was the first to observe that antagonism with an external foe has a positive integrative effect within the unit. He wrote: "Conflict may not only heighten the concentration of an existing unit, radically eliminating all elements which might blur the distinctions of its boundaries against the enemy; it may also bring persons and groups together which have otherwise nothing to do with each other" (98–99). Lewis Coser (1956, 95) has elucidated Simmel's concepts: "Conflict with another group leads to the mobilization of the energies of group members and hence to increased cohesion of the group. Whether increase in centralization accompanies this increase in cohesion depends upon both the character of the conflict and the type of group. Centralization will be more likely to occur in the event of wartime conflict."

Also, conflict with an adversary will result in associations and coalitions with other groups (Coser 1956, 155). Sociologists have found ample empirical evidence to support the Simmel-Coser propositions. For instance, in lobbying the U.S. Congress to recognize the Armenian genocide of 1915, Armenian Americans stand united against the persistent denial of the Turkish government. This is remarkable given that their communal institutions are divided into two contentious political/ideological factions (Bakalian 1993). While we find the Simmel-Coser theorem to be highly relevant to our case study, we are more concerned with mobilization than with group cohesion.

Theories of intergroup relations have attributed the cause of conflict to competitive minority-majority relations in the host society. For example, the structural theory of ethnic competition deals with some form of economic or political contest between groups (Olzak and Nagel 1986; see also Okamoto 2003). Susan Olzak (1992) has argued that ethnic conflict is caused by increased rivalry when inequalities between groups diminish. This would explain the rise of hate crimes in the 1980s as new immigrants attempted integration into previously white-majority neighborhoods and institutions, threatening whites' privileged position and access to scarce societal resources (Olzak, Shanahan, and McEneaney 1996). Taking globalization into account, Olzak (2006, figure 1.1) has expanded the competitive ethnic relations model by adding several levels of analysis—world, country, and group. This reformulation improves the static nature and U.S. focus of the original model. Still, it does not question the nature of the relationship between sending and receiving societies and the role of the state vis-à-vis minorities. The competitive ethnic relations model is silent on the state's repressive policies and practices as a source of conflict and violence, a central concern of ours.

The transnationalism literature has improved the explanatory power of intergroup relations by stressing the positive connections between transnational migrants and their homelands—for example, remittances and reinforcement of ethnic ties. Because of global forces, economic cycles, shifting patterns of immigration, new political conflicts such as the resurgence of ethnic nationalism, and terrorist acts or threats, the level of strife and violence may escalate in any given society even after years of harmonious coexistence. When the sending and receiving societies experience international tension and conflict, the receiving society tightens its control of immigrants, thereby mitigating transnationalism (Waldinger and Fitzgerald 2004). Still, the literature on transnationalism does not go far enough in addressing the types of oversight and restrictions that the government imposes on minority populations.

Edna Bonacich and John Modell (1980) have argued that middlemen minorities—small business owners who straddle producers and consumers in modern economies—face host hostility because of their visible concentration in niche markets. Their economic success can provoke hostility in the majority population and envy in disadvantaged minority groups. This host hostility, in turn, reinforces the middleman's ethnicity and group solidarity. Pyong Gap Min (1996) distinguishes *ethnic solidarity* from *ethnic attachment,* terms used interchangeably in the middleman minority literature (see also Min 2008). While ethnic attachment is "the degree to which members are culturally, socially, and psychologically" connected to their ethnicity, ethnic solidarity "is the degree to which members use ethnic collective actions to protect their common interests" (5). Members claiming a given ethnicity must first feel attachment to enact their solidarity. For Min, "Collective goals and ethnic mobilization [are] the central components of ethnic solidarity" (5). Like the competitive ethnic relations model, middleman minority theory focuses on economic factors and thus is not applicable to our case study.

In their reading of U.S. immigration history, Kathleen Conzen and her associates assert that ethnicity is a "process of construction or invention which incorporates, adapts, and amplifies preexisting communal solidarities, cultural attributes, and historical memories. That is, it is grounded in the real life context and social experience" (1992, 4). It is now widely accepted that ethnicity is dynamic, socially constructed, and fundamentally relational in nature, involving the binary "us" versus "them" categories. This often means that there is no ethnic minority without a majority. The very definitions of ethnicity and nationality presuppose an "institutionalized relationship between delineated categories whose members consider each other as culturally distinct" (Eriksen 1993, 18). Dichotomies or contrasts, as well as complementarization or shared discourse and interaction, are inherent in systems of majority/minority classification (28). This dialectical process of competition, conflict, and contestation changes both the immigrants and the host society.

Frederick Barth (1969) argues that boundaries, whether imposed objectively by outsiders (e.g., state, majority population) or subjectively determined by insiders, are a more powerful gauge of ethnicity than the "contents" of a culture or other inherent qualities of the collectivity. When boundaries are not maintained, they become porous, allowing for traffic in and out. This may eventually lead to the obliteration of boundaries and the demise of the collectivity. Extending Barth's concept of ethnic boundary formation, Rogers Brubaker (2004), in *Ethnicity without Groups,* takes on the vast literature on ethnicity and race for reifying "groups," whether national, communal, ethnic, religious, or other. He recommends an analytical perspective that focuses on group-making projects rather than groups per se. Ethnic categories are often "backed by political entrepreneurs and entrenched in governmental and other organizational routines of social counting and accounting" (Brubaker 2004, 20). For instance, the Office of Management and Budget is responsible for the classificatory system that prevails in the United States. The "ethnoracial pentagon" is a cultural product that provides "standardized cognitive maps over categories of relevant others" (Eriksen 1993, 60).[16] Likewise, "the notion of a universally acknowledged 'core culture' has lost all its plausibility since the late 1960s" (Brubaker 2004, 126; see also Conzen et al. 1992). We use *American* or *mainstream* here not as monolithic but as relational, oppositional terms.

In the case of Middle Easterners and Muslims after 9/11, the "us" versus "them" has gone beyond minority/majority relations to include the U.S. government. Thus the relational dimension here is above all political. Political circumstances, at home and abroad, have transformed immigrants and their descendants from the Middle East, North Africa, and South Asia into suspicious aliens or noncitizens in the United States. They struggle to find a place for themselves and their children in American society in the face of governmental targeting, popular stereotypes, and scapegoating.

## THEORIES OF PAN-ETHNICITY AND PAN-ETHNIC MOBILIZATION

The theoretical literature on the mobilization of Asian Americans shortly after the civil rights movement and the subsequent development of Asian American pan-ethnicity provides yet another framework for our case study. *Pan-ethnicity* is defined as "the development of bridging organizations and solidarities among subgroups of ethnic collectivities that are often seen as homogenous by outsiders" (Lopez and Espiritu 1990, 200). This requires similarities in culture, such as language and religion, or certain structural conditions, such as social class, race, generation, and geographical dispersion. Yet David Lopez and Yen Espiritu argue that "structural factors, not cultural commonalties, better explain the emergence and success of panethnicity" (218).

The structural factors that were instrumental in developing Asian pan-ethnicity include (1) targeted violence, (2) outsiders' perception that Asian ethnics are "foreigners" (Espiritu 1992; Tuan 1998), (3) racial lumping (Min 1999, 29), which is a result of the government's classification of Asians as a minority population, and consequently (4) entitlement to affirmative action and other programs. Moreover, (5) as professionals of Asian descent have realized the benefits of set-aside programs, they have been fighting to sustain these advantages. Asian American umbrella organizations have participated in electoral politics, engaged in activism, and established social service organizations (Espiritu 1992).

More recently, Dina Okamoto (2003, 813) has defined "pan-national mobilization as the public action of people from two or more national-origin groups who express grievances or claims on behalf of the collective, pan-national group. These collective efforts are often directed at local, state, or federal government agencies, other public institutions, or the general public." She further points to the shifting and layered nature of pan-ethnicity due to external structural factors. The "layering" of identity, which implies the multiplicity of possible affiliations and identities an individual can claim (e.g., Druze, Lebanese, Arab, Middle Easterner, or Sunni, Muslim, Egyptian, Arab, Middle

Eastern), allows for the contraction and expansion of ethnic boundaries of organizations.

Although the terrorists in the 9/11 attacks originated from different nation states, they had a common ethnicity (Arab) and religion (Islam). Consequently, the U.S. government targeted Arabs and Muslims. Like the Chinese, who originate from several countries, Arabs are a supranational ethnic group; and like Asians, Middle Easterners are a pan-ethnic group. Though there was no emergence of Middle Eastern Americans as a pan-ethnic group, Arab and Muslim Americans crystallized as pan-ethnic/pan-religious groups in the aftermath of the events.

American Islam is a post-9/11 "invention" as a distinct new category in the nation's classificatory system. Ironically, Islam is not an ethnic category, so it cannot be codified into laws. In the post-9/11 era, the label has been used awkwardly alone and/or in conjunction with Arab Americans, as in phrases like "Arabs and Muslims." As a religion, Islam encompasses a broad range of sects, nationalities, ethnicities, languages, generations, and political ideologies. Additionally, *Islam* implies religiosity. Like American Christians and American Jews, a significant proportion of Muslim Americans are secular in their outlook and, if asked to identify themselves, may not give "Muslim" as a first response. Islam is both a religion and a cultural tradition. Many immigrants from the Middle East (the Arab world, Iran, and Turkey) identify more strongly with their national origin than with their religion.

## A MODEL OF BACKLASH AND MOBILIZATION

Figure 1 illustrates our general theory of backlash and mobilization, resulting in civic and political integration. Figures 2 and 3 lay out the specific components of backlash and mobilization.

### TYPES OF BACKLASH

After an extensive search of the social science literature, we realized that the term *backlash* has not been conceptualized, though it has been widely used in both scholarship and the popular media.[17] Generally, backlash consists of harassment and hate crimes, but it may also subsume a state's actions that unjustly target a minority population or "outgroup."[18] Therefore, we define backlash as an excessive and adverse societal and governmental reaction to a political/ideological crisis against a group or groups.

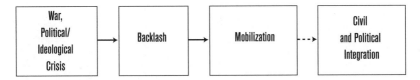

Figure 1. A model of backlash and mobilization.

We argue that during times of war or political/ideological crisis, populations that share the same ethnic and/or religious background as the "enemy" of the state are subject to backlash. This backlash may take several forms (figure 2). First, members of the majority population may engage in acts of intimidation, harassment, verbal abuse, and physical violence against persons or property of members of the targeted population. More extreme forms of such behaviors are categorized as hate crimes, although scholars have not agreed on what constitutes a hate crime. Violent behaviors motivated by hatred and bias, such as vandalism, destruction of property, assault, arson, theft, rape, and murder, were criminalized in the United States in 1990 (see chapter 5).

Second, the state may respond to threats to the nation's security and sovereignty by singling out the targeted ethnic and/or religious group(s) within its borders for policed scrutiny, suppression, and repression. Governmental reprisals in American history have included internment, detention, deportation, mandatory identification cards, surveillance, and prosecution. While the state may not condone citizens' vigilante actions, its own policies are likely to send a different message. In chapter 2, we draw on Michael Mann's work to elucidate the types of violence that the state inflicts on "outgroups" or minority populations when they are deemed undesirable. This violence is often disguised as preventive or in the interest of the state. In its extreme form, the mistreatment of an "outgroup" may be considered ethnic cleansing. Moreover, governments may control minority populations—those contending for power or seeking a larger share of benefits—through a variety of repressive measures such as "institutional coercion," "policed repression," or "violent repression" (Mann 2005). In the 9/11 case, Arab, Iranian, and Muslim immigrant men suffered inordinately from detention, deportation, special registration, and profiling. The affected populations also experienced FBI monitoring and surveillance, largely made possible by the PATRIOT Act.

While political scientists have studied the state's role in immigration, the state has not been examined as a repressive agent. For example, in his *magnum opus,* Zolberg (2006) details the U.S. government's long

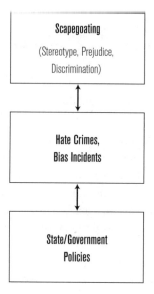

Figure 2. Types of backlash.

history of determining the extent to which immigrants were allowed into the country and the countries from which they came. He argues that the United States was a "nation by design," challenging popular assumptions that until 1924 the gates were completely open. Nonetheless, his focus is on the receiving state's role as gatekeeper, whereas we concentrate on its repressive, punitive domestic tendencies.

Third, hate crimes and government initiatives are mediated though deeply rooted prejudices and stereotypes. Stereotypes are culturally constructed, crystallized, and perpetuated by "moral entrepreneurs," consisting of the political, cultural, and business elite, and are facilitated by the media (Cohen 2002). Thus preexisting negative stereotypes of Middle Easterners and Muslims fuel the actions of the hate-mongers, thereby resulting in more bias incidents and hate crimes.[19] A feedback loop invariably reinforces the various forms of backlash, often resulting in renewed cycles of violence against the targeted ethnic or religious group(s).

## COMPONENTS OF ETHNIC MOBILIZATION/CLAIMS MAKING

Olzak offers the most succinct definition of ethnic mobilization: "Collective action based upon ethnic claims, protests, or intergroup hostility that makes reference to a group's demands based upon one or more cultural

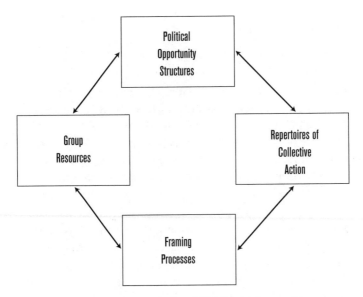

Figure 3. Components of mobilization/claims making.

markers" (2006, 4–5). We go beyond this definition, however, to describe the components of mobilization. For this we have consulted the general social movement literature, whose central concept has been "contentious politics" (Tilly and Tarrow 2006; McAdam, Tarrow, and Tilly 2001). Any contention involves interactions between actors making claims that almost invariably impinge on someone else's interests, including governments and third parties. According to Ruud Koopmans and his associates, claims making is "a unit of strategic action in the public sphere. It consists of the purposive and public articulation of political demands, calls to action, proposals, criticisms, or physical attacks, which, actually or potentially, affect the interests or integrity of the claimants and/or other collective actors" (2005, 254). In this volume, we use the two terms interchangeably.

We contend that backlash promotes mobilization/claims making in the short or long term, depending upon favorable structural and cultural conditions, namely political opportunities, resources, repertoires of collective action, and framing processes. These conditions, while affecting each other, as well as the form and content of the mobilization, are in turn influenced by collective action, resulting in a continuously modified feedback loop. Ethnic mobilization/claims making is a dynamic, circular process, so our model (figure 3) cannot be reduced to a linear, discrete representation.

## POLITICAL OPPORTUNITY STRUCTURE

The literatures on social movements, immigration, and ethnic and racial studies demonstrate that political opportunity structure is a key component in mobilization/claims making. Susan Olzak and Emily Ryo theorize that "movement mobilization is a function of changes in the political climate that make collective action more likely to succeed, such as an increase in the level of elite receptivity to protestors or a restructuring of existing power relations" (2004, 2). In other words, the "institutional structure[s] and ideological dispositions of those in power" must be sufficiently open to the demands of the group of claimants (McAdam and Snow 1997, 3).

While some studies of immigration in Europe have addressed issues most pertinent to our case (Koopmans et al. 2005; Statham 1999), these works precede the terrorist attacks in Europe and thus are not applicable to the post-9/11 situation. It is imperative that claimants be able to influence and manipulate those in power and state policies; otherwise they will not achieve their objectives. Policies on citizenship, a component of institutional contexts, vary significantly among the European host states, thus affecting the outcome of immigrant mobilization in each case. Also relevant here are policies regarding religious accommodation in Europe's liberal democratic societies. As the use of religious symbolism in public places is excluded, Muslim immigrants have been forced to make "exceptional" demands on the state that have led to heightened opposition in the "native" population. Examples of exceptionalism include not only wearing the *hijab* (head covering) at work, amplifying the *azaan* (call to prayer) from minarets, and offering *halal* (permissible) food in school cafeterias but also pushing for *sharia* (Islamic law) divorce, polygyny, and female circumcision (Koopmans et al. 2005, 148–49; Statham 1999).

Major changes in a society give birth to mobilization/claims making on the part of disenfranchised groups who see opportunities opening up or disadvantages to maintaining the status quo. Collective action in response to different levels of repression tends to follow the form of a bell curve (Benford 1992). Medium levels of oppression tend to motivate mobilization, but extreme forms of despotism make the costs of struggle too high. Historically, acts of war, like the Japanese attack on Pearl Harbor, and perceived threats from political ideologies, like the threat of communism in the Red Scare of 1919–20 and then McCarthyism, have led to extreme forms of repression by the U.S. government.

We contend that in the post–civil rights era state-sponsored backlash has been tempered by the law and the belief of the American public in the principles of civil rights. Therefore, lower levels of government subjugation have triggered mobilization and activism by the targeted populations. Leaders of preexisting community-based and advocacy organizations have galvanized their constituents to seize the moment. To maintain the status quo, to do nothing or to accept the backlash, would have been detrimental for the reputation of the leaders and the longevity of their organizations. Thus they moved forward with the goal of political integration.

## FRAMING MECHANISMS

To achieve success in contentious collective action, movement leaders must "frame" their demands in language, symbols, and forms that are likely to be understood by their opponents and their general audience. Erving Goffman was first to introduce the term in *Frame Analysis*. Frames are "schemata of interpretation" (1974, 21) that selectively control human perception by identifying and labeling cognitive structures and providing meaning. Social movement scholars have adapted the concept to attribute cognitive, cultural, and historical beliefs and ideologies to actors. According to Steven Buechler, "Framing means focusing attention on some bounded phenomenon by importing meaning and significance to elements within the frame and setting them apart from what is outside the frame. In the context of social movements, framing refers to the interactive, collective ways that movement actors assign meanings to their activities in the conduct of social movement activism. The concept of framing is designed for discussing the social construction of grievances as a fluid and variable process of social interaction" (2000, 41).

Robert Benford and David Snow (2000) emphasize that frames have to be "culturally resonant" and morally justifiable if a claim is to be accepted and supported by the larger society. In other words, framing processes must garner a sympathetic audience in the mainstream and, just as important, must win concessions from those with political power (Buechler 2000). According to Douglas McAdam and David Snow, those who articulate frames are "not merely . . . carriers of existing ideas and meanings, but . . . signifying agents actively engaged in producing and maintaining meaning of their constituents, antagonists, and bystanders" (1997, 232). This implies that frames must be shaped and reshaped continually so that they remain relevant to contemporaneous sensitivities.

Ultimately, the way a group of claimants frames or constructs its grievances and demands will affect its ability not only to gain a wider membership base among the populations of concern and reach its goals but also to sustain the interest of its own rank and file. As Olzak notes, "Ethnic markers (such as skin pigmentation, language, religious distinctions, dialect, cultural practices, or regional/homeland identification) delineate a potential membership pool, which may or may not be activated" (2006, 4–5). Mobilization does not occur ex nihilo, as it were— not unless group membership is sustained even among the "natural" base of co-ethnics or co-religionists. This point is evidenced in this book in the differences in the degree of mobilization among the various subgroups that are subsumed under the "Middle Eastern" category. Advocacy organizations and their leaders must use frames that win the hearts and minds of potential recruits; otherwise they will remain bystanders.

## REPERTOIRES OF COLLECTIVE ACTION

Whether framing processes can be "translated" into action depends on whether the group can identify and effectively use social movement repertoires. In his seminal book *From Mobilization to Revolution* (1978), Charles Tilly describes repertoires as the political action tactics that are recognized within a culture as legitimate forms of claims making. In the Western world, the current repertoire or "ensemble of performances" consists of a wide array of methods, used alone or in combination with others. They include forging coalitions or forming special-purpose organizations; distributing press releases; and holding public meetings, rallies, demonstrations, strikes, petition drives, conferences, solemn processions, and vigils (Tilly 1978, 1986; McAdam, Tarrow, and Tilly 2001; Traugott 1994). We have also found that Middle Eastern and Muslim Americans in the post-9/11 era have used interfaith projects, plays, films, songs, stand-up comedy, and other artistic venues as powerful, though indirect, methods of claims making. Though kidnappings, blowing up of symbolic buildings or structures, targeted murders, and other forms of terrorism may be tactics of protest, they are obviously not considered legitimate for groups playing by the rules.

According to James Ennis, repertoires have two features: breadth and structure. "Breadth consists of the number and variety of options available. Groups with long and active histories of resistance will have wider repertoires of conceivable action, as will those with cosmopolitan rather than sectarian outlooks. Ample resources and effective organization will yield broader tactical repertoires" (1987, 522). Clearly, then, there is a strong relationship between repertoires and resource mobilization, a structural influence in determining the outcome of mobilization.

## RESOURCE MOBILIZATION

John McCarthy and Mayer Zald (1977), among others (e.g., Tilly 1978; Oberschall 1973; Zald and McCarthy 1979), have established that the success of a collective movement depends on the organizational resources available to aggrieved claimants and not on the grievances themselves. Resources shape the very form and content of mobilization. According to David Cress and David Snow (1996, 1094), resources can be "moral, material, informational [or] human." First, an organization gains moral "credits" if it endorses causes that are considered socially worthy, such as caring for the injured. Likewise, social legitimacy, or "symbolic resources of a legitimate and officially recognized 'status'" (Statham 1999, 601), may be considered moral resources. Second, material resources comprise "tangible goods and services" such as (1) finances (including levels of affluence among leaders/members); (2) facilities and space for meetings and offices; (3) equipment and supplies; and (4) access to transportation. Third, informational resources include (1) strategic "know-how" of lobbying and claims making in general; (2) technical support; and (3) referrals. Fourth, human resources include (1) captive audiences; (2) leaders or spokespersons; (3) a cadre of committed volunteers and supporters with the ability to recruit more members; (4) group cohesion or internal solidarity, on McCarthy and Zald's assertion that those who "are highly organized internally (either communally or associationally) are more likely to spawn other organized forms" (1977, 1218); (5) access to elites, communication media, and expertise in using these media as resources; and (6) preexisting coalitions with outside groups, labor, organizational/social networks, and political connections (McCarthy and Zald 1977, 216; Statham 1999).

In summary, our model of backlash and mobilization makes the following points. First, we attribute a large repressive role to the host state in dealing with immigrant/minority populations during times of war or political/ideological crises. We argue that the backlash consists of scapegoating and hate crimes perpetrated by members of the host society, as well as by government initiatives. Second, theories of intergroup relations, host hostility, and solidarity focus primarily on economic issues, leaving out political issues, which are central to our model. Third, we go beyond the usual explanations of group solidarity and group cohesion in response to hostility and analyze the mobilization of the groups affected by the backlash. Fourth, our analysis of mobilization involves an investigation of political opportunity structures, resources, repertoires, and framing processes. Last but not least, our model of backlash and mobilization bridges the literatures of immigration, ethnic and racial studies, and social movements.

## CROSS-NATIONAL COMPARISONS

Since 9/11, terrorist attacks and civil unrest involving Muslims in Europe have added a comparative dimension to our study. Although the circumstances and contexts are different, these incidents and their repercussions are worth a closer look. On March 11, 2004, simultaneous bombs exploded in three Madrid train stations, killing 191 persons and leaving more than 1,500 injured. Within a few days of the events, the electorate voted for a new socialist government, breaking away from the pro-Iraq war policies of its predecessor.[20] Surprisingly, few incidents of backlash were reported in Spain. The low incidence of hate crimes in Spain may be attributed to Spaniards' anger regarding the ruling party's alleged politically motivated misidentification of the terrorist group responsible for the bombing.[21]

On July 7, 2005, three British citizens of Pakistani descent and a fourth Jamaican-born British resident detonated three bombs in as many underground trains in London, and a fourth one blew off the top of a double-decker bus. Fifty-five individuals died and about seven hundred were wounded. These blasts were immediately followed by a higher incidence of hate crimes,[22] and soon thereafter there were reports of suspects being rounded up for interrogation and detained beyond the mandated period. Radical clerics in the United Kingdom were jailed and deported.

On October 27, 2005, young people of mostly North African descent began rioting in the suburbs of Paris. The riots were triggered by the visit of then-interior minister Nicolas Sarkozy, who had described the inhabitants of their run-down neighborhoods as "rabble" and as "gangrene" deserving to be "cleaned with a power hose."[23] The violence peaked on November 7, affecting 274 communes. Official tallies indicate that 8,973 cars were torched, 2,888 youth were arrested, and 126 police officers were injured. A state of emergency was declared, and subsequent restrictions were imposed on immigrants and minorities, especially Muslims.[24]

On August 10, 2006, British authorities revealed that they had thwarted a terror plot to blow up as many as ten airplanes over the Atlantic Ocean heading to the United States. Twenty-four Muslim men, once again all born in the United Kingdom, were arrested after several months of surveillance. They had planned to smuggle liquids in drink bottles and mix them as explosives on board. Though the British believed they had arrested the key conspirators, they imposed extra security measures in case some of their associates were still at large. The British Muslim extremists alarmed authorities on both sides of the Atlantic,[25] leading to comparisons of Muslims in the United States, the United Kingdom, and the rest of Europe.[26]

The arrest of seventeen Muslim men of mostly South Asian origin in Toronto in June 2006 revealed how close Canada had come to an attack.[27] They were charged with plotting to bomb targets in southern Ontario. Five of the accused were under eighteen years of age, although most were in their twenties. The leader, forty-three-year-old Qayyum Abdul Jamal, was a reputed "fiery figure," the imam (cleric) of the mosque in Missisauga. Tarek Fatah of the Muslim Canadian Congress was quick to denounce the terrorists, saying: "Law enforcement agencies have done a great service to the Muslim community by busting this terrorist cell."[28] The reaction of the Canadian government and citizenry did not follow the U.S. example.

The main differences between the British and North American cases can be summarized as follows. First, while the 9/11 terrorists were foreign-born visitors (Zolberg 2002), the instigators in the U.K. incidents were home-grown, second-generation immigrants. Second, Muslim immigrants in Britain tend to come from former colonies in Asia, and their children tend to harbor anticolonial sentiments. Third, the U.K. terrorism plotters have been generally marginalized youth with few prospects for social mobility, compared to the relatively more economically advantaged and upwardly mobile American Muslims (see chapter 3 of this book and the cover story in *Newsweek* for July 30, 2007).[29] This profile, however, may be changing, for the terrorists who plotted the bombing of London's West End and Glasgow Airport in July 2007 included foreign-born suspects with professional degrees and credentials.[30]

A leadership change in the United Kingdom in June 2007 produced new policies. Prime Minister Gordon Brown parted ways with his predecessor by eschewing the divisive phrase *war on terror;* with the goal of reaching out to the Muslim communities, he mandated that public officials call the perpetrators of violence simply "criminals." Writing in the *New York Times Magazine,* David Rieff observed: "So far, it seems, Brown has had more success in getting influential Muslim groups to denounce terror than Blair did. . . . Particularly in light of the U.S. National Counterterrorism Center's recent report that Al Qaeda is as strong today as it was before 9/11, Gordon Brown's bet on the criminal model, however risky, seems the more sensible course."[31]

No doubt colleagues in Spain, England, France, and elsewhere will be examining governmental reactions to the attacks, riots, and alleged terrorist cells. We hope that in the future, when studies have been conducted, there will be opportunities for comparative analysis. Meanwhile, we hope that our work will provide a benchmark for research on backlash against Arabs and Muslims after terrorist attacks in Western societies.

## METHODOLOGY

This study was initiated by a Request for Proposals sent out by the National Science Foundation (NSF) a week after the events of 9/11. Coincidentally, our center, the Middle East and Middle Eastern American Center (MEMEAC), had just received official approval from the Board of Trustees of the City University of New York. Given our interest in Middle Eastern Americans and our concern about the hate crimes reported in the media, we sent out a proposal to examine empirically the backlash that had been triggered by the terrorist acts.[32]

We considered a number of options in studying the backlash. The first was to examine the attitudes of the general American public toward Middle Eastern and Muslim Americans for the purpose of understanding stereotypes and biases. Another option was to explore the experiences and perceptions of Middle Eastern and Muslim Americans themselves. Both of these projects required the use of surveys, which the NSF's budget constraints prohibited. A third option was to monitor incidents of hate crimes through a content analysis of newspapers. However, this type of research could be carried out later, and we sought to tap information that was time sensitive. We wanted to gather the data as events unfolded, an approach that in hindsight turned out to be critical with the shift from hate crimes to government initiatives. We decided to focus on the responses of community-based organizations (CBOs) to the backlash, since such organizations mediate between their constituencies and the larger society. We believed that by interviewing the officers or leaders of national and grassroots organizations we could collect rich and insightful data, not accessible otherwise, in the most cost-effective, rapid, and feasible manner given our constraints.

We wrote the proposal in about three days, and the NSF responded in less than twenty-four hours—an unprecedented turnaround, yet understandable given the urgency demanded by the nature of the events. We were given a Small Grant for Exploratory Research for one year. Initially, we aimed to interview the national Middle Eastern and Muslim American advocacy organizations in Washington, D.C., and the bulk of the social service and grassroots organizations in metropolitan New York. We chose those two cities because they were the sites of the attacks on the World Trade Center and the Pentagon as well as the sites of national CBOs.

At first, we were concerned mainly with hate crimes and bias incidents. But as the Bush administration churned out one initiative after another, we shifted gears to account for the impact these directives were having on the targeted populations. By the beginning of June 2002, we realized that a study of governmental backlash warranted a wider scope and the inclusion of organizations in other parts of the country. Through their reports and public appeals, civil liberties organizations had also taken the lead in informing Americans about the backlash and the erosion of civil liberties allegedly in the interest of improving security. Additionally, we decided to include in our sample representatives of civil liberties groups, legal experts on immigration, and government officials who could inform us on the situation as "knowledgeable sources." In summary, we have been closely following the post-9/11 backlash against Middle Eastern and Muslim Americans from its inception to the present.

## RESEARCH DESIGN

We have conducted seventy-five in-depth interviews—sixty of them with high-ranking representatives of Middle Eastern and Muslim American organizations and fifteen with knowledgeable sources. In collaboration with the September 11 Digital Archive, we conducted seventy-two additional interviews with Arab and/or Muslim Americans about their personal experiences following the terrorist attacks.[33]

We first developed a list of organizations across the country by ethnic/religious groupings of the Middle East. Our initial source was a "Curriculum Guide" of Middle Eastern American philanthropies (Bozorgmehr and Baron 2001). We also checked the Internet and used snowballing to generate information about new and little-known organizations. Several of the organizations on our master list existed only on paper or had a very narrow focus (e.g., an annual ethnic parade organized by one man). Additionally, we discovered disconnected telephone numbers and mailing addresses with no forwarding destination. We contacted almost all the organizations on our list at least twice by phone, e-mail, or letter.

We were persistent in our efforts to reach and interview the leaders of the most prominent organizations. The national organizations were professional in granting us interviews and generous with their time in spite of their very hectic schedules after 9/11. We did not encounter any refusals among those we managed to contact, though a handful of small grassroots organizations did not respond to our repeated phone messages, letters, and e-mails. However, the cause of nonresponse may have been a defunct organization or mislabeling, as in the case of an Arab American corporation that we mistook for a CBO.

We interviewed sixty Middle Eastern and Muslim American leaders, but our sample consists of fifty organizations. This is because in five organizations we interviewed at least two representatives and in two of the largest national organizations we conducted three interviews at different times (at one organization with the same person all three times). We conducted sixty-nine out of the seventy-five face-to-face interviews ourselves, either together or individually. The interviews were mostly held in the offices of the organization, or occasionally at a place designated by the respondent, such as a café or a park bench. In a few cases, respondents chose to come to MEMEAC's offices in midtown Manhattan. Outside New York and New Jersey, both of us visited Washington, D.C., twice (in 2002 and again in 2003) and took a trip to Dearborn (Michigan) in October 2002. Bakalian visited Chicago, and Bozorgmehr went to Los Angeles and again to Washington, D.C. To ensure that our sample would represent most of the ethnic/religious/national groupings in the Middle East, one of our research assistants conducted six interviews over the phone with spokespersons of groups that we had missed.

In April 2005 we presented our preliminary findings at an immigration workshop at the Baldy Center of the State University of New York at Buffalo. We took advantage of our visit to upstate New York to talk to several Arab and Muslim representatives in the area.[34] Our pressing concern was to discuss a border-crossing incident that had involved several members of the local Muslim community in December 2004. When these individuals attempted to return to their homes in Buffalo after attending a convention in Toronto, the border police detained a number of them for several hours despite their presentation of U.S. passports. Our conversations confirmed what we had read in the press.[35] We also wanted to visit Lackawanna, the home community of six Yemeni American men who had received training in an Al Qaeda camp in Pakistan,[36] but it was impossible. The community had become even more closed to outsiders after all the media attention, making us doubt that our short visit would have permitted access and yielded much significant information. Time is needed to gain the trust of such a wounded community. Also in January 2006, Bakalian attended the four-day convention of the National Network for Arab American Communities (NNAAC) in Dearborn, Michigan, where about a dozen CBOs were represented.

In addition to interviewing, we have been engaged in participant observation of the Middle Eastern and Muslim communities in New York City since September 2001. This is partly because of our professional affiliation as directors of a center whose mission is to promote the study of the Middle East and its diaspora, and partly because of Bakalian's volunteer service on three Middle Eastern nonprofit boards in New York City. We have also observed fourteen "know your rights" forums, town hall gatherings for community members, and meetings of advocacy groups in greater New York and Washington, D.C., between 2001 and 2003. We have kept abreast of research on the affected communities by collecting a large amount of documentation issued by Middle Eastern and Muslim CBOs. Since 9/11, we have subscribed to ethnic publications and listservs and have monitored their coverage continuously, selecting relevant articles and messages for subsequent use in the book.[37] The bulk of our evidence on mobilization comes from the Web sites and listservs of the Middle Eastern and Muslim CBOs, since our interviews predated this stage. While our last formal interview was in November 2003, we have continued to consult some of the leaders in our sample. Curiously, since embarking on this project, we have ourselves become a resource for foundations, journalists, and filmmakers seeking to learn more about Arab and Muslim American organizations. We can certainly say that as researchers we have not been sequestered in the proverbial ivory tower.

All interviews were tape recorded and later transcribed verbatim. In a couple of cases respondents did not want us to record the conversation, so we took extensive notes instead. Two graduate student assistants coded all the transcribed interviews using the qualitative software program N-Vivo.[38] Though this process was labor intensive and time consuming, it was essential for managing the voluminous amount of data we amassed. Searches for recurring themes and patterns in the data set yielded extensive quotes from respondents. We painstakingly read these quotes, organizing them into sections and subsections in the chapters. Our goal was to present the perspective of Middle Eastern and Muslim American leadership on the post-9/11 backlash. To validate our interviews, we cite corroborative evidence whenever possible.

## THE CASE FOR INTERVIEWING LEADERS OF COMMUNITY-BASED ORGANIZATIONS

Social scientists have documented the pivotal historical role that pioneering immigrant CBOs or ethnic voluntary associations played in helping newcomers adapt to life in America (e.g., Breton 1964; Handlin 1973; Mirak 1983; Thomas and Znaniecki 1918–20/1958; Warner 1963). However in recent decades, analysis of immigrant/ethnic organizations has fallen out of favor (see chapter 4). The main reasons for this waning interest are probably shifts in methodology and a preoccupation with sample representativeness. Sociologists are discouraged from collecting information from organizational leaders because arguably they are not "typical" community members.

We are cognizant of the pitfalls of attributing authority to community leaders. We agree with Brubaker that "rarely is a single 'leader' recognized as authoritatively entitled to speak in the name of the group. As a result, ethnic groups generally lack what states ordinarily possess, namely a leader or leaders capable of negotiating and enforcing settlements" (2004, 104). Since the 1980s, interest in nonprofit organizations has brought back attention to differences among organizational actors. It has become increasingly evident that disregarding the input of organizational and community leaders results in loss of knowledge on important topics that the average member cannot possess. Leaders can inform researchers about an organization's social context, institutional memory, relations with other organizations, organizational culture, and funding streams, as well as the political climate that helps or hinders their work. Caroline Nagel and Lynn Staeheli concur that "leaders are easier to find, at least initially, and they are more likely to respond to questions about websites, organizational goals . . . and the politics of citizenship the organization and its members may pursue" (2004, 11).

Leaders of CBOs have a unique vantage point as knowledgeable and articulate persons. When the terrorists attacked, the media were totally unaware of the Middle Eastern and Muslim American communities and thus had to educate themselves quickly by seeking out visible CBOs and their leaders. Given the crisis-driven nature of our study, we too found the organizational representatives most informed and communicative. They were uniquely positioned to answer questions not only about their communities but also about the larger picture—the government, the civil rights networks, the media, the justice system, and the American public.

Indirect evidence for interviewing leaders as opposed to rank-and-file members comes from the September 11 Digital Archive. Between June 2002 and March 2003, we collaborated with the archive in recruiting, training, and supervising three interviewers charged with finding Arab and/or Muslim individuals in New York City who would be willing to talk about their experiences on 9/11 and its aftermath. Initially, convincing people to be interviewed in the aftermath of the attacks was difficult, but assurances of complete anonymity resulted in seventy-two interviews (September 11 Digital Archive 2002–3).[39]

There was much overlap in the type of questions we asked the organizational leaders and the respondents in the September 11 Digital Archive project. We had hoped that the latter would provide insights about what members of the affected communities felt on the day of the attacks and what their experiences were afterwards. The yield from the individual interviews was very low. The vast majority of respondents did not experience backlash but had heard of such cases. There were a couple of interviews with persons who formed organizations in reaction to the attacks, which we have quoted from in this volume. The nonprobability sample of the September 11 Digital Archive makes it even more difficult for us to generalize the results to a larger population. In hindsight, this confirmed our decision to interview organizational leaders to learn about the backlash.

## PLAN OF THE BOOK

This book consists of eight chapters. In chapter 2, we compare and contrast the post-9/11 backlash with watershed cases in American history when the U.S. government targeted minorities or outgroups during times of political crises. We begin with the case of the Germans during World War I; next we analyze the Palmer Raids or Red Scare of 1919–20, when the rise of Bolshevik power in Russia was believed to pose a threat to the United States. The internment of the Japanese during World War II is no doubt the best-known example and the most egregious, having targeted all Japanese Americans, including the U.S.

born. During the Cold War, McCarthyism ignited many Americans' fears and imaginations of a communist threat and unfairly discriminated against individuals who had once been party members or sympathizers. A less-known episode is the mistreatment of Iranian foreign students in the United States during the hostage crisis in Iran (1979–81).

Chapter 3 examines the immigration patterns as well as the demographic and social characteristics of Middle Eastern, North African, and South Asian immigrants, since the foreign born were especially targeted. Unlike other minority groups such as Asian Americans or Hispanics, Middle Easterners are not considered an official minority. Individuals who trace their ancestry to the Middle East and North Africa are categorized as white. Sociologically, it makes sense to group Middle Easterners and North Africans from various countries in one category because they share many cultural, religious, historical, and political characteristics; the same applies to South Asians. The lack of accurate statistical data on these populations is a major handicap. They are too small to be included in most nongovernmental surveys. Even though it is possible to extract data from the open-ended ancestry question in the 1980, 1990, and 2000 censuses, the number of Middle Eastern Americans is believed to be undercounted. We are on firmer footing in identifying the foreign born through census data on country of birth. Arab Americans are "not quite white," and some have even argued that this supranational ethnic group has been "racialized" since 9/11, so we conclude with a brief discussion of identity politics.

In chapter 4 we review the sociological literature on CBOs as it applies to our study. We analyze how the structure and capacity of the organizations in our sample were transformed by the crisis. In particular, we focus on changes in their mission, personnel, and funding sources. We conclude by sampling a handful of new organizations that emerged after 9/11.

Next, we examine the impact of the post-9/11 backlash against Middle Eastern and Muslim American communities. In chapter 5, we begin with an exploration of hate crimes, profiling, bias incidents, discrimination in the workplace, and responses to women's wearing of the *hijab*. We also discuss how media biases and their inflammatory anti-Islamic rhetoric fuel hatred against the targeted populations and perpetuate stereotypes. Chapter 6 focuses on government initiatives. Though Arab and Muslim immigrant men have been most affected by the policies, their families, who depended on them for their livelihood, have also suffered. We conclude with a discussion of the repercussions of the backlash on the communities, namely their fear, anxiety, and growing mistrust of the government.

Chapter 7 examines the mobilization of Middle Eastern and Muslim American organizations. We analyze each of the components of their mobilization or claims making. We argue that with the passage of the civil rights laws new political opportunity structures opened up for Middle Eastern and Muslim groups, who were able to mobilize relatively rapidly. Framing mechanisms used by the CBOs in our sample included distancing from and condemning the terrorist attacks, demonstrating allegiance to the United States, and educating their fellow Americans about Islam and the Middle East. The CBOs relied on standard tactics in claims making, whereas the repertoire of the second generation included various cultural productions such as theater, comedy, and poetry. We analyze coalition building and political socialization as forms of resource mobilization. We conclude by exploring the three types of coalitions we identified—coalitions based on identity politics, situational alliances, and social justice alliances—and by discussing conflict within coalitions, which in our case means disagreements over domestic and foreign policy.

The final chapter centers on integration, since it has been the ultimate goal of mobilization for Middle Eastern and Muslim Americans. We begin by exploring the accommodations Muslim immigrants have to make to practice their faith in America. We devote the remainder of the chapter to civic engagement and political incorporation. We examine how the respondents in our study defined and envisaged integration: as a call to leave the "ghetto," become proficient in English, and engage in the civic and political life of the society, particularly voting and electoral politics, even at the risk of assimilation. We conclude this chapter with the summary and conclusions of the book.

# 2

# The Post-9/11 Backlash in Comparative and Historical Perspectives

For American historians the post-9/11 situation must seem like déjà vu. When France opposed the United States' invasion of Iraq, the congressional cafeteria replaced French fries with "freedom fries." David Kennedy reminds us that during World War I a hamburger was called a "liberty sandwich" and sauerkraut was dubbed "liberty cabbage" (1980, 68). Today, the "Bolshevik menace" has been replaced by the "Islamic menace." Some twenty books published within one year after 9/11 depict Muslims as a threat. According to the *Los Angeles Times* journalist Teresa Watanabe, "Two of those books are the best-selling titles among 7,219 books on Islam at Amazon.com: 'American *Jihad:* The Terrorists among Us,' by Steven Emerson, and 'Militant Islam Reaches America,' by Daniel Pipes."[1] During McCarthyism, communists were not granted fishing permits lest they contaminate New York City's reservoir (Schrecker 1998, 154). After September 11, a young Pakistani who delivered pizza for Domino's near Albany was accused of terrorism and detained. He was "caught" taking photos of a picturesque vista overlooking a water reservoir.[2] Sociologist Neil Smelser observes that "the impulse to blame is quick to spread symbolically to other groups believed to be related to or sympathetic with the identified perpetrator" (2007, 146).

President Bush declared the September 11, 2001, terrorist attacks to be an act of war against the United States. Whether the terrorist attacks qualify as war will no doubt be debated for years to come, but it is clear that the government effectively treated them as such, waging a "War on Terror" not only internationally, by invading Afghanistan and Iraq, but also domestically.[3] Historian Gary Gerstle has written on the remarkable similarity between the Red Scare of 1919–20 and the War on Terror. He argues, "Both campaigns crystallized around terrorist acts. . . . Both acts were the work of revolutionists. . . . The terrorists in both instances belonged to small cells. . . . Both acts of terrorism occasioned frenzied roundups by U.S. government authorities of thousands of immigrant suspects who were held for a long time, often without access to bail, attorneys, or decent conditions. Both of these roundups yielded remarkably little information about those who had been involved in terrorist acts while spreading fear in America at large about those populations of immigrants with whom the terrorists shared a nationality or religion" (2004, 106–7).

Government abuses of civil rights after 9/11 are not without historical precedent. In *All Laws but One: Civil Liberties in Wartime,* Chief Justice William Rehnquist shows how U.S. presidents have pushed the limits of the law during periods of war or political and ideological crisis (cited in Mark, Masters, and Metha 2002). On several occasions the U.S. government has targeted immigrant and ethnic populations who originated from the country with which the United States was either at war or in a warlike situation. The Japanese internment during World War II stands out as the most egregious case. Others include the mandatory registration and detention of German immigrants and citizens during World War I; the harassment and deportation of communist sympathizers after the Palmer raids (1919–20); the witch-hunt against suspected Communist Party members during McCarthyism; and the mandatory registration and threatened deportation of Iranian students in the United States during the hostage crisis in 1979–81.

In March 2002, Operation TIPS (Terrorism Information and Prevention System; see chapter 6) proposed that service personnel, such as mail carriers, "spy" on fellow citizens, but this initiative was defeated by American grassroots opposition. The TIPS project's historical precedent was Iowa's American Protective Association a century ago; it charged 250,000 volunteers to keep an eye on fellow Americans who had been born in Germany and Austria-Hungary and was supported with $250,000 from the Department of Justice (Painter 1987, 335). In this chapter, we compare these historical precedents to the post-9/11 government initiatives, highlighting their similarities and differences and accounting for the observed disparities.

Nativist backlash following a major national crisis has rarely been studied while still unfolding. Attempts to carry out impartial research were deemed imprudent since scholars ran the risk of being labeled unpatriotic. Historians will surely examine the 9/11 backlash in due course, and they have cautioned us from jumping to conclusions. Roger Daniels, the foremost historian of the Japanese internment, writes, "Historical analogies are always tricky, particularly when one of the things being compared is a current event. Contemporary history is, after all, a contradiction in terms. Nevertheless, the ways in which our memory of what was done to Japanese Americans has evolved over six decades can shed some light on our contemporary situation."[4] In the next section, we explore each of the historical precedents, including the stereotypes, discrimination, and scapegoating suffered by Middle Eastern and Muslim immigrants in America. Then we develop a typology of the scope of minority targeting in times of war or political/ideological crisis.

## PRECEDENTS IN U.S. HISTORY
### GERMAN AMERICANS DURING WORLD WAR I

Xenophobia reached unprecedented levels by the time the United States entered the Great War, and the Espionage Act of 1917 gave the government the tools to turn prejudice into policy. Those who obstructed military operations during wartime were threatened with fines of $10,000 and twenty years in jail. The U.S. government cited the anti-immigrant Aliens Act of 1798 as justification for the arrest of German Americans. Over 250,000 German immigrants, called "enemy aliens," were required to register at their local post office and carry their identity card at all times. German men over the age of fourteen were not allowed to own guns, radios, or explosives or to live near munitions factories or military areas. Fifteen states passed laws making English the official language, and the governor of Iowa banned the German language in public places such as streetcars and telephone booths (Kennedy 1980). Teachers and other school personnel had to take an oath of loyalty to continue their employment. History books deemed to be "pro-German" were banned. Such measures encouraged zealous groups to spy on and harass German Americans. Altogether, during the Great War, over six thousand Germans were arrested and over two thousand Germans were interned without charge (Luebke 1974).

As David Reimers (1998, 19) aptly says, "It seemed as if the war against Germany in Europe had degenerated into a 'War against German America.'" Past admiration for Germans' scientific and artistic accomplishments soon turned into hostility and race-based vilification of "Huns" or barbarians (Gerstle 2004). German ethnic organizations were attacked, and nativist anger was aimed at all things German. The hysteria led to the banning of Beethoven's music in Boston and the burning of German books in Lima, Ohio. Many German American institutions and organizations conformed to the demands of superpatriots. For example, Lutheran churches switched their service to English, and many German Americans anglicized their names (Gerstle 2004; Luebke 1974; Reimers 1998). The declaration of war led to the development of an ideology of "unhyphenated Americanism," including the 100 Per Cent Americanism movement.

## THE PALMER RAIDS

As World War I came to a close, Americans' new fear became the "Red Scare," shorthand for communism. In April 1919, thirty-two mail bombs were sent to the mayor of Seattle, a U.S. senator in Atlanta, and prominent businessmen and government officials (Gerstle 2004). Next, on June 2, 1919, bombs exploded in eight cities, including Washington, D.C., where the house of A. Mitchell Palmer, the attorney general, was partially destroyed. The culprit, who died in the blast, was an Italian anarchist. Palmer attributed the country's problems of economic recession and labor militancy to the "Bolshevik menace."

Under the Espionage Act of 1917 and the Sedition Act of 1918, Palmer and his young assistant J. Edgar Hoover compiled a list of supposedly subversive elements and proceeded, without search warrants, to raid a large number of labor union offices and headquarters of communist clubs and organizations.[5] Over 1,500 persons were imprisoned under the wartime statutes of the Espionage Act of 1917 (for obstructing the draft), the Sedition Act of 1918 (for any harsh criticism of the government and its war effort), and the Immigration Act of 1918 (the deportation of any alien who was an anarchist or "believed in the violent overthrow of the American government or advocated the assassination of public officials") (Camp 1995, 100).

Several thousand aliens were rounded up in the Palmer raids of late 1919, but only 591 were deported (Camp 1995, 102). The immigrants of the 1920s were Catholics, Orthodox Christians, and Jews from Russia and eastern Europe. The prominent radicals Emma Goldman and Alexander Berkman were among those extradited to the Soviet Union (Schrecker 1998). The arrests continued, and in January 1920 over four thousand radicals, many from the Industrial Workers of the World union, were caught in a sweep that spanned thirty-three cities in twenty-three states. "Meant to expose the extent of revolutionary activity, these raids netted exactly three pistols, no rifles, no explosives, and no plans for insurrection. Nevertheless, those arrested were jailed for weeks and, in some cases, for months without being charged with a crime and often under harsh conditions. Of these, 591 would be deported by the spring of 1920 and the rest would be released" (Gerstle 2004, 99). Unmistakably, Palmer used public hysteria to target revolutionaries and anarchists whom he deemed enemies of the United States.

## THE JAPANESE INTERNMENT

Following the bombing of Pearl Harbor, President Roosevelt issued Executive Order 9066 on February 19, 1942, directing the U.S. military to designate areas "from which any or all persons may be excluded." All Japanese Americans, including the U.S. born, were removed from western coastal regions and "relocated" to guarded camps in isolated regions of the country. They were forced to liquidate their property and were transported to ten detention camps in California, Idaho, Wyoming, Utah, Colorado, Arizona, and Arkansas. The War Relocation Authority records indicate that 120,313 Japanese Americans were held in custody between 1942 and 1946 (Daniels 1988, 241). Of these, over 70,000 were U.S. citizens (187). The camp population comprised the young and the old—77.4 percent were under twenty-five years old, but among the foreign born 57.2 percent were over fifty (Daniels 1993, 104). Camp conditions were poor because of overcrowding, the cost of food was rationed at forty-eight cents per internee, and there was a limited supply of coal for heating. Later in the war, even when American-born Japanese men joined the U.S. armed forces, the government was slow in freeing their families. President Roosevelt rescinded his order after two and a half years, but the last camp was shut down in 1945 (Daniels 1988). The right to become a U.S. citizen was not granted to Japanese immigrants until the McCarran-Walter Act of 1952 repealed the blanket exclusion laws.

Executive Order 9066 was also responsible for the arrest of 3,200 resident aliens from Italy and some 11,000 Germans, including naturalized citizens. Of these, over 300 Italians and 5,000 Germans were interned during World War II (Daniels 1972). There was no mass internment, even though the German American Bund was "a dangerous pro-Nazi organization" and "German submarines regularly prowled the Atlantic coastline . . . [and] debark[ed] saboteurs . . . to blow up key American army, munitions and communications facilities" (Gerstle 2004, 104).

The Japanese, and other Asians, had been denied a right that whites had always enjoyed and that freed slaves had received after the Civil War.[6] What explains the massive removal of Japanese men, women, and children from the Pacific Coast region? Some have blamed special interest groups, but this does not explain why the Japanese were unpopular throughout the nation. There is also little support for the hypothesis that military purposes required evacuation. If the Japanese were indeed a threat to security in California, where they constituted less than 2 percent of the population, why were fewer than 2,000 Japanese rounded up out of the 158,000 living in Hawaii, where they constituted 35 percent of the population? Moreover, the evacuation was deemed a "military necessity" by politicians, not by the military. Historians have argued that if generals had been the decision makers they would have acted differently, knowing quite well that the Japanese military did not have the capacity for a full invasion of the United States. Harry Kitano notes that wartime exigency trumped constitutional guarantees as the Supreme Court turned down several cases. Eventually in 1944, in *Endo v. United States*, it found the detention and relocation of loyal Japanese Americans unlawful. Kitano concludes, "The incarceration of an entire ethnic group without any hearing or any formal charge having been brought against a single member has been described as the worst assault on civil rights in American history" (1980, 567).

## MCCARTHYISM

Joseph McCarthy, Republican senator from Wisconsin, was the point man of the anticommunist crusade after World War II. Even though he gave his name to the movement, historian Ellen Schrecker argues that it would have been more accurate to call it "Hooverism" (1998, 203). Between 1950 and 1954, the FBI's Security Index of purportedly dangerous individuals grew from twelve thousand to twenty-six thousand. Moreover, the FBI "checked out two million federal employees and conducted 20,000 full-field investigations. Its roster of agents increased from 3,559 in 1946 to 7,029" in 1952 (211). Communist Party members could not apply for a passport, and radio and television broadcasts and mailings by suspect organizations were heavily restricted. Though an estimated 74,000 individuals were officially registered with the Communist Party in 1947, Hoover calculated that another 486,000 were "fellow travelers" (Navasky 1980, 24). Ironically, "there was no realistic need for this kind of surveillance," as the Communist Party's power had dissipated by 1952 (Schrecker 1998).

Immigrants were also considered dangerous. Victor Navasky explains that the 1952 Immigration and Nationality Act was used to arrest aliens without a warrant, hold them without bail, and deport them: "Among the grounds for deportation was membership in any subversive organization as defined by the Internal Security Act. Information from anonymous informers could be invoked at the deportation hearings, and no hearing needed to be granted to deportees if the disclosure of evidence was found 'incompatible with national security'" (1980, 23). Mere allegations of communist sympathies were enough to ruin immigrants' careers and reputations.[7]

The House Un-American Activities Committee (HUAC) is best known for its investigation of communism in Hollywood in 1947 (Navasky 1980). It pioneered many of the methods that have become the trademark of McCarthyism—accusations with little evidence, hearings where those questioned or even mentioned were automatically assumed to be guilty, and witnesses strong-armed to implicate their colleagues. Joseph McCarthy was not a member, but the senator and the committee had similar goals and tactics.

## THE IRANIAN HOSTAGE CRISIS

After the Iranian Revolution of 1978–79, relations between the United States and Iran became strained, as Washington was a longtime supporter of Mohammad Reza Shah Pahlavi. When the exiled shah entered the United States in October for medical care, many Iranians feared a repetition of the U.S.-assisted coup that had put the shah back on the throne in 1953. This concern instigated the "Iranian Hostage Crisis," which began when a crowd of about five hundred militants stormed the U.S. Embassy in Tehran on November 4, 1979, and captured about ninety employees who were inside. Fifty-two Americans were held hostage for 444 days. In retaliation, the federal government and several states enacted measures that specifically targeted Iranian students in the United States. In November 1979, the attorney general, at the direction of President Carter, required all Iranian nationals who were in the United States on student visas to report to the Immigration and Naturalization Service (INS) for registration by mid-December. Each nonimmigrant alien was required to provide proof of residence and full-time school enrollment and a passport with a valid visa (Bozorgmehr 2000). The regulation implied that noncompliance would be considered a violation of the conditions of the alien's stay in the United States and thus grounds for deportation under the Immigration and Nationality Act.

The hostage crisis prompted a presidential order known as the Iranian Control Program, which screened almost fifty-seven thousand Iranian students, the single largest group of foreign students in the United States at the time. However, the program was not aimed at students only. According to the INS Annual Report, the new policy "effectively prohibited the entry of most Iranians into this country" (1980, 7). Because of the permanent closure of the American Embassy in Iran, Iranians, even over a quarter of a century later, must still first travel to a transit country to obtain a U.S. visa.

## PRECEDENTS OF BACKLASH AGAINST MIDDLE EASTERNERS AND MUSLIMS
### STEREOTYPES AND SCAPEGOATING

As anti-Japanese racism provided the backdrop for Japanese Americans' internment during World War II, so too did anti-Arab, anti-Muslim, and anti–Middle Eastern stereotypes in American popular culture facilitate the backlash after 9/11. At the turn of the twentieth century, early immigrants suffered from prejudice and discrimination. With their "olive skin, dark eyes, large mustaches, and shabby clothes," the new immigrants were unable to "pass" as white (Naff 1985, 247). In Birmingham, Alabama, the local congressman called these immigrants "the most undesirable of the undesirable peoples of Asia Minor" (quoted in Naff 1985, 250). In the 1920s, Syrian children, especially Muslims, were called "camel jockeys," "black," "dirty Syrians," and most often "Turks" (Naff 1985, 252). The word *Turk* was particularly offensive because these groups had emigrated to escape the Ottoman Turks. A century later, Arab and Muslim Americans continue to be taunted "with epithets such as *sandnigger, dune coon, camel jockey, towelhead,* and *raghead*" (Salaita 2006, 13).

According to Jack Shaheen's *Reel Bad Arabs* (2001), between 1896 and 2001 Hollywood produced more than nine hundred movies depicting Arabs as terrorists, rapists, con men, and other unsavory characters—without one positive portrayal.[8] Many of these films, such as *The Sheik* (1921), starring Rudolph Valentino, have entered mainstream iconography as classics. Shaheen has also documented stereotypes in television (1984) and comic books (1994). Iconic images vilifying Middle Easterners continue to appear insidiously in American popular culture.[9] Therefore, stereotypes of Arabs have been not only perpetuated but also reinforced.[10]

Nabeel Abraham has argued that anti-Arab racism is not only tolerated but manipulated by the government and political figures "to garner public support for domestic or foreign policy objectives" (1994, 195). Michael Suleiman explains that after the 1967 Arab-Israeli war, "Arabs in America, both newcomers and third-generation descendants of the early pioneers, deeply resented the extreme partisanship . . . America . . . showed toward Israel and the occasional hostility toward Arabs" (1999, 13). They started to organize in order to counter the stereotypes and offer alternative perspectives to American foreign policy in the Middle East (see Shain 1999 and chapter 4 of this book).

During the last decades of the twentieth century, newsworthy incidents involving or affecting Americans in the Middle East resulted in increased anti-Arab/Muslim backlash in the United States.[11] These included the 1973 oil embargo,[12] the Iranian Hostage Crisis, the 1983 bombing of a U.S. Marine barracks and the U.S. Embassy in Beirut,[13] the hijacking of TWA flight 847 to Beirut,[14] the killing of passenger Leon Kinghoffer on the *Achille Lauro* cruise ship,[15] the First Gulf War (1990–91), and the 1993 World Trade Center bombing.[16] With each incident, Middle Eastern and Muslim Americans were scapegoated and the terrorist stereotype was reinforced. The most extreme backlash incident was the murder of Alex Odeh in the wake of the *Achille Lauro*. At the age of forty-one, Odeh, the regional director of ADC, was blown up by a booby-trap bomb attached to his office door in Los Angeles on October 11, 1985 (Abraham 1994, 163). It was not surprising that when the terrorists bombed the federal building in Oklahoma City on April 19, 1995, killing 168 innocent people, some Americans were quick to blame Middle Easterners.[17] Understandably, when news of 9/11 broke out, Middle Eastern Americans immediately feared for their lives.

Public opinion polls have consistently reflected the American people's negative stereotypes of Middle Easterners and Muslims. Here we offer a sample. A national survey of a random sample of 2,910 Americans, conducted between September 18, 2002, and February 25, 2003, for the Religion and Diversity Survey found that 5 percent said they were very familiar with Islam while 33 percent said they were somewhat familiar with it. Only 8 percent of sampled Christians had ever attended a service at a mosque, in contrast to 25 percent who had attended a synagogue (Wuthnow 2005, 206). Remarkably, 32 percent of the sample had had no contact with Muslims. Of those who had had a "fair amount of contact" (24 percent), almost two-thirds found Muslims "mostly pleasant" (213). Additionally, this survey showed that 47 percent of the sample considered Muslims fanatical, 40 percent violent, 34 percent backward, 57 percent closed-minded, and 44 percent strange (the percentage exceeds 100 because of multiple responses). While 38 percent of respondents wanted to make it harder for Muslims to settle in the United States, 71 percent said they would "not object at all" if their child wanted to marry a Muslim. When asked how they would feel if a mosque were built in their community, 40 percent of the sample said they would not be bothered, and 16 percent said they actually would welcome it (216–17, 219). As can be seen, there are discrepancies in the findings. The polls show that an acquaintance with a Muslim enabled respondents to debunk some of the most egregious stereotypes.

A national opinion poll conducted by Cornell University in November 2004 revealed increasing bias and anti-Islamic prejudice among the American public (Nisbet and Shanahan 2004). Nearly half (47 percent) of the 715 individuals who participated in the survey agreed that "Islam is more likely to encourage violence compared to other religions." Only 27 percent agreed that "Islamic values and beliefs are similar to Western/Christian values and beliefs." Respondents who described themselves as highly religious Christians tended to have more negative views of Islam and Muslims. More specifically, 42 percent said Muslim Americans should register their whereabouts with the government, 29 percent said the government should profile Muslim citizens, and 40 percent said Muslim civic and volunteer organizations should be infiltrated.

Right after the London bombings in July 2005, the Pew Research Center for the People and the Press and the Pew Forum on Religion and Public Life commissioned a national opinion poll (N = 2,000) on Islam and Muslim Americans, which they then compared to previous surveys conducted in July 2003 and March 2002. While they found an increase in Americans' positive attitudes toward Muslim Americans (55 percent, up from 50 percent in 2003 and 45 percent in 2002), opinions about

Islam as a religion were stagnant. More than half of those surveyed believed that Islam was very different from their religion—59 percent in 2005 versus 60 percent in 2003 (see Pew Research Center 2005).

The Genesis Research survey commissioned by CAIR (2006a) used random-digit sampling to generate one thousand telephone interviews in June/July 2004 and again in November 2005. The results indicate that negative comments about Muslims had decreased slightly between 2004 and 2005 (32 percent vs. 26 percent) and that positive comments had slightly increased (from 2 percent to 6 percent). There was a statistically significant decline in the percentage of respondents who believed that all Arabs were Muslims (from 25 percent to 18 percent between 2004 and 2005). Likewise, there was a drop in the proportion of people who believed that Muslims should be locked up (from 21 percent to 17 percent). It was ironic that while the majority of Americans admitted that they did not know much about Islam (CAIR 2006a) they still had strong opinions about this religion and its practitioners.

A national sample of 1,007 adults conducted in July 2006 by *USA Today*/Gallup Poll reiterated the results of previous surveys. Americans harbor stereotypes against Muslims, with only 39 percent acknowledging their prejudice. More specifically, 49 percent do not think Muslims are loyal to the United States; 31 percent get nervous when they realize that a Muslim man is flying on the same airplane as they are; 57 percent favor Muslims' undergoing more intensive security measures at airports; and 59 percent think Muslims should be required to carry an identity card. A personal acquaintance with a Muslim made respondents less likely to favor ID cards for Muslims, more willing to have a Muslim neighbor, and slightly less approving of airport profiling.[18] In summary, anti-Muslim racism or Islamophobia persists in the United States.[19]

## THE "L.A. 8"

One of the noteworthy legal cases of pre-9/11 government harassment of Arab Americans is that of the "L.A. 8." Six Palestinian men and the Kenyan wife of one of these men were arrested in their homes in Los Angeles on January 26, 1987. A week later, an eighth person was detained while taking an exam in a community college. When prosecutors were unable to prove subversion, six of the members were indicted for visa violations. The two permanent residents, Michel Ibrahim Shehadeh and Khader Musa Hamide, were charged with circulating and distributing material endorsing the overthrow of the U.S. government and with preaching world communism because of their association with the Marxist Popular Front for the Liberation of Palestine (PFLP) (Abraham 1994; Moore 1999; Motomura 2006).

Arguing that they were merely engaged in lawful political activities protected by the First Amendment, ADC defended the case of the L.A. 8. In *American Arab Anti-Discrimination Committee (ADC) v. Reno*, the Court of Appeals of the Ninth Circuit affirmed in 1997 the rights of noncitizens to free speech and association, stating: "Aliens, who often have different cultures and languages, have been subjected to intolerant and harassing conduct in our past, particularly in times of crises. . . . It is thus especially appropriate that the First Amendment principle of tolerance for different voices restrain our decisions to expel a participant in that community from our midst" (quoted in Moore 1999, 93).[20] However, the U.S. Supreme Court's 1999 ruling in *Reno v. American Arab Anti-Discrimination Committee (ADC)* argued for prohibiting access to courts during deportation proceedings and allowing only one appeal at the conclusion of the process, thereby further limiting the rights of noncitizens (Moore 1999, 94).

Two decades after the arrest of the L.A. 8, Bruce E. Einhorn, an immigration judge in Los Angeles, dismissed the case of Hamide and Shehadeh, ruling that the government had failed to show evidence of their membership in PFLP and that it could not deport permanent residents just because they advocated for Palestinians' right to a homeland. None of the L.A. 8 had been accused of criminal wrongdoing. Ironically, one of them, Aiad Barakat, had been sworn in as a U.S. citizen in 2006, three others were permanent residents, and one had an application for permanent residency pending. The *Los Angeles Times* reported that while the "Constitution does not permit 'guilt by association'" the government had "twice persuaded Congress to change laws and make them retroactive in an effort to be able to deport the two men." In October 2007, the United States dropped its charges against the remaining two defendants, finally bringing the case of the L.A. 8 to a close.[21]

## LEGAL DISCRIMINATION IN THE 1990S: SECRET EVIDENCE

President Clinton signed into law the Antiterrorism and Effective Death Penalty Act of 1996 to alleviate heightened anxieties about illegal immigrants.[22] It allowed INS to arrest, detain, and deport noncitizens on secret evidence if they were deemed to be national security threats. The defendant and his lawyer would be denied access to documents revealing the nature of the charges and their provenance. Additionally, the 1996 Illegal Immigration Reform and Immigrant Responsibility Act allowed courts to deny bond to noncitizens facing criminal charges and deportation based on secret evidence. Thus not only was the accused incarcerated and unable to post bail, but the defense was handicapped in preparing its case adequately.

Secret evidence clearly violates the due process rights of defendants guaranteed by the Fifth Amendment. According to AAI, secret evidence in deportation hearings was used in the 1990s almost exclusively against about two dozen Arab and Muslim men. In most cases the government attorney, using undisclosed documents, persuaded the immigration courts that the defendant was associated with an enemy of the United States. An ADC Action Alert elaborates: "Secret evidence has included rumors, innuendo, racist stereotyping, faulty translations, and the testimony of a vindictive ex-spouse or girlfriend."[23]

We were fortunate to interview a leader charged with secret evidence.[24] He told us:

> Secret evidence means it is classified information; it cannot be shared with the defendant or the defense attorney. It can only be presented to the court and also can be shared with the judge. And the judge even cannot view these matters before he or she obtains a security clearance. In order for this evidence to be presented and accepted as secret evidence, it has to have an executive order signed by the INS commissioner. . . .
>
> At that time, me and my attorney were stunned because I was simply waiting to receive my adjustment of status, my green card. All of a sudden, I received a letter stating, "You are to be at the INS office at this date with luggage, and you will be deported." When I called my attorney, I said, "What's going on here?" He said, "Beats me. I don't know." . . . My case was supposedly processed and reviewed by the immigration judge, and the BIA [Board of Immigration Appeals], and there were no problems. . . . The first round . . . took place in [date]. This was where the judge was stunned. The judge said, "I assume this case is over in fifteen or twenty minutes if all documents are in order," simply because the BIA overruled the INS, canceled the deportation, restored my work permit, and sent my files to the immigration judge reopening my case for adjustment of status. So the judge . . . was smiling. He had no idea about what was going on.
>
> Then the INS attorney said, "No, your honor. It is not ten or fifteen minutes. We have evidence to present to argue against adjustment of status." The judge said, "What kind of new evidence? This case was reviewed by the BIA and sent to reopen. I don't see anything here." They said, "It's secret." The judge said, "What do you mean, secret?" They said, "Secret in that we cannot share it with the defendant, or the attorney. We can only share it with you. And even you, sir, Your Honor, you need to check with

the court about the procedures." He said, "What do you mean, I have to check?" They said, "Well, there are certain procedures." The judge was in disbelief about what he was hearing, because it was the first time for him to hear about it. . . .

I had a ruling in my favor. So what happened here is that the judge put the court in recess. And then he came back half an hour later, smiling again. He said, "Guess what, I learned something new. I never knew that I needed a security clearance even to see this evidence." My attorney said, "Your Honor, I would like the court to order the INS to give us a brief about this secret evidence." He did, but the INS, as usual, never did tell you what is this. They give you maybe a sentence or two words, just saying, "linked to terrorism," or "membership in a terrorist group," or something.

So we had to go through the full-course hearing. That was held on [date]. We went through a five-hour hearing. They went to the judge's chambers and discussed the secret evidence. At the end of the day, the judge came and he asked my attorney to put his final argument against the secret evidence. My attorney said, "Your Honor, I don't know what is the secret evidence. So how do you expect me to put an argument against evidence you only saw and debated with the government?" He said, "I understand, Mr. [name], but you have to say something." He said, "What should I say?" He said, "Say something. You have been doing a good job of speculation." The judge was even confused, so he was telling my attorney, "Say anything. Just go along with what you were saying. Just put the final argument."

At the end of the day, he ruled in my favor. He stated clearly that he had reviewed the evidence. He didn't see it as of a nature to incriminate me and to pluck my adjustment of status. He granted me to become a permanent resident. We thought that was the end of it.

However, the respondent's saga took over five years to be resolved. Even after the Board of Immigration Appeals ruled in his favor in 1999, his citizenship papers were put on hold, and he did not get his citizenship until 2001. When we asked him, "What was the evidence against you?" he replied:

It stated that I had been working at places that I never worked at. One of the evidences was that I was working in a [name] shop that is located in [place], and this [name] shop is operated and owned by the Popular Front for the Liberation of Palestine. We brought [in] the owner. The owner is an engineer in [name] who worked with the most sensitive military authorization. He testified that I [had] never worked there. He had never heard of me. And it was stated that I was part of this [name] shop. Another thing was that it was stated, "Subject wearing a T-shirt." They circled the T-shirt by saying I was wearing the PFLP logo. It was obvious to whoever saw the photo that it was the Lebanese and the Palestinian flag. And it was like from [date] and said, "Unity is strength." It had nothing to do with that specific group.

Though INS made his "life miserable" for many years, this respondent remained gracious and forgiving. Like many other respondents whose voices resonate in this book, he survived his ordeal with an even stronger faith in the American Constitution and the sense of fairness and justice of the American people. He vouched, "I trust always that justice will prevail and the true fabric of this nation will prevail. The other thing that helped me is that if I were to face this ordeal in any other part of this world, I might not have a chance even to speak about it." Our respondent acknowledged that being a community leader "only helps, because it gives you the visibility and opportunity to present your case to all of these people involved and who care about justice, and to deal with injustices."

## A TYPOLOGY OF MISTREATMENT OF MINORITIES (OUTGROUPS)

We draw on Michael Mann's controversial and provocative book *The Dark Side of Democracy: Explaining Ethnic Cleansing* (2005) to explain how the state may be an instrument of repression, even murder. Drawing on the history of the development of democracy in the twentieth century, Mann asserts that "democracy has always carried with it the possibility that the majority might tyrannize minorities, and this possibility carries more ominous consequences in certain types of multiethnic environments" (2). Stable democracies in North America, Europe, and Australia have had murderous episodes in their history, though now minority populations are relatively more protected by law. Mann is convinced that it is futile to stop most ethno-nationalist movements from claiming their people's autonomy because the "nation-state is too strongly entrenched in the modern world for them to be simply repressed or ignored" (2005, 523). Yet he is careful not to suggest that ethnic cleansing is necessary or a fundamental element of human nature.

To clarify the "types of violence and cleansing in intergroup relations," Mann develops a sophisticated typology with two axes (2005, table 1.1). The first axis deals with the degree of an ethnic group's purging or "cleansing" from society: "none," "partial," or "total." The second axis focuses on the degree of violence used to reach this end, ranging from "none," to "institutional coercion," to "policed repression," to "violent repression," to "unpremeditated mass deaths," and finally to "premeditated mass killing." Thus, when there is no violence and no cleansing, ethnic groups are tolerated or allowed to coexist in a multicultural society. At times the ethnic group will negotiate with the

TABLE 1. TYPOLOGY OF STATE POLICIES TOWARD MINORITIES (OUTGROUPS)
IN TIMES OF WAR OR POLITICAL/IDEOLOGICAL CRISIS

| Characteristics of Crisis | Times of War or Political/Ideological Crisis | | | | | |
|---|---|---|---|---|---|---|
| | *World War I* | *Palmer Raids* | *Japanese Internment* | *McCarthyism* | *Iranian Hostage Crisis* | *Post–9/11 Backlash* |
| Cause of crisis | U.S. entry into the war in 1917 | "Bolshevik menace" | Foreign attack on Pearl Harbor | Cold War (Fear of Soviet invasion) | Taking of American hostages in Iran | Terrorism on U.S. soil |
| Targeted ethnic minorities (outgroups) | German Americans | Communist Party members (many Jews and Italians) | Japanese Americans | Communist Party members and sympathizers | Iranian students | Middle Eastern and South Asian immigrants |
| Legal status of targeted population | Naturalized citizens and immigrants | Citizens, naturalized citizens, and immigrants | Citizens and naturalized citizens | Citizens and naturalized citizens | Foreign nationals | Noncitizens and immigrants |
| U.S. government policy | Internment, cultural suppression, involuntary assimilation | Expulsion to Soviet Union | Internment | Detentions, loss of livelihood, becoming a pariah | Deportation | Detention, deportation |
| Yield from government investigations | None | Minimal | None | Minimal | None | Minimal |
| Response of affected groups | Rapid assimilation | Limited challenge | Short-term acquiescence, long-term redress | Limited challenge | Few lawsuits, no response | Mobilization and political integration |

host society a "consociational" agreement or confederation. At the other extreme, the highest level of violence ("premeditated mass killing") combined with total cleansing leads to genocide.[25]

Mann's less severe forms of violence, "institutional coercion" and "policed repression," illustrate the mistreatment of minorities (or what Mann calls "outgroups") during periods of crisis or war. The mildest form of institutional coercion is "discrimination." However, if there is partial cleansing, the outcomes are "official language restriction" and "segregation," measures that remind us of the Japanese experience during World War II. Total cleansing at this level implies "cultural suppression" of an ethnic group, as in Germany during World War I. The combination of no cleansing with a more severe form of violence, "selective police repression," applies to the deportations of Middle Easterners and Muslims after 9/11. But the combination of "partial cleansing" with "selective police repression" could involve partial repression of the minority group's language and culture through policing. More ruthless forms of cleansing result in total police suppression of the group's language and culture, as well as deportations and pressure to emigrate. As Mann argues, and we attest in the case of the 9/11 backlash, the presence of civil rights laws can prevent implementation of the more ruthless measures of state repression.

Next we develop a similar typology of the historical watershed events we discussed above by focusing on (1) the cause of the crisis; (2) who was the target; (3) the legal status of the targeted group(s); (4) the U.S. government's reaction; (5) the yield from the investigations; and (6) the response of affected groups (see table 1). Then we delve into a more extensive comparison of the Japanese internment and the post-9/11 backlash. We conclude this chapter with a discussion of the legality of the governmental measures taken in the 9/11 backlash and the factors that have restrained the post-9/11 governmental response.

## THE CAUSE OF THE CRISIS

In the historical precedents that we analyzed above, identifiable sovereign states attacked American interests, and the United States targeted persons of those nationalities or their sympathizers in retribution. The treatment of Germans during World War I, the Japanese internment during World War II, and the Iranian Hostage Crisis in 1979–81 followed the belligerent actions of specific foreign nations. On the other hand, the Palmer raids and McCarthyism were responses to alleged threats of communism to national security and as such targeted communist sympathizers of all stripes. In contrast, the 9/11 attacks were masterminded by a terrorist network extending beyond national boundaries. Bin Laden, the assumed 9/11 mastermind, was born in Yemen, became a Saudi national, and operated Al Qaeda out of Afghanistan. Al Qaeda leaders and members hailed from a variety of Arab and Muslim countries, and some were studying or working in Europe and the United States. Given the mix of the terrorists' nationalities, all Arabs and Muslims in the United States became the target of retribution.

## TARGETED GROUPS

During World War I, German Americans were under attack. Though the Japanese were the prime targets during World War II, some Italians and Germans were also apprehended. During the Red Scare, Bolshevik sympathizers and anarchists were suspected of sedition. Many were immigrants from Russia and eastern Europe, and a sizable number were Jewish. McCarthyism most severely affected former Communist Party members, who again were largely of immigrant stock. Iranian students in the United States were targeted during the hostage crisis. Since the 9/11 hijackers were young Arab/Muslim men, the government profiled immigrants with these personal characteristics.

Estimates of the size of the Arab population in the United States range from 1.2 to 3 million, and those of the Muslim population range from 2 million to 6 million (see chapter 3). Even if one excludes African Americans, who make up about one-third of Muslim Americans, the residual figure is still substantial. Clearly, even the low estimates make the post-9/11 targets more numerous than the historical precedents. Their case might best be compared to that of the two million Germans in the United States in 1917 (Higham 1988).[26]

## CITIZENSHIP STATUS

Perhaps the most outstanding difference among all these cases is that the German and Japanese victims, as well as the communist sympathizers, included *citizens* as well as *aliens* or *noncitizens*. The Iranian foreign students who were subject to deportation were noncitizens. The post-9/11 government initiatives almost exclusively targeted noncitizen men from twenty-five Arab or Muslim countries. Only the 9/11 backlash and the Iranian Hostage Crisis have targeted overwhelmingly noncitizens.

The only person in the United States to be charged in connection with the 9/11 terrorist attacks, Zacarias Moussaoui, is a French citizen of Moroccan descent. He was indicted on six terrorism conspiracy charges and pled guilty even though he was in prison on an immigration violation at the time of the attacks. Though the prosecutor asked a federal jury to sentence Moussaoui to death for concealing knowledge of the 9/11 plot, he was sentenced to life in prison in May 2006.[27]

Most of the detainees charged with terrorism have been noncitizens, but a handful, including John Walker Lindh, Jose Padilla, Yaser Hamdi, Hamid Hayat, and the Lackawanna Six, have been U.S. citizens. Lindh, "the American Taliban," was born in California and captured in Afghanistan. He was charged with "conspiring to kill Americans and aiding Al Qaeda" (D. Cole 2003, 1, 3). His trial in criminal courts in the United States was settled when he pled guilty to minor charges (D. Cole 2003). Padilla, a Puerto Rican convert to Islam, was detained in 2003, but his trial did not begin until April 2007 because the Bush administration repeatedly changed its accusations. Padilla was incriminated for planning to detonate a "dirty bomb," for planning to blow up an apartment complex, and, finally, for conspiring to support terrorism as an Al Qaeda operative.[28] In August 2007, he was found guilty of conspiracy to murder and kidnap overseas.[29] Hamdi is a U.S.-born Saudi who was captured in Afghanistan in November 2001 and subsequently indicted for fighting with the Taliban, though his family claimed he was on a humanitarian mission. In June 2004, the U.S. Supreme Court ruled that even terrorism suspects like Hamdi have the right to appeal to the U.S. courts to challenge their imprisonment. They affirmed, however, that the administration has the authority from Congress to hold U.S.-born citizens as enemy combatants. On September 15, 2004, Hamdi was released from military prison without facing any allegations of terrorist-related activity and was allowed to fly to Saudi Arabia.[30] Hamid Hayat, a U.S. citizen of Pakistani descent from Lodi, California, was convicted for aiding terrorists and providing false statements to the FBI and was sentenced to twenty-four years in prison. An informer who received $200,000 from the FBI testified that Hayat had attended a training camp in Pakistan and had a connection with Al Qaeda. Hayat's lawyer has questioned the validity of the government's case to no avail.[31] In the case of the Lackawanna Six, which involved U.S.-born Yemenis, the FBI postponed its arrests until a witness testified that the men had been trained by Al Qaeda.[32]

That post-9/11 government policies have been directed against noncitizens cannot be attributed to the nature of the threat. Terrorism can easily be carried out by citizens: we need only recall that the bombing of the Murrah Federal Building in downtown Oklahoma City on April 19, 1995, was carried out by Timothy McVeigh, a U.S.-born white supremacist.[33] Thus the focus on noncitizens is a very significant and a sharp departure from the historical patterns in this chapter.

The governmental backlash against foreign nationals is clearly demonstrated by its actions at Guantánamo Bay, in Abu Ghraib, and in rendition cases. These have been widely publicized as examples of the Bush administration's disregard for human rights. Some may contend that Guantánamo Bay, Abu Ghraib, and rendition practices should be considered part of the backlash.[34] Although these fall outside the framework of our U.S.-focused arguments, we will briefly describe them to make an analytical distinction.

Shortly after 9/11, the U.S. naval base in Guantánamo Bay, Cuba, began holding "enemy combatants" (D. Cole 2003; D. Cole and Lobel 2007), foreign nationals captured abroad (Amnesty International 2005). Most had been seized during the war in Afghanistan, allegedly for involvement with the Taliban or Al Qaeda.[35] The Guantánamo detainment center quickly gained media attention when allegations of unfair treatment and abuses of justice surfaced. On December 30, 2005, President Bush signed the Detainee Treatment Act, prohibiting cruel treatment of detainees but limiting their right to judicial review of their detention conditions. In October 2006 he authorized the Military Commissions Act, further subjecting Guantánamo Bay detainees to laws significantly deviating from traditional U.S. standards of justice.[36] By December 2006, over 750 individuals, all labeled "enemy combatants," were being held at the base without having been tried or even formally charged (Amnesty International 2006). The mishandling of detainees in Guantánamo has led to both domestic and international protests. Citing "arbitrary detention" and human rights abuses, a United Nations report called for the closure of the detention facilities in 2006.[37] By late 2007, the Bush administration was considering closing Guantánamo and transferring the detainees.[38]

Abu Ghraib, a prison complex in Iraq originally built in the 1960s and notorious for its role in Saddam Hussein's repressive regime, was used by the American military to hold Iraqi prisoners following the U.S. invasion.[39] A report by U.S. Major General Antonio Taguba in early

2004 disclosed severe mistreatment of prisoners at Abu Ghraib. By late April 2004, *60 Minutes* and the *New Yorker* released evidence of abuses of prisoners by American soldiers, including photographs of prisoners in humiliating positions.[40] This publicity partly contributed to the American military's March 9, 2006, decision to transfer the approximately 4,500 detainees to other prisons, thereby ending Abu Ghraib's tenure as a detention facility.[41]

To formally sidestep United Nations rulings, President Bush pronounced the Geneva Conventions inapplicable to terrorist detainees at Guantánamo Bay in February 2002. He thereby discounted the federal war crime statute's application to the Guantánamo Bay case.[42] Furthermore, the Justice and Defense Departments also drew their own definitions of permissible "coercive interrogation" techniques; these included sleep deprivation and the experience of painful physical conditions. The government had originally declared Abu Ghraib subject to the Geneva Conventions, but in 2003 a Pentagon-initiated study suggested that Guantánamo Bay's interrogation techniques be extended to Abu Ghraib. The Pentagon's study recommendation thus blurred the line between what the Geneva Conventions "permitted" at Guantánamo Bay and at Abu Ghraib.[43]

The practice of rendition, which involves transporting foreign nationals suspected of terrorism to a third country for interrogation, has been documented in governmental directives since the 1990s (ACLU 2005; Human Rights Watch 2006), but its use became widely publicized after 9/11. Rendition is questionable on two counts: first, that due process is not offered to the detainee prior to rendition, and second, that the rendition is carried out because the United States presumes that the foreign country uses torture as an interrogation technique to obtain information the United States cannot obtain. The American Civil Liberties Union (ACLU 2005) cites expert estimates that approximately 150 foreign nationals were subject to rendition between 2001 and 2005 and reports that four criminal investigations of CIA rendition activities in Europe have been initiated.[44] Perhaps the most famous case of rendition is that of Maher Arar, who was arrested at JFK Airport while changing planes on September 26, 2002. He was rendered to Syria, where he was tortured during interrogation. Ultimately he was released for lack of evidence (see D. Cole and Lobel 2007).

While the cases of Guantánamo Bay and Abu Ghraib as well as rendition clearly represent some of the most extreme examples of American governmental flaunting of universal human rights principles, the scope of our book deals principally with domestic American issues and persons arrested on U.S. soil. Instances involving international territory, United Nations conventions, and the detention of foreigners captured abroad are beyond the scope of this volume.

## U.S. GOVERNMENT POLICY

The U.S. government's reaction to political/ideological crises has depended not only on the nature and scope of the crisis but also on the domestic political and legal situation at the time. The most extreme response, in terms of the number of persons targeted, was during World War II. As noted above, over 120,000 Japanese Americans, 70,000 of whom were U.S. born, were relocated to camps. The next most extreme case was during World War I. The government arrested over six thousand German Americans and interned two thousand. Additionally, over 250,000 German immigrants were required to register.

The Red Scare led to the arrest of over ten thousand Bolsheviks and the deportation of a few hundred, most of whom were Jews or Italians. During McCarthyism, several thousand individuals and their families whose communist sympathies were declared by suspicious neighbors, coworkers, and even friends in front of the hearings of the House Un-American Activities Committee and other official boards lost their jobs and were stigmatized. Many were unable to earn a living for several years afterwards. The U.S. government reacted to the Iranian Hostage Crisis by threatening Iranian students with deportation. After holding 7,177 deportation hearings, it ordered 3,088 students to leave the United States, and the departure of 445 was verified (Bozorgmehr 2000).

The Bush administration may have used the Iranian hostage crisis in support of its initiatives against Middle Eastern and Muslim immigrants after 9/11. However, the regulation requiring Iranian students to register with INS had a narrower focus. It was based on national origin—not ethnicity, race, or religion (Chishti et al. 2003). Perhaps this explains why the civil rights community did not step in to help the Iranians. At that time, there was no established Iranian community, let alone an Iranian advocacy group. It is ironic that newly arrived Iranian exiles, who were opposed to the Islamic regime, faced unfair targeting and scapegoating in their adopted country, making them double victims.

In the post-9/11 case, Arab and Muslim noncitizen men have suffered the most from U.S. government policies, but it is not yet known how many of those detained, interviewed, and registered have been deported because the government has not published these statistics. Even less is known about how many decided to leave the country voluntarily. However, about six thousand Arab and Muslim absconders were sought;[45] 42 percent of those invited for "voluntary interviews" were questioned; about twenty were arrested on immigration and criminal charges; at least 231 individuals were deported, more than half of them Pakistanis; and fewer than 1 percent of the five thousand Iraqis were detained after interviewing. Estimates of the detainees vary from the inspector general's estimate of 762 illegal immigrants from the Middle East or South Asia to 1,200 from other sources (Chishti et al. 2003, Appendix F). By May 2003, about eighty-two thousand had obeyed the "special registration" orders of NSEERS (the National Security Entry-Exit Registration System), and almost 1,200 were detained. While Iranian nationals were detained and deported in relatively modest numbers, they became victims of NSEERS in larger numbers.

It is patently unfair to quantify a people's suffering and declare that one group has suffered more than another. Yet unless we assess and observe the qualitative differences in mistreatment of minorities, we will not be able to account for what has changed over time and why. Relative to earlier political/ideological crises, the tangible government reaction to 9/11 to date appears to be relatively moderate. Zolberg (2002, 287–88) seconds this opinion, noting, "In contrast with previous surges of securitarian nationalism provoked by international conflicts, most notoriously in the wake of Pearl Harbor when the U.S. government treated all ethnic Japanese as suspects, including American citizens, governmental responses to 9/11 were restrained. Not only were there no wholesale denunciations of particular groups, but instead, the President pointedly visited a mosque and the mayor of New York explicitly admonished the city's residents not to seek revenge on Arabs or Muslims." From a historical perspective, this marks a positive development. It is important to note that many Americans have shared the values of the decision makers and executors of discriminatory policies and have acquiesced to their actions. During McCarthyism, for example, the entertainment industry, philanthropic foundations, and even civil rights and professional organizations such as the National Association for the Advancement of Colored People (NAACP), the ACLU, Americans for Democratic Action, and the American Association of University Professors did little publicly to change the status quo (Schrecker 1998).

## YIELD FROM GOVERNMENT INVESTIGATIONS

Although none of the drastic measures taken by the U.S. government since the beginning of the twentieth century have proven that there was a real threat from the groups under scrutiny,[46] discriminatory practices have generally created precedents, thus making it easier for future administrations to target outgroups. The Japanese redress movement may have served as a major deterrent to the large-scale detention of Middle Easterners and Muslims. In 1976, President Ford declared, "Not only was that evacuation wrong, but Japanese Americans were and are loyal Americans" (Daniels 1993, 90). In 1989, President George Bush authorized redress, and the attorney general held a small ceremony on October 9, 1990, to distribute checks in the amount of $20,000 to elderly camp survivors (Daniels 1993, 105). A presidential apology letter was sent to the Japanese who had been interned or evacuated or who had lost property or liberty. Additionally, there was a public education effort to send the message "never again," including mention in textbooks and museum exhibits. In his book on reparations, John Torpey writes that "the history of the Japanese American internment has had some effect on recent discussions of the treatment of Arab Americans, reminding the public of a dishonorable past experience and a warning against repetition" (2006, 105).

## RESPONSE OF AFFECTED GROUPS

As table 1 shows, the affected groups in times of war or political/ideological crisis have responded in a variety of ways. At one end of the continuum is German Americans' rapid assimilation, while at the other end is the Japanese Americans' long-term redress movement, preceded by short-term acquiescence. Between these extremes, we find limited challenge in the case of the Palmer raids, McCarthyism, and the Iranian Hostage Crisis. Clearly, the post-9/11 mobilization and potential for integration stand out in historical context.

In response to anti-German attacks by the U.S. government and overt discrimination during World War I, German Americans defended their loyalty, enlisted in the army, changed their names, and removed the word *German* from institutional names and commercial labels. The vast majority of German-speaking immigrants and their children felt that they had no choice but to publicly declare their support for the war

(Higham 1988). In summarizing the situation during this period, Kennedy (1980, 54) writes, "The perpetrators of these measures cared little for President Wilson's nice distinctions between the German government, with which the United States was at war, and the German people, toward whom Wilson wished to extend the hand of respect and conciliation." Kathleen Neils Conzen writes that the outcome "was the rapid dismantling of the associational structure of German America. The total number of German-language publications declined from 554 in 1910 to 234 in 1920; daily newspaper circulation in 1920 was only about a quarter of its 1910 level. Language shift accelerated rapidly in the churches as elsewhere; in 1917 only one-sixth of the Missouri Synod Lutheran churches held at least one English service a month, while by the end of the war, three-quarters were doing so. The National German-American Alliance dissolved in April 1918 under Senate investigation" (1980, 423).

In response to the Red Scare and McCarthyism, Bolsheviks and the targeted communities were mostly focused on defending their members. The National Civil Liberties Board (NCLB) asked Elizabeth Gurley Flynn, a veteran of the Industrial Workers of the World (IWW), to organize a separate foundation through which labor-related groups could support defenses of such cases. She thus headed the Workers Defense Union (WDU), which drew membership from over 170 organizations, including labor unions and radical groups. "In the first year-and-a-half of its existence the WDU distributed over \$12,500 for defense and raised over \$35,000 for bail" (Camp 1995, 90). The WDU also asked prominent liberals to write letters of protest to the government (Camp 1995, 100). By 1920, there was a shift in public opinion through the efforts of the WDU, and with internal dissensions in the Wilson administration, many more deportations were averted (Camp 1995, 99–101). The WDU also helped the defense of nonalien radicals on trial (Camp 1995, 102–3).

During World War II, Japanese Americans complied with Executive Order 9066 and cooperated overwhelmingly with the authorities. For example, immediately after Pearl Harbor, the Japanese American Citizens League (JACL) wired President Roosevelt, pledging the loyalty of its members (Daniels 1972).[47] There was both active and passive resistance among the internees,[48] but even when they resisted the draft and challenged the constitutionality of drafting interned citizens, the JACL director disassociated his organization from them (Daniels 1972). After the war, JACL's major political activities shifted to eradicating anti-

Japanese discrimination and commemorating the wartime achievements of Japanese servicemen.[49] Many U.S.-born men and women of Japanese ancestry enlisted in the armed forces as soon as they were given permission to demonstrate their loyalty to the United States. "The record of the 42nd Combat Team and the 100th Battalion composed of 33,000 Japanese Americans from Hawaii and the mainland was unparalleled. The most decorated units in American military history, they suffered more than 9,000 casualties" (Kitano 1980, 567). The redress movement was born after the war; almost twenty years later President Ford acknowledged the mistake of the U.S. government, and another decade elapsed before the distribution of monetary compensation for all those who had been interned.

The trials of communist leaders under the 1940 Smith Act were a direct response to McCarthyism. Twelve of them were on trial in the case that went to the Supreme Court in 1951 as *Dennis v. United States* for the act of having reconstituted the Communist Party of the United States in 1945. Elizabeth Gurley Flynn, who was also a Communist Party leader, orchestrated the defense and raised $500,000 from 1948 to 1950 from party members and affiliated groups (Camp 1995, 211). Flynn also tried to mobilize liberal public opinion, but even groups like Americans for Democratic Action (ADA) and the American Civil Liberties Union (ACLU) were very reticent in their responses (Camp 1995, 214).

In response to President Carter's decree that all Iranian nonimmigrant aliens register with the INS, several Iranian students sued the government to overturn the order. The plaintiffs used the protection of personal rights under the Fifth Amendment to argue that the government had unfairly singled out Iranians. The defense retorted that the regulation served "overriding national interests." The district court dismissed this claim, finding only a dubious connection between protecting the lives of American hostages in Iran and singling out Iranians for registration with INS. It asserted instead that the regulation seemed to appease the American public's demand for action in response to the hostage crisis. When the government appealed, the D.C. Circuit Court of Appeals reversed the lower court's order, noting that the Immigration and Nationality Act had given the attorney general sufficiently broad authority to screen aliens of certain nationalities (Chishti et al. 2003, 139–40).

In this book we argue that in contrast to historical precedents, the post-9/11 mobilization of Arab and Muslim Americans has been exceptional. Chapters 7 and 8 describe their response.

## COMPARING THE JAPANESE INTERNMENT AND THE POST-9/11 BACKLASH

The Japanese internment was on the minds of many Middle Eastern and Muslim Americans after 9/11. Several respondents wondered anxiously whether history would be repeated. An American-born woman told us, "I think a lot of people in the community after [9/11] . . . were talking about . . . Japanese Americans. Could that kind of internment situation occur [again]? Could we all be shipped out? Is it relevant that you have an American passport if your last name is [Arab name]?" As time passed, there was some relief: "Thank God, we have to admit that the officials in the United States . . . did not make the mistake that our leaders previously did when they [made] a massive arrest of the Japanese."

Hadi Jawad, an Iraqi-born American citizen, told journalists that when the FBI came knocking at his door "it reminded me of what was done to . . . the Japanese during the Second War."[50] Likewise, in Southern California, during the special registration initiative, Reuters quoted Ramona Ripston of the ACLU: "I think it is shocking what is happening. It is reminiscent of what happened in the past with the internment of Japanese Americans. We are getting a lot of telephone calls from people. We are hearing that people went down wanting to cooperate and then they were detained."[51] Among thousands of Iranian Americans who protested special registration in mid-December 2002 in Los Angeles, some carried banners asking: "What's next? Concentration camps?"[52]

There is ample evidence that Japanese Americans were quick to draw the same parallels and that they observed the gravity of the 9/11 backlash with empathy.[53] For instance, a study that interviewed a sample of Japanese who had been interned on the subject of reparations found that many compared the experiences of Arab and Muslim Americans after 9/11 to their own during World War II. One respondent said, "I cringe when I see the government bypassing judicial procedure by using military tribunals." Another noted that "the current climate is an echo of everything that was said in 1942." Yet another echoed, "Every Arab could be targeted and the administration won't care about the Constitution and government protocol" (quoted in Torpey 2006, 102). The comparison was the subject of a 2004 documentary by the Japanese American filmmaker Lina Hoshino, *Caught in Between: What to Call Home in Times of War.*[54]

Japanese Americans reached out to the affected communities in solidarity and goodwill. Several of their activities have been documented, as in the following *Los Angeles Times* story:

Among the Muslim community's new friends is Japanese American activist Kathy Masaoka of Nikkei for Civil Rights and Redress. Listening to the radio after the terrorist attacks, Masaoka said fears expressed by Muslims struck an instant emotional chord, reminding her of her own family's ordeals after Pearl Harbor. Two weeks after Sept. 11, she helped organize a candlelight vigil for the victims of terror and to express support for innocent Muslims, Arabs and South Asians. Since then, she has helped form a committee to forge friendships with her community through picnics, dinners, cultural exchanges and Buddhist-Muslim dialogues.

"I don't think they should have to feel responsible for all of the actions done by others from other countries who don't represent them," Masaoka said, adding that her Muslim friends have shown her a faith of compassion and good deeds. "We weren't responsible for Pearl Harbor, and we don't have to prove our loyalty any more than anyone else. They shouldn't have to, either."[55]

In support of Arabs and South Asians detained after September 11, three grandchildren of interned Japanese Americans filed an amicus brief opposing a Brooklyn federal judge's June 2006 ruling that gave the government the right to detain noncitizens indefinitely on the basis of their race, religion, or nationality. They argued that the Brooklyn judge "overlooks the nearly 20-year-old declaration by the United States Congress and the president of the United States that the racially selective detention of Japanese aliens during World War II was a 'fundamental injustice' warranting an apology and the payment of reparations." It must be noted that this third-generation activism among Japanese Americans has been rare compared to the activism of the second generation, who devoted their lives to seeking reparations.[56]

Middle Eastern and Muslim American respondents in our study were forthcoming with compliments about the sympathy they had received from an ethnic group that had experienced backlash in the past. A leader in Dearborn noted how much he appreciated their support, adding, "I don't think anyone is as sensitive to what is going on in the Arab American community as the Japanese Americans." Another respondent stated, "The only thing that I can say for sure is that there's a lot more sense of closeness between the Japanese American community and the South Asian community" (see also Naber 2002). Since 9/11 the Muslim Political Affairs Council (MPAC) and other organizations have regularly reported interfaith activities with Japanese Americans, such as the *iftar* (breaking the fast of Ramadan) that brought together Muslim, Japanese, and Mexican Americans at the Senshin Buddhist

Temple in Los Angeles in 2003.[57] And on September 19, 2001, a multi-ethnic, multireligious gathering held a press conference at the National Japanese American Memorial in Washington, D.C., to mourn those who had lost their lives to the terrorist acts and to show solidarity in the various alliances being forged between Japanese/Asian American and Middle Eastern American organizations. The location of the meeting was undoubtedly strategically chosen. The symbolism could not be ignored. Respondents praised Transportation Secretary Norman Minetta, who presided over the ceremony and had been interned with his family during World War II, as "a great guy [who] understands" the plight of Arab and Muslim Americans.

In response to our question about the lack of public outcry during the Japanese internment, an Arab American noted, "At the time, they were not as sophisticated, the civil rights laws were not in place." A knowledgeable source of Japanese descent chimed in:

> In 1941, they didn't have any options, they were facing guns. It was a situation beyond their control. There is a Japanese saying that goes, "It can't be helped." This was the pre–civil rights era. . . . Asian ethnic groups, including the Japanese, have the cultural value of going with the consensus. So they went with the government's edict. Everyone else thinks that it was fault of the Japanese leadership at the time. The leaders in 1941 . . . reasoned that if we fight, more damage will be done. There are people who said JACL was responsible. But there was no community that had power or sway. . . . Even the ACLU didn't support the Japanese community in 1941–42.

A high-ranking government official replied more defensively to our question: "If you look at the case of the Japanese Americans in the 1940s and compare it with today, there is no comparison. We're more respectful of civil rights today than one or two generations ago. There will always be criticism, we're not going to say that we are perfect; we could always do better. . . . The media misinformed people about what we are doing. Once people understand, they will realize that we are serious about protecting civil rights. We are open to people's ideas in the community."

Although the post-9/11 governmental initiatives targeting Middle Eastern and Muslim Americans are most reminiscent of the Japanese internment, Daniels warns us to not push the comparison too far: "Many commentators have compared the two cases—some seeing a disturbingly similar pattern in the reaction against a feared nonwhite population, others praising what they see as the relative moderation of today's government. . . . But when compared with what was done to

Japanese Americans during World War II, government actions before and after September 11 do not seem to amount to very much. Indeed, many media commentators have objected that even to mention them in connection with the massive violations of civil liberties by the Roosevelt administration is inappropriate."[58]

## THE LEGALITY OF THE POST-9/11 GOVERNMENT INITIATIVES

There has been considerable debate since 9/11 regarding the legality of the government initiatives that targeted Arab and Muslim noncitizens. Some have argued that these initiatives are merely legitimate immigration control measures—appropriate responses to the profile of the terrorists and the fact they used tourist (and, in one case, student) visas. And indeed, as Bill Ong Hing writes, "After the tragic events of September 11, 2001, perpetrated by foreign nationals who entered as nonimmigrants, a call for more restrictive immigration policies might seem the natural response" (2006, 46). Hing goes on to point out, however, that "while such a response was predictable, it was misguided and has inevitably resulted in overreaction" (47). He argues that a less, rather than more, restrictive immigration policy is more in the interests of U.S. national security. Similarly, David Cole and James Dempsey, who have aptly given their book *Terrorism and the Constitution* the subtitle *Sacrificing Civil Liberties in the Name of National Security* (2002), argue that in delicately balancing liberties and security the U.S. government should not trample on the rights of vulnerable immigrants. They state that "while the post-September 11 response does not yet match . . . historical overreactions, it nonetheless features some of the same mistakes of principle" (151). Elsewhere, Cole argues that in spite of "talk about the need to sacrifice liberty for a greater sense of security, in practice we have selectively sacrificed *noncitizens'* civil liberties while retaining basic protections for citizens. It is often said that civil liberties are the first casualty of war. It will be more accurate to say that noncitizens' liberties are the first to go" (2003, 955; italics in original). He challenges this "double standard" not only on the grounds that it is against U.S. security interests both normatively and constitutionally but also on the grounds that it is likely to end up encroaching on citizens' liberties as well.

Cole contends that the line between citizen and noncitizen can easily be crossed. He finds ample support for this in U.S. history, corroborating our analysis in this chapter. The Sedition Act of 1918 punished political dissidents during the Palmer raids for allegedly disrespecting the government—noncitizens and citizens alike. Japanese Americans were interned for fear of potential subversive action. During the McCarthy era, communist ideology and political association trumped race in the arrests and the eventual deportation of radical citizens along with radical aliens. Undisclosed evidence was used to incriminate the L.A. 8. The underlying rationale has been that aliens should not benefit from due process in the same manner as citizens. However, Cole contends that "contrary to widely held assumptions, the Constitution extends fundamental protections of due process, political freedoms, and equal protection to all persons subject to our laws, without regard to citizenship" (2003, 221).

Some legal scholars have argued that post-9/11 government policies are less about citizenship status than about Arab or Muslim identity and that they exemplify unconstitutional racial/religious profiling. Susan Akram and Maritza Karmely (2005) argue that the government has targeted Arabs and Muslims, both aliens and citizens, beginning long before 9/11 and suggest that their alien versus citizen status is actually a "distinction without a difference." Elsewhere, Akram and Kevin Johnson (2004) point out that as far back as the 1970s U.S. laws and policies targeting Arab and Muslim noncitizens have been predicated on the assumption that Arabs and Muslims in general are potential terrorists. Leti Volpp (2002) similarly maintains that those who appear Middle Eastern, Arab, or Muslim, regardless of their citizenship status, are excluded from being considered American because of the legitimization of racial profiling and the redeployment of Orientalist stereotyping. Still, Volpp holds that a clear distinction exists between the treatment of citizens and that of noncitizens, which underscores the fact that formal, legal rights do make a difference.

According to law professor Hiroshi Motomura, after 9/11 the U.S. government adopted a double standard in the justice system—one for citizens and another for noncitizens[59]—for reasons of convenience: "Noncitizens can be arrested, detained, and deported under immigration law with little recourse to the constitutional protections that would limit the government outside of immigration. For this reason, the government found it easier after September 11 to proceed against noncitizens in the United States who were suspected of terrorist ties by enforcing immigration laws, rather than initiating criminal prosecutions" (2006, 174). Immigration law is now being used as antiterrorism law through "new patterns of enforcing laws that have long been on the books" (177), and those singled out on suspicion of terrorism are Arabs and Muslims.

However, racial/ethnic profiling as a law enforcement technique can be sloppy and irrational, and the yield in this case has been negligible. Motomura writes, "The thousands of detentions that resulted from the post-September 11 immigration law enforcement against Arabs and Muslims led to virtually no terrorism convictions. Racial or ethnic profiling can cause ethnic communities to mistrust enforcement agencies, and the failure to enlist these communities' assistance may be fatal to investigate terrorism" (181). Further, Motomura points to the harm that targeting Arab and Muslim noncitizens inflicts on citizens: "The assumption was that profiling in immigration law enforcement hurts only the noncitizens who are arrested, detained, or deported. Even the administration's critics seemed to accept this assumption and did not press the point that post-September 11 enforcement treads too much on *citizens'* civil rights" (182, italics in original). Motomura's argument rests on the belief that the function of immigration policy is to ensure the nation's safety and the well-being of its citizens. The Bush administration has ignored the fact that noncitizens have strong intimate, professional, and civic ties to U.S. citizens. Profiling burdens loved ones and ethnic/ religious communities with the stigma of guilt and increases their vulnerability to hate crimes. As Motomura says, "The real test of profiling is how it affects citizens, and the worst aspect of plenary power is that it disregards the interests of citizens in choosing new citizens, and thus in shaping their national future" (2006, 183). Motomura asserts that just as settlers on the western frontier circled their wagons to defend themselves against Native American raids, the Bush administration has kept Middle Eastern and Muslim Americans outside the circle. The problem is that "as soon as enforcement of immigration law relies on race and ethnicity, then a person's race and ethnicity will matter more than whether he is a citizen" (187).

## FACTORS LIMITING THE POST-9/11 GOVERNMENTAL POLICIES

Why have the post-9/11 government initiatives differed so markedly from their historical predecessors? There are several plausible explanations. First, the passage of the civil rights laws of 1964 and 1965, with their far-reaching legal consequences, has undoubtedly made a dramatic difference. Networks of rights-oriented grassroots advocacy nonprofits have emerged since the 1960s as watchdogs of the nation's constitution and legal framework. Activists have been able to mobilize their constituents whenever they see threats to the erosion of hard-won civil rights. Among others, the American Friends Service Committee and the ACLU were at the forefront of advocating for the rights of individuals held in detention centers in New Jersey and New York City. They tend to be successful whenever a large proportion of the public believes in a specific right, as was the case with the TIPS program, which proposed to enlist thousands of mail carriers, electricians, and other service providers as "citizen observers." TIPS was defeated when extensive media exposure resulted in outrage among the American public. The ACLU orchestrated the media blitz and the subsequent repeal (see Appendix).

Civil rights organizations have filed lawsuits against the government's excesses during the post-9/11 backlash.[60] In the first class-action case to reach a federal court, the Center for Constitutional Rights represented brothers Hany and Yasser Ibrahim, who were detained in the weeks after 9/11 and then deported to their native Egypt. They had overstayed their tourist visa. The judge, who heard the case in June 2006, allowed that the government had the right to detain noncitizens but faulted its abusive and unconstitutional confinement conditions. The judge's decision implies that former attorney general John Ashcroft and FBI director Robert S. Mueller will have to appear in court to answer these accusations. Constitutional scholars and the civil rights community found the ruling problematic because it would encourage profiling, and they have vowed to appeal.[61]

A second, related explanation for the relative restraint in the case of 9/11 is that, as Richard Alba and Victor Nee write, "*In the post-civil rights era, the institutional mechanisms for monitoring and enforcing federal rules have increased the cost of discrimination in non-trivial ways*" (2003, 54, emphasis in the original). Torpey argues that in response to the civil rights movement "the architects of the movement for Japanese American redress believed that it was strategically important to frame their demands in terms of constitutional violations—transgressions against the rule of law itself—rather than in terms of the wrong inflicted on a particular groups. Instead, they stressed that, as a violation of the Constitution, it was a wrong done to the entire country" (2006, 87). The Japanese redress movement, which resulted in the passage of the Civil Liberties Act of 1988, cost the U.S. government $1.6 billion. It is no wonder that the consensus at the highest levels of government not to repeat "our worst wartime mistake" seems to hold, at least for now.

Third, pluralism and multiculturalism have replaced the assimilation ideology of the early twentieth century. Since the civil rights movement, minority populations have fought for greater inclusion in the Anglo/ WASP mainstream. Both quantitatively, because of the influx of new immigrants, and qualitatively, because of the increased acceptance of ethnic and other minority diversity, American society has become more accepting of cultural pluralism. Even the "system" is more careful to respect minority and ethnic cultures.[62]

Fourth, the role of the major U.S. newspapers, such as the *Washington Post*, the *New York Times*, and the *Los Angeles Times*, in exposing government abuses of civil rights has been critical. Globalization, especially in communications, has made news dissemination instantaneous, and the Arab and Muslim world is watchful. When the U.S. government profiles Middle Eastern and Muslim Americans and violates their human rights on our home turf, its proposals for improvement of human rights in the Middle East appear hypocritical and foment anti-American sentiments.

In conclusion, in the parlance of social movement literature, the institutionalization of civil rights laws opened new political opportunities for the affected communities. In the last quarter of the twentieth century, the United States experienced a major shift in its institutional structure and ideological outlook that has made minority/outgroup mobilization not only possible but also supported by the large oversight organizations that monitor governmental action/inaction.

Additionally, the passage of several decades since the civil right laws has allowed the American people to become more familiar with the implications of the laws. Though race remains a heinous discriminatory marker in the United States, there is widespread acceptance of cultural diversity: that is, "discursive opportunity structure" (e.g., Koopmans et al. 2005). Therefore, the political climate at the turn of the twenty-first century has been more conducive to claims making, an opportunity the Japanese and Germans did not have when they suffered backlash in the twentieth century.

# 3

# Immigration Patterns, Characteristics, and Identities

Given the dearth of information on Middle Eastern and South Asian immigrants and the extent of misinformation about them, it is necessary to address their migration patterns as well as their demographic and socioeconomic characteristics. These patterns and characteristics, in addition to cultural similarities stemming from their ethnic/religious traditions and historical roots, form the structural basis for their pan-ethnic categories. We begin by exploring the variety of labels and names given to these groups by insiders and outsiders. Next, we list the sources of information about these populations, such as the census. Finally, we analyze patterns of Middle Eastern and South Asian immigration, population size and distribution in the United States, socioeconomic characteristics, and contested identities.

## TERMINOLOGY

The term *Middle East* refers to an almost contiguous area stretching from Morocco in the west to Afghanistan in the east. There is no consensus on which countries make up the Middle East, but the core countries include the following geographical clusters: Turkey, Syria, Lebanon, Israel, Palestine (the West Bank and Gaza), Jordan, Iraq, Iran, Saudi Arabia, Yemen,

Oman, United Arab Emirates, Qatar, Bahrain, Kuwait, Egypt, Libya, Tunisia, Algeria, Morocco, and Mauritania. Afghanistan is a special case, as it is alternatively included in the Middle East, South Asia, or Central Asia. Similarly, Sudan and Somalia are alternatively included in the Middle East or North Africa, given their cultural and linguistic affinities with both regions.[1]

Some international organizations (e.g., the World Bank, the International Monetary Fund) use the combination *Middle East and North Africa (MENA)*, and the United Nations separates North Africa from western Asia (Armenia, the Arab countries, Israel and Turkey, and South Central Asia), Iran, and Afghanistan. In his widely used book *The Middle East and Central Asia*, Dale F. Eickelman confirms that "the region's inhabitants did not coin the term 'Middle East.' Like older, geographically restricted labels such as 'the Near East' and 'the Levant,' it originated with nineteenth-century European strategists and is unabashedly Eurocentric" (2002, 5). *Mashreq* (east) and *Maghreb* (west) are indigenous words that have entered Western, especially French, dictionaries. *Asia Minor* and *Mesopotamia* are historical references. The Arabian Peninsula, the Persian Gulf region, and the Arab world are some of subregions in the area.

This book uses the broadest definition to demarcate the Middle East and, by implication, its diaspora. We focus mainly on the countries that have sent a relatively large number of immigrants to the United States. Since immigrants from predominantly Muslim Bangladesh, Pakistan, and Afghanistan were affected by the post-9/11 backlash as well, we include them in our analysis separately.[2] Afghans, Bangladeshis, and Pakistanis are often classified as South Asian, though they have much in common with Middle Easterners culturally and religiously.

## SOURCES OF DATA

Because the literature on Middle Eastern Americans is sparse, studying this pan-ethnic group is daunting.[3] The task is further hampered by the lack of official data, since these populations are classified as "white" by the Office of Management and Budget. Middle Eastern Americans did not take part as a group in the civil rights movement of the 1960s, which was instrumental in mobilizing several pan-ethnic groups for inclusion in the nation's minority preference programs. As Michael Omi and Howard Winant explain, "The ability of racially based movements to *rearticulate* traditional political and cultural themes—first among blacks, and later among Latinos, Asian Americans, and Indians—permitted the entry of millions of racial minority group members into the political process" (1994, 138, italics in original). The lobbying efforts of the Association of Indians in America in the 1970s entitled them to be subsumed under Asian Americans[4] (Kibria 2006, 215). Since Middle Easterners did not make similar demands, they remained in the "white" category. At the time, many relatively high-status Arab Americans resisted being lumped with disadvantaged blacks and Hispanics, and even today affluent Iranian Americans feel the same. Moreover, this historical moment occurred before the influx of large numbers of new Middle Eastern immigrants.

The race question on the short form of the decennial census, which every household in the United States receives, has been one of the primary tools for generating demographic information on minority groups. Subsumed under the "white" racial category, people of Middle Eastern descent can be traced only through their first and second responses to the open-ended ancestry question. The ancestry question first appeared in the 1980 census and was repeated in the 1990 and 2000 censuses. The long form of the census questionnaire, which included the ancestry question, was sent to one in every six households, and the results were adjusted statistically. Many Middle Easterners who did not receive the long form and therefore were not able to report their ancestry dismiss the census enumeration of these populations. Respondents were asked: "What is this person's ancestry or ethnic origin?" Only two responses could be given in the blank spaces provided. By necessity, the ancestry question was open-ended: that is, no options were presented for the respondent to choose from. While some wrote in "Lebanese," "Arab," or "Iranian," it is possible that others did not understand the question, left it blank, or gave problematic religious responses (e.g., "Muslim" or "Jewish") that were not coded by the census. Additionally, later-generation Lebanese and Syrians with known high rates of intermarriage may not have listed their Arab ancestry as their first or second choice, so that they would not be counted as Arab American. Moreover, when parents reported a specific Middle Eastern ancestry (e.g., Arab) but left that of their children blank, the U.S. Census Bureau did not assign the parents' ancestry to the children, as it did with race. These issues resulted in an undercount of Middle Eastern Americans.

AAI has successfully lobbied to serve as one of the forty-seven national Census Information Centers that collaborate with the U.S. Bureau of the Census for improved data collection and analysis on Arabs. Since 1996, AAI has also been a member of the Working Group on Ancestry in the U.S. Census because of the issue's importance for its constituents.[5] It appears that the 2010 census will consist only of the short form.[6] The American Community Survey will be used in place of the long form to collect ancestry data. Since a survey involves a smaller sample size than a census, its use increases the likelihood of underestimating the Middle Eastern population,[7] creating further challenges for data analysis on them.

Middle Easterners are hardly mentioned in the vast social science literature on immigration and in ethnic and racial studies. Even *Immigrant America*—the most widely used textbook on immigration, now in its 2006 expanded third edition—pays little attention to Arabs and Muslims in spite of the authors' acknowledgment of public hostility against them since September 2001 (see Portes and Rumbaut 2006, 335–39). Members of this population are often placed in a residual category after all other specific and broad ancestry categories have been defined (e.g., Lieberson and Waters 1988). Even the burgeoning literature on the various ethnic and religious groups from the Middle East is not cited in the mainstream literature.

Despite these problems, the absence of an official minority status has been the main reason for the invisibility of Middle Easterners in the American ethnic mosaic, especially before 9/11. Legal minority status is a U.S. government designation that affords members access to affirmative action preferences, as well as many set-aside programs. Omi and Winant explain these entitlements or benefits as follows:

> How one is categorized is far from a merely academic or even personal matter. Such matters as access to employment, housing, or other publicly or privately valued goods; social program design and the disbursement of local, state, and federal funds; or the organization of elections (among many other issues) are directly affected by racial classification and the recognition of "legitimate" groups. The determination of racial categories is thus an intensely political process. Viewed as a whole, the census's racial classification reflects prevailing conceptions of race, establishes boundaries by which racial "identity" can be understood, determines the allocation of resources, and frames diverse political issues and conflicts. (1994, 3)

Because data are not available separately for Middle Easterners, it is difficult for these groups to prove that they suffer from systematic discrimination. For instance, the National Iranian American Council encountered difficulty assembling sufficient evidence to demonstrate discrimination against Iranians. The objective was to qualify for U.S. Small Business Administration programs, which would have entitled Iranian Americans to government contracts and financial aid loans as disadvantaged minority members.

The dearth of demographic data and statistics on Middle Eastern Americans only reflects their larger sense of invisibility, which several community leaders and activists have noted. One respondent stated: "Lebanese and Syrian population in Brooklyn, they've been here for such a long period of time, but people really have no sense of them being here, except for Atlantic Avenue." Another respondent elsewhere in the country said: "We usually describe ourselves as the unnoticed community . . . the invisible community." Community organizations have encountered difficulty in applying for grants for social and mental health services and legal clinics. Before 9/11, mainstream philanthropic foundations were largely unfamiliar with this population. Members of these groups must repeatedly explain why they are victimized in renting, buying property, applying for loans, getting admitted to college, or applying for jobs.

In spite of these shortcomings, even the existing official governmental statistics on these populations have not been tapped. We use the most recent census (2000) on demographic and socioeconomic characteristics of Middle Eastern and South Asian groups. We also draw on data from INS and from DHS, which since 9/11 has replaced INS: *Annual Reports* (U.S. INS 1968, 1970), *Statistical Yearbooks* (U.S. INS 1978, 1980–81, 1987), and the *Statistical Yearbook of the Immigration and Naturalization Service* (U.S. DHS 1996–2005). Focusing on immigration patterns and socioeconomic characteristics provides a clearer background about Middle Eastern and South Asian immigrant (foreignborn) populations, the targeted segments of the groups under study.

## IMMIGRATION PATTERNS

### THE PIONEERS

In the aftermath of September 11, the American public's attention increasingly focused on Arab and Muslim Americans. They were suddenly "discovered" in spite of their presence in the United States for over a century. Middle Easterners began arriving to the United States in large numbers during the classical period of mass migration (1880–1930). The first wave of immigrants started arriving from the eastern Mediterranean shores of the Ottoman Empire in the last two decades of the nineteenth century. Immigration statistics show that 34,207 people were admitted from 1881 to 1900. The numbers rose tenfold to a total of 325,259 for the years 1901–30.[8]

Several factors encouraged the emigration of the pioneers.[9] During the waning years of the Ottoman Empire, economic and social problems were widespread. Additionally, several massacres in the late nineteenth century and the genocide of 1915 led to the mass exodus of the Armenian refugees from present-day Turkey. While some of the survivors joined relatives in the United States, most settled in Middle Eastern countries, notably Syria, Lebanon, Iraq, Iran, Palestine, and Egypt. Ironically, by the second half of the twentieth century, many of the children and grandchildren of the survivors had left for North America.

It has been assumed that the bloody sectarian civil war in Mount Lebanon in 1860 impelled the departure of thousands of peasants from that area to the United States, Brazil, and Argentina. In *Inventing Home*, Akram Khater (2001) refutes this argument by showing that the heightened expectations of the peasantry, rather than persecution, precipitated emigration. In the 1850s, the daughters of poor subsistence farmers had joined the cash economy as day laborers in the silk cultivation that supplied the industries of France. Once the French started buying their silk from China and Japan, ambitious youth hit a barrier in employment. This triggered the mass movement across the Atlantic to *Amrika*. Other historical studies corroborate that the immigrants from Greater Syria sought better economic opportunities (Khater 2001; Naff 1985, 77; Saliba 1983; Younis 1995, ch. 6). American missionaries in the Middle East further contributed to emigration by increasing the migrants' exposure to the West. They were responsible for bringing the first printing press to Beirut in 1834, establishing schools, opening the doors to education for girls, founding universities, training physicians in modern medical schools, spreading innovative notions of public health, and encouraging social change (Younis 1995; Khater 2001).

About one-third of Syrian Lebanese immigrants were single women (Gualtieri 2004), and almost 95 percent were Christian (Naff 1985, 112). New York was the "Mother Colony" (Benson and Kayal 2002) of the Syrian Lebanese in the United States; however, their dispersal and relatively rapid assimilation have become legendary. Pack peddling, their economic niche, encouraged a frugal existence that promoted financial saving, dispersion, intermarriage, and, consequently, expedited assimilation. An analysis of the 1990 census shows that a remarkably high percentage of Arab men (79 percent) and women (73 percent) were intermarried. Even among the foreign-born Arabs, 67 percent of the men had married outside their ethnic group, compared to only 38 percent of the women (Kulczycki and Lobo 2002). This reflects a very high rate of intermarriage, the most significant indicator of assimilation. Yet some second- and third-generation Syrian Lebanese Americans have continued to maintain the values of their ancestors: "family unity and honor, hospitality, and generosity" (Naff 1985, 319; Hooglund 1987a). Like other ethnic groups in America whose attachment to their ancestral culture is by now primarily symbolic, they continue to display the cuisine, music, and *dabké* (line dance) of that culture to punctuate celebrations and affirm their ancestral legacy (Naff 1985). The pioneers included a small number of Muslims, especially after 1909, when the Young Turk government was stricter in enforcing mandatory military service. Some escaped conscription by paying the exorbitant *bedel* (fees), but others emigrated. A small town in North Dakota is reputed to have been the first Muslim community in America (Younis 1995, 183–91).

## POST-1965 IMMIGRATION

The Immigration and Nationality Act of 1965 abolished the restrictive national-origins quotas enacted in 1924 and established a seven-category preference system based on family reunification and skills. A per-country limit of twenty thousand persons annually was set for the Eastern Hemisphere, and, for the first time, a cap on immigration from the Western Hemisphere was imposed (amended in 1976). These changes facilitated a second major wave of migration, including newcomers from the Middle East and South Asia. However, the impetus to emigrate came primarily from the disruptive political developments in the region, such as the Arab nationalist movement.[10] The antielitist and populist-socialist policies of Egypt, Syria, and Iraq between the 1950s and 1970s led to the nationalization of many industries and the confiscation of property, spurring an exodus of minority populations, including Jews, Greeks, Italians, Armenians, and Arab Christians, as well as former members of the majority elites.[11] Many of them made their way to the United States.

The oil boom, which enriched oil-exporting countries and brought about massive social change, triggered more Middle Eastern immigration to the United States after the 1970s.[12] Given the limited number and capacity of institutions of higher education in the region at the time, the Middle East became the number one exporter of foreign students to the United States. Citizens of Saudi Arabia, Kuwait, the Emirates, Iran, and other oil-producing countries benefited directly from generous government subsidies or indirectly through personal wealth. Additionally, Arab and Muslim expatriates who worked in the Gulf economy after the 1970s earned high salaries that financed their children's American education.

Yemeni immigrants began largely as cultivators in California or laborers in the auto and steel industries in the Midwest and on the East Coast in the 1970s (see Friedlander 1988). Subsequently, many turned to small business ownership and other employment. There are sizable Yemeni communities in Dearborn, Buffalo, and New York City. Kuwaitis, Saudis, and Algerians came to the United States mostly after the 1980s. For the first time, the 2000 census added Palestine to Israel to create an "Israel/Palestine" category. Cross-tabulating national-origin data by ancestry shows that 21 percent of Israeli-born immigrants in the United States can be considered Arab.[13]

The first South Asian immigrants to America were Punjabi men at the end of the nineteenth century. Though they were mostly Sikhs, there were a few Muslims among the agricultural settlers in California.[14] The new South Asian immigrants consist of Indian and Pakistani doctors, engineers, and other professionals. In the 1980s and 1990s, many came on the H-1B visa, which granted highly skilled migrants work permits valid from three to six years. Family reunification visas and the 1990 Diversity Visa Lottery or "Green Card Lottery" allowed for more varied immigration patterns based on national origin, religion, and socioeconomic status. Among the newcomers were Bangladeshis, 40 percent of whom entered the country through the visa lottery (Kibria 2006, 207–8). Afghans are new arrivals (Gold and Bozorgmehr 2007).

Tables 2 and 3 present the numbers of immigrants admitted to the United States from major Middle Eastern and South Asian countries in five-year intervals since 1965.[15] By and large, these tables indicate an upward trend in the number of immigrants from both regions. Iranian immigration has fluctuated; it increased steadily and substantially from 1965 to 1994 but has declined precipitously ever since. The number of immigrants admitted from Egypt, the second-largest post-1965 group, increased considerably from 9,848 during 1965–69 to 15,197 during 1970–74 and remained fairly steady until 1990–94, when it rose again dramatically to 20,243. It peaked to 26,125 during the 1995–99 period but ebbed to 23,395 during the 2000–2004 period. The number of immigrants grew fairly steadily for Syria during each of the five-year intervals from 1965 to 1989 and then reached a peak of 14,108 in the subsequent five-year interval (1990–94). Immigration from Syria declined after a peak in 1990–94 but stayed fairly steady during the 1995–99 and 2000–2004 periods at about 12,500.

TABLE 2. NUMBERS OF IMMIGRANTS ADMITTED TO THE
UNITED STATES FROM SELECTED MIDDLE EASTERN COUNTRIES, 1965–2004
(in five-year intervals)

| Years | Egypt | Iran | Iraq | Israel | Jordan[a] | Lebanon | Syria | Turkey | Yemen[b] |
|---|---|---|---|---|---|---|---|---|---|
| 1965–69 | 9,848 | 5,935 | 3,755 | 7,340 | 8,258 | 3,922 | 2,691 | 8,490 | N/A |
| 1970–74 | 15,197 | 12,901 | 7,244 | 9,733 | 13,474 | 10,131 | 5,199 | 9,567 | N/A |
| 1975–79 | 12,402 | 24,666 | 14,704 | 15,329 | 15,624 | 21,482 | 7,508 | 8,847 | N/A |
| 1980–84 | 14,241 | 56,799 | 13,569 | 16,720 | 15,226 | 17,764 | 9,546 | 11,919 | 1,895 |
| 1985–89 | 15,901 | 83,491 | 6,884 | 18,486 | 16,357 | 22,372 | 9,712 | 8,689 | 3,164 |
| 1990–94 | 20,243 | 84,042 | 17,458 | 21,868 | 21,475 | 27,265 | 14,108 | 11,528 | 8,082 |
| 1995–99 | 26,125 | 45,013 | 19,913 | 11,946 | 18,794 | 18,164 | 12,599 | 14,650 | 8,393 |
| 2000–2004 | 23,395 | 49,730 | 21,269 | 17,373 | 18,848 | 19,016 | 12,509 | 16,115 | 7,778 |
| Total | 137,352 | 362,577 | 104,796 | 118,795 | 128,056 | 140,116 | 73,872 | 89,805 | 29,312 |

SOURCES: U.S. INS (1969, 1979, 1982, 1988); U.S. DHS (1996–2005).

NOTE: N/A = not available.

[a]Includes Arab Palestine from 1965 to 2003. Beginning in 2003, Palestine is not included and is placed under "unknown" in DHS's *Statistical Yearbook of the Immigration and Naturalization Service*.

[b]Prior to 1991, Yemen consisted of two separate countries (Aden and Sanʿa) whose populations were summed up to indicate the number of immigrants for those years.

Immigration from Iraq doubled from 3,755 during 1965–69 to 7,244 during 1970–74, and once more to 14,704 in 1975–79. Coinciding with the First Gulf War, the number of Iraqi immigrants admitted during 1990–94 was over twice as large as the number during 1985–89 (17,458 and 6,884, respectively). There has been a consistent increase in the number of Iraqi immigrants ever since (from 19,913 in 1995–99 to 21,269 in 2000–2004). The Iraq War has spurred a mass exodus, and the vast majority of Iraqis have sought shelter in neighboring countries (Syria and Jordan). There is a lengthy (up to two-year) wait in processing and admitting Iraqi refugees to the United States.[16] In an Op-Ed piece in the *New York Times* about the plight of 1.5 million Iraqi refugees, four prominent members of the Board of the International Rescue Committee assert: "There is absolutely no denying that the United States has a special responsibility to help. The sectarian violence these Iraqi refugees have fled is a byproduct of the invasion and its chaotic aftermath—yet America has paradoxically done far less than its traditionally generous response." They note that "fewer than 5,000 Iraqi refuges" have been resettled in the United States, and they urge the government to meet its target of welcoming 12,000 Iraqis, thus "fulfilling its commitment to admit 5,000 Iraqis (and their dependents) who have worked for the United States and are eligible for special immigrant visas."[17]

Immigration from Iran grew steadily after 1965, thanks to the influx of foreign students in pursuit of advanced degrees from American universities. The number of Iranians admitted (mostly exiles), however, increased dramatically after 1980 because of the Iranian Revolution of 1978–79. As table 2 shows, the number of immigrants from Iran more than doubled from 24,666 during 1975–79 to 56,799 during 1980–84 and topped off at 84,042 during 1990–94. These numbers have subsequently declined (Bozorgmehr 2007).

War has served as a leading catalyst of immigration for a number of other Middle Eastern countries. The 1990–94 period also marked the peak years for immigration from Jordan (21,475, which includes Palestinians from the occupied territories), Lebanon (27,265), and Israel (21,868).[18] Another large influx of immigrants from Lebanon (21,482) arrived during 1975–79, coinciding with the beginning of the civil war. A total of 17,764 Lebanese immigrants were admitted during 1980–84, a period coinciding with the Israeli invasion in 1982. The continuation of the strife led to more immigration, with 22,372 Lebanese nationals admitted in 1985–89. Sizable numbers of Yemeni immigrants began to be admitted only after 1990. When Yemen sided with Iraq during the

First Gulf War, Saudi Arabia, which had employed the lion's share of Yemeni migrant workers, no longer welcomed them in the country. This may have redirected Yemeni emigration elsewhere, including the United States. The number of immigrants from Turkey showed a spike (11,919) in 1980–84, a period that coincided with the era of military rule (1980–83). Although it dropped to 8,689 during 1985–89, it has since regained momentum, marking the beginning of a steady rise to 16,115 during 2000–2004.

Among immigrants from South Asian countries (table 3), those from Bangladesh and Pakistan have shown a tremendous and steady increase in numbers since changes in immigration law. Data are available only after 1975 for Bangladesh, but they show more than tenfold growth from 2,921 in 1975–79 to 32,564 in 2000–2004. Similarly, the number of Pakistani immigrants started at a low of 2,704 in 1965–69 but grew exponentially to 66,256 in 2000–2004. A considerable spike in Afghan immigration occurred after the Soviet invasion in 1979–89 and subsequent political turmoil leading to the advent of the Taliban in Afghanistan. While in 1975–79 only 929 Afghan immigrants were admitted to the United States, this number grew tenfold to 9,960 during 1980–84. It then increased to about 14,000 during the next two five-year intervals. However, it dropped sharply to 5,525 during 1995–99 and 7,377 during 2000–2004. The last period coincides with the U.S. overthrow of the Taliban in 2001 and the hope for a stable and prosperous future for Afghanistan

We obtained additional information on the types of immigrants admitted from the countries listed in tables 2 and 3 by their "selected class of admission," as provided in the *Statistical Yearbooks of the Immigration and Naturalization Service* (INS 1996–2005). During this decade, the latest for which data are available, a total of 66,498 Middle Eastern and South Asian immigrants were admitted because of "employment-based preferences,"[19] indicating a skilled and educated crop of newcomers. While Egyptians, Iranians, Bangladeshis, and Pakistanis ranked high among employment preferences, Afghans and Yemenis ranked quite low. At the same time, 67,502 persons came either as refugees or as asylee adjustments, mainly from Iran, Iraq, and Afghanistan. Another 62,936 were admitted under the U.S. Diversity Program, which primarily benefited immigrants from Egypt, Morocco, Turkey, Bangladesh, and Pakistan. By far the largest number (366,366) entered under family-sponsored preferences and as immediate relatives of U.S. citizens. The totals for each selected class of admission for immigrants from Israel, including Arabs, in 1996–2005 are as follows:

TABLE 3. NUMBERS OF IMMIGRANTS ADMITTED TO
THE UNITED STATES FROM SELECTED SOUTH ASIAN
COUNTRIES, 1965–2004
*(in five-year intervals)*

| Years | Afghanistan | Bangladesh | Pakistan |
|---|---|---|---|
| 1965–69 | N/A | N/A | 2,704 |
| 1970–74 | N/A | N/A | 11,228 |
| 1975–79 | 929 | 2,921 | 17,282 |
| 1980–84 | 9,960 | 3,537 | 24,405 |
| 1985–89 | 14,154 | 7,934 | 31,495 |
| 1990–94 | 14,059 | 25,393 | 57,923 |
| 1995–99 | 5,525 | 37,641 | 61,850 |
| 2000–2004 | 7,377 | 32,564 | 66,256 |
| *Total* | 52,004 | 109,990 | 273,143 |

SOURCES: U.S. INS (1969, 1971, 1979, 1982, 1988); U.S. DHS (1996–2005).

NOTE: N/A = not available.

19,583 persons entered on the basis of family-sponsored preferences
and as immediate relatives of U.S. citizens; 10,680 individuals entered
because of employment-based preferences; 395 entered as refugee and
asylee adjustments; and 1,377 entered with the U.S. Diversity Program.
In summary, the post-1965 Middle Eastern and South Asian immigrants
are far more diverse in terms of types and national origins than their
predecessors, as is the case for immigrants in general (Portes and Rumbaut 2006).

## CONTESTED CLASSIFICATIONS AND IDENTITIES

Sociologists define "minority groups" by the following criteria: (1)
members suffer various disadvantages at the hands of a majority population; (2) they are easily identified by a visible characteristic; (3) their
status is ascribed; (4) they have group consciousness; and (5) by choice
or necessity they tend to be endogamous, confining their primary group
relations (i.e., friendships and marital partners) to fellow members.
These conditions apply to some degree to Middle Eastern Americans.
Many share visible physical characteristics—olive skin, dark hair,
prominent facial features—and outsiders have difficulty distinguishing
people of the differing nationalities. For example, an Iranian is rarely
distinguished from an Egyptian or a Lebanese. After 9/11, even Fil-
ipinos, Mexicans, and other Hispanics have been mistakenly victimized.
Though Middle Eastern Americans are ascribed a broadly "Middle

Eastern" status, their individual and group consciousness is more ethnic than pan-ethnic. Nostalgia for their native culture (e.g., cuisine, music, theater, sense of humor) spurs many to seek the company of their compatriots. These factors as a whole point to Middle Easterners as a sociological minority group.[20]

Individuals of Middle Eastern descent identify themselves by national (e.g., Iranian, Israeli), ethnic (e.g., Arab), or ethno-religious (e.g., Armenian, Druze, Jewish) categories. South Asian Muslims, such as Bangladeshis, Pakistanis, and Indians, on the other hand, favor a religious label. The term *Middle Eastern* entered the American lexicon only after 9/11 and has been more frequently used in the media since. Though immigrants from Iran, Israel, and Turkey tend to generally identify with their national origin as Iranian, Israeli, and Turkish, the ethno-religious minority populations from within those countries, such as Armenians from Iran, tend to identify themselves as Armenian or Armenian Iranian.

There is much disagreement as to what the term *Arab American* means. Does it imply a primordial connection to the Arab world? Does it refer to a shared cultural heritage that includes the Arabic language, beliefs about the primacy of the family and the values of respect for elders, hospitality, generosity, and honor? Or does it have a political connotation with regard both to nations of origin, in terms of support for the "Arab cause" in the Middle East, and to efforts to mobilize as an ethnic group in the United States? The identity of Arabic-speaking immigrants to North America and their descendants in the last century has fluctuated with the social and political changes in both their countries of origin and the host society.[21]

If someone were to ask the early Arabic-speaking immigrants to America how they thought of themselves, they would have probably identified first with their family, next with their village or town of origin, and last with their sect.[22] The Ottomans had organized their society along religious lines, better known as the *millet* (people) system (see Cahnman 1944). This made sectarian affiliation, mainly for the non-Muslim populations, more consequential for one's well-being.

Many of the early immigrants were either Armenians or Christian Arabs.[23] The latter included Maronites, Antiochian/Syrian Orthodox, Melkites, and Protestants.[24] Most were from the Ottoman province of Syria, which was made up of Syria proper, Mount Lebanon, and Palestine. Eric Hooglund (1987b, 88) writes, "In a new country, where they were surrounded by different peoples who identified themselves on the basis of ethnicity, it became necessary for the Arabic-speaking immigrants to find a similar identity. As early as the 1890s they had begun to refer to themselves as 'Syrians.'" These Christians tended to use the term *Arab* to identify native Muslims of Syria. Therefore, *Syrian* came to identify an Arabic speaker who was from the ancient Syrian churches rather than a Muslim. Hooglund adds that U.S. immigration officials promoted the label *Syrian* as an ethnicity because they favored provid- ing designations of nationality to varied groups from multiethnic empires. Common practice also designated the Arabic language as "Syr- ian," and in 1899 the United States officially adopted this term for Ara- bic speakers from Ottoman Syria. Today most immigrants from the Middle East are Muslim,[25] but some Jews have also emigrated from the Arab world.[26] Immigrants from the three non-Arab countries in the Middle East—Iran, Israel, and Turkey—tend to be newcomers.[27]

Race has been a central issue in the question of citizenship since the formation of the United States. The Naturalization Act of 1790 made any free white persons of satisfactory character eligible for naturaliza- tion after a two-year residence. After the Civil War, aliens of African descent were also eligible to become U.S. citizens (Zolberg 2006). How- ever, as large numbers of immigrants, including Middle Easterners, arrived in the latter part of the nineteenth century, their "whiteness" became a contentious issue. According to Tehranian (2008), between 1878 and 1952 (when naturalization laws changed), fifty-two cases were litigated after immigration officials denied an immigrant the right to become a U.S. citizen on the basis of race. These cases presented the first challenge for the federal government in dealing with the Middle Eastern- ers, and the subsequent jurisprudence settled their classification as white.

In 1910, the U.S. Census Bureau classified Syrians, Palestinians, Armenians, Turks, and others from the eastern Mediterranean as "Asi- atics": that is, nonwhite. However, thanks to the editors of the Arabic press in New York City, Syrians galvanized support and raised funds to fight this decision. Several cases came before the courts across the United States with the argument that Syrians were Caucasians, there- fore white. Naff (1985, 257) summarizes the conclusion of the case of George Dow of Charleston, South Carolina, in 1914: "After deliberat- ing, the court accepted the definition of the Dillingham Report of the Immigration Commission, namely that 'Physically the modern Syrians are of mixed Syrian, Arabian, and even Jewish blood. They belong to the Semitic branch of the Caucasian race, thus widely differing from their rulers, the Turks, who are in origin Mongolian.'" Before that, the federal court in Georgia had allowed a Syrian with a dark complexion to be naturalized (*In re Najour*).[28] Similar cases were settled for Armenians with *In re Halladjian* in 1909 and *United States v. Cartozian,* on whose behalf the anthropologist Franz Boas testified in 1924–25 (Alexander 2005, 112–18; see also Suleiman 1987, 44; Younis 1995, Appendix 4, "The Syrian Naturalization Issue").[29] However, the Syrians' Caucasian identity was predicated on their Christian faith. In 1942, the naturalization of Ahmed Hassan was disputed in a court in Detroit. His case was resolved with the stipulation that Arab Muslims were white but only when their religious affiliation was left undeclared. Thus Muslims became "honorary whites" (Gualtieri 2001). As these cases illustrate and as Tehranian (2008) explains, those who won their lawsuit were able to show good character, Christian faith and beliefs, association with the upper class, educational credentials, wealth, English proficiency, intermarriage—that is, generally, an ability to pass as white in a cultural sense.

Helen Samhan (1999) argues that race has remained an issue for Arab Americans. In an article appropriately entitled "Not Quite White," she demonstrates that "Arabs who contest, resent, or misunderstand their white classification . . . in school and medical forms, job and loan applications, political caucuses, polls, even market surveys" are denied all identity and are classified as the "other" who is not counted. She illustrates her point by citing, among others, the "1988 national longitudinal study of eighth graders" that overreported the Asian/Pacific Islander category by 15 percent because of the (mistaken) inclusion of students of Middle Eastern descent (219). Because of this error, the voices of these Arab American students were silenced.

Suad Joseph contends that Arab Americans, in spite of their white citizenship, go "against the grain of the nation" (1999, 257). She avoids racial or color designations in claiming difference but asserts that the situation is more subtle and damning because Arabs are painted as the opposite of the independent, autonomous, individual, modern, and free person (260). Several Arab American scholars have applied the racial formation perspective to explain the relentless stereotyping and escalating scapegoating of Arab and Muslim Americans, especially after 9/11 (Naber 2000; Alsultany 2005; Cainkar 2006). Using representations of Arabs in the media before 9/11, Nadine Naber argues that Muslims and Arabs are considered "tainted" but not enough to be colored: "While Arab Americans . . . have been forced into the binary classification 'either entirely white or entirely non-white,' . . . [they] do not quite fit into the U.S.'s either/or racial labeling system" (2000, 51). She believes that distortions have racialized Arab Americans "through religion rather than phenotype" (53).

Evelyn Alsultany (2005) draws on Edward Said's *Orientalism*, which argues that identity is constructed in relation to the "other," and on Michael Omi and Howard Winant's (1994) theory that racial formation is the outcome of historical and sociological processes to contend that Arab and Muslim Americans are racialized. Since the beginning of the "War on Terror," the U.S. media have turned these populations into the "enemy-other," terrorist noncitizens in opposition to American citizens. Racializing Muslims as dangerous extremists produces national unity through fear, which in turn leads to public endorsements of government initiatives such as the PATRIOT Act, detentions, deportations, and special registration. According to Alsultany, speeches by government officials, television dramas, talk shows, and nonprofit advertising create the "feeling" that the United States is, in contrast to reality, "unique, harmonious, equal, democratic, in relation to other countries" (2005, 5). Alsultany borrows from Omi and Winant (1994) to emphasize politics' influence in establishing difference, arguing that "racialization is not solely based on phenotype but relies heavily on racing politics and religion" (Alsultany 2005, 7).

According to Louise Cainkar (2006), Arab Americans have experienced increased marginalization and racialization since the 1960s. This is not due to "the domestic distribution of power and resources" (273) or even religious differences and distinctive institutions formed by Arab immigrants. Rather, international political developments, America's relationship to the region, and the media's negative depictions of Arabs as violent have led to their exclusion from political and civic life and a heightened incidence of discrimination and hate crimes against them.

Cainkar's historicizing of Arab American marginalization fits in well with Omi and Winant's theory of racial formation: "[The] sociohistorical process by which racial categories are created, inhabited, transformed, and destroyed . . . is a process of historically situated *projects* in which human bodies and social structures are represented and organized. . . . [It is linked] to the evolution of hegemony, the way in which society is organized and ruled. . . . From a racial formation perspective, race is a matter of both social structure and cultural representation" (Omi and Winant 1994, 55–56; emphasis in original). Similarly, Bonilla-Silva notes in *Racism without Racists* (2006) that contemporary racism is covert discriminatory behavior embedded within systematic, institutionalized structures. A racial ideology then becomes a political instrument that justifies the status quo and those in power.

Andrew Shryock explores the racialization of Arab and Muslim Americans though a more critical lens. Analyzing the DAAS data on racial and ethnic identification, he finds that the vast majority of respondents (70 percent) identified as "Arab American" and the remaining 30 percent offered about "one hundred" alternative identities. "Not a single person opted for an extant 'racial' alternative: no one said white, black, Asian, or even 'of color'" (2008, 89). On the basis of these findings, Shryock argues that racialization should be seen as a "'moral analogy' that give[s] Arabs and Muslims a more secure place within a dominant structure of American identity politics" (2008, 98). As race represents a central element of American society from which Arab Americans often feel excluded due to their perceived racial ambiguity (e.g., Samhan 1999; Tehranian 2008), activists and emerging young scholars have adopted the racialization perspective to challenge their invisibility. Indeed, as Shryock observes, "The fact that many Arab Americans now believe antiterrorism policies have constituted them as 'a distinct racial group' says a great deal about the trauma of 9/11, the experience of marginalization and stigma, and how these are reshaping identity politics amongst Arabs and Muslims in the United States" (84).

We contend that these racialization arguments in and by themselves have become claims for the inclusion of Arab Americans within the larger American society. Furthermore, it is ironic that Arab American advocates and scholars have adopted racialization as a perspective to fight marginalization, stigma, and discrimination. Racialization lacks clarity and specificity as an analytical tool. It is at best a sensitizing concept rather than as an empirically verifiable one.

Before 9/11, the Arab community in the United States tended to be mobilized by events in the Middle East. Most scholars working in this field concur that the 1967 Arab-Israeli war was a watershed event ushering in a renewed consciousness for Arab Americans. By the end of the century, this identity had become "a matter of justice and honor to defend the Arab cause and specifically the rights of Palestinians" (Kayal 1995, 252). Yet precisely because of the conflicts in the Middle East, the *Arab American* label has not produced cohesion for Arabic-speaking peoples and their descendants in the United States. A number of Lebanese Maronites and Iraqi Chaldeans have resisted it for political and ideological reasons, especially after 9/11 (see chapter 1).[30]

Muslims consider identity as the "mother of all issues (*umm al masaʾil*)" (Y. Haddad 2000, 22). Every time political or other leaders announce publicly that the United States is a Judeo-Christian nation,

Muslims feel powerless and believe that the notion of separation of church and state in the U.S. Constitution is being violated (23). Muslims see contradictory behavior in American society when Christian values are encouraged by the president but efforts to build a moral and just Islamic state in the Middle East are denounced. Government support of the Jewish state, coupled with continual denunciation of Islamic states as "extremist," presents another double standard. According to Yvonne Haddad, during the last third of the twentieth century U.S. foreign policy toward Muslim nations "continue[d] to trouble and alienate the majority of Muslim citizens" in the United States (24). U.S. foreign policy in the region remains a thorny issue for Arab and Muslim Americans.

American scholars who work in the fields of immigration and ethnic and racial studies seem to have their own trends and fashions in ethnic labels and groupings. In 1980, the *Harvard Encyclopedia of American Ethnic Groups* had an entry under "Arabs" (Naff 1980), whereas the 1997 *Encyclopedia of American Immigrant Cultures* did not. The editors of the latter publication, however, provided separate entries for the Iranians, Druze, Egyptian Copts and Muslims, Jordanians, Lebanese Christians and Muslims, Palestinians, Syrians, and Yemenis. The complementary volume to the *Harvard Encyclopedia, The New Americans*, focuses on immigrants rather than ethnic groups. It includes an entry on immigrants from the Middle East and North Africa (Gold and Bozorgmehr 2007) and a separate entry for immigrants from Iran (Bozorgmehr 2007). As more Middle Eastern and South Asian scholars conduct research on their own diasporas, they are likely to draw more public attention to their previously "invisible" groups and increase the odds that their studies will be cited in mainstream literatures (see Okamoto 2005).

## DEMOGRAPHIC AND SOCIOECONOMIC CHARACTERISTICS OF MIDDLE EASTERN AND SOUTH ASIAN GROUPS

### POPULATION SIZE

According to the 2000 census, the population of persons of Middle Eastern ancestry in the United States was 2,150,635 (see table 4). We used both first and second responses to the open-ended ancestry question (in the long form) to ensure the inclusion of all hyphenated Middle Easterners. Surprisingly, Arabs only slightly exceeded non-Arabs in population size (i.e., 1,120,313 Arabs vs. 1,030,322 non-Arabs). Both groups were

TABLE 4. POPULATION SIZE OF MIDDLE
EASTERN AND SELECTED SOUTH ASIAN GROUPS IN
THE UNITED STATES, WITH PERCENTAGE
OF FOREIGN BORN, 2000

| Ancestry/Race[a] | Population | Foreign Born (%) |
|---|---|---|
| Arab | 1,120,313 | 39.1 |
| "Arab/Arabic" | 205,822 | 49.8 |
| Egyptian | 142,832 | 64.5 |
| Iraqi | 37,714 | 71.9 |
| Jordanian | 39,734 | 63.7 |
| Lebanese | 440,279 | 22.4 |
| Moroccan | 38,923 | 57.5 |
| Palestinian | 72,112 | 49.7 |
| Syrian | 142,897 | 23.7 |
| Non-Arab | 1,030,322 | 56.7 |
| Armenian | 385,488 | 44.3 |
| Assyrian/Chaldean/Syriac | 82,154 | 58.0 |
| Iranian | 338,266 | 68.3 |
| Israeli | 106,839 | 57.2 |
| Turkish | 117,575 | 55.3 |
| *Total Middle Eastern* | 2,150,635 | 47.8 |
| South Asian | | |
| Afghan | 53,709 | 73.1 |
| Bangladeshi | 41,428 | 82.9 |
| Pakistani | 155,909 | 75.5 |

SOURCE: U.S. Bureau of the Census (2000b).

[a]The population of Middle Eastern groups was determined from the ancestry question, while the population of South Asian groups was determined from the race question in the 2000 U.S. Census. Ancestry data are not available for Algeria and Tunisia.

further divided by major national and ethnic differences. Among Arabs, the old-timer Lebanese were by far the largest group (440,279), followed by Syrians (142,897), and newcomer Egyptians (142,832).

Persons who traced their ancestries to Iran, Israel, and Turkey are regarded as non-Arab. Christian ethno-religious minorities such as Armenians and Assyrians/Chaldeans are also non-Arab. Among non-Arabs, Armenians have the largest population (385,488), followed closely by Iranians (338,266). Among North Africans, ancestry data were available only for Moroccans (38,923). The population sizes of Algerians, Libyans, and Tunisians were too small to report, though the census identified 11,664 foreign-born Algerians (Gold and Bozorgmehr 2007, table 1).

All Arab populations contained substantial proportions of foreign-born individuals, but the ratios were smaller for the Lebanese and Syrians, who included descendants of the pioneers. The majority of Iraqis (71.9 percent) were foreign born, followed closely by Egyptians (64.5 percent) and Jordanians (63.7 percent). Among non-Arabs, with the exception of old-timer Armenians, over half of all other groups were foreign born. Iranians topped the list (68.3 percent), followed by Assyrian/Chaldean/Syriac individuals, who were mostly from Iraq and Iran (58 percent), Israelis (57.2 percent), and Turks (55.3 percent). The census data show that Middle Eastern groups had a sizable foreign-born population. The South Asian populations, however, reflected an even newer migration pattern: 75.5 percent of Pakistanis, 82.9 percent of Bangladeshis, and 73.1 percent of Afghans were foreign born.

An analysis of the data for earlier censuses (1980 and 1990) on Arabs by ancestry and country of birth reports similar findings (Kulczycki and Lobo 2001). The foreign born made up 41 percent of Arab Americans in 1990. Over half of Arab Americans claimed Lebanese (41 percent) and Syrian (19 percent) ancestries. Of these, almost 75 percent and 67 percent, respectively, were U.S. born. The next largest groups were Egyptians (9 percent of Arab Americans) and Palestinians (5 percent of Arab Americans).

## IMMIGRANT (FOREIGN-BORN) POPULATIONS

With 362,577 immigrants admitted between 1965 and 2004 (see table 2), Iranians are by far the single largest group among foreign-born Middle Easterners. Lebanese, Egyptians, Jordanians (which includes Palestinians), and Iraqis are the largest foreign-born Arab groups. The vast majority of all groups have immigrated since 1970. At least about one-third and at most over two-thirds of all groups arrived between 1990 and 2000. Not only are the South Asian groups predominantly foreign born, but they are also relatively new immigrants, the vast majority having immigrated since 1980 (see table 3).

Like most other immigrant groups, Middle Easterners are concentrated in a few states. Arabs are the most dispersed, with large concentrations in California, New York, and Michigan, in that order.[31] Both Armenians and Iranians are heavily concentrated in California, though there are sizable Armenian communities in Massachusetts, New York, and New Jersey, and there are large Iranian populations in New York and metropolitan Washington, D.C. The majority of Israelis reside in New York and Los Angeles (Gold 2002). California has emerged as the largest center of Middle Easterners in the United States, since three of the four largest Middle Eastern populations are concentrated there, mainly in the Los Angeles area (Bozorgmehr, Der-Martirosian, and Sabagh 1996). California is followed by New York and Michigan.

Half of Bangladeshis reside in New York, and another 5 percent live in New Jersey. Bangladeshis are also numerous in California (7 percent) and Texas (6 percent). New York has the highest concentration (21 percent) of Pakistanis, followed by California (13 percent), Texas (12 percent), and New Jersey (8 percent) (Kibria 2006, figure 9.1). Jackson Heights in Queens, Coney Island in Brooklyn, and Devon Avenue in North Chicago are business centers for "Indo-Pak-Bangla products," including *halal* foods, for Muslims from neighboring countries.[32]

The metropolitan region of Detroit is home to a large and diverse Middle Eastern, especially Arab, population. It is a microcosm of the history of this population in terms of its immigration waves and characteristics (see Abraham and Shryock 2000). In the suburbs, the groups include Christian Syrian/Lebanese and Armenians, all descendants of the first wave of immigration who tend to be more affluent, and Chaldeans from Iraq. The city of Dearborn has the highest density of Arab immigrants, with Shi'a from South Lebanon making up a significant proportion of this Arab American community. Some arrived as laborers in the 1950s, but the civil war in Lebanon was responsible for later waves of immigration. Yemenis were also drawn to this area by industrial jobs, especially in the automotive field (Aswad 1974; Abraham 1983; Friedlander 1988).

Shi'a refugees from southern Iraq arrived after the First Gulf War (1990–91). As a local community leader told us, Dearborn has borne the burden of large migrations of traumatized refugees from Iraq:

> There is a constant immigration. We always get a couple thousand a year. But the last influx was the Iraqi refugees, the marsh people. . . . [The] U.S. abandoned them and Saddam brutalized them. He massacred them. Then they spent three or four years in Saudi Arabia in deplorable living conditions until the U.S. brought them here. . . . This is the most messed-up community that we have seen—birth defects, mental conditions, depression. A lot of them were victims of torture. There are learning disabilities. . . . They are legal refugees. . . . They spread them all across the country, but they all immigrated to Detroit.

The Arab Community Center for Economic and Social Services (ACCESS) and other local social service agencies have been addressing these problems as best they can with mental health professionals and social workers.[33]

TABLE 5. EDUCATIONAL LEVEL OF FOREIGN-BORN
MIDDLE EASTERN AND SELECTED SOUTH ASIAN
GROUPS IN THE UNITED STATES, 2000

| National Origin | Population[a] | Bachelor's Degree Only (%) | Post– Bachelor's Degree (%) | Total: Bachelor's Degree or More (%) |
|---|---|---|---|---|
| Middle East | | | | |
| Iran | 219,071 | 29.4 | 25.5 | 54.9 |
| Iraq | 65,708 | 14.3 | 8.9 | 23.2 |
| Israel/Palestine | 88,629 | 23.1 | 20.3 | 43.4 |
| Jordan | 38,745 | 23.8 | 11.4 | 35.2 |
| Kuwait | 13,190 | 35.3 | 18.8 | 54.1 |
| Lebanon | 86,150 | 22.2 | 19.5 | 41.7 |
| Saudi Arabia | 10,405 | 31.5 | 20.4 | 51.9 |
| Syria | 40,001 | 18.0 | 19.4 | 37.4 |
| Turkey | 61,726 | 22.8 | 23.4 | 46.2 |
| Yemen Arab Republic | 11,490 | 10.6 | 4.4 | 15.0 |
| Egypt | 86,567 | 39.0 | 23.9 | 62.9 |
| Algeria | 8,932 | 23.9 | 28.8 | 52.7 |
| Morocco | 31,764 | 25.9 | 12.0 | 37.9 |
| South Asia | | | | |
| Afghanistan | 30,076 | 19.7 | 11.4 | 31.1 |
| Bangladesh | 63,301 | 26.6 | 21.7 | 48.3 |
| Pakistan | 164,232 | 28.5 | 23.1 | 51.6 |
| *All Foreign Born* | 22,034,522 | 15.2 | 10.9 | 26.1 |

SOURCE: U.S. Bureau of the Census (2000a).

NOTE: Data are not available for Tunisia.

[a]Population twenty-five to sixty-four years old.

## SOCIOECONOMIC STATUS

To gauge the socioeconomic status of Middle Eastern and South Asian Americans, we analyzed the data from the 2000 census. The educational attainment of Middle Eastern immigrant groups is generally high, and for some remarkably so. For this reason, we disaggregate the category of "bachelor's degree or more" into "bachelor's degree only" and "post–bachelor's degree" in table 5.

As of 2000, Egyptians had the highest levels of education (62.9 percent have a bachelor's degree or more), followed by Iranians (54.9 percent had a bachelor's degree or more). As a frame of reference, 26.1 percent of all foreign born, who made up a population of about twenty-two million in 2000, had a bachelor's degree or more. Only Iraqis and

TABLE 6. ENGLISH PROFICIENCY AND CITIZENSHIP
OF FOREIGN-BORN MIDDLE EASTERN AND
SELECTED SOUTH ASIAN GROUPS
IN THE UNITED STATES, 2000

| National Origin | Population | Speaks English Well or Very Well[a] (%) | Naturalized U.S. Citizen[b] (%) |
|---|---|---|---|
| Middle East | | | |
| Iran | 293,021 | 74.6 | 61.6 |
| Iraq | 93,565 | 70.0 | 49.3 |
| Israel/Palestine | 125,325 | 72.7 | 62.5 |
| Jordan | 50,193 | 80.2 | 61.2 |
| Kuwait | 22,600 | 81.4 | 37.1 |
| Lebanon | 112,702 | 77.2 | 68.6 |
| Saudi Arabia | 27,819 | 59.6 | 35.5 |
| Syria | 55,500 | 71.8 | 62.7 |
| Turkey | 93,245 | 62.0 | 51.2 |
| Yemen Arab Republic | 19,672 | 64.5 | 56.3 |
| Egypt | 118,081 | 74.4 | 61.2 |
| Algeria | 11,664 | 75.2 | 27.9 |
| Morocco | 39,995 | 67.4 | 48.3 |
| South Asia | | | |
| Afghanistan | 44,690 | 72.9 | 58.5 |
| Bangladesh | 92,235 | 77.5 | 33.2 |
| Pakistan | 233,020 | 80.7 | 42.6 |
| *All Foreign Born* | 33,055,462 | 51.2 | 43.7 |

SOURCE: U.S. Bureau of the Census (2000a).

NOTE: Data are not available for Tunisia.

[a] Population five years or older who speak a language other than English at home.

[b] Naturalized U.S. citizen rates include persons born abroad of American parents.

Yemenis had a lower educational level than the "all foreign born" category. Over half of Kuwaitis, Saudis, and Algerians also had a bachelor's degree or more. As noted above, with the exception of Algerians, these groups originated as students from major oil-producing countries.[34] In the Iranian case, the 1978–79 revolution spurred the immigration of elite exiles. In general, Middle Eastern groups also exhibit high levels of English fluency. The percentage that report speaking English well or very well is higher for every Middle Eastern group than for the "all foreign born" category (51.2 percent) (see table 6).

As expected, the Lebanese and Syrians, who have a long history of immigration to the United States, show the highest rates of citizenship. Yet despite their recent arrival, several other groups—Afghans, Iranians, Israelis/Palestinians, Jordanians, and Egyptians—also show high rates of citizenship (see table 6). This reflects in some cases (e.g., Egyptians) their high levels of educational and occupational achievement and in other cases (e.g., Iranians) the irreversibility of migration of exiles or political refugees (see Portes and Rumbaut 2006). Even though the second wave had been in the United States for only a short period, by 1990 Arab Americans already had a high rate of naturalization. Only Kuwaitis, Saudis, and Algerians have naturalized at a rate lower than the U.S. average for the "all foreign born" category (43.7 percent). The first two groups are sojourners, usually students and businessmen. Algerians are very new arrivals and as such are probably ineligible for naturalization (Kulczycki and Lobo 2001).

Community leaders claim that applications for citizenship have increased since 9/11. They postulate that the targeting of noncitizens may have jump-started the process of naturalization. A leader observed:

> I tell you one of the post-9/11 reactions: so many people used to think and believe that being a permanent resident and a citizen is the same, that you enjoy the same equal rights and equal protection, and that there was maybe no need for the citizenship. That is not the case. They used to see only the differences in the voting or what have you. But they never felt that they were not to be treated equally. Now there is a big belief that that is not the case. Even with you being a citizen and happening to be of foreign descent, there is a question mark. So imagine if you are not a citizen. So there is a rush, a flow, an increase in inquiries of people who never bothered to pursue citizenship. Now they are trying to pursue it more than before. They believe that it is more secure. They don't believe now that having a green card means a lot and entitles you to equal protection, as they used to believe.

Similarly, journalists have reported that immigrants with Arab- or Muslim-sounding names have had to wait for several years to obtain their citizenship. For example, Jodi Wilgoren, writing for the *New York Times*, noted, "There have been some significant spikes in the number of legal immigrants seeking citizenship in the months following Sept. 11, but it is too early to see an overall trend because the naturalization process is long. But the increase is reminiscent of similar surges in naturalization after Word War I and during World War II."[35] Another article reported that in April 2006 ADC "launched a national legal campaign to get the government to resolve hundreds of [stalled naturalization] cases. More than 40 lawyers filed lawsuits in federal courts, requesting that a judge step in and force U.S. Citizenship and Immigration Services to complete the stalled naturalization cases."[36]

While there has been a surge in citizenship applications in general from 2005 to 2007, most of this is by Hispanics and is due to the controversy over undocumented immigration.[37] DHS data are not readily available by country of birth of applicants for smaller populations such as Middle Easterners. Therefore, it is difficult to corroborate assertions about a drive for naturalization among Middle Eastern and South Asian groups. However, the naturalization data do not reflect an appreciable increase after 2001. DHS data on the numbers of persons naturalized for any country of birth originating in the Middle East, North Africa, and South Asia show that the totals for the two consecutive five-year periods before and after 9/11 (1997–2001 and 2002–6) are comparable.

Many self-employed Middle Easterners come from a premigration culture of entrepreneurship, and some bring capital. Others turn to self-employment as a result of discrimination in hiring and promotion in the labor market. In fact, Middle Easterners outpace most other major ethnic groups by a considerable margin in self-employment (Gold and Bozorgmehr 2007; Zenner 1982). Many post-1965 immigrants have educational credentials that they have pursued further in the United States, becoming professionals in medicine, architecture, engineering, law, and high-tech fields. Therefore, Middle Easterners hold top occupational categories (professionals and managers). These factors contribute to economic success in the United States.

According to the 2000 U.S. Census, five Middle Eastern immigrant groups (Israelis/Palestinians, Syrians, Jordanians, Iranians, and Lebanese) ranked among the top nine most entrepreneurial groups. Nearly all Middle Eastern immigrants have total rates of self-employment (unincorporated, incorporated, and unpaid family worker) that exceed the 10.8 percent average for all foreign-born Americans (see table 7). The immigrant groups with the highest rates of self-employment are Israelis/Palestinians (33.4 percent), Syrians (26 percent), Jordanians (23.4 percent), Lebanese (22 percent), Iranians (21.8 percent), Yemenis (18.7 percent), and Iraqis (18.5 percent). Even Saudis', Moroccans', and Algerians' rates of self-employment (10.9, 11.5, and 9.7 percent respectively) are about on a par with "all foreign born." Middle Eastern immigrants are unlikely to follow the traditional immigrant pattern of starting out at the bottom of the socioeconomic ladder. Since entrepreneurship generally confers higher returns than wage and salary incomes (all else being equal) and allows the second generation to pursue higher education rather than enter the workforce at an early age, these groups tend to be economically successful and to experience significant social mobility.

TABLE 7. SELF-EMPLOYMENT RATES OF FOREIGN-BORN MIDDLE EASTERN AND SELECTED SOUTH ASIAN GROUPS IN THE UNITED STATES, 2000

*(percentages)*

| National Origin | Population | Not Incorporated[a] | Incorporated[a] | Unpaid Family Worker[a] | Total Self-Employed[a] |
|---|---|---|---|---|---|
| Middle Eastern | | | | | |
| Iran | 160,539 | 11.8 | 9.6 | 0.4 | 21.8 |
| Iraq | 43,015 | 9.6 | 8.6 | 0.3 | 18.5 |
| Israel/Palestine | 63,110 | 12.0 | 12.1 | 0.3 | 33.4 |
| Jordan | 25,794 | 13.6 | 9.6 | 0.2 | 23.4 |
| Kuwait | 8,876 | 5.0 | 6.5 | 0.6 | 12.1 |
| Lebanon | 59,006 | 10.6 | 10.8 | 0.6 | 22.0 |
| Saudi Arabia | 5,209 | 4.1 | 6.5 | 0.3 | 10.9 |
| Syria | 26,191 | 15.8 | 9.7 | 0.5 | 26.0 |
| Turkey | 44,008 | 8.7 | 7.0 | 0.4 | 16.1 |
| Yemen Arab Republic | 7,078 | 11.0 | 6.5 | 1.2 | 18.7 |
| Egypt | 62,172 | 7.9 | 6.2 | 0.4 | 14.5 |
| Algeria | 6,363 | 5.9 | 3.6 | 0.2 | 9.7 |
| Morocco | 24,314 | 6.4 | 4.8 | 0.3 | 11.5 |
| South Asian | | | | | |
| Afghanistan | 19,068 | 9.9 | 5.0 | 0.0 | 14.9 |
| Bangladesh | 42,065 | 6.0 | 3.1 | 0.3 | 9.4 |
| Pakistan | 107,786 | 7.9 | 6.8 | 0.3 | 15.0 |
| *All Foreign-Born* | 15,170,448 | 6.8 | 3.7 | 0.3 | 10.8 |

SOURCE: U.S. Bureau of the Census (2000a).

NOTE: Data are not available for Tunisia.

[a]Population twenty-five to sixty-four years old in the labor force.

Several Middle Eastern groups hold top occupational positions (managerial/professional) at a higher level than that of all foreign born (29.7 percent) (see table 8). Egyptians, Iranians, Kuwaitis, and Israelis, who have the highest educational credentials among Middle Easterners, are also most likely to occupy the top occupational categories. This is not to suggest that all Middle Easterners are professional/managerial or entrepreneurial, for there is variation across and within groups. The most visible exceptions are the Arab working-class population in and around Detroit, Michigan. In addition, there are new Algerian and Moroccan migrant workers in the New York metropolitan area. Groups such as Afghans and Yemenis are also overrepresented in service occupations (see table 8). Nevertheless, the combination of self-employment and professional careers, two time-honored routes to success in America (see Portes and Rumbaut 2006), largely accounts for the successful economic adaptation of most Middle Easterners in the United States.

The socioeconomic data for Bangladeshis and Pakistanis are very similar to those for many Middle Eastern groups. Their educational and occupational achievements are particularly impressive for newcomers, reflecting their relatively high social class origins. About half of Bangladeshis and Pakistanis, and one-third of Afghans, have a bachelor's degree or more, and about three-quarters to four-fifths of each of these three South Asian groups speak English very well (table 5). Over half of Afghans (58.5 percent), about one-third of Bangladeshis, and 42.6 percent of Pakistanis became naturalized citizens soon after arrival (table 6). The occupational distribution of Afghans, Bangladeshis, and Pakistanis is tilted toward white-collar jobs (table 8). The only economic characteristic of Bangladeshis that sets them apart from Middle Easterners is their relatively low rate of self-employment; they tend to concentrate in service occupations and as laborers/operators (table 8). Afghans and Pakistanis tend to be almost as entrepreneurial as many Middle Eastern groups. As a founder and representative of a new South Asian grassroots organization in New York told us: "In the South Asian community, there is definitely a history of a class division. . . . We work with the folks who migrated here in the second wave [over] the last ten to fifteen years and who are predominantly working-class communities. . . . A lot of times, internally in the community, the people that we're organizing against, or have a campaign against, are the first wave of migrants who are employers or business owners."

Foreign-born Middle Eastern women have unusually low rates of labor force participation. In fact, immigrant Arab women have some of

TABLE 8. MAIN OCCUPATIONS OF FOREIGN-BORN MIDDLE EASTERN AND SELECTED
SOUTH ASIAN GROUPS IN THE UNITED STATES, 2000

| National Origin | Population | Occupation[a] (%) | | | |
| | | Managerial/Professional | Technical/Sales/Administration | Service | Operators/Laborers |
| --- | --- | --- | --- | --- | --- |
| Middle East | | | | | |
| Iran | 161,774 | 50.2 | 29.5 | 7.5 | 12.0 |
| Iraq | 43,337 | 24.4 | 34.2 | 9.9 | 30.7 |
| Israel/Palestine | 63,342 | 50.0 | 31.1 | 6.7 | 11.7 |
| Jordan | 25,965 | 33.0 | 38.1 | 9.8 | 18.2 |
| Kuwait | 8,902 | 48.9 | 36.0 | 4.1 | 10.3 |
| Lebanon | 59,399 | 44.4 | 29.9 | 8.9 | 16.1 |
| Saudi Arabia | 5,299 | 44.0 | 32.0 | 5.7 | 15.6 |
| Syria | 26,343 | 37.3 | 31.5 | 8.3 | 22.3 |
| Turkey | 44,252 | 43.4 | 25.8 | 10.6 | 19.3 |
| Yemen Arab Republic | 7,116 | 16.6 | 45.3 | 11.6 | 25.0 |
| Egypt | 62,687 | 47.4 | 26.1 | 9.9 | 15.6 |
| Algeria | 6,384 | 44.1 | 24.7 | 12.1 | 18.5 |
| Morocco | 24,430 | 34.6 | 28.5 | 17.7 | 18.1 |
| South Asia | | | | | |
| Afghanistan | 19,283 | 30.5 | 32.1 | 14.7 | 21.4 |
| Bangladesh | 42,585 | 30.8 | 31.1 | 16.0 | 20.9 |
| Pakistan | 108,408 | 40.1 | 32.5 | 6.6 | 19.9 |
| All Foreign Born | 15,299,536 | 29.7 | 22.2 | 16.3 | 29.0 |

SOURCE: U.S. Bureau of the Census (2000a).

NOTE: Data are not available for Tunisia.

[a]Population twenty-five to sixty-four years old in the labor force. The total percentages of occupations do not add to 100% because of the omission of military,
farming/forestry/fishing, and "unemployed, or not classified."

the lowest rates of labor force participation among all immigrant groups, regardless of their educational level. Religiosity, endogamous marriages,[38] and women's responsibility for maintaining traditional families are among the main factors accounting for Arab women's low employment rate (Read 2004a, 2004b); however, men's generally high earnings may also account for these low numbers. Read and Oselin have further argued that Arab American husbands and wives, whether Christian or Muslim, "support female education as a resource, not for economic mobility, but to ensure the proper socialization of children, solidarity of the family, and ultimately the maintenance of ethnic and religious identity" (2008, 296). The immigrant generation was more likely to uphold beliefs and practices than later generations.

## DEMOGRAPHIC AND SOCIOECONOMIC CHARACTERISTICS OF MUSLIMS IN THE UNITED STATES

The U.S. Constitution prevents government agencies, including the Census Bureau, from collecting data on religious affiliation. This makes it difficult to know how many Muslims live in the United States. The population size and characteristics of Muslim Americans are thus estimated from polls and surveys, although the results vary widely. In the American Religious Identification Survey, a total of 50,281 American residential households in the continental United States were reached through random-digit phone calling between February 2001 and June 2001. Respondents were asked, "What is your religion, if any?" The results of the survey estimated that 1,104,000 Americans identified themselves as Muslims in 2001 (Kosmin, Mayer, and Keysar 2001).

Project MAPS: Muslims in the American Public Square is another source of data on Muslim Americans.[39] The American Muslim Poll claims to be the "first ever systematic poll" of Muslims in the United States. Phone interviews were conducted in November 2001 with individuals over age eighteen who identified as Muslims. Starting with the zip codes of three hundred randomly selected Islamic centers, the researchers matched the phone numbers of common Muslim surnames from local telephone exchanges. Since the surnames of African American Muslims are less readily identifiable, in-person interviews were conducted in New York, Washington, D.C., Atlanta, and Detroit, areas of high African American Muslim concentration. This survey reached 1,781 individuals, of whom 26 percent identified themselves as Arab, 32 percent as South Asian, and 20 percent as African American. The poll estimated the total Muslim population at 5,745,100 in 2001 (Ba-Yunus and Kone 2004, 314), without giving a clear rationale for this high estimate.

In October 2004, Project MAPS/Zogby International released the results of another survey conducted in August and September (Project MAPS and Zogby International 2004). The sample size consisted of 1,846 respondents, 64 percent of whom were foreign born and 58 percent of whom were male. About one-third (34 percent) were South Asian, 26 percent were Arab, 20 percent were African American, 7 percent were African, and the remaining 13 percent had other ethnicities. As for socioeconomic status, 59 percent had completed college or more, 42 percent held managerial, medical, and professional/technical occupations, and 33 percent earned more than $75,000. The 2004 survey matched the demographic characteristics of the 2001 respondents.

The Pew Research Center (2007) has conducted a survey with a sample of 1,050 Muslim adults eighteen years and older nationwide, using random-digit dialing. It estimates that there are 1.4 million Muslims of age eighteen or older in the United States: that is, Muslims constitute less than 1 percent of the total U.S. adult population. The majority of Muslims (65 percent) are foreign born, with 37 percent coming from the Arab region and another 27 percent coming from Pakistan, India, Bangladesh, or Afghanistan. One-third of the foreign born arrived in the 1990s, 28 percent after 2000, and 23 percent in the 1980s. A majority (77 percent) are citizens, with 65 percent of the foreign born having been naturalized.

The main advantage of this poll is its comparability with the U.S. population. Income and education for Muslims in the Pew study mirror those of the larger population: 24 percent have a college degree and 10 percent have continued with their graduate education. Income levels between Muslims and the general population are at parity: 41 percent of Muslim households report an income of $50,000 or more annually, compared to 44 percent for the general population. Sixteen percent report an income of $100,000 or more, which is almost identical to the percentage of the public at large. Over one-third (35 percent) report an income of $30,000 or less, again comparable with the figure for the general public.

American Muslims belong to diverse Islamic traditions: 50 percent say they are Sunnis; 16 percent say they are Shiᶜa; 22 percent say they are just Muslim; 5 percent say they are of another Muslim tradition; and 7 percent offer no response. Sunnis constitute 50 percent of the native born and 53 percent of the foreign born, whereas 21 percent of the foreign born identify as Shiʿa and 18 percent have no affiliation. Twenty percent of U.S. Muslims are native born African Americans: of these, 48 percent identify as Sunni, 34 percent as just Muslim, and 15 percent as other. About a quarter (23 percent) of American Muslims say they converted to Islam; 91 percent of them were born in the United States.

Each of the surveys reported has methodological shortfalls, but they are still useful given the dearth of data on Muslim Americans. While the American Religious Identification Survey was a random survey of a cross section of the American people, it did not ask questions on ethnicity. The use of high-Muslim-density zip codes and "common Muslim names" makes the MAPS sampling problematic. The Pew poll suffers from somewhat similar sampling problems, but mostly from a relatively high refusal rate. Such issues illustrate the difficulty in reconciling the various polls and surveys and agreeing on a reliable estimate of Muslim Americans.

In conclusion, Middle Eastern and South Asian Americans are one of the most ethnically and religiously diverse populations in America, yet their cross-cutting allegiances to various religious, linguistic, historical, and cultural groups have unifying tendencies. Third-generation Armenians, Lebanese, and Syrians have integrated into American society. The second wave of immigrants from both the Middle East and South Asia has unusually high socioeconomic status and English proficiency, characteristics that have facilitated their adaptation. Nevertheless, they have experienced adjustment difficulties because of obstacles that have arisen as a result of the continuous political crises in the Middle East and the Muslim world. Needless to say, the post-9/11 backlash and the wars in Afghanistan, Iraq, and Lebanon have aggravated the situation, feeding stereotypes, prejudice, and discrimination. Yet in spite of the backlash, new immigrants from the Middle East, North Africa, and South Asia continue to arrive and strive to make the United States their home.[40]

# 4

# Organizational Structures and Transformation

Our evidence in this study centers on Middle Eastern and Muslim American community-based organizations (CBOs). We relied heavily on interviews with high-level representatives of these organizations. We should stipulate that this chapter is not what sociologists call an "organizational analysis." As noted in chapter 1, we believe that organizations and their leaders offer the most advantageous angle for our purpose. The social service agencies, as well as local and national chapters of the Middle Eastern and Muslim national advocacy organizations, were the first-line response to families of detainees and those affected by special registration and other governmental policies. Our study contributes to the literature on ethnic nonprofits and how they respond to crises. We believe the latter contribution is most significant because it has been overlooked in the literature. Here we examine how the fifty organizations in our sample responded to a massive crisis, then analyze the changes in their structure, capacity, visibility, and growth. We also highlight a few of the new CBOs that emerged after the events.

## ETHNIC/RELIGIOUS COMMUNITY-BASED ORGANIZATIONS

Historically, immigrant voluntary associations have played a pivotal role in helping newcomers adapt to life in America by providing information about jobs, housing, language classes, and other resources. In the absence of public welfare institutions such as Medicare and Medicaid, unemployment benefits, Social Security, and private insurance policies for health care, disability, and death, these associations were indispensable. Moreover, they fulfilled essential emotional and social needs as immigrants gathered for festive occasions and commemorations. CBOs functioned as a buffer, providing a safety net for immigrants (e.g., Lissak 1989). At the same time, Old World organizations such as the *Landsmanshaftn* (the hometown aid societies of East European Jews) retarded assimilation (e.g., Weisser 1985).

American society was also conducive to associational life. During his visit to America in 1831–32, Alexis de Tocqueville observed that "Americans form associations for the smallest undertakings" (1945, 115). He wrote: "Americans of all ages, all conditions, and all dispositions constantly form associations. They have not only commercial and manufacturing companies, in which all take part, but associations of a thousand other kinds, religious, moral, serious, futile, general or restricted, enormous or diminutive" (114). While members of the *Landsmanshaftn* and other imported benevolent organizations found a welcoming environment for their associational activities, ethnic groups that did not have such premigration traditions felt the need for specialized associations. For example, German Jews modeled B'nai B'rith (Sons of the Covenant) after the Freemasons (Soyer 1997, 38). Yet historian Daniel Soyer notes that Jewish "immigrant organizations in the United States resembled each other so remarkably that it is hard to escape the conclusion that they were largely American in form, if not in inspiration" (1997, 43). Indeed, Jose Moya's historical analysis of immigrant associations indicates that the major stimulus was "the migration process itself" (2005, 839).

Timothy Smith (1978) would agree with Moya's analysis but notes that religion was a significant component of associational life in American immigrant history. He writes, "Ethnic organizations coalesced out of both economic and psychic need and found meanings for personal and communal life in the cultural symbols and the religious ideas that their leaders believed were marks of a shared inheritance and, hence, of a common peoplehood. Both the structure and culture of these emerging ethno-religious groups helped participants compete more advantageously with members of other groups" (1978, 1168). Thus Catholics from Germany, Ireland, Poland, Italy, and elsewhere in Europe found common ground against the Protestant elite. Likewise, Jews came together in the United States irrespective of their provenance (see also

Herberg 1960). This observation is relevant to our study, given the focus on the mobilization of American Muslims, as we shall see in chapter 7.

The study of immigrant organizations was at the height of its popularity at the beginning of the twentieth century, but with only a few notable exceptions (e.g., Glazer and Moynihan 1970) it has fallen out of favor. Philip Kasinitz suggests that the increased professionalization of the discipline of sociology sought advances in theorizing and empirical research.[1] In particular, sociologists of immigration and ethnic studies shied away from organizations and their leaders as unrepresentative. They used large national databases and conducted surveys, using representative samples to improve generalizability of the data. There was little use for case studies of organizations. Even ethnographers avoided organizational leaders, opting for interviews with rank-and-file members.

The renewed awareness of CBOs seems to have coincided with the burgeoning network of nonprofit organizations among post-1965 immigrant groups (see, e.g., Hagan and Baker 1993; Kasinitz 1992; Marquez 2003; Marwell 2004; Schrover and Vermeulen 2005a). From his large survey of CBOs in New York City, Hector Cordero-Guzman shows that contemporary immigrant organizations fulfill the same functions as their predecessors: (1) they help with the immigration process by providing citizenship, legal, and translation services; (2) they facilitate adaptation and integration by offering employment training and referrals, English as a Second Language (ESL) classes, benefits counseling, and family support; (3) they link the immigrant community to the home country; and (4) they act as political representatives of the immigrant group by "articulating the needs of the community to metropolitan-level policy makers; serving as an advocate and network for their ethnic groups; activities that can be categorized as 'community building'; providing representation in politics; and representing the community in policy making, management and implementation" (2005, 17; see also Cordero-Guzman 2001a, 2001b).

Raymond Breton's (1964) concept of "institutional completeness"— that is, the degree to which ethnic communities develop formal organizations to meet their needs—is useful in classifying groups into low or high degrees of institutionalization. Moya adds that the critical variables are "size and the demographic and socioeconomic complexity of the immigrant community. Smaller and simpler immigrant communities . . . [tend] to form a narrower organizational spectrum even if participation [is] often higher than in larger communities" (2005, 851–52). Another development in the literature is the recognition of the role of governments in the associational life of immigrants and their descendants (856). This pertains to both transnational activism of diaspora communities with governments back "home" (e.g., Waldinger and Fitzgerald 2004; Shain 1999) and the host society's interventions in immigrant communities through policies and the allotment of public monies (e.g., Chung 2005; Marwell 2004). Drawing on Europe's experience with immigrants at the end of the twentieth century, Schrover and Vermeulen conclude that a "non-linear, bell-shaped relationship is found between government interference (as part of the political opportunity structure) and associational behavior, and between the size of the immigrant population (as a characteristic of the immigrant population) and associational behavior" (2005b, 826).

More specifically, sociologists of disaster have observed that "grassroots organizations acting on crises collaboratively create the most effective and adaptive responses to emergency problems within their communities. The flexibility, existing social ties, and knowledge of the community embedded in these organizations makes networks of local organizations more effective than hierarchical bureaucracies attempting to operate in turbulent environments characteristic of disasters."[2] Moreover, these organizations can be responsive to the immediate location. As Kathleen Tierney, an expert on disasters, says: "The centralized commander is too far away for that. You generally see people taking responsibility themselves."[3]

## MIDDLE EASTERN AND MUSLIM AMERICAN CBOS

Though Middle Eastern immigrants have traditionally been more invested in informal family and village/town networks than in formal institutions and nonprofits, in the New World there was a need to establish compatriotic societies as well as literary, theatrical, and musical associations that served mainly local consumption (Mirak 1983, ch. 9; Naff 1985).[4] The renowned Lebanese American historian Philip Hitti observed in his book *Syrians in America* (1924) that "Syrians cut no figure in the political life of this nation. Very few of them interest themselves in politics or aspire to office" (quoted in Suleiman 1987, 49). Consequently, it has been assumed that the early immigrants were apolitical.

New scholarship, however, has discovered that the pioneers forged a sense of identity around political issues upon arriving in appreciable numbers in the late 1800s. Hani Bawardi (2008) contends that a number of activists rallied countrymen around Greater Syria's nationalist cause much earlier than previously thought. Bawardi debunks the popular notion that Arab American political mobilization emerged after the Six-Day War in 1967. On the basis of primary sources in Arabic-language manuscripts and archives, he argues that political mobilization among early immigrants in the United States originated in late nineteenth-century Arab nationalism, which helped to forge an Arab American identity between 1890 and the 1950s. In the first stage, the immigrants defended Syria against Turkification; then, after 1911, they defended it against explicit French, British, and Russian colonial territorial ambitions in the Middle East. During this period the United Syrian Society was the largest such organization and included in its ranks a cross section of sectarian, village, and clan affiliations from Greater Syria. In 1915 the secret Free Syria Society, founded by Ameen Farah, from Nazareth in "southern Syria," was the first attempt to create political networks with the aim of achieving Syria's complete independence in stages—decentralization, autonomy, then complete independence.

The second stage of mobilization, which utilized pragmatic efforts by the New Syria Party to influence the U.S. political establishment on behalf of Syria, occurred at the end of World War I when that country's inhabitants were facing the French. In the third stage, U.S.-educated and highly qualified individuals, including Fuad Shatara, Habib Katibah, and Khalil Totah, established the Arab National League (1938–42) and the Institute of Arab American Affairs (1945–50). Bawardi notes that the league was one of most sophisticated national political organizations at the time. During this stage, the plight of Palestinians emerged as a core issue. Palestine took center stage when the British made good on the Balfour Declaration, which promised to create a "national home for the Jews in Palestine." Bawardi suggests that these Arab American political organizations suffered an early demise when the death of their leaders was eclipsed by the calamity of the Holocaust and the legitimation of Zionist designs. After World War II, Israel gained special status as an outpost against communism, whereas pan-Arab nationalism was deemed antagonistic to U.S. regional security.

Michael Suleiman concurs that the pioneers were not at all averse to getting involved in homeland politics. Yet he suspects that their "avoidance of political activity, especially when such activity involved a challenge to specific laws or opposition to authority figures," was motivated by a desire to keep their "good citizen" image in the United States untarnished (1987, 50). The dismantling of the Institute of Arab American Affairs at the end of World War II left a political void in the community.

After the 1967 Arab-Israeli War, a new generation of activists founded the Association of Arab American University Graduates, which became "the first post-World War II national, credible, nonsectarian organization seeking to represent different elements of the Arab American community and to advance an Arab (as opposed to regional or country) orientation" (Suleiman 1994, 47). Its goal was to "provide accurate information about the Arab world and Arabs in the United States, . . . [to] educate the Arab countries and people about the true nature of the problems facing the region, and to educate Arab intellectuals and political leaders about U.S. policies and the U.S. political process" (47). It devoted its resources to "political lobbying, attacks against defamation of and discrimination against Arabs and Arab Americans, and activism among Arab Americans in order to get them to participate in politics" (48). Other organizations were formed later: the National Association of Arab Americans in 1972, ADC in 1980, and AAI in 1985.

In Dearborn, grassroots activists formed ACCESS in 1971. It was the first Arab American CBO committed to empowering the local community (Rignall 2000). The founding members, who included established later-generation Syrian Lebanese and more recent immigrants, realized that they needed to "engage the community overall in helping itself by helping those in need" (Checkoway, Rignall, and Ramakrishnan 2005, 29). Their strategy has paid off; today ACCESS˙is the premier Arab American CBO, with over seventy programs and a budget exceeding $10 million.[5] ACCESS has also taken the lead to professionalize Arab American CBOs by creating NNAAC. Additionally, ACCESS spearheaded the effort to establish the Arab American National Museum in Dearborn, Michigan, which opened in 2005.

Since Muslim immigrants to the United States are relative newcomers, their institutions were founded in the last decades of the twentieth century. The earliest organizations were the Federation of Islamic Associations, established in 1953 by Lebanese Muslim immigrants, and the Muslim Students' Association, founded in 1963 by foreign students studying in the United States (Y. Haddad and Lummis 1987; Abdo 2006; Schmidt 2004). By 1982, the Islamic Society of North America had taken over most of the functions of its predecessors (Leonard 2003). The Islamic Center of North America, another major organization, was founded in 1963. Pan-Islamic advocacy organizations such as MPAC and CAIR are much younger (founded in 1988 and 1994, respectively). MPAC was founded in Southern California, but in 1999 an office was opened in Washington, D.C. The National Council of American Muslim

Non-Profits was established in March 2005 in response to the shutdown of over twenty-five Muslim American organizations by the U.S. Treasury Department, allegedly for "aiding terrorism." The council's goal is to work proactively with the government and the CBOs to ensure transparency and protect Muslim American institutions.[6]

## CHARACTERISTICS OF THE ORGANIZATIONS IN THE STUDY

All but three of the fifty organizations in our sample (6 percent) were founded after 1969, a time that coincides with the beginning of a large influx of immigrants from the region. The exceptions were two compatriotic societies established in 1908 and 1947 and an Islamic center founded in 1952. Almost half (44 percent) of the organizations were founded in the 1990s, 16 percent in the 1980s, and another 16 percent in the 1970s. A remarkable 18 percent of CBOs emerged between 2000 and 2003. The data indirectly reflect the time it takes for new immigrants to get organized (see table 9).

In terms of ethnic/religious background, 50 percent of the organizations in the sample are Arab American. Most of these were established after 1970. The 1990s were particularly active, with the emergence of a large proportion of new Arab American CBOs (22 percent). Muslim American religious institutions and advocacy organizations made up 22 percent of our sample. Again, most were established in the 1990s. The South Asian category encompasses Pakistani, Bangladeshi, and Sikh CBOs (14 percent of sample). The remaining 14 percent are classified as "other." They represent Afghan, Armenian, Chaldean, Druze, and Iranian organizations (see table 9).

We divided the Middle Eastern and Muslim American organizations in our sample into six types according to their primary mission and scope of outreach (i.e., national, regional, or local). The majority (44 percent) of the organizations were devoted to advocacy, itself an indicator of the pressing needs of these communities. This was followed by hometown associations or compatriotic societies (16 percent); religious institutions—mosque, church, or *gurdwara* (Sikh temple) (14 percent); social service agencies (10 percent); professional associations, such as ethnic/religious legal or business associations (8 percent); and media outlets—radio, newspaper, or magazine (8 percent). Half of the organizations we sampled served local needs, and the other half were almost equally divided between national (26 percent) and regional (24 percent) concerns (table 10). The social service organizations and almost all

TABLE 9. PERCENTAGES OF ORGANIZATIONS OF SPECIFIC
ETHNIC/RELIGIOUS BACKGROUNDS BY YEAR OF FOUNDING

| | 1900–1969 | 1970–1979 | 1980–1989 | 1990–1999 | 2000–2003 | Total |
|---|---|---|---|---|---|---|
| Arab American | 2 | 6 | 12 | 22 | 8 | 50 |
| South Asian American | — | 6 | — | 6 | 2 | 14 |
| Muslim American | 2 | 2 | 2 | 14 | 2 | 22 |
| Other | 2 | 2 | 2 | 2 | 6 | 14 |
| Total | 6 | 16 | 16 | 44 | 18 | 100 |
| N | (3) | (8) | (8) | (22) | (9) | (50) |

NOTE: Although the 1970–99 period is given by decade, the other periods are not comparable. The first period spans sixty-nine years and the last period only three years.

TABLE 10. TYPES OF ORGANIZATIONS BY SCOPE OF OUTREACH
*(percentages)*

| | National | Regional | Local | Total |
|---|---|---|---|---|
| Advocacy | 76 | 33 | 32 | 44 |
| Social Service | — | — | 20 | 10 |
| Religious | 8 | — | 24 | 14 |
| Professional | 8 | 25 | — | 8 |
| Compatriotic | 8 | 17 | 20 | 16 |
| Media | — | 25 | 4 | 8 |
| Total | 26 | 24 | 50 | 100 |
| N | (13) | (12) | (25) | (50) |

the religious institutions were local, but advocacy organizations were mostly national in scope.

As a category, Middle Eastern and Muslim American organizations tend to have limited financing (table 11). Those with annual budgets of under $40,000 were most common (34 percent of total). These CBOs raise most of their funds through dues, gifts, and fundraising events. The next most common category in our sample was at the other end of the spectrum: organizations whose annual budgets ranged between $100,000 and almost $1 million (28 percent), followed by those with budgets between $40,000 and almost $100,000 (18 percent). Only 14

TABLE II. ORGANIZATIONAL OUTREACH TYPE
BY ANNUAL BUDGET, 2003
*(percentages)*

|  | $0–39,999 | $40,000–99,999 | $100,000–999,999 | $1 million–4,999,999 | $5–10 million | Total |
|---|---|---|---|---|---|---|
| Advocacy | 10 | 12 | 10 | 10 | 2 | 44 |
| Social Service | 2 | — | 2 | 4 | 2 | 10 |
| Religious | — | — | 12 | — | 2 | 14 |
| Professional | 2 | 2 | 4 | — | — | 8 |
| Compatriotic | 14 | 2 | — | — | — | 16 |
| Media | 6 | 2 | — | — | — | 8 |
| *Total* | 34 | 18 | 28 | 14 | 6 | 100 |
| N | (17) | (9) | (14) | (7) | (3) | (50) |

NOTE: Budget intervals do not match.

percent of organizations had budgets exceeding $1 million but less than $5 million, and, not surprisingly, only 6 percent (three organizations) had a budget between $5 million and $10 million. Analysis of organizations' budgets by their mission shows that the ethnic media and compatriotic societies had very small budgets. The financial resources of religious institutions (mosques and *gurdwaras*) mostly fell between $100,000 and $1 million. However, one of the oldest national agencies providing educational and social services to Muslim Americans had a budget of over $5 million. In general, social service organizations tended to have larger budgets, except for two agencies in our sample that were established recently and still relied mostly on volunteers. Advocacy organizations came in all stripes: at one extreme were organizations that raised almost $10 million annually, and at the other were those with budgets under $40,000, some not even half of that (table 11).

Only three organizations had received funding from corporations. Two of them were professional associations that lent themselves to close corporate ties. The third was a newly formed advocacy organization. Three of the largest social service agencies relied heavily on government contracts to deliver welfare, child care, and other programs for impoverished co-ethnics or new immigrants. One Arab American group relied on local government funding, largely a tribute to city elders who believed in multiculturalism. Three organizations—two advocacy and one social service agency—relied primarily on grants and foundations. This means

80 percent of the organizations were dependent on raising funds from their communities through dues, gifts, donations, and fundraising events such as banquets and picnics. Such self-reliance is no doubt admirable. It could be argued that the CBOs' small membership and budgets do not warrant going through the arduous formal grant application process. Generally unfamiliar with the American philanthropic and corporate worlds, many immigrants do not have adequate knowledge about where to seek funding or adequate skills in writing grant applications. They are also not connected to the networks where one could hear about Requests for Proposals (RFPs), and they do not have ties to program officers in mainstream philanthropies. Indeed, the estrangement goes both ways. Until recently, foundations almost totally neglected Middle Eastern and Muslim CBOs. Even since 9/11 their support has been patchy. There was a burst immediately after 9/11, but it has dwindled over time.

Thirty-eight percent of the organizations in our sample relied totally on volunteers (no paid employees), many of whom poured in immediately after 9/11 (table 12). The leader of an Arab American organization told us: "When we asked for volunteers, we had over 1,200 people! I mean, that's amazing! That says something, you know?" When we probed about the ethnic background of the volunteers, we learned that most were mainstream Americans. "No, they were not Arab. I mean there were some, but not the majority, that's for sure. They were mostly Americans. A lot of Jewish names—of course you can't tell who's Jewish and who isn't, but there are some that you can tell somewhat from their names." Organizations serving other ethnic groups and civil/immigration rights agencies stepped up to the occasion and offered their expertise and services. A knowledgeable source told us that "HELP [Human Rights Education Law Project] and DRUM [Desis Rising Up and Moving, an Asian American organization] immediately came out and provided interpreters. They got the community involved and provided interpreters. They were key in this whole process of making it work because we couldn't do it without interpreters." However important volunteer contributions are, a professionally run organization still requires professional staff. As a leader observed, "If we just depended on volunteers . . . it wouldn't work." As is typical with most disasters, once the urgency subsided, the volunteers evaporated. As for paid employees, 44 percent of the organizations in our sample employed between one and ten workers, 14 percent had a workforce of eleven to twenty-five employees, and only 4 percent (one organization) had twenty-six or more paid employees.

TABLE 12. STAFFING OF ORGANIZATIONS
BY ANNUAL BUDGET, 2003
*(percentages)*

| | $0–39,999 | $40,000– 99,999 | $100,000– 999,999 | $1 million– 4,999,999 | $5–10 Million | Total |
|---|---|---|---|---|---|---|
| No paid employees | 88 | 33 | 7 | — | — | 38 |
| Small (1–10 employees) | 12 | 67 | 93 | 14 | — | 44 |
| Medium (11–25 employees) | — | — | — | 86 | 33 | 14 |
| Large (26 or more employees) | — | — | — | — | 67 | 4 |
| N | (17) | (9) | (14) | (7) | (3) | (50) |

About two-thirds of the organizations (68 percent) had regular boards, though the number of board members varied enormously from small (five or six) to over a dozen. Fourteen percent of the organizations were not formally organized, while 18 percent had an executive board and advisory boards with large numbers of directors. By law, a 501(c)3 organization must have a board; the names and addresses of its members are part of its official record with the Internal Revenue Service (IRS). Many organizations in our sample recognized the importance of boards but struggled to recruit and keep board members. A leader noted, "The real backbone of [name] is the people that are the trustees themselves. They're the ones that bring in other people. They're the ones that reach out to their friends because they're trusted by them. They don't necessarily trust the organization, but they trust Mr. such-and-such." When a board is not effective, the organization does not function to its full potential.

## DEMOGRAPHIC AND SOCIOECONOMIC CHARACTERISTICS OF ORGANIZATIONAL LEADERS

We conducted sixty interviews with spokespersons of Middle Eastern and Muslim American organizations. One of these interviews was with the same person after a gap of fifteen months; therefore, we present the individual characteristics of fifty-nine respondents (table 13). Men dominate by far (83 percent) as leaders and directors of CBOs in our sample. The average age of this sample was fifty years, though almost one-third of the respondents were between forty and forty-nine years of age (30.5 percent); the youngest respondent was twenty-five years old, and the oldest was seventy-six. Two-thirds of the sample were foreign born (66 percent). The U.S.-born second generation made up 27 percent of the sample, and the remaining 7 percent were from the third generation and beyond. In terms of religious affiliation, the majority of this sample (64 percent) identified as Muslim, 24 percent were Christian, and the other 12 percent included Hindus, Sikhs, Druze, Buddhists, and Zoroastrians.

In terms of ethnic background, the highest proportion (27 percent) of the leaders and officials were Palestinian, followed closely by the Lebanese (20 percent). Our sample also included Egyptians (8.5 percent), Pakistanis (5 percent), Iranians (5 percent), Jordanians (3.4 percent), and "Americans" who were converts to Islam (3.4 percent). There was also one person from each of the following ethnic backgrounds in the "other" category (27.7 percent): Afghan, Algerian, Armenian, Bangladeshi, Libyan, Iraqi, Somali, Syrian, and Yemeni (see table 13). The large proportion of Palestinian leaders in the sample is noteworthy given that they made up only 5 percent of the Arab population in the 2000 U.S. Census. We attribute this strong presence to the political mobilization of the Palestinian people in their struggle for an independent homeland. On the other hand, the Lebanese make up 20 percent of the sample because they represent almost 34 percent of the Arab population in the 2000 census and have the longest history of residence in the United States.

Overall, our respondents were highly educated. This partly reflects the high levels of educational achievement of these populations (chapter 3), but it also reflects their self-selection in becoming organizational leaders. Only 8.5 percent of the respondents in the sample had just a high school diploma or some college. Over one-third (37.3 percent) of the leaders had a master's degree, 16.9 percent had completed college, 10.2 percent had earned a law degree, 6.8 percent held a PhD, another 6.8 percent were in the process of getting a doctorate, and 6.8 percent had a medical degree (MD or DSS). Most of the degrees were from top American universities, including Columbia, Cornell, Georgetown, and Michigan. About a fourth of the respondents had earned their degrees from universities overseas, including three from the prestigious American University of Beirut. In terms of employment, only 42 percent of the leaders in our sample were salaried staff of the organizations they

## TABLE 13. DEMOGRAPHIC AND SOCIOECONOMIC CHARACTERISTICS OF RESPONDENTS (ORGANIZATIONAL LEADERS)

| Characteristics | Percent |
|---|---|
| Gender | |
| Male | 83.0 |
| Female | 17.0 |
| Age | |
| 20–29 | 11.9 |
| 30–39 | 23.7 |
| 40–49 | 30.5 |
| 50–59 | 18.6 |
| 60–69 | 13.6 |
| 70–80 | 1.7 |
| Generation | |
| Foreign born | 66.0 |
| Second generation (native born) | 27.0 |
| Third generation or higher (native born) | 7.0 |
| Religion[a] | |
| Muslim | 64.0 |
| Christian | 24.0 |
| Other | 12.0 |
| Ethnicity[b] | |
| Palestinian | 27.0 |
| Lebanese | 20.0 |
| Egyptian | 8.5 |
| Iranian | 5.0 |
| Pakistani | 5.0 |
| Jordanian | 3.4 |
| American converts to Islam | 3.4 |
| Other | 27.7 |
| Education[c] | |
| High school/some college | 8.5 |
| Bachelor's degree | 16.9 |
| Master's degree/MBA | 37.3 |
| Law degree | 10.2 |
| PhD/doctorate | 6.8 |
| Medical degree (MD or DDS) | 6.8 |
| Doctoral candidate | 6.8 |
| Missing | 6.8 |
| Occupation[d] | |
| Salaried staff of organization | 42.0 |
| Volunteer | 58.0 |
| Physician | 13.0 |
| Lawyer | 13.0 |
| Entrepreneur | 20.0 |
| Banker/accountant | 13.0 |
| Computer scientist | 13.0 |
| University professor | 7.0 |
| Publisher | 7.0 |
| Midlevel bureaucrat | 7.0 |
| Doctoral candidate/retired | 7.0 |
| N | (59) |

[a]There was one missing case for religion.  [b]There were two missing cases for ethnicity.  [c]There were four missing cases for education.  [d]There were four missing cases for occupation.

administered; the rest served pro bono. Among these voluntary work-ers, 13 percent were physicians, another 13 percent were lawyers, 20 percent were entrepreneurs (business owners), 13 percent were bankers/accountants, 13 percent were computer scientists, 7 percent were uni-versity professors, 7 percent were publishers, 7 percent were midlevel bureaucrats, and the remaining 7 percent consisted of a doctoral candi-date and a retired government employee (see table 13).

## CHARACTERISTICS OF KNOWLEDGEABLE SOURCES

We supplemented our data with fifteen interviews with "knowledgeable sources" (chapter 1), two of whom represented the same agency. Of these fifteen experts, five represented advocacy organizations for ethnic groups other than Middle Eastern and Muslim Americans; five worked for organizations specializing in immigration and civil rights; one was employed by an interfaith agency; and the remaining four were govern-ment employees at local and federal levels.

All fifteen knowledgeable sources in our sample were professional, salaried employees of their respective associations and institutions. Two-thirds were female (67 percent). In terms of religion, they covered many of America's faith communities—Christians, Muslims, Jews, and Buddhists. They also represented America's broad ethnic groups—His-panics, Jewish Americans, Asian Americans, and Anglos. Only one of these experts was of Arab descent and had been hired after 9/11. All were native born except for two immigrants, one of whom had arrived as a child. All had graduate degrees.

## THE SIGNIFICANCE OF LEADERS

American historians have shown that ethnic leaders play a critical role in the adaptation process of their group. According to Kathleen Conzen et al. (1992, 10), though "the process was fraught with internal conflicts and dissension over the nature, history, and destiny of its peoplehood," ethnic leaders strategized their future. They used accommodation, advo-cacy, negotiation, protest, and other tactics to chart a future for their people. Unquestionably, Middle Eastern and Muslim American leaders after 9/11 have played a crucial role in the struggles of their peoples.

Charisma is highly valued in leaders, but most leadership skills are acquired. A cursory search of published material or programs on leadership will yield a voluminous amount of material for corporate and non-profit leaders.[7] Today, even high school students are targets of leadership training programs.[8] Respondents were aware of the importance of grooming leaders, and some acknowledged opportunities in their own lives. A respondent said, "I learned a great deal by getting involved in the interfaith organization. . . . [I learned that] it is important that we speak with one voice, even though we may have differences. So when this 9/11 happened, the first reaction was to come together and speak with one voice." Through participation in rallies, ceremonies, and other public gatherings, leaders advocated for their constituents' inclusion in multiethnic/religious America. For instance, on September 19, 2001, a press conference was organized at the National Japanese American Memorial in Washington, D.C. A respondent who attended observed, "It was the first press conference that included leaders from the Asian American, Muslim, Sikh, and Arab American communities. It was actually quite a large crowd; it was standing room only. It was the first time, I think, that national leaders got to address the backlash in a unified manner."

Effective leaders also develop broad social networks to facilitate their organizational goals. A Muslim leader observed, "We're going to be working with a number of Asian American groups. . . . Those are easy alliances for us because some of our board members have had a lengthy history of working with those groups—including myself. So we already have, at least personally, some credibility that we're able to take and use on behalf of the organization." As the quote suggests, some professional ties gain strength over time through mutual respect and trust. The outcome is fulfilling for the actors and productive in reaching organizational goals. A knowledgeable source with a long track record in ethnic mobilization emphasized the importance of informal ethnic networks: "It is . . . hard for me not to describe this in a way which makes it sound incredibly exclusive . . . but that is, to a certain extent, how this works. . . . [Of] the two models I outlined—the sort of formal civil rights community and the informal, more flexible immigrants' rights community—I by far prefer the latter, 'cause we get more done and we're much more flexible."

Many respondents in our sample held multiple leadership roles. For instance, a physician in private practice was the president of a CBO that offered social and youth services; he was also chairman of the board of his local mosque, served on the board of trustees of an Arab American nursing home, and was part of the founding team of the local Islamic school. Another respondent noted that she was on three boards, two with an Arab American focus and one that helped Palestinians in Gaza and the West Bank. Still another person hosted a weekly Arabic-language radio program, read the news on an Arabic TV channel, and was president of a cultural association that promoted the folklore, music, literature, and arts of Egypt. When leaders serve several organizations, their relationships and knowledge facilitate community-wide organizing (see also Cristillo 2004, 115, 255).

The post-9/11 backlash brought the leadership of grassroots organizations into the national and international media limelight. The president of a hometown association bragged, "I was in two meetings in Washington, and we met with the Assistant Secretary of State Burns. As a matter of fact, tomorrow . . . [there is] a meeting with Secretary of State Powell." Leaders were assumed to represent the communities, and their opinion filled an important void in the public's (and government's) hunger for knowledge about Arabs and Muslims in America. Those who were articulate in English and presented well on TV screens were repeatedly sought by major networks to explain the Arab and/or Muslim perspective. The legitimacy of their expertise and the accuracy of their views were rarely questioned.

Many Middle Eastern and Muslim leaders became minor celebrities. Some enjoyed being in the public eye and justified their visibility in terms of community goals, such as the person who told us, "September 11th to us is horrible, but it is again an opportunity to reach out and tell people [our] story." Another respondent acknowledged that the tragedy had opened up new opportunities for educating the public about Islam. A national spokesperson boasted about the ability of his advocacy organization to produce media-savvy leaders. Accordingly, one person specialized in the Arabic media, another appeared on the American national media, and a third covered the regional outlets. He went on to say, "We're polyphonic. And the voice is not all exactly the same. My point is this: . . . there's much more depth here in this office. There is much more than one person with a bunch of different support staff." In this respondent's estimation, an organization is stronger when more than one person represents it to the larger community.

At an academic conference we witnessed a national leader show off his celebrity status. After introducing the speaker as someone who had appeared over two thousand times in the media since the terrorist attacks, the moderator was duly corrected that the speaker had actually made over three thousand media appearances. Although the speaker was well educated, highly eloquent, and a persuasive debater, almost any leader is likely to become media savvy after three thousand trial runs. While credentials and skills are valued in leaders, elitism is not an admirable characteristic. A respondent complained about the local chapter president of a national organization: "They mostly select people who are elitist to run these chapters. . . . You want to go to the masses, and that's where . . . you're going to find the Arabs." Irrespective of class background, effective leaders need to bridge the needs of their constituents and mainstream resources. The events of 9/11 gave a young leader with only a master's degree the opportunity to fine-tune his advocacy skills and the courage to critique the old guard:

> Because "Oh, we're doctors," this and that, they [physicians] think that they know politics, they think that they know architecture, they think they know everything. We would like to make them understand that if I have a toothache or a pain somewhere in my body, you're the man. Other than that, if you haven't studied politics, if you don't know how to go through political analysis, or have good writing skills, or be a good diplomat, then you're not the man or the woman for the job. Usually it's a man. They actually tell themselves that it's not that difficult, it's easy. They just don't understand this concept that you have to be a specialist or something in that field. This is the way of thinking I would like to change.

Several leaders in our sample reflected on the importance of leadership. Here are some of their comments:

> I think that to be working for an organization that's not designated as an "Arab" organization, I think was meaningful for our community. . . . Being in that position, I was able to open up doors for our community because resources are scarce. . . . I think my strong background in terms of the political work that I have done and my commitment to social justice help in keeping that vision going in terms of creating that inclusive community.
> When you think about the leadership development piece, it starts by being on your local school council, on your local park district, reforming the public aid office, so it also will respect the needs of our community and reach out to them—if we want to build capacity, and that's what it takes to organize the community.

Middle Eastern and Muslim American organizations are newcomers to advocacy and especially need grooming of future leaders. Organizations such as ADC, AAI, CAIR, MPAC, and SAALT have begun to offer internship opportunities for college students and young professionals, but much more is required if these communities are to compete effectively for their place in the American mainstream.[9]

## ORGANIZATIONAL TRANSFORMATION

### ORGANIZATIONAL CAPACITY

Capacity issues were a source of tension in practically all the organizations in our sample, even government institutions and civil rights groups. There were shortages of experienced professional staff and board members; even funding, space, and equipment were limited. Clearly, this was due to the magnitude of the crisis. The post-9/11 backlash changed the scope, nature, and intensity of the work of almost every organization. Respondents recalled the first few weeks after the terrorist attacks: "Nobody knew what was going on." "There were just so many things that were happening. . . . It's like your worst nightmare come true." They felt "stretched," "overburdened," and "overwhelmed." The representative of a large national organization said, "What did we do? . . . We did what we do normally, but in a much more frantic pace and in a much greater volume than we did before." No matter how well established and resourceful some of these organizations were, almost invariably our respondents confessed that they were frustrated because they were inundated with tasks they could not possibly handle. The speed and secrecy with which new initiatives were issued by the administration, sometimes described as a "shifting landscape," aggravated the situation. In an interview more than a year after 9/11, a knowledgeable source in Washington, D.C., explained that the "only thing that's harder about the post-9/11 environment is that it's uglier." She continued: "We spent a year careening from crisis to crisis to crisis, starting with all the stuff the Justice Department has been doing, as in the appointing of local police to engage in immigration enforcement, and then the . . . profiling that's been going on. . . . So we sort of raced from one to the other."

Middle Eastern and Muslim organizations encouraged their constituents to report hate crimes and bias incidents and offered them guidelines and referrals; this added another dimension to the increased workload. A respondent explained that his agency had received three hundred discrimination complaints in two months' time, a number that before 9/11 they would have received in six to nine months. He added, "It was way over our ability and capability and the limited resources we were dealing with." The director of a social service agency that offered help to the families of the detainees noted: "This department was swamped with all of those people coming with all different stories and all different experiences. . . . Some of them still receive our counseling services."

The national and international media and the American public wanted to learn more about Arabs and Muslims and often approached the CBOs since they were readily identifiable. Thus public relations and outreach became paramount concerns of the leaders. The president of a nascent social service organization explained to us that after 9/11 there was an urgent need for outreach to "improve the image of Arabs or Middle Easterners in general." Leaders responded by granting interviews to journalists and lecturing at churches, synagogues, universities, and other public forums. A nationally recognized leader we interviewed explained: "Up until September 10, our Web site was on track to get about five million visitors. . . . By the end of the year, we had ten million." This attention, though often positive, further stretched the capabilities of the CBOs.

The amount of printed information disseminated is another indicator of the exponential increase in the demands placed on Middle Eastern and Muslim American organizations. A respondent noted, "We used to do a mailing of about twenty-five to thirty pieces of Islamic material and brochures every day before this. After this, it increased in the initial two months; it was something like 125–30 pieces of mailing every day. Now it has gone again down a little bit, but still it is in the range of 50 to 60 mailings, which is still higher than we were doing before September 11." A young Afghan leader noted, "Before September 11 we used to do three, four, five, at the most, events per year. Now in the span of four months, we're doing more than twenty-five." In an interview in January 2002, a prominent Arab American respondent observed, "I would say at least ten thousand sets of educational information went out; a couple [of] thousand posters. [Name] and I have done probably six hundred media [appearances] since September 11."

While the immediate demands on organizational capacity were pressing, the leadership also had to evaluate the new situation and develop strategies for meeting the needs of their constituents. In an interview about five months after 9/11, an eloquent respondent explained the situation succinctly:

> And, of course, we had to, at the same time, really sit back and rethink. . . . We had to try to get a sense of how the political landscape had shifted. . . . It was fairly clear that some reevaluation, some . . . serious analysis was going to be required before we would be able to make a strategy for moving forward on . . . many of the issues that are most important to our constituents. And that's a process that's been in place since the 12th. I don't think it's completely resolved yet. . . . I think we've managed to do a lot of it, but there are still some serious challenges.

At the time of our interviews, professional personnel, especially those with work experience and cultural sensitivity, were in short supply. Moreover, the existing staff of most Middle Eastern and Muslim American organizations were ill prepared for the challenges. For instance, the leader of a Muslim organization explained to us: "We get requests from prisoners who feel that they are not getting their rights, so we try to contact the chaplain and the prison authorities. We do not have that many resources to hire attorneys and fight the cases." When we asked this man if the caseworkers were trained and licensed as social workers, he replied that they were "learned Muslims, with not only Islamic knowledge."

Immigration experts were even harder to find. An attorney working in an agency dedicated to immigrant rights explained the scarcity: "There has never been enough attention paid to this issue, to the issue of detention, to the issue of the undocumented. There have never been enough agencies. In the state of New Jersey, until this year there were six nonprofit agencies that did immigration work. And the state of New Jersey has the fifth highest number of immigrants in the country. Six little agencies with one attorney each are not going to cut it."

There were hardly any immigration lawyers on the staff of Arab and Muslim organizations on the eve of 9/11, and fewer who could speak Arabic, Urdu, or another South Asian language. When the government initiatives warranted legal expertise, the CBOs scrambled to find reputable legal services for referrals or developed their own legal departments. A social service agency partnered with a local law school so that students could advise clients on a pro bono basis.

A civil rights organization with no ties to the Middle East or South Asia pitched in after 9/11 with its legal clinic and outreach. The services needed from legal offices varied. At times, they even involved arbitration and negotiation with a client's employer, as the following case illustrates:

> I have a client who was literally beaten on the [subway] train because he was [of] Bangladeshi descent, and they misperceived him to be Arab. He . . . didn't go to work for eight days because he was scared. He works the midnight shift at the post office. The post office's response was: "Sorry, dude. I can't change your schedule. Live with it. Deal with it. Why don't you put on a New York Yankees cap, and maybe that'll protect you?" So what we tried to do was deal with some of the employment situation, getting him to change his . . . night shift to day shift.

Given the dearth of experienced immigration attorneys from the affected communities, the major civil rights organizations were invaluable in lending their support at this juncture. Here is how a respondent explained their involvement:

> A lot of these people are white lawyers, white Christian or Jewish or atheist lawyers who are not really familiar [with the Middle East]. . . . Many of them have dropped a lot of what they're doing to work on these [immigration] issues. I mean, many of them are getting outside their comfort zone. . . . It takes a lot for some of these people to get up to go to a mosque and to say, "I want to know what's happening here and I'm here to help." And the fact that hundreds of [these] lawyers are doing this around the country says a lot.

Several organizations created new positions to accommodate the new programmatic changes. One of the elders of a mosque we visited in the New York region observed, "We developed an outreach department to express *insaf* [fairness to Muslims]. We developed packages and references for mosques and organizations. . . . We used to do this before 9/11, but not as much. In the past we didn't need a department." When we visited a national organization for a second time, about two years after our initial visit, we learned that they had added a Government Relations Department and had expanded the Community Affairs Department. Representatives traveled around the country offering workshops on civil rights or media relations and distributed "know your rights" literature. A well-known organization recognized the need to create a new position for an Arab and Muslim advocate. They hired a lawyer of Arab descent in summer 2002. However, the rapid creation of new positions did not necessarily guarantee the support the employee required to accomplish his or her job. When we asked a new hire, "What is it you do?" the response was "It's constantly evolving. . . . There's no clearly defined role for my job. In fact, the job description was crazy. They just put a laundry list of things down. . . . It's a lot more . . . than one person can do."

## ENGAGING IN ADVOCACY

In response to our question "Have your goals and objectives changed since 9/11?" we learned that most organizations shared the views of the following respondent: "The mandate of the organization has not changed, but . . . we had to try to redefine ourselves to some extent in order to cope with the radically altered circumstances . . . in the country. . . . The cultural and political circumstances in which our community relates to the rest of American society changed drastically as a result of the 9/11 attack." Safety was a new concern in the first few weeks after 9/11. The representative of a social service agency told us that they had to develop a program to escort Arab and Muslim women, especially those wearing the *hijab*, around their neighborhood to perform such basic daily chores as taking their children to school and buying food at the local supermarket. Several organizations established a hotline to address the fears of their constituents and provide advice and referrals. While some of the emerging needs called for short-term solutions, others, such as engaging in advocacy, required more long-term programmatic changes.

Regardless of their original mission and goals, the 9/11 backlash necessitated that Middle Eastern and Muslim American organizations engage in claims making on behalf of their constituents (table 11). Even social service agencies, professional associations, ethnic media outlets, and religious institutions, whose original mission was not advocacy, were in some way drafted into this activity and politicized. The president of a nascent social service agency explained:

> Before 9/11 we were just an organization trying to help the immigrants understand the laws, how to cope with the new system, not to leave your children unattended at home, if there is a dispute don't go to the police, come to the organization to solve your problem. If you need Medicaid, or financial assistance, this is the program. . . . So we—by circumstances— have tended to become politicized because of September 11. . . . [Now] we had to reach out to the community and give them a new dimension to the needs of the community, whether it is fighting the fear factor, the detention issue, or profiling.

An ethnic lawyers' association issued a white paper about the backlash that received national attention, and a Muslim law enforcement association made public appearances at community forums and town meetings to speak about relations with the police.

Advocacy organizations tend to have a not-for-profit status: that is, they are registered with the Internal Revenue Service as a tax-exempt 501(c)3 association. They are prohibited by law from lobbying: that is, endorsing specific political candidates and policies. Some respondents in our sample were quick to clarify the technical differences between advocacy, lobbying, and political action committees (PACS). These are their definitions:

> We're a 501(c)3. And the way the 501(c)3 rules work, you're not supposed to get too involved in politics, especially in terms of campaigning and things like that. So we've steered clear of that level of politics. But we've

certainly expressed to the community the need to be involved in the process. . . . Unfortunately, in our community political participation often means running for office. . . . We're trying to dissolve that notion, or that perception.

We actually don't do lobbying at all. . . . We give an opinion. . . . Lobbying means, I go to members of Congress and say, "Go and vote or do this." We don't do that. . . . When there's an issue, we say, "This is how we think Muslims should support, or this is what the [name of organization] thinks [of] this issue."

Most communities do have political action committees. And if we are able to raise that amount of money we will be known to the parties. They will know us. And with that kind of money, they would be coming to us instead of us going to them.

Evidently, the word *support* mentioned above connotes financial donations that respondents expected to receive from their trustees and friends. They even had specific dollar goals: "Our goal as a PAC is to raise half a million dollars a year. I mean, that's our objective, and that would make us a one million dollar per election cycle PAC, and that would place us in the top fifty PACs in the nation."

The following leader elucidates the tasks involved in mobilization:

We're sending people to these hearings, to the different think tank seminars, just to report completely objectively who said what and make sure that we make it accessible for the Arab American community to start understanding that this is where ideas are started. . . . We are very careful, particularly when it comes to the State Department and the Hill, always telling them: We can help you by bringing you information or putting you in contact or answering your questions, but we can never take sides. We can never help you in that sense. We're not here to lobby. . . . But we can tell you that if you introduce a bill that we judge is going to have an impact on Arab Americans, then we will do an alert on it and then we will tell people, "Make your voice heard, if you're in favor, against, whatever, just make your voice heard on it."

In spite of the legal distinctions between advocacy, lobbying, and PACs, these activities rely on mobilized constituents. One might say that while lobbying and PACs are in the realm of formal politics, advocacy is politics with a lower-case *p*.

## CHANGES IN SOURCES OF FUNDING

Funding is undoubtedly the engine that drives nonprofit organizations. As noted already, the majority of the organizations in our sample raised their own funds. We learned that initially after the 9/11 attacks, contributions slowed down to a trickle and some organizations began to worry. Yet this situation was only temporary. "For the first month, it was very, very difficult. The Arab American community was frozen. . . . But what saved us is that some of our friends on the Arab side started to say, 'You guys need some help.' And so those donations started coming. . . . Then our regular membership base came out of their lethargy."

The closure of Muslim charities in December 2001, allegedly for funneling money to "terrorist" organizations overseas, contributed to the initial halt in donations (see chapter 6). Nonetheless, the government's surveillance of financial transactions of the targeted communities has been problematic since then. A respondent explained, "Every time an Arab American sends $1,000 to their families, they feel threatened or they feel this may come back to haunt them." Another respondent said: "Several mosques have been established in the last three months, and the money for all of them was raised locally. People are giving. Money is given to the needy, charitable organizations that people can trust. People don't want to be investigated by the authorities for giving money to 'suspect' organizations." The establishment of the National Council of American Muslim Nonprofits, a coalition that gives its seal of approval for organizations that meet its criteria, is an institutional response to the giving crisis.[10] Both nonprofits and individual donors have changed their methods of philanthropy. People are more likely to donate cash to their local institutions, help needy persons they know, give but not claim tax deductions, or give money to more secular institutions.[11]

Perhaps what made the biggest difference in funding was the unprecedented donations that many of the affected 501(c)3 organizations received from major American philanthropic foundations.[12] Before the terrorist attacks, Middle Eastern and Muslim American communities had not been on the foundations' radar screen since they had not been considered official minorities. Unquestionably, the 9/11 backlash increased the foundations' awareness of these previously overlooked populations. These donations were unsolicited, onetime, unrestricted funds, averaging $100,000. A respondent concurs, "A lot of foundations—unexpected ones—were looking to do something, had some emergency money, and realized there was a need in the Arab American community."

Likewise, major immigrant rights and human rights organizations realized that the pressing issue of the day involved Arabs and Muslims. A representative of one such organization explained their use of funds:

> We got involved in the 9/11 work partly because the national board of [name] immediately released emergency funds after September 11th, recognizing that nationally and internationally we were going to want to work to create strong advocacy response, whether it be a peace response to the war, or working on immigration issues, or humanitarian aid in Afghanistan. . . . After a couple of months, what became clear was that the problem of detention was the one that really needed the most attention. So that is where we decided to focus that piece of emergency funding, which was temporary. It was six months of funding.

In summary, Middle Eastern and Muslim CBOs in the United States are limited in number, capacity, and scope of outreach. What exists tends to be in the nascent stages of development.

## EMERGING ORGANIZATIONS

Several new organizations were established as a result of the gaps and needs observed after 9/11. Mostly young, foreign-born or second generation, U.S.-educated men and women established these organizations. Here we feature four organizations that are very diverse in their mission and modus operandi but similar in their overarching goal of advocating for Arab, Muslim, and Iranian Americans. The Human Rights Education Law Project (HELP) was founded after 9/11 by a group of men from an Islamic Center in New Jersey mobilized without legal expertise, "for the sole purpose of helping the detainees." They learned quickly and benefited from a course offered by a major philanthropic organization to become "accredited to do immigration representation." HELP filled a unique niche, reaching out to the detainees in New Jersey prisons, assigning their cases to lawyers, and, when no other options were available, providing assistance to detainees' families. HELP was organized very quickly; it had a handful of board members but no office. They hired an answering service to take calls from detainees and family members. In early 2005, HELP terminated its legal services and detainee representation. It had outlived its original mission.

The Association of Patriotic Arab Americans in the Military (APAAM) was founded after 9/11 to organize Arab Americans in the U.S. Armed Forces.[13] It is the first organization of its kind and boasts about 3,500 members—both current and former servicemen and women. The Web-based September 11 Digital Archive features one of our interviews with its founder, a thirty-eight-year-old U.S. Marine Corps gunnery sergeant who was born in Cairo of a Yemeni father and

a. Vietnamese mother and grew up in the United States after the age of ten (September 11 Digital Archive 2002–3). He describes his reactions to the collapse of the Twin Towers and how it was followed with news about Arab American children who were called derogatory names, picked on, and beat up in school. These feelings galvanized him to take action: "I wanted to come out in the forefront and educate Americans about Arab Americans: that there's a difference between the Arab nationals and Arab Americans, that the terrorists were not Arab Americans. They weren't the ones here pursuing their dreams to raise their children, to live a free life. . . . Honor for me would be to [be buried] in the Arlington National Cemetery. . . . So I wanted to make a difference, to let people know that we're just as American as anyone else and that it was wrong for them to alienate us after September 11th."

The Network of Arab American Professionals (NAAP) traces its origins to university student associations in the late 1990s, but 9/11 heightened the need for activism. NAAP's mission is to educate the public about Arab culture and identity by offering "a positive face to Arab Americans," to empower the Arab American community, and to promote networking and social interaction among Arab Americans and professionals from the Arab world.[14] NAAP chapters rely entirely on volunteers.[15] The work is handled by committees. NAAP—New York, for instance, has grown remarkably since its establishment in 2002. Its events have attracted large numbers of twenty- and thirty-something professionals in the metropolitan area in purposive but socially entertaining activities. The pages of *Aramica,* an Arab American biweekly newspaper also established in 2002, show that NAAP events have been featured at least nine times in three years.[16] Even though social events seem to outnumber more serious events, this chapter has engaged in advocacy.[17] One cannot help but surmise that these gatherings have the latent function of serving as a marketplace for those searching for friends and mates.

The Iranian American Political Action Committee (IAPAC) is a good example of a Middle Eastern American PAC. It raises money from the community to distribute to candidates running for political office. IAPAC was established after 9/11, specifically after the passage of Enhanced Border Security and Visa Entry Reform Act of 2002 into law, which made it more difficult for Iranian nationals to obtain visas to come to the United States. IAPAC's mission is to encourage the civic participation of Iranian Americans and support candidates for office who are responsive to the needs of this community. During its short tenure, IAPAC has campaigned to get candidates elected for office; it has also worked with elected officials to address immigration issues and violations of civil liberties such as NSEERS that have resulted in the detention and mistreatment of Iranian nationals.

## EVALUATION OF ORGANIZATIONAL PERFORMANCE

How do Middle Eastern and Muslim American organizations evaluate their performance in the aftermath of the terrorist attacks? How do they rate their effectiveness in meeting their goals? How have they addressed their shortcomings? The persons we interviewed were realistic. They recognized their successes but also identified the need for improvement in several areas; after all, they saw themselves as "the new kids on the block." Some respondents viewed unity between organizations as a positive and productive force. In a pluralistic society like the United States, inclusion in local and national coalitions is indispensable for any immigrant group trying to carve a place for itself. One leader provided an example: "When Mr. Ashcroft announced these 'voluntary interviews,' . . . members of the Arab community, the Islamic community, the Southeast Asian community came together and said, 'We need to address these issues.' We then met also with the ACLU, with the National Lawyers Guild, and said, 'How can we deal with this?'" Another respondent said, "It's been encouraging to find allies. We've had solidarity and support from many organizations. We've begun to develop coalitions; 9/11 has kick-started us into advocacy work" (chapter 7).

The leaders we interviewed were also aware of their organizations' shortcomings. One respondent noted that Arab American groups are "not as effective as, say, Jewish organizations because, again, they are well established." Another suggested, "I think that research right now is essential." Several offered solutions: "I think new organizational forms should be coalitions of existing organizations, as opposed to more organizations. For example, in the Arab American community, between us and the American Muslim communities, I think we have everybody covered. The question is coming up with a common strategy." Another respondent prescribed ways of avoiding intergroup conflict: "You work with organizations where you have common interests and you don't where you don't. . . . When it comes to civil rights, we're going to work with the ACLU. . . . They've been in this game long enough where they know that they'll work . . . with whoever. . . . But when you're trying to . . . fight something like the PATRIOT Act, . . .

you come together on that common interest, and then where you don't have common interest you sort of separate."

The 2003 Detroit Arab American Study (DAAS), which used a random sample of the local population, included questions on participants' level of confidence in Arab ethnic associations. Amaney Jamal (2005c), one of the DAAS researchers, shows that 28 percent of the sample believed civil liberties and antidiscrimination organizations to be very effective, and 56 percent said they were somewhat effective. Respondents were also pleased with Arab American social services (43 percent believed that they were very effective and 48 percent that they were somewhat effective).[18] In contrast, hometown associations were deemed the least effective (25 percent). Moreover, the study found that Muslim Arabs who identified strongly as Muslim were more likely to approve of their community institutions. Jamal (2005c) concludes that the more vulnerable an Arab American feels, the greater his or her confidence in ethnic institutions but the lower his or her confidence in mainstream institutions.

We have found that the extent and significance of the backlash far exceeded the ability of the Middle Eastern and Muslim American organizations to respond to the post-9/11 crisis. Given the relatively recent immigration of most of the Middle Eastern and Muslim populations, their communities were not sufficiently organized and their infrastructure was not well developed on the eve of September 11. A few organizations that expanded rapidly right after 9/11 through philanthropic funding were unable to sustain their growth. When funding dried up, they had to let go of some of their newly hired staff, close some of their new programs, and shrink to their pre-9/11 size or dissolve. Even if they had been mobilized and well organized institutionally, the events would still have been overwhelming. Nevertheless, the majority of the organizations weathered the crisis fairly well. The more successful ones increased their programming and developed a national and regional reputation. The CBOs in our sample were at the forefront of the struggle not only to safeguard but also to advance the interests of their constituents.

# 5

# Hate Crimes and Bias Incidents

The post-9/11 backlash against Middle Eastern and Muslim Americans followed a chronological sequence. Leaders initially acknowledged that repercussion from the terrorist attacks was mild when compared to historical precedents such as the Japanese internment. Within about six months, however, there was a consolidation of opinion among the leadership that the government policies were going after their constituents. While at the beginning of the crisis the organizations used the law of the land to fight the hate crimes, they could no longer do so with the detentions and the PATRIOT Act. In a sense, they were fighting the law itself. This was a more complicated, even risky, undertaking. In chapters 5 and 6, we analyze the impact of the backlash on the targeted populations. On the basis of our theoretical model in chapter 1, we conceptualize backlash as (1) hate crimes and bias incidents; (2) stereotypes and scapegoating; and (3) government initiatives. Here we analyze hate crimes and bias incidents perpetrated by ordinary citizens. The difference between the two is that hate crimes are codified into law. In the next chapter, we focus on the government initiatives.

## DEFINING HATE CRIMES

The term *hate crime* was "coined by Representatives Conyers, Kenally, and Briggs in their 1985 sponsorship of a hate crime statistics bill" (Perry 2003, 2–3), and the topic has been addressed mostly in the deviance and criminology literature (e.g., Hopkins Burke and Pollock 2004; Jacobs and Potter 1998; Perry 2003; Poynting 2002, 2004). Barbara Perry offers the following definition: "Hate crime is a mechanism of power and oppression involving acts of violence and intimidation against already stigmatized and marginalized groups, and intended to re-affirm the precarious hierarchies that characterize the given social order" (2001, 10). Perry argues that hate crimes have not been theorized because of problems with definitions, measurement, and a lack of systematic data. A serious impediment is the emphasis on individual-level analysis. Perry places hate crimes squarely in the intersection of several contemporary issues such as "violence, victimization, race/ethnicity, gender, sexuality, and difference." Yet she notes that "in spite of the centrality of violence as a means of policing the relative boundaries of identity, few attempts have been made to understand theoretically the place of hate crimes in the contemporary arsenal of oppression" (2003, 16).

In the United States, it took a social movement to bring discriminatory violence to public consciousness. The effort was spearheaded by the Anti-Defamation League (ADL) and the Southern Poverty Law Center. In 1981, a model law was proposed. Initially it focused on violence motivated by racial, religious, and ethnic bias. Later three other categories—gender, sexual orientation, and disability—were added. Even though there is no consensus among scholars about the meaning of hate crimes, most recognize that there is a continuum of behaviors ranging from hate speech to intimidation, arson, mugging, and murder. The "sites" of hate crimes tend to be public spaces—the street, public transportation, stores, work, and school. It has been argued that "these spaces of fear and incivility also become landscapes of exclusion because they define not just what but who is acceptable. Racial vilification, by its nature, emphasizes a sense of cultural difference . . . but this sense of difference is also a sense of not belonging" (Poynting 2004, 24).

In summary, defining hate crime remains problematic because the concept is socially constructed; it depends on context, place, and historical timing. Perry observes that "what constitutes a hate crime differs dramatically between jurisdictions. Across the United States, there are dramatic differences in how bias is defined, what classes of victims are protected, and the extent of bias motivation necessary for classification" (2003, 7). Though violent behaviors motivated by prejudice were criminalized in 1990,[1] they have "a long historical lineage" in the United States (6) and globally. For practical purposes, however, we use the U.S. Department of Justice's definition, since it has been codified into criminal law.

> A crime which in whole or part is motivated by the offender's bias toward the victim's status. A hate incident is an action in which a person is made aware that her/his status is offensive to another, but does not rise to the level of a crime. Hate crimes are intended to hurt and intimidate individuals, because they are perceived to be different with respect to their race, color, religion, national origin, sexual orientation, gender or disability. The purveyors of hate use physical violence, verbal threats of violence, vandalism, and in some cases weapons, explosives, and arson, to instill fear in their victims, leaving them vulnerable to subsequent attacks and feeling alienated, helpless, suspicious and fearful. These acts of hatred can leave lasting emotional impressions upon their victims as well as entire communities. (U.S. Department of Justice, Community Relations Service 2003)

In a special issue on hate crimes and ethnic conflict in *American Behavioral Scientist,* Jack Levin and Gordana Rabrenovic argue that individual-level acts of hate and bias, often motivated by vengeance, "can easily become part of a vicious cycle of violence that spirals out of control and ultimately escalates into pervasive intergroup hostilities" if left unpunished (2001b, 575). Rapid economic, social, and political changes are likely to trigger interethnic conflict and violence because someone's status or "birthright" may be threatened. The media often incite the escalation of ethnic hatred, and the situation becomes especially dangerous when a minority group becomes a national scapegoat (581). However, it is important to remember that "scapegoating and other types of hostility are more likely to occur in situations of maximum ambiguity" (Cohen 2002, 162).

The term *scapegoating,* which refers to the biblical goat that was blamed for the sins of the Israelites, refers to the punishment of a visible, vulnerable, and accessible target rather than the culprit. Stereotypes and scapegoating tend to work in tandem. Stereotypes are used as tools by the majority population to exaggerate social distance from an outgroup. They can be employed as part of a political agenda when cherished values of "civilized" society are supposedly threatened. Stanley Cohen (2002) argues that stereotypes are social constructions by politically powerful people in the government, business, and media. The media become a conduit in the process of vilification of the "enemy" and the crystallization of stereotypes. Stereotyping entails the development of a stylized, one-dimensional caricature of the other. The mold is often borrowed from a repertoire of suspect characters. This argument applies to the defamation of Arabs, Muslims, and Middle Easterners as long as the post-9/11 political/ideological crisis continues.

In discussing ethnic or religious violence, it is important to remember that violence is not intrinsic to any group.[2] A fundamental component of ethno-national conflicts are the symbols of group identity. During crises, symbols come to possess political power to mobilize members into opposing camps (Cohen 2002). When a situation becomes volatile, an all-out "war" becomes politically legitimized through the endorsement of organized factions, and its causes are justified or legitimized as social or political in nature. Though the distinction may be artificial, "all hate crime is political in the sense that it involves a statement that goes far beyond a particular act of violence or intimidation. It involves the identification of a target, the objectification of the targeted individual(s), and the depersonalization of the victim. Often, hate crimes have a deliberately public aspect that is meant to convey a warning to a wider community" (Mac Ginty 2001, 650). Perry (2003) concurs that the damage that a hate crime inflicts is beyond the immediate physical and financial effects. Hate crimes generate fear, hostility, and suspicion.

Jack McDevitt and colleagues argue that "hate crimes are inherently more harmful to the social fabric of society than comparable crimes without bias motive" (2001, 698). Targets' group membership is likely to cause secondary victimization to members of the victim's family and community. Perry (2003) adds that beyond the impact on the victim and his or her group and family, hate crimes have repercussions on the national community because they are "message crimes." One study concluded that minority group members are unable to control the psychological sequelae as the news of the incident spreads and resonates in the community as a personal threat. The outgroups that share the characteristics of the enemy run the risk of becoming victims of scapegoating, and the state has the capacity to vilify an internal "enemy." During political/ideological crises, backlash may occur if the state's interests coincide with ingrained stereotypes against a minority or outgroup.

## MEASURING HATE CRIMES

Several statistical reports have been published on post-9/11 hate crimes by civil rights agencies and Middle Eastern and Muslim CBOs, including CAIR, which has been compiling anti-Muslim incidents since the Oklahoma City bombing in 1995.[3] They all indicate an increase in anti-Arab and anti-Muslim hate crimes, discrimination, profiling, and harassment. One might fault these tallies for being prone to self-selection bias in reporting, multiple counts, and other tabulation errors. *Hate Crimes Statistics,* published by the FBI annually, is a national systematic gauge, but it is not error-free either, due to underreporting.

Hate crime reporting was particularly problematic after 9/11. Government initiatives may have prevented persons of Middle Eastern and Muslim origin from coming forward and reporting experiences of bias to the police. Some feared that their names would be entered into government databases and that they would risk subsequent retribution. In any case, there is little consensus on which incidents should be classified as hate crimes, even in the clear-cut case of a homicide. The U.S. Department of Justice lists nine murders as possible hate crimes against persons of Middle Eastern origin in September and October of 2001.[4] CAIR (2002a, 30) cites a dozen murders related to 9/11, while ADC (Ibish 2003, 69–70) enumerates four "confirmed hate crime murders" and seven "suspected" cases.[5]

The first case of hate crimes related to the post-9/11 backlash was that of Balbir Singh Sodhi in Mesa, Arizona. This was a case of mistaken identity because the victim was a Sikh. A respondent who was part of his legal defense team said, "[He] was one of the three casualties of the backlash. He was shot and killed by . . . a white man. . . . [The murderer] then went on to a Lebanese family as well as to another gas station owned by an Afghan. Luckily for the latter two families, they were okay; they weren't killed or anything. But unfortunately for my client, he was shot and killed. He left three children, all adults, sons, a wife who's in India."

Because of their traditional turban, Sikhs have been inordinately victimized, given that they have nothing to do with Bin Laden or Al Qaeda. At a *gurdwara* in New York City, a respondent told us that he personally knew of three Sikhs who had been beaten right after 9/11 (see also Das Gupta 2005, 216). One victim was a sixty-six-year-old man who was severely injured and eventually died. Another was a student who was beaten up with a custom-made baseball-style bat with nails. The third was a man in his late fifties who was stabbed on his way to do volunteer service. Sikhs were also mistaken during the Iranian hostage crisis, about twenty-five years before 9/11, because of their physical resemblance to Ayatollah Khomeini, who, like Osama Bin Laden, wore a turban and had a long beard. A Sikh respondent reminisced, "I had just arrived in

1979. . . . In our homes and in temples, we discussed that we should not wear black turbans because we . . . would be confused with Khomeini."

It was only in 1990 that the U.S. Congress passed the Hate Crime Statistics Act.[6] Data are collected on five major categories of hate crimes: (1) race, (2) religion, (3) sexual orientation, (4) ethnicity/national origin, (5) disability. Out of these, only two bias-motivation categories—religion and ethnicity/national origin—are relevant to our study. Within the religious crimes classification, statistics are reported for crimes against Jews, Catholics, Protestants, Muslims, other religious groups, multiple religions/groups, and atheists or agnostics. The anti-Jewish rates have been historically the highest. Here we report the data on crimes against Muslims and crimes against "other religious groups," which includes Sikhs, who have mistakenly suffered from post-9/11 hate crimes.

The total hate crime numbers motivated by religion were relatively steady from 1999 to 2006 (the last year for which data are available), with the exception of a sharp increase in 2001 (see table 14). More specifically, the anti-Islamic category went up 1,600 percent from 2000 to 2001, though admittedly it started at a low base. In 2000, there were 33 anti-Islamic offenses compared to 546 offenses in 2001—a jump from 2.1 percent to 27.2 percent of the total hate crimes. Between 2001 and 2006, anti-Islamic hate crimes had stabilized in the low teen percentages. Using the anti-Jewish hate crimes statistics as a benchmark, we note that 2001 is an atypical year since the number of cases show extremely high levels of hate crimes. Curiously, for the category of hate crimes against "other religions" (which includes Sikhs) the percentage for 2001 was 10.5, a slight decrease from the previous year. There was a slight increase in 2002, but there has been a decrease since then.

The ethnicity/national-origin category has only two values: anti-Hispanic and anti–other ethnicity/national origin. Here we report on the latter because Middle Easterners are most likely to be classified under this category (table 15). There was also a spike in hate crimes motivated by ethnic/national origin from around 1,011 in 1999 and 1,164 in 2000 to 2,507 in 2001. However, the number of such crimes has since subsided slightly and remained steady. According to the FBI report, "Crime incidents motivated against ethnicity/national origin were the second most frequently reported bias in 2001, more than doubling the number of incidents, offenses, victims, and known offenders from 2000 data. Additionally, the anti-other ethnic/national origin category quadrupled in incidents, offenses, victims, and known offenders" (FBI 2001, 1). "Other ethnic/national origin," the category that includes Arabs, jumped from

TABLE 14. SELECTED CATEGORIES FROM RELIGIOUS
HATE CRIME STATISTICS, 1999–2006
*(percentages)*

|  | 1999 | 2000 | 2001 | 2002 | 2003 | 2004 | 2005 | 2006 |
|---|---|---|---|---|---|---|---|---|
| Anti-Jewish | 78.2 | 74.6 | 55.7 | 65.9 | 69.2 | 67.8 | 68.5 | 64.3 |
| Anti-Islamic | 2.2 | 2.1 | 27.2 | 10.8 | 10.9 | 13.0 | 11.1 | 11.9 |
| Anti-other-religion | 11.1 | 12.0 | 10.5 | 13.8 | 8.3 | 9.5 | 7.8 | 8.8 |
| *Total number of religious hate crimes* | 1,532 | 1,556 | 2,004 | 1,576 | 1,426 | 1,480 | 1,314 | 1,597 |

SOURCE: FBI (1999–2006).

NOTE: Percentages do not add up to 100 because these statistics are reported for selected religious categories.

ª Reported here are single-bias offenses. Single-bias offenses occur when one or more offense types within the incident are motivated by the same bias.

36.9 percent of total anti-ethnic/national-origin hate crimes in 2000 to 69.9 percent the following year. In the next year, the percentage dropped to 55.3 percent, a proportion higher than pre-9/11 rates. But there have been more decreases since.

Between September 11, 2001 and May 15, 2006, the Department of Justice's Civil Rights Division investigated over seven hundred cases of bias-motivated backlash crimes involving Muslim, Sikh, Arab, or South Asian victims. Of these, twenty-seven cases were brought against thirty-five defendants in federal courts. Additionally, the department collaborated with state and local agencies across the country to secure nearly 150 criminal prosecutions.[7] The Civil Rights Division has promoted the initiative to combat post-9/11 backlash and has posted updates and complaint filing on its Web site, printed in Arabic, Urdu, and other languages read by the groups suffering the most backlash. It has also appointed a Special Counsel for Religious Discrimination and has been active in outreach.[8] We witnessed a couple of their information sessions presented to the Middle Eastern and Muslim American communities.

Surveys can be another source of information on hate crimes. Unfortunately, given the small numbers of Middle Eastern and Muslim Americans in the general population, the cost of using probability samples is prohibitive. Polls are much less costly and faster to conduct than nongovernmental surveys. The Pew Research Center's poll of Muslim Americans conducted in 2007 has a probability sample of 1,050, making it perhaps the most representative of the national Muslim population to

## TABLE 15. SELECTED CATEGORIES FROM ETHNIC/NATIONAL-ORIGIN HATE CRIME STATISTICS, 1999–2006

|  | 1999 | 2000 | 2001 | 2002 | 2003 | 2004 | 2005 | 2006 |
|---|---|---|---|---|---|---|---|---|
| Anti-other ethnic/national-origin hate crimes as % of total ethnic/national-origin hate crimes | 43.0 | 36.9 | 69.9 | 55.3 | 57.2 | 49.1 | 42.3 | 37.5 |
| Total number of ethnic/national-origin hate crimes | 1,011 | 1,164 | 2,507 | 1,345 | 1,236 | 1,201 | 1,144 | 1,233 |

SOURCE: FBI (1999–2006).

NOTE: Percentages do not add up to 100 because these statistics are reported for selected ethnic/national-origin categories.

[a]Reported here are single-bias offenses. Single-bias offenses occur when one or more offense types within the incident are motivated by the same bias.

date.[9] Respondents were asked to report their experiences as Muslims; 26 percent had been treated or viewed with suspicion, 15 percent had been called offensive names, 9 percent had been singled out by police, and 4 percent had been physically attacked or threatened in the previous year. Those between the ages of eighteen and twenty-nine years reported slightly more incidents. While 32 percent of the entire sample had encountered at least one of the four types of intolerance, 42 percent of the youth subsample had (Pew 2007, 38).

## IMPACT OF HATE CRIMES

### RESIDENTIAL ENCLAVES AS SAFETY ZONES

When we asked the leaders of Middle Eastern and Muslim American CBOs about the impact of the backlash, most acknowledged that it had been initially mild. A respondent in Bay Ridge, a district with a high concentration of Arab immigrants in New York City, noted, "Some, they were harassed. No major attack in this neighborhood." In another part of Brooklyn we heard, "We haven't had any major incidents that someone got hurt badly. . . . There was some harassment."[10] In Paterson, another Arab/Muslim enclave in New Jersey, a respondent observed, "There's [sic] nothing happened, and I don't think . . . anything will happen." In Chicago we were told, "In terms of backlash, not a major problem after 9/11."

In Dearborn, which has the highest concentration of Arabs in the nation, a leader concluded, "I tell you; we were lucky to witness just one hate crime. I understand that nobody tolerates that. It is unfortunate, sad. But still, it is just one that we witnessed here in the city of Lincoln Park, where a citizen of Arab descent was shot to death."[11] Another respondent in the area observed, "I think a couple of windows got broken, but as far as violence, not that much happened here in Detroit, not as bad as it did in some other parts of the country, where people were actually murdered."

DAAS, which randomly sampled 1,016 adults of Arabic and Chaldean descent in metropolitan Detroit between July and December 2003, found that 15 percent had had "a bad experience" personally after 9/11. Verbal slurs were most common, with 24 percent of the sample saying that someone in their household had been subjected to verbal abuse because of his or her ethnicity or religion. Another 13 percent reported threatening gestures. Four percent of the sample reported vandalism, 4 percent said they had lost their job, and 2 percent said they had been physically attacked (Jamal 2005c).

In comparing the DAAS data to a Zogby International poll in 2002, Howell and Jamal (2008) note that Arab Americans in the Detroit area experienced fewer incidents of backlash than the national average (15 percent vs. 25 percent). In Dearborn, where about thirty thousand immigrants from the Arab world live, there were only two hate crimes.[12] They conclude, "Overall, our data suggest that Arab Detroit weathered the post-9/11 backlash with fewer scars than the Arab American community nationwide and the Arab Detroiters, relative to Arab Americans elsewhere, are more confident about their future in the U.S. and more assertive of their rights as citizens. These findings are most pronounced among those Arab populations that are most vulnerable nationwide: namely, immigrants and Muslims" (Howell and Jamal 2008, 58).

The "Detroit exceptionalism" is attributed to the presence of Arabic-speaking peoples in the state of Michigan for over a century; several decades of political activism; the development of extensive community-based organizations and infrastructure; and, most importantly, the success achieved by many Arab Americans in holding high-ranking positions in the region's government, corporations, and civic life. More specifically, 39 percent of those surveyed by DAAS reported being involved in Arab ethnic organizations such as ACCESS, ADC, the Yemeni Benevolent Association, and the Chaldean Federation. At least sixty deputized law enforcement officers in Wayne County, thirty-eight political appointees in the state, and twenty-three elected officials are Arab Detroiters who have "power and influence." There is also a "much larger number of Arab Americans who sit on the boards of local hospitals and the United Way, serve as regents of state universities, or are active participants in the local ACLU, UAW, Civil Rights Board, or many of the state's important nonprofit organizations" (Howell and Jamal 2008, 53).

Evidence shows that in places like New York City, Paterson, Dearborn, Chicago, and Los Angeles, where there are high concentrations of Middle Eastern and Muslim Americans, there have been fewer hate crimes. We attribute this outcome to the fact that members of these minority populations are known to the larger society as co-workers, neighbors, customers, classmates, and even friends.[13] This confirms opinion polls where personal acquaintance with a Muslim/Arab decreases negative attitudes about the group (chapter 2). Additionally, ethnic/

religious communities are fairly well connected to city and county services such as police, the mayor's office, and politicians. The leaders in our sample made use of these networks immediately after the terrorist attacks and received protection. Even in the city of Philadelphia, which has a lower density of Arabs and Muslims but good relations with the local authorities, a police car was parked in front of every mosque by noon on September 11.[14] Yet it is paradoxical that while hate crimes were not numerous in areas with a high concentration of Arabs and Muslims, these very ethnic neighborhoods and enclaves felt most intimately the effects of detention, deportation, voluntary interviews, and special registration (chapter 6).

## RELATIONS WITH LAW ENFORCEMENT AGENCIES

Participants in DAAS were questioned on their level of confidence in public institutions. Arab Americans were more approving of public schools, local police, and the American legal system in their locality than the comparative subsample of the American mainstream population. For example, 86 percent of Arab Americans versus 71 percent of the general sample had high confidence in the local police. Likewise, 66 percent of Arab Americans versus 47 percent of the general population had "a lot" or "a great deal" of confidence in the U.S. legal system. These results suggest that Arab Americans enjoyed well-established institutional linkages with the local government. The issue of fair trial, however, deviated from this pattern: 50 percent of Arab Americans believed that Arabs and Muslims accused of terrorism could receive a fair trial, whereas 66 percent of the general population believed so (Jamal 2005c).

Respondents were suspicious of the police and fearful of the FBI because of their covert operations in mosques and other community centers after 9/11. However, the bulk of the negative comments had previously been directed toward INS. The director of an advocacy group in Michigan said:

> I can assure you that INS is at the bottom of the list of people to look up to or to trust. Before September 11th, it is so ironic, people used to have these hard feelings more towards the FBI. Always the FBI was seen as this "devil" that watched people and came after people. . . . The INS regulations are so vague, so general, that it gives the INS maybe the extreme, unbelievable discretionary power. They can twist and use the [regulations the] way they please. I think that if I were to cite a governmental agency that in my mind very often conducts governmental abuse, it is the INS with no question.

A knowledgeable source had similarly vexing relations with the INS:

> Well, the head of the INS in New York has never responded to our demands for a public meeting. So that is still part of the active letter-writing campaign that we are having. The head of the INS in New Jersey . . . agreed to have a public meeting. So we were in active conversation to have this meeting set up. . . . [However,] a week before the public meeting . . . [she said] she would no longer participate in the meeting where the media were present. . . . So she had reneged on her promise that she had made, citing two recently filed lawsuits, the Center for Constitutional Rights lawsuit and the ACLU lawsuit.

Our own interviews indicate that relations with local police precincts depend on the local captain and his or her willingness to work with the local ethnic/religious communities. Many respondents mentioned police bias and mistreatment, fear of the police (especially among the undocumented), and co-optation of neighborhood cops to enforce immigration laws. But there was also praise of specific precinct officers. An Arab American respondent offered a nuanced picture: "You have very traditional community members who meet the police, embrace the police . . . [because they want the] police to keep an eye on their stores. . . . Those of us that are working more on the community capacity have kind of a dual role that we play with the local police. . . . We understand that the police are important stakeholders in the community and that we need to cultivate strong relations with them. But at the same time, they are public institutions that we need also to hold accountable when mistakes are made." Nonetheless, community-police relations remained contentious, and high turnover in police leadership—six officers in the span of four years in one area we visited—was another obstacle to building strong relationships. A high-ranking law enforcement officer in our sample observed: "I have a community relations officer. Not all federal agencies do that. I have someone in the community with an ear to the community, listening to what people are saying. I'm the longest-sitting federal person here. The feds want to believe that we are gaining more trust. If you hear the community people, they say no, that's not true."

Not surprisingly, the data generated from law enforcement interviews indicated discrepancies in perception. The appropriateness of deputizing state and local police to enforce immigration laws remained an unresolved issue among the FBI rank and file. Some thought it was not their mandate; the blurring of boundaries would undermine the trust of the targeted communities. They believed that community policing would prevent terrorism. However, only five of the sixteen sites in the study had an active community liaison officer. In two additional sites, the community was active but the department was passive. Nine of the FBI field offices in the study were characterized as active in outreach, six as passive, and one as inactive (Henderson et al. 2006, 73–74).

Our sample of knowledgeable sources included police officers, but time and funding constraints precluded a more systematic analysis of law enforcement's interaction with the leaders of the affected communities after 9/11. The Vera Institute's national study on the topic fills that gap.[15] Its interviews conducted with Arab Americans support most of our findings:[16] "increased victimization and harassment; heightened suspicion; anxiety about their place in American society, particularly fuelled by new federal policies; and concerns about civil liberties" (Henderson et al. 2006, 50).

Both the Vera Institute's report and our respondents suggested that cultural awareness training, foreign language skills, town meetings, recruitment from within the community, appointment of community-police liaisons, and increased resources for outreach would improve cooperation with Arab and Muslim Americans.[17] Police departments in cities with high concentrations of Middle Eastern and Muslim immigrants, such as Dearborn, Paterson, and New York, are making concerted efforts to "reach out" to these populations.[18]

## ORGANIZATIONS AS TARGETS

Because of their visibility, Middle Eastern and Muslim American organizations in our sample were frequently the targets of hate crimes. The storefront center of the Arab American Action Network in Chicago was destroyed by a suspected arsonist after 9/11. Innumerable death threats and hate speeches were sent by phone or e-mail to the leaders of several prominent organizations. One respondent explained, "Within an hour [of the terrorist attacks], we started to receive death threats. [Name of organization's president] had a death threat against him. He was doing media the entire time. I was working with people in the community. We started to get a lot of hate e-mails." Another leader concurred, "Well, we got a million e-mails saying that they're coming after us, and we should run, and things of that nature."

A couple of the organizational representatives shared with us the hate messages they had compiled from the first few weeks after 9/11. The following is a selection of unedited e-mails received by one organization in the first thirty days:

If you want to prevent anti-Muslim sentiment in this country, convince Muslims to stop being delusional and anti-American.

How many of your members donated money to the people responsible for the previous days actions??? Get off of your asses and go beyond your religion and aid the authorities in removing your communities filth from the face of the planet.

Tell all your pig members to go home.

You must be very proud! Your brothers have struck again. I'm sure you know that a bus has been blown up in Israel, killing more innocent people. The only thing your brothers would like more is to blow one up in the U.S.A.!! If I was the leader of Israel I would NEVER negotiate with these animals! You must be very proud!

Get a life, Arabs and moslems [sic] are cave dwellers, just look at Afghanistan and Irac, iran [sic] and throughout the mideastm [sic] because you have known that these people are doing these injustices and abusing children and woman from day one before 9/11. Treating woman like property is the way you keep order in you home instead of doing your job, like hillbillies. You have never done anything about it until now and that is only lip service. I still see no Arabs or Moslems anywhere doing anything about what is going on today, nothing. And you or your people want special rights when you use suicide and children and innocent people to get what you want, the cave man way. If I was an arab or muslim [sic] would be ashamed of my people and fear for my children's future in a world where people walk upright.

A respondent showed us a postcard he had received after being interviewed on ABC News. Published by St. Patrick's Cathedral, the card depicted a photo of Pope John Paul II with a cardinal; on the reverse, the typed message stated that Muslims have no right to complain and that they deserve what they get because they reject Israel, America's loyal ally. It was signed "a Catholic Veteran."

## PROFILING

In *Profiles, Probabilities and Stereotypes* (2003), Frederick Schauer provides one of the most cogent discussions of the topic. Profiling, he argues, "paints with a broad brush," makes a generalization, and stigmatizes an entire category of people while ignoring the context. As long as all probable options are included in the algorithm, profiles that are constructed for a particular case are reasonable tools in investigations; however, *ad hoc* profiles tend to be either under- or overinclusive. Schauer elucidates, "The issue is not about profiling at all, for profiling is inevitable. Rather, the debate that masquerades as a debate about profiling is a debate about rules, and is a debate, therefore, that is centrally about circumstances under which we will and we will not rely on the unconstrained discretion of enforcement officials. The risks of this discretion are nowhere more apparent than in the area of race. . . . It is the use of race that has caused the hitherto largely unobjectionable practice of profiling to become so laden with political, moral, and emotional baggage" (174). In summary, "the exercise of individual discretion is often, though of course not always, inferior to decision-making based on more systematically compiled actuarial information" (Schauer 2003, 179; see also Motomura 2006, ch. 9).

Rogers Brubaker offers another critique: profiling assumes the existence of a cohesive group with clear boundaries whose members share "ways of seeing, thinking, parsing social experience, and interpreting the social world" (2004, 79). He argues that although "there is no doubt . . . that conscious and unconscious 'racial profiling' exists . . . it may also be that event schemas such as [no-fly lists] can generate the interpretation and experience of racial profiling even in marginal and ambiguous situations, thereby further 'racializing' social experience" (77). As Arabs, Muslims, and Sikhs travel through airports garnering new stories of stigma and victimization, these tales become part of collective memory and end up defining, in part, one's identity and personhood.

Airport profiling has been a common practice since it most closely responds to the hijackers' mode of terrorism. Reports by ADC (Ibish 2003), CAIR (2002a, 2002b, 2004, 2005, 2006a, 2006b, 2007), the Pew Research Center (2007), and others indicate that profiling is a persistent source of frustration and humiliation for community members.[19] Many Middle Easterners and Muslims have developed an understanding of the experience of African American men in this regard. One respondent told us: "We always believed that racial profiling is not something that was born on September 11th. It has always been an ongoing challenge to all of us in America. It became more inclusive, more dangerous, more comprehensive. It is no longer to say 'driving while you are black'; now you say, 'driving while you are black, or Arab, or Muslim, or flying while you are brown, etc.,' because of the many incidents that we register and people face." Individuals looking "Middle Eastern" or having an Arab/Muslim name have been most likely to be profiled at airports by security officials, but there were cases, especially in the first few months after 9/11, of individuals who were asked to leave a plane because flight attendants or fellow passengers were not comfortable. This happened so frequently that T-shirts with the following slogan on them became popular among Arabs: "My name causes national security alerts. What does yours do?"[20] Some community activists advertised their new status: "We're the new blacks."[21]

Even those who can "pass" easily (i.e., their complexion, appearance, accent, or name does not attract attention) have not been spared the insults of profiling. Congressman Darrell Issa (R-CA), a highly assimilated individual of Lebanese descent, was not allowed on the plane because he had a one-way ticket to Saudi Arabia and an Arabic last name. Congressman Issa protested unsuccessfully: "I'm a member of Congress. Here's my House ID. . . . I'm a Republican, on the right wing of the party."

Many of our respondents shared with us their personal experiences of profiling, harassment, bias incidents, and discrimination with regard to air travel. An American-born Arab woman told us, "I travel very frequently . . . internally in the U.S. . . . There has been twice since September 11th that I did not receive an 'S' on my boarding pass. An 'S' meaning . . . right before you board the plane, all of your things get checked again. Everything gets taken out of your bags and checked again." A similar incident happened at Dulles Airport to a Pakistani respondent. He was in the passport check line when the security officer, noting his Pakistani passport, asked him to step aside and interrogated him and searched his suitcase. Then, before boarding the plane, he was searched again.[22] In New York, a respondent recounted another incident: "I spoke to Yemeni men who arrived in plenty of time but were detained for hours at check-in, were questioned repeatedly, then eventually thrown off the flight because people didn't like the look of them. . . . The next day, his fellow passengers didn't say anything, and he was able to go to Sanᶜa via London. That's simply racism. People are offered flights on subsequent days, and there's no additional security because the only problem was the distaste of their fellow passengers for them."

Almost a year after 9/11, the Associated Press reported that travelers with darker complexions and Arabic/Muslim names were modifying their behavior to avoid the indignities of "interrogations, body searches and suspicious stares" at airports. Prominent Arab Americans were interviewed for the story, including forty-five-year-old Khaled Saffuri, director of the Islamic Institute in Washington, D.C., who said, "I don't open my mouth in the plane." It was reported that he "makes sure he shaves closely and puts on a suit every time he has to fly, even on weekends." Similarly, Nidal Ibrahim, the thirty-five-year-old editor of *Arab American*

*Business Magazine,* "tries to get a seat in the back of the plane, far away from the cockpit, lest he make the flight attendants or other passengers nervous. He also makes sure to go to the restroom before boarding to avoid making others fearful by getting out of his seat mid-flight."[23]

On November 29, 2004, Salam Al-Marayati, executive director of MPAC, was detained for over two hours at Los Angeles International Airport as he was returning with his family from a vacation in Mexico. Articles in the *Los Angeles Times* and phone calls to Congressman Adam Schiff speeded up an investigation and a formal apology for "rude and unprofessional behavior" from officials of U.S. Customs and Border Protection, a division of DHS.[24] This makes one wonder what happens to ordinary people who do not have the phone number of their representative or the wherewithal to protest an unlawful profiling. Advocacy groups such as the Iranian American Bar Association, the Council of Pakistan American Affairs, the Free Muslims Coalition, and the Sikh Society have been working with the FBI to clean up security warning lists at airports that lead to unnecessary delays and detentions. However, Arab and Muslim Americans continue to travel with trepidation years after 9/11.[25]

Indeed, Raed Jarrar was prevented from boarding JetBlue Airways in New York on August 12, 2006, because he wore a T-shirt that read "We will not be silent," in English and Arabic. He was told, "Going to an airport with a T-shirt in Arabic script is like going to a bank wearing a T-shirt saying, 'I'm a robber.'"[26] In November 2006, six imams who had attended a conference of the North American Imams Federation were taken off their U.S. Airways flight and detained after several passengers and crew members complained that they had been engaging in suspicious activity: more specifically, praying before boarding the plane, changing seats, and requesting seat-belt extensions. CAIR promptly called for congressional hearings on religious and ethnic profiling at airports. Its executive director stated, "CAIR is receiving more reports of 'flying while Muslim' and racial profiling incidents from members of the Islamic community nationwide." In March 2007, the imams brought a discrimination lawsuit to a federal district court. Their complaint emphasized that the key issue to be determined was the right to practice one's religion and to travel without fear of being detained on the basis of unsubstantiated allegations.[27]

Currently, the Computer-Assisted Passenger Prescreening System (CAPPS) is used to inspect checked and carry-on luggage. The White House Commission on Aviation Safety and Security, chaired by Al

Gore, generated CAPPS in 1997. Even though race is statistically relevant, the commission decided not to include race in its formula in order to avoid type II errors.[28] However, critics such as Schauer argue that race/ethnicity is not spurious in the post-9/11 era:

> The argument is thus not that all people of Middle Eastern appearance (which could include name as well as physical appearance) should be targeted, but that Middle Eastern appearance may be a permissible component of an algorithm that also includes gender, age, form of purchasing the ticket (cash or credit card, last minute or well in advance, direct or through a travel agent), membership in a frequent flyer program, time of check-in, type of luggage, presence or absence of a hotel or rental-car reservation at destination, demeanor, and all the other factors that are part of the current CAPPS system. (2003, 184)

The problem is that in the real world, when law enforcement officials are deluged with information overload, they tend to overuse some factors such as race/ethnicity. Yet the profiling of Middle Easterners imposes a heavy cost on those who have done no wrong. Society needs to decide what type of a price it is willing to pay. Will vulnerable populations be profiled for the sake of security? Or will officials "distribute the cost more broadly, and in doing so raise the cost without lowering the degree of security" (Schauer 2003, 190)? In the latter case, instead of profiling Middle Easterners only, the system would require all passengers to arrive at the airport two to three hours before their flight to endure extensive searches.

Sikhs were particularly aggrieved with the profiling and insulted by demands to give up their ritualistic *kirpan* (ceremonial dagger) and remove their turban in public, which for them was tantamount to getting undressed. Sikh advocacy groups worked with the U.S. Department of Transportation and the Federal Aviation Administration to issue the fact sheet "Answers to Frequently Asked Questions Concerning Air Travel by People Who Are or May Appear to Be of Arab, Middle Eastern or Muslim Descent and/or Muslim or Sikh." Efforts to accommodate the ethnic/religious communities as well as educating security officers and airline personnel earned the praise of Sikhs and other targeted groups.[29] Sikhs traveling in 2002 and 2003 printed the guidelines from the Internet to show to security personnel. Sikh organizations continue to advocate for their religious rights (see chapter 7).

Profiling does not only take place at airports. Immediately after 9/11, there were some puzzling incidents, such as the one involving a Boy

Scout troop from Dearborn on a field trip to Mackinaw Island in Michigan. The troop members, U.S.-born youth of Arab descent, were held by the police for two hours for taking photos near a bridge. Generally, anonymity governs behavior in public spaces. However, at times of crisis, a person bearing telltale markers of the "enemy" may rouse the stereotype-based suspicions of zealous law enforcement officials or citizen vigilantes and lead them to act on their fears and misconceptions.

We interviewed an Arab American lawyer who had experienced the following incident about one month after 9/11 but had had the opportunity to protest profiling effectively:

> I was driving downtown dressed the way I am [business suit] in my car, and a marked police car pulled next to me and asked me where I was going. And I was right in the heart of the downtown immigration area. And he said to me, "Well, you don't have your seatbelt on." So I put my seatbelt on and turned around to thank them. They were two white police officers, and he just laughed and said, "You know, we follow the law in my country," with a very sarcastic Arabic accent that he was trying to conjure up. He didn't hit me, he didn't punish me, didn't do anything, but those words alone bothered me. So I took his number down and debated what to do with it. I followed them. I was very upset, 'cause if it happens to me, imagine the poor taxi driver. . . . When we finally had this meeting with . . . the police and they're encouraging people to speak up, I finally spoke up. . . . They published [the story in] their magazine article. I said, . . . "All the good words of the leadership don't mean anything if it doesn't trickle down to the people on the streets who deal with the people."

Given that all the terrorists on 9/11 were Arab/Muslim men, it has been argued that the government had the right to profile Arab and Muslim men. Our respondents seemed to be well aware of the debates regarding ethnic and religious profiling. One of them offered a passionate and succinct critique of the practice.

> Ethnicity is a false lead. Stereotyping—racial and religious stereotyping—is a waste of time. It directs limited law enforcement and intelligence resources away from people who might be suspicious for real law enforcement reasons, and onto a whole group of people who are just generically something or other in terms of national identity or ethnicity or religion. . . . Stereotyping as a tool of law enforcement is also lazy. It's also a shortcut. It's also a substitution of a formula for actual information. And we know that's not going to make people more secure. . . . We have a profiling system in this country since 1996 in airports [CAPPS program]. And we have documented that it led to hundreds of cases of abuse. . . . It certainly didn't stop the September 11th attack.

## BIAS INCIDENTS AND HARASSMENT

Middle Eastern and Muslim Americans have encountered numerous incidents of bias. For example, a Palestinian woman we met at a community forum in Brooklyn told us: "I live on the second floor. I came down and somebody write [sic] on the door, 'Why you live here, go back to your country.'" Her landlord was obliging enough to paint over the graffiti. Another respondent in New Jersey had somebody throw a rock at his house. A Sikh leader confirmed that harassment and name-calling were widespread: "Wherever we would go in public, somebody would taunt us, 'Go back!' or 'Go back, Iranians!'" Likewise, a Palestinian leader who was at an anti-Israel demonstration in New York City in spring 2002 was accosted by a man who yelled, "Aha, tell me when are you going to prepare the next bomb to bomb one of our towers?" A lawyer in our sample was working on a discrimination case in which a group of Muslims had wanted to buy a church and turn it into a mosque but the local mayor had blocked the sale by threatening eminent domain. In Chicago, a Christian Arab respondent's ten-year-old son was accused of stealing at school. When he protested, "I swear to God I did not take it," his teacher replied, "You are Muslim, you have no God."

A sampling of stories of bias shared by our respondents includes the attorney who was handling the discrimination case for an association of second- and later-generation Lebanese/Syrian Christian clubs whose hotel reservation for the annual convention had been canceled after 9/11 for alleged security reasons. The officers of the association filed a complaint with the Justice Department. The matter was eventually settled, and the corporation "issued an apology. They are going to give a $100,000 grant to their association," and they agreed to develop a sensitivity training program for their employees about Arab Americans (see AAI 2002, 7). A mosque congregation in New Jersey had a similar experience. "They were trying to rent space for Eid [a holiday], and the hotel refused. They said that they were booked that day. And some people went for brunch . . . and found that the hotel was not booked. . . . So they're suing the hotel."

A representative of an Arab American advocacy group recounted that two Arab storeowners had called the police over a bill dispute that ended up in a fistfight. The Arab men were held overnight while the attackers were released. The Arabs were interrogated "about their activities, their political affiliation, where they were on 9/11." This respondent added, "We're seeing a lot of racism in general in society towards Arabs and Muslims. For example, I've heard a case just yesterday about a neighbor calling the police against a friend of mine on the New Jersey shore because she was speaking Arabic with some friends on the front lawn. The police came and ultimately gave them a noise violation, but they were clearly called because of the Arabic."

Our respondents were familiar with incidents in public spaces, such as schools, the workplace, and the marketplace, where members of outgroups are most vulnerable. Typically, students were "getting into fights and being beaten up simply because they had an Arabic surname." In Chicago, the mother of seven-year-old Osama "finally went to the Board of Education and said, I have had enough of this, I love my child's name; he loves his name. . . . Leave him alone."[30] In New York, a teenage Osama attempted suicide twice after years of being called "bin Laden" and "terrorist" by classmates. He finally changed his name to Sammy.[31] A leader was anxious about his son's future: "I worry about [him], why did I name him [Mohammad]. . . . It may cause him some trouble sometime in his life."

Ironically, one of our interviewers for the September 11 Digital Archive was so angered by an experience she had on the New York subway that she wrote a piece entitled "Subway Negotiations." Sherien Sultan, an Egyptian American who emigrated to the United States at the age of four, described how she was reading the Quʾran one morning on her way to work, trying to brush up on her Arabic, when a man pointed at the book in her hands, saying, "You're making people uncomfortable," and then added an expletive. Sherien's innocent act was interpreted by one of her fellow riders as a threat. She found it offensive that the English, Spanish, and Cantonese Bibles that she saw that morning in the subway did not solicit the same reaction. Sherien was later vindicated when her article won a writing contest and was published (Sultan 2006).[32]

After 9/11, women donning the Islamic *hijab* were readily marked scapegoats.[33] In Chicago we were told that "a woman in the Southside was walking with the *hijab* and a white Caucasian man [ran] after her [and said], 'Go back, you f——ing whore [to where you came from].' She said, 'I'm American!' . . . She's married to an Arab. She said, 'I'm more American than you are. I'm from Detroit! Where do you want me to go?'" We learned that a young Michigan woman's scarf was taken off her head and she was spat at. Also in Michigan, a high school student was assaulted by another student who "pulled her scarf and kicked her, and basically said, 'You f——ing terrorist.'" At Baltimore's Washington

International Airport, a teenage Muslim girl was forced to remove her *hijab* when passing through security. When she questioned the reasoning and tried to explain that it was a religious symbol, she was surrounded by military personnel carrying rifles; out of fear, she then removed her *hijab* (CAIR 2002a, 46).

In New York, we heard that a woman wearing a *hijab* went to the Department of Motor Vehicles to take her driver's exam. "The inspector refused to test her and literally said: 'Get out of the car.' She says: 'Why? Is it because I'm a Muslim?' He says, 'Yeah.'" A respondent in Long Island told us about a similar incident: "A Muslim woman student from Nassau Community College came to us one day; she said the other students were pulling her scarf and making fun of her. These things do happen. But there were also some friends of hers who defended her and told off those who were harassing her."

In New York, an obstetrician we interviewed noticed that right after the terrorist attacks his patients were camouflaging their *hijab* with a hat because, they said, "I'm afraid if I put the *hijab* I'll be harassed or attacked." In Dearborn, immediately after the terrorist attacks, women who wore the *hijab* "stopped taking their kids to school. They stopped even going shopping. . . . Basically they didn't drive outside of Dearborn." As a respondent commented, "The *hijab* issue was very clear. The idea was, if you start blaming the incident of September 11th on Islam, the *hijab* issue will be a problem." Incidents involving the *hijab* have not subsided since the terrorist attacks. The national press continues to feature *hijab* stories involving "death threats and other offensive telephone calls salted with expletives."[34] Like the African American activists in the civil rights era who began sporting Afros and dreadlocks, many young Muslim women wore the *hijab* in defiance, in solidarity, and to claim their identity as Muslim Americans (see Cainkar 2004b; Peek 2003).[35]

## WORKPLACE DISCRIMINATION

Title VII of the Civil Rights Act of 1964 prohibits workplace discrimination on the basis of an employee's religious affiliation, national origin, race, color, or sex. The law covers harassment on the basis of membership in an ethnic group or religious faith, as well as harassment based on accent or traditional dress. It also penalizes discrimination based on association, as when the spouse of an Arab is denied a promotion or an employee attends a mosque. Discrimination due to misperception is likewise punishable under this statute, as in the case of Sikhs who are harassed because they are mistaken for Muslims. According to the 2003 report by the General Counsel of the Equal Employment Opportunity Commission (EEOC), "Since the terrorist attacks of 9/11, the Commission has used a variety of tools, including litigation, to combat discrimination against Muslims and people of Middle Eastern, African and Asian national origin" (U.S. EEOC 2003).

There was a 33 percent increase in the number of religious discrimination charges received by the EEOC between 2000 and 2002. National-origin discrimination similarly increased by almost 21 percent in the same period (2000–2002). The number has remained far above the numbers reported in 2000. In 2000, 1,939 charges were received, compared to 2,531 in 2006. Whereas 7,792 cases were filed in 2000, there were 8,327 cases in 2006. In the five years after the terrorist attacks, "991 charges were filed with the EEOC under Title VII alleging post-9/11 backlash employment discrimination against individuals who are, or are perceived to be, Muslim, Arab, Afghani, Middle Eastern or South Asian."[36] Between September 11, 2001, and September 11, 2004, the EEOC processed and resolved more than nine hundred charges of 9/11-related discrimination. They litigated fifteen of these cases, obtaining almost $3.2 million.[37] For example, the EEOC brought Alamo Car Rental to court for terminating Bilan Nur's employment because she refused to remove her *hijab*. A jury in Phoenix, Arizona, awarded Nur $287,640 on June 4, 2007.[38] On October 2004, the chair of the EEOC received the "Friend in Government" award from the ADC at their annual banquet in Dearborn.

By the first anniversary of the tragic events, we had heard several blatant cases of workplace discrimination. One respondent observed:

> The employment arena . . . continues to be the challenge. It seems like the workplace is truly left unattended, with all due respect to diversity programs and awareness and what have you. . . [There is now a] hostile working environment . . . for those who are Middle Eastern or Muslim. We had cases where people worked for five years to twenty-five years for certain employers who all of a sudden felt unwelcome, unaccepted, and even pressured to be rejected, isolated. Even when they have coffee, people avoid them. Some of them went so far as to be interviewed about their loyalty and commitment. . . . Personal lockers were tampered with and searched without their consent. . . . Some sites used to allow people to pray freely. All of a sudden, they told them, "Go home, pray to your God at your home."

A lawyer we interviewed concurred:

> Employment discrimination is now a more serious issue. I am handling several cases right now. . . . There are some horror stories. People are being fired, disciplined. It is happening a lot to women who wear the *hijab*. They are being told, "You look like a terrorist." Most of my clients [who] did not want to remove the *hijab* thought it was a matter of principle; that is why they are taking legal action. I have a woman in her thirties; she is from Guyana. She went to Mecca for the pilgrimage in February. When she came back she had decided to wear the *hijab*. . . . She was terminated for her religious-looking appearance.

Jennifer Bryan similarly says of her research in Jersey City after 9/11, "Nearly all of the Muslims I interviewed mentioned feeling hostility from employers, coworkers, store clerks and bank tellers, police officers, neighbors, random passerby, and even former friends" (2005, 143).

Middle Eastern businesses that are readily identifiable by name or signage experienced a drop in customers immediately after 9/11. An Arab-owned restaurant in Michigan was the target of an e-mail campaign alleging that its employees were celebrating the terrorist attacks. Its business dropped significantly until the culprit was found and threatened with a lawsuit. In Brooklyn and Paterson, several respondents noted that customers stayed away from Arab and Turkish stores, thus causing loss of revenue and even forcing a handful of businesses to declare bankruptcy. Since many Middle Easterners are self-employed, economic "boycotts," as locals interpreted the situation, can affect them harshly.

More systematic studies of economic discrimination against Arab and Muslim men are beginning to appear. One such project, by Neeraj Kaushal, Robert Kaestner, and Cordelia Reimers (2007), extracted data on 4,300 Arab and Muslim men from the 2001 FBI annual hate crime report, the Current Population Surveys for 1997–2005, and the census. They found a drop in real wage and weekly earnings somewhere between 9 and 11 percent. They attribute this to increased discrimination in the labor market, though 9/11 did not affect employment rate or hours worked.

New York City's taxi drivers, who are overwhelmingly Muslim immigrants from Afghanistan, Bangladesh, Egypt, India, and Pakistan, have been particularly vulnerable to the backlash because of their easy identification in this niche. Forty-five drivers who were surveyed by Monisha Das Gupta (2005) in August 2002 reported increases in unfair ticketing by police and overt hostility among some passengers who refused to ride with them or yelled, "You Muslims are the same. You're terrorists." Das Gupta argues that drivers were operating under the punitive policies of the Taxi and Limousine Commission:

> In the face of such xenophobic and anti-Muslim treatment, South Asian and Middle Eastern drivers found the attention paid to the hack licenses frightening. As one driver put it: "Most customers look for the name. When they see a Muslim or Asian name, they are not friendly. . . . " Passengers' ability to feel free to tell their drivers to "go home," regardless of their citizenship status, demonstrates the perception that immigrants are perpetual outsiders. . . . Before the attacks, drivers found their interactions with passengers to be "frank and easy." . . . But after 9/11, the pleasure of meeting different people and getting the chance to talk about their home country and family evaporated. In the words of an Egyptian driver, drivers and passengers now approached each other with some "trepidation." But while passengers were formally and discursively empowered to act on their fears about terrorism, drivers were not. (2005, 231)

## PROVOCATIVE ROLE OF THE MEDIA AND ISLAMOPHOBIA

In the epilogue to *Wounded City: The Social Impact of 9/11,* Kai Erikson notes, "When the fact of being Muslim trumps all other distinguishing characteristics in the minds of the people among whom one lives, it is very likely to have the same effect on one's self. Other ways of identifying one's position in the world—occupational, national, some other—begin to pale in significance because of the sheer weight of the anti-Muslim hostility" (2005, 358). Second to anti-Muslim hostility was anti-Arab hostility. Indeed, negative portrayals of Arabs and Muslims and Islamophobia (D. Cole and Lobel 2007) in the mainstream media had the effect of continuously adding fuel to a raging fire (see also Y. Haddad 2004; Mamdani 2004; Muscati 2003; Varisco 2004). Years after the terrorist attacks, slanderous speech against Muslims and Islam persisted unabatedly.[39] Some Arab and Muslim haters were prominent evangelical preachers, others academics, still others journalists. Their targets were Arab and Muslim individuals, organizations, or projects.

The terrorist attacks on 9/11, followed by the "War on Terror," the Afghanistan and Iraq wars, the political stalemate in Israel/Palestine, the terrorist bombings in Madrid and London, and several plots that were thwarted in Europe are the obvious reasons why Middle Eastern and Muslim Americans have been turned into the "enemy." Stanley Cohen explicates vilification and "othering" in *Folk Devils and Moral Panics,* which explores how political/ideological crises ("moral panics" in his title) are generated and outgroups ("folk devils" in his title) are blamed. "Our society as presently structured will continue to generate problems for some of its members . . . and then condemn whatever solution these groups find" (172). Boundaries are maintained by the powerful, such as politicians, scholars, and editors, and outgroups are "visible reminders of what we should not be" (2). The media act as "moral entrepreneurs," or agents of indignation, generating anxiety and concern and "amplifying" threats, whether real or imagined.

In the 9/11 era, Islamist terrorists have become identified as killers of innocent bystanders. Likewise, Bin Laden, jihad, and Al Qaeda are symbols of the enemy threatening America's security. Objects or images, such as a man's bushy beard, a woman's *hijab,* the collapse of the Twin Towers, and the explosion of a double-decker bus have also come to symbolize Islamists. Consequently, Samuel Huntington's book *The Clash of Civilizations* and President Bush's reference to the Crusades have become crystallized as emotive.[40] Cohen writes, "The process of spurious attribution is not, of course, random" (2002, 41). The state may, at times, create "a climate of hostility" that safeguards "the interests of political and media elites: legitimizing and vindicating the enduring patterns of law and order politics, racism and policies such as mass imprisonment" (xxix). The state may also generate "inchoate social anxieties, insecurities and fears" that include risks of terrorism (xxv).[41]

## THE ROLE OF THE MEDIA

The mainstream media play a significant role in transmitting the discourse of fear and hatred, assessing evaluations of risk before passing them on to the masses, and using their power to magnify a crisis. For this reason they are a major cause of anger and frustration among Middle Eastern and Muslim Americans. When these populations watch TV or read the newspaper, they tend to find stereotypical assumptions, false interpretations, and overall unfavorable representations of Middle Easterners, Arabs, and Muslims. They are thus skeptical of journalists who purport to report the "truth." A respondent said, "If I want to know what is going on in America, I don't read the American media. I read the British media. I read the European. I read the Israeli media, for God's sake; the Israeli media has more freedom on writing about what is happening in America than the American media. The American media has become a mouthpiece for the government. Walter Cronkite, the legend who is the godfather of the electronic media, said it, that it seemed like the American media rolled over and died."

The subject of the media solicited lengthy diatribes from the community leaders. Despite their anger, they tried to be fair in their assessment and distinguish among the various media outlets. A Muslim leader echoed:

> I think all of the Muslims were frustrated by the role the media played, and when you look at the big American picture, our Muslim representation in America is like zero. I think that is why when it comes to experts talking on Islam they are mainly non-Muslims. . . . After this, the good thing which has happened is that we developed a lot of contacts with the media, and we realized that there are a lot of people out there who are in the media who are very open and supportive. I think that [there were] several good articles in papers and also Peter Jennings did some good programs; Ted Koppel did some good programs.

In a public lecture that we sponsored at our center, a public relations expert spoke of her experience assisting Middle Eastern and Muslim American organizations in the immediate aftermath of the attacks.[42] While handling the deluge of media demands for interviews from a client (a small Arab American organization), she realized that on the eve of the terrorist attacks few editors and commentators were well informed about the Middle East. Moreover, there was no time to do research. Many searched the Yellow Pages and called the first organization they spotted under "Arab" or "Muslim." They demanded, "We want to talk to a Muslim." In particular they were eager to televise interviews with women wearing a *hijab*. There was a dearth of Arab or Muslim experts who could communicate effectively to larger audiences. Some with no particular expertise in community affairs or their ancestral history, religion, or Middle Eastern politics became spokespersons overnight. Many Middle Eastern and Muslim American CBOs were equally ill prepared for the crisis.

Left in a vacuum with major time pressures, many in the news business toed the official line, using the often-repeated cliché "You are either with us or against us." But many journalists, editors, producers, and publishers should be credited for their steep learning curve in gaining a better understanding of the Middle East and its diaspora very quickly. They started probing and asking pertinent questions that were more in keeping with the ideals of fair and balanced reporting. Indeed, thanks to some reporters, the public was informed about not only detainee families, prison conditions, and even detention protests but also activists in the civil rights community and other organizations. Their stories filled some of the significant gaps in the jigsaw puzzle created by government's secrecy, such as information on detainees.

Some newspapers must be recognized for their extensive coverage of specific government initiatives. The *Washington Post* divulged the national origins of the detainees and humanized their case,[43] and the *Los Angeles Times* exposed the special registration initiative, which led to the detention of Iranian Americans in Los Angeles.[44] The Lackawanna Six purportedly received the longest cover story (three and a half pages) in the history of the *New York Times*.[45] Of course, other publications, radio programs, and television channels have also attempted to challenge stereotypes and biases, but certain news outlets still continue to be particularly biased against Arabs and Muslims at home and abroad.

*Aliens in America,* a television series shown in 2007–2008, and *Little Mosque on the Prairie,* a 2006 Canadian series, have been acclaimed by many advocacy organizations for their sympathetic portrayals of Muslims. Even Jack G. Shaheen, the author of several studies on the vilification of Arabs and Muslims in popular culture, told a reporter for the *New York Times* that the pilot episode of *Aliens* "use[d] comedy extremely well to debunk myths about Muslims. It's the first that I can recall in a TV show that I laugh with, and also respect, the character."[46] Whatever the reason for this departure from the norm in the American media, it is indeed welcome.

## ISLAMOPHOBIA

Our respondents did not spare any words in venting their anger at the born-again Christian evangelists who tried to denigrate Islam. "Billy Graham! His son! He's an ignorant! *[sic]* And he's defaming Islam . . . without knowing anything about it." A Muslim organization described the changes they had observed between our visits (January 2002 and March 2003) as follows: "Some of the new phenomena, after you guys had left, were the increasing [hate speech of] the Christian evangelical movements. I mean, you began to hear Jerry Falwell, Pat Robertson, Franklin Graham, all saying statements to the effect that Islam is evil." CAIR has publicly accused Franklin Graham of "smearing Islam" by calling it an "evil religion" and saying it "preaches violence."[47] In its 2003 report, ADC also devoted a whole section to "Media Bias and Defamation," which included evangelical preachers (Ibish 2003, 119–31).

The Khalil Gibran International Academy, a bilingual Arabic-English public school for grades six to twelve that opened in Brooklyn in September 2007, received a barrage of defamation press coverage as soon as news of this school was made public.[48] The conservative *New York Sun* called it a *madrassa* (school),[49] implying a religious school that would be in sympathy with the Taliban. The Web site of Daniel Pipes, director of the Middle East Forum, named it a "jihad" school and maintained that the school would be "imbuing pan-Arabism and anti-Zionism, proselytizing for Islam, and promoting Islamist sympathies."[50] According to an article in the *Christian Science Monitor,* New York's Jewish establishment was particularly concerned by fears of "ethnic triumphalism . . . [found] in many of the Islamic academies."[51]

Critics, especially a group known as Stop the Madrassa Coalition, caricatured the Yemini American founding principal, Debbie Almontaser, who was pressured to resign a month before the beginning of the school year.[52] According to the *New York Times* writer Andrea Elliott, a 2007 Pulitzer Prize winner, this "conflict tapped into a well of post-9/11 anxieties. But Ms. Almontaser's downfall was not merely the result of a spontaneous outcry by concerned parents and neighborhood activists. It was also the work of a growing and organized movement to stop Muslim citizens who are seeking an expanded role in American public life. The fight against the school, participants in the effort say, was only an early skirmish in a broader, national struggle."[53] The most prominent academic leaders of what could be construed as the backlash against the response to the backlash are Daniel Pipes, founder of the Middle East Forum and Campus Watch, which scrutinizes Middle East faculty, courses, and programs in higher education, and David Horowitz, founder of Islamo-Fascism Awareness Week, which runs a campaign on college campuses.[54] Another vocal critic of the Gibran Academy is Jeffrey Wiesenfield, a CUNY trustee, who alleges the school is teaching "soft jihad" to the students. By singling out Muslims, Pipes, Horowitz, and others who share their ideology "lean heavily on guilt by association" (A16). For the record, the Gibran Academy is named after the Christian author of the highly acclaimed and best-selling book *The Prophet,* who immigrated as a child to Boston from a village in Mount Lebanon in the late 1800s. It is partially funded by the Gates Foundation's New Visions for Public Schools, which has helped create dozens of new schools. As a New York City Department of Education school, the academy is obligated to comply with all of the department's rules and procedures, especially regarding curriculum.

Middle Eastern and Muslim American organizations and their leaders were themselves subjected to bias and Islamophobia. CAIR, for example, has been accused of having ties with Hamas and Hezbollah. Politicians on both sides of the aisle protested against allowing its D.C. offices to use the meeting room in the Capitol Building. When CAIR's executive director in Sacramento received a certificate for "outstanding service" from Senator Boxer, critics attacked Boxer's Web site with "Senators for Terror" messages until she revoked the certificate. CAIR has successfully defended its actions and blamed widespread prejudice for these suspicions.[55]

In the political sphere, African American Keith Ellison (D-MN) has contended with Islamophobia on a personal level. Upon becoming the first Muslim congressman, he was vilified for wanting to swear his oath of office on the Qu'ran. Representative Virgil Goode Jr. (R-VA) objected to the idea and wrote to his constituents that if immigration was not overhauled "there will likely be many more Muslims elected to office demanding to use the Qu'ran."[56] Furthermore, Goode refused to apologize for his lack of sensitivity. Eventually, Ellison used a two-volume Qu'ran once owned by Thomas Jefferson, thus "paying respect not only to the founding fathers' belief in religious freedom but the Constitution itself," according to his spokesman.[57] He has since responded to further anti-Islamic sentiment in the legislature. For example, when Congressman Peter King (R-NY) argued that there were too many mosques in the United States and that the existing ones should be infiltrated by the government, Ellison spoke out, urging Muslim Americans to refrain from judging all of Congress on one congressman's statements.[58]

Another instance of media bias involves Imad Hamad, the executive director of ADC Michigan, and his significant contributions to the Building Respect in Diverse Groups to Enhance Sensitivity (BRIDGES) project, which has become a national model for community–law enforcement relations. When the FBI in Washington, D.C., wanted to honor his work with the Exceptional Public Service Award in September 2003, Hamad was slandered by the media. Because of public accusations that he supported terrorism, the FBI decided not to give him the award after all (Howell and Jamal 2008, 70). The advocacy and civil engagement of Middle Eastern and Muslim American organizations exert a heavy toll on the affected leaders and their communities. Howell and Jamal explain, "When Arab organizations are included in 'public diplomacy' and 'community policing' efforts but they are not treated as full partners with a voice in setting agendas and negotiating strategies, then they risk weakening their grassroots strength and eroding Arab confidence in American public institutions and government" (2008, 71).

Physical, verbal, and symbolic incidents against Middle Eastern and Muslim Americans have clearly increased since 9/11. Hate crimes soared immediately after the terrorist attacks, and though they have subsided somewhat since, they remain much higher than they were in the pre-9/11 era. Incidents at home or overseas perpetuate the scapegoating of innocent Arab or Muslim people.[59] Bias incidents, particularly incidents of employment discrimination, have continued to escalate in spite of victims' courageous reporting of their grievances and the EEOC's ability to mete out justice. All this has been fueled by deeply entrenched stereotypes slandering Arabs and Muslims and the rhetoric of "the clash of civilizations." Nonetheless, our respondents did not find the acts of hatred and bias as damaging as the administration's initiatives. In the next chapter, we turn our attention to the government dragnet.

# 6

# Government Initiatives and the Impact of the Backlash

Coming immediately on the heels of the hate crimes and bias incidents, the government initiatives were interpreted among the Middle Eastern and Muslim American populations as an undeserved infliction of discrimination and suffering. In the language of sociologists (e.g., Mann 2005), this was state repression (chapter 2). These groups were being targeted for no other reason than sharing the terrorists' ethnic origins (Arab) and religious affiliation (Muslim); they were scapegoats. Unanimously, the leaders we interviewed considered the actions of the administration more harmful to the overall well-being of their communities than the incidents of harassment and hate crimes by ordinary citizens. A respondent stated: "I think it is the biggest thing we have seen since the Japanese internment. It is not just one issue; it is the collection of things, the whole cumulative effect of the various court decisions and other legal processes. . . . The attorney general, Ashcroft, proceeded through executive fiat to take over more and more power. The story is that the country behaved quite well on this issue, it is Ashcroft who didn't. Single-handedly he managed to take unprecedented types of powers. It is a big dragnet." The Appendix provides a detailed list, in chronological order, of the series of measures that the U.S. government instigated after 9/11. In this chapter we first provide a brief overview of these directives and the PATRIOT Act; then we discuss the cumulative repercussions of the backlash as they were viewed by the affected communities.

## GOVERNMENT INITIATIVES

### DETENTIONS

Almost immediately after 9/11, Arab and Muslim immigrant men began disappearing. The process was shrouded in secrecy. Nobody knew where detainees were kept, why they were charged, or how long they would be kept, and even their names were not made public. Due process laws were disregarded. There were also allegations of custodial abuse (U.S. Department of Justice, Office of the Inspector General 2003). The detentions pitted Middle Eastern and Muslim American advocacy organizations against the former INS and other government agencies. It also mobilized the civil rights community, particularly Japanese Americans who had bitter memories of incarceration.

Our respondents found the administration's actions contradictory. We heard this refrain again and again. "The biggest problem we have is: on the one side, the president has come out and said, 'Don't blame Arab Americans. Don't blame American Muslims. Don't blame South Asians.' But on the other hand, they're saying, 'We're going to round up these five thousand. We're going to round up these six thousand. We're holding a thousand, but we're not going to tell you who they are or where they're from.' It's a real mixed message." Their first contention was that the detentions were a form of ethnic/religious profiling. A prominent national spokesperson said:

> We're not arguing that [the terrorists] weren't Muslims and Middle Easterners! We're arguing that it's so broad that it makes it very difficult for law enforcement to do the job. What law enforcement has said to us . . . it is very difficult because they are trained to be investigators for criminal [cases]. . . . These laws are administrative and not criminal. . . . So they're asking them to use criminal procedures to find people who are not criminals. So that's number one. Number two: the leads aren't the same. In a criminal investigation, you have fingerprints, you have patterns of behavior. . . None of this is here. . . . What I keep saying is that . . . this is political smoke to make people feel good.

Another respondent observed that Middle Easterners and Muslims were arrested and investigated "because they broke the visa [sic], but we know that many people in the United States are undocumented. I'm not defending them because they broke the law, because of course they have to be deported, but what worried us as a community was that they were subjected [sic] by the authorities just because of their names and their origin and their religion." Our representatives were also critical of the government's assumption of guilt. A lawyer we interviewed argued, "Due process doesn't apply when you are a Muslim or an Arab. What kind of justice is that? The very reason for due process is that it doesn't matter if you are a murderer. . . . [Now it is] guilty until proven innocent. . . . Just get them all in jail and then we will sort it out."

The reasons for detention ranged from being out of status—typically a visa overstayer—to mistaken identity, incorrect INS records, or false incriminating information sent to law enforcement officials by jealous or nervous acquaintances. Muzaffar Chishti, a prominent immigration lawyer and policy expert, has aptly referred to the latter as "collateral damage."[1] A sheriff we interviewed explained that such information was sent to his precinct in the form of fax messages and letters with no return address. The messages read something like "This individual, I've seen him carrying guns into his house. He's out all hours of the night. Different people come in and out of the house at two, three, four o'clock in the morning." Or "I know he has relations in Beirut and he flies in every other week." The sheriff justified the seriousness with which such tips were received: "You've got to understand. It sounds crazy to you. It sounds crazy to me. But my God, the World Trade Center would have sounded crazy to anybody a year ago."

The volume of tips received by the police increased exponentially in the first few weeks after 9/11, considering that historically hardly any allegations of this nature had been made against Arabs and Muslims. The Vera Institute report on community relations with law enforcement after 9/11 concurs that false reporting compromised good policing (Henderson et al. 2006). An officer told the Vera team: "Suppose I get a call about suspicious activity. I have to respond, even if it's based on prejudice. If I show up, the Arab American feels he is being profiled and trusts the police less. If I don't show up, I get an angry call or complaint that I am not doing my job. It's a lose-lose situation" (quoted in Henderson et al. 2006, 61).

Leaders in our study vehemently opposed Operation TIPS, proposed by the Bush administration. Mail carriers, electricians, and other government employees who had access to people's homes because of the nature of their jobs were to check for suspicious signs of terrorism. The case of the three Muslim medical students who were detained for seventeen hours by the police in Florida on September 13, 2002, demonstrated the vagaries of such programs.[2] A woman had allegedly overheard these men in a restaurant "laughing at September 11" and plotting a terrorist attack. Two of the men were American born, and the third was a foreign student with a valid visa. They were released without any charges after their ordeal was aired on national television.[3] The TIPS program was defeated when it met with massive popular opposition from the American public (chapter 1).

A law enforcement official we interviewed emphasized community informants' role: "A lot of people . . . have a long grudge against someone. Then they start throwing these names out. These leads came to us from somewhere. . . . The only reason we would get involved with anybody, the federal authorities or whatever, is because of information generated by someone." Discrepancies in the INS records led to other detentions. A respondent told us that his cousin in Florida had been picked up for terrorism. His American wife took her children to the FBI offices and said, "You have two choices, either you raise my kids or you get my husband out [of jail]. . . . I lived with him for eighteen years; he's not [a terrorist]!" Our respondent conjectured that his cousin had been detained because his citizenship papers were pending. In the weeks after the terrorist attacks, being in the vicinity of high-security locations was another cause for detention. Several respondents recounted the case of an Arab American civil engineer who had worked on New York City's bridges for thirteen years but who, because of his proximity to a bridge, was picked up and detained for several hours.

Because one of the airline tickets used by the terrorists had been purchased from a travel agent in Paterson, New Jersey, we were told that Main Street was swamped with FBI agents for several weeks after the attacks. Months later when we visited that travel agency, all the employees had disappeared out of fear, except for one who informed us that the owner was out of the country on business. Similarly, in the suburbs of Washington, D.C., it was discovered that Mohammed Atta, the ringleader of the 9/11 terrorists, had used a certain copy center. Coincidentally, a nineteen-year-old Pakistani had also made copies that day and charged his credit card. Once he was identified, the FBI arrested him. According to a respondent, "They took him in. He was kept in the prison for four months. . . . When he was brought to the Embassy of Pakistan, he was all in chains, in orange dress, with chains that go from your neck to your feet, shackles. . . . He was at the wrong place at the wrong time."

Though the majority of detainees were male, a handful of women were arrested. A twenty-three-year-old Egyptian woman enrolled at the City College of New York was detained with her family on February 27, 2002. She was a good student who planned to graduate in May in biochemistry. She was the eldest of six siblings, having lived in New York since she was ten. The family had asked for asylum and their case was pending. The FBI came to their home at 6:00 a.m. and arrested her, her twenty- and sixteen-year-old brothers, her seventeen-year-old sister, and their parents. Her two American-born younger siblings were left at home. According to the campus newspaper, "Handcuffs were placed on their hands and ankles and around their waists. No one was allowed to ask any questions or talk to one another. Everyone was put in a separate vehicle, and the caravan took them to Federal Plaza in Manhattan where they were interrogated and then given to the INS for deportation."[4]

We attended an interfaith concert in Brooklyn whose proceeds were earmarked for detainee families. The son of a Pakistani detainee, a tenth grader, addressed the audience. His father was a successful businessman, yet he was facing charges of grand larceny because one of his associates had accused him of being a "terrorist." Moreover, there was a dispute regarding money he had sent to the old country for his grandfather, who suffered from diabetes. In mid-June 2002, when we met, the father had been in detention for 105 days in the second-highest-security facility at Riker's Island, housed with the general inmate population. Furthermore, the government had seized the family's home and several cars they owned.

Detention centers in Paterson (Passaic County) and Kearny (Hudson County), New Jersey, housed the vast majority of post-9/11 detainees. With reputedly the worst conditions, the Metropolitan Detention Facility in Brooklyn also had a major depot for Arab and Muslim detainees (see Chishti et al. 2003). The detainees in these jails suffered abuse and denial of *halal* food and other accommodations, charges that were later substantiated by an official report (U.S. Department of Justice, Office of the Inspector General 2003). Several months after 9/11, we asked a respondent if conditions had improved. He replied, "They just elected a new sheriff who really is trying to, for example, facilitate praying. . . . But his hands are tied, though. He said, 'Policy I cannot really do anything [about]; if it is actually in the administering of the jail, maybe I can help. Like, for example, allowing an imam to go and visit and preach . . . or to [provide] *halal* meat.'"

Effectively, the civil rights community was taken by surprise by the large number of detentions. An immigration lawyer who works for a civil liberties agency showed us the lists of lawyers who speak Spanish and other languages but confessed that she did not know of any Arabic-speaking immigration lawyers. Her office had to cull together such a list in great haste after 9/11 and prepare immigration guidelines for Arabic-speaking lawyers who wanted to help but did not specialize in immigration. In spite of these shortcomings, the civil rights watchdog organizations were at the forefront in challenging the government's secrecy and infractions of due process and other legal procedures (see Chishti 2003, 27).

Several Middle Eastern and Muslim agencies devoted many of their resources to the detention problem. The representative of a small agency with a handful of employees told us: "Right now we work with about two hundred detainees and family members on a direct basis. . . . When someone gets detained, we write down all the information, including the name, the date of birth, the phone number. We work with a group . . . in New Jersey, which includes the ACLU New Jersey, the Center for Constitutional Rights, this group called HELP. . . . They have helped set up this network to try to represent people in New Jersey. We even refer folks to [the Islamic Center of North America] for services. We visit folks inside. In many cases, we get them in contact with their families."

The detainees left behind wives, children, and many obligations. As men are often the breadwinners in Middle Eastern and Muslim immigrant households, the detentions had an adverse ripple effect on their dependents. In their absence, the community mobilized to provide food and other funds to secure the basic needs of the detainee families. A respondent explained, "We know the families are truly suffering, because they don't know where their heads of household [are], they don't know how to support themselves. . . . These women . . . some of them don't go out, don't speak English." Another respondent recalled what he had witnessed: "I joined one of the reporters of the *New York Times* to translate, . . . and we visited two families in Jersey City [whose] husbands were taken away because they broke the visa *[sic]*. They were in very bad condition because they were not eligible for public assistance. They can't pay the rent, they have little children, and both of them were pregnant and about to have babies, and their husbands were away."

According to the ACLU (2004c), the deportations of Pakistani and Arab immigrants have torn apart families and shattered communities (see also ACLU 2004a). One such community was "Little Pakistan" in Coney Island (Brooklyn), where more than thirty businesses failed after 9/11.[5] Moreover, shopkeepers who remained continued to struggle with revenue decreases of 30 to 40 percent (ACLU 2004c, 10–11). The report also features eleven cases of persons caught in the detention-deportation nightmare, revealing forced family separations and economic and psychological distress (see also Nguyen 2005). All the pain and suffering caused by the detentions yielded a few criminals but no terrorists.

A respondent from a civil rights agency summed up the challenges of the detentions as follows:

> There were several things happening: legal groups were working to help detainees get representation; . . . community groups were organizing family members, . . . also providing help to the community; advocacy groups were speaking out without a lot of constituency, because you just need time to do that on basic civil liberties violations. . . . We had the emergence of all these new groups working on detention issues who weren't connected to the old detention people [experts]. So people didn't know what everybody else was doing. . . . And then in Brooklyn, because of the demographics, there sprang up a couple of grassroots groups.

## THE PATRIOT ACT, VOLUNTARY INTERVIEWS, THE ABSCONDER INITIATIVE, AND NSEERS

The PATRIOT Act brought about changes to laws dealing with crimes, immigration, banking, and intelligence. Bill Ong Hing writes, "The act passed Congress with near unanimous support, and the president signed it into law a mere six weeks after 9/11. The vast powers embodied in the law provide expanded authority to search, monitor, and detain citizens and noncitizens alike, but its implementation since passage has preyed most heavily on noncitizen Arabs, Muslims, and Sikhs. Authority to detain, deport, or file criminal charges against noncitizens specifically is broadened" (2006, 142).

Some of the changes called for by the PATRIOT Act were necessary to address the emerging needs of law enforcement agencies in the age of new technologies. However, constitutional scholar David Cole (2003) notes that the provision created a double standard: one set of rights for citizens and another for noncitizens. Noncitizens were basically deemed guilty for associating with or contributing "material support" to "terrorist" organizations. Cole faults the PATRIOT Act for authorizing "secret searches and wiretaps in criminal investigation without probable cause to believe that the target is engaged in criminal conduct or that evidence of a crime is found" (2003, 67).

From the perspective of the civil rights community and many of the Middle Eastern and Muslim American advocacy organizations, the

PATRIOT Act was a major setback in the nation's civil rights. A respondent commented: "The enormity of the 9/11 attacks . . . on American soil changed the climate totally, as to the whole passing of the PATRIOT Act and moving ahead on the war on terrorism, and not having the kind of congressional second-guessing that you normally would have." Another respondent reaffirmed this point: "I think that, from our perspective as an advocacy organization, the minute the PATRIOT Act went to Congress our only recourse was to lobby Congress, because they were the ones that were going to pass it." Unfortunately, their efforts proved unsuccessful.

Another respondent placed the PATRIOT Act in a larger political framework:

> The 9/11 attacks were a real opportunity for those who wanted to accrue power, essentially take power away from other branches of government like the judiciary or the legislative—especially the judiciary—or from ordinary people and transfer it to the government. . . . There was no time for a public debate. The PATRIOT Act is about 312 pages long. . . . It's like the size of the phonebook. . . . Even most of the people who voted for it in the Congress did not read it. . . . Almost everything in the PATRIOT Act is something the government has asked for in the past, in the past ten to fifteen years, and the Congress said no. Every bit of it: roving wire taps, indefinite detentions, guilt by association, new powers of search and seizure, reduced level of probable cause, reduced need for warrants, reduced role for judges. . . . Basically, they got what they wanted.[6]

The PATRIOT Act stipulated that financial contributions to questionable nonprofits were a punishable crime. In December 2001, the U.S. Treasury Department froze the assets of the Holy Land Foundation for Relief and Development, the Global Relief Foundation, and the Benevolence International Foundation, allegedly for funneling funds to terrorist organizations, though no criminal charges were filed (Bozorgmehr and Bakalian 2005b). According to a report by CAIR (2002b), about fifty thousand American Muslim donors were affected by the closures. CAIR also noted that these organizations had a solid track record in aiding widows and children and financing several development projects in Palestinian refugee camps.

Established in 1989, the Holy Land Foundation for Relief and Development, a humanitarian and disaster relief organization, was the first casualty. The U.S. government maintained that funds it sent to Hamas were used to support schools that encouraged children to become suicide bombers in Israel. As Hamas encompasses a social service arm, it is difficult to separate its dual, often contradictory objectives. Federal agents closed down the Holy Land Foundation's headquarters in Richardson, Texas, and its three offices in Bridgeview, Illinois; Patterson, New Jersey; and San Diego, California. The Holy Land Foundation was the largest Muslim charity in the United States, having raised $13 million in 2000. It claimed that it supported humanitarian causes in the West Bank and Gaza, earthquake victims in Turkey, and refugees in Kosovo, Chechnya, Jordan, and Lebanon, as well as in the United States. The Holy Land Foundation denied the allegations of supporting terrorism. The Global Relief Foundation, headquartered in the Chicago suburbs, raised about $5 million in 2001 to send to clinics in Israeli-occupied territories and refugee camps in Kosovo. The Benevolence International Foundation reported $3.6 million in contributions for 2001. It entered a plea bargain to cooperate with the authorities, though it denied any ties to Al Qaeda.

Many Muslim Americans viewed the U.S. Treasury's intensification of surveillance during the month of Ramadan (November–December 2001) as a highly provocative act. Muslims customarily donate more than the usual amount during this holy month of fasting. More basically, the closure of Muslim charities curtails the ability of Muslim Americans to fulfill their *zakat* (almsgiving) duties. Giving alms is one of the five pillars of Islam, a religious duty of all Muslims. Muslims are required to give charitable donations annually, consisting of 2.5 percent of their net worth, not just income.[7] These legal issues have proved so problematic that three prominent Muslim organizations met with the U.S. Department of Treasury in 2007 to create an almsgiving guide for American Muslims during Ramadan.[8]

Several court cases have subsequently acquitted American Muslim men of providing aid to terrorist organizations.[9] New evidence has shown that the Bush administration had relied too much on foreign intelligence. A central component of the prosecution's case against the Holy Land Foundation rested on evidence provided by Israeli intelligence. "Federal prosecutors, accusing charity officials of aiding terrorists, have disclosed receiving 21 binders of documents from the Israeli government . . . [with] an estimated 8,000 pages . . . including Israeli military, police reports, translated interrogation transcripts and financial analyses."[10] American legal experts question the accuracy of the translations and the inherent biases, given the enmity between Hamas and Israel. Neil MacFarquhar writes in the *New York Times*, "The case is extremely complicated and has been delayed three times since first scheduled in October 2004. . . . The prosecution's list of un-indicted co-conspirators runs to more than 10 pages with some 300 names, including some of the larger Muslim American organizations."[11] The jury could not come to a unanimous decision regarding the charges, and on October 22, 2007, the case ended in a mistrial.[12]

The "voluntary interviews" (see the Appendix) created huge turmoil in Arab and Muslim communities. They were puzzled as to who was being called in and why. The government had initially said that it would question five thousand young men who had arrived on student or work visas after January 2000. Then it issued a twenty-day waiting period. Middle Eastern students wondered whether they should go back home for the holidays; they feared they might not be allowed to return on the same visa.

As time passed, leaders and their constituents were engulfed by feelings of anger and resentment for the unfair targeting of these "voluntary interviews." One respondent put it eloquently:

> The announced policy was that it would apply to men aged sixteen to forty-five from a list of countries. . . . [There was also] the entry of the 6,000 Middle Easterners among the 350,000 visa absconders, deportee absconders, into the national crime database. In other words, in terms of deportation policy, the government is going to focus on Middle Easterners first and everybody else second. . . . You can see, I think, very clearly, the notion being articulated that young Arab men are a particular class of people, dangerous, suspicious by definition, and of interest to the authorities by definition, and that they are being treated as a particular category. So we have two kinds of immigration policy and two kinds of immigration law enforcement: one for young Middle Eastern and Muslim men, one for everybody else.

An immigration lawyer in our sample reflected on the interviews: "They were very far from being voluntary. . . . Let's take the case of Florida. . . . When you have FBI agents knocking on your door at midnight, you are pretty much going to let them in, especially if you are an immigrant and you are coming from perhaps a country where authority is to be feared—not respected, but feared. You are going to comply, especially post-9/11. You are just going to take the interview because you don't know your rights." Another immigration lawyer expounded the dilemma many immigrants felt: on the one hand, they felt outrage for being profiled, but on the other hand, they had nothing to hide. "The first thing we said was, 'Listen, these are voluntary. You have to hold the government to its word. If you don't want to do it, you don't have to do it.' But whatever offense people felt, they also felt the need to respond, to say, 'If I don't respond, it is going to look like I'm guilty. I want to talk.'"

The "voluntary interviews" were followed by the "absconder initiative."[13] Considering that there were about three hundred thousand absconders in the United States at the time, mostly from Latin America, rounding up the 2 percent of them who were Middle Easterners or South Asians was enough reason to get the leaders fuming. Particularly egregious was the fact that INS was entering its data into the federal crimes database. A respondent surmised: "If you get stopped for speeding, I check it against the database because I think you might be a Middle Easterner. So what that means is that state and local officials and the FBI . . . [started] carrying out the tasks of the INS."

NSEERS, otherwise known as "special registration," was another government initiative that called for foreign nationals from twenty-six countries—mostly in the Middle East and South Asia—to be registered, fingerprinted, and photographed upon entering the United States. They were ordered to report to INS within thirty days of arrival and annually afterwards. They also had to report their departure. Community activists and civil rights professionals such as Hing found NSEERS a prime example of "the failure and ill-advisedness of immigration-related laws and policies" (2006, 148). It was voluntary, so that real terrorists would be unlikely to report their whereabouts, and "the sweeping roundup diverted resources from more pressing counter-terrorism needs, strained relationships with some Arab and Muslim nations, and alienated immigrants who might otherwise have been willing to help the government hunt for terror cells in this country" (149).

Between June 2002 and January 2003, the tenure of NSEERS, approximately 82,000 Arab and Muslim immigrant men complied with the special registration, but only about 1,200 men were placed in deportation proceedings for immigration irregularities, and no one was charged with terrorism (see the Appendix and D. Cole and Lobel 2007, 10). Since Iranian nationals were among the detainees, massive demonstrations ensued in Los Angeles.[14] The Washington-based Iranian American Bar Association interviewed thirty-four Iranians who had been arrested and published a report cataloging abuses and violations of their rights (Bozorgmehr 2007).

An Arab American respondent told us: "Now we are dealing with the question of fingerprinting for visitors from selective countries. It always suggests a selective approach focused on those of Middle Eastern descent or Muslim faith." The Arab American Family Support Center, a social service agency in Brooklyn, called a press conference on the topic of "Families without Fathers" around Father's Day in 2003. The goal was to sharply criticize NSEERS for discriminating against immigrants on the basis of national origin and demonstrate the economic and emotional suffering of detainee families. To prove its point, the center provided in its PR packet five "family portraits" to humanize the impact of special registration on the families.[15]

In retrospect, there is no doubt that the government employees who were handling the initiatives were as overwhelmed as the Middle Eastern and Muslim leaders and the civil rights advocates.[16] The decision makers in the administration were themselves grappling for solutions when none were obvious. After all, the challenge of terrorism was new and monumental. Community observers acknowledged the many false starts, trials and errors, and often-incomprehensible tactics that added to the confusion and exhaustion of the post-9/11 era. In spite of the outreach efforts of the FBI, the Justice Department's Civil Rights Division, local law enforcement agencies, and politicians, the Bush administration's message remained mixed. A respondent said, "I have to give credit to [the FBI] Hate Crimes Unit, [which] has done a lot of outreach. They go to communities, though sometimes it's a little confusing, . . . and people have said, 'We don't know whether or not they came to interview us or they're coming to let us know what our rights are because oftentimes the next day they'll come and say, well, we'd like to talk to this person and this person.' . . . There's a schizophrenic kind of relationship."

Ultimately, the words of a high-ranking INS official we interviewed confirm some of these impressions: "Most of Ashcroft's initiative is a lot of make-work with few returns, but it gets good press. It hasn't helped our community relations. It hurts the agency because the FBI and other agencies make arrests using INS statutes. . . . We are overreacting. . . . There are some initiatives that are good and should be followed by INS. For example, the greater attention at entry and exit is not symbolic. The absconder initiative is not symbolic. The interviews were symbolic, the detentions were symbolic." Even as policy, the government initiatives had serious shortcomings. They "equated national origin with dangerousness" (Hing 2006, 150). They were counterproductive because "othering" Arabs and Muslims "deepened the perception abroad that the United States is anti-Muslim and that its democratic values and principles are hypocritical" (Hing 2006, 160). Profiling creates a false sense of security, and when carried out by private citizens, as the TIPS program proposed, it is totally unreliable, even dangerously akin to racial (religious) profiling (see Hing 2006, 150–51).

## REPERCUSSIONS OF THE BACKLASH ON THE AFFECTED COMMUNITIES
### PSYCHOLOGICAL IMPACT

Given the major backlash against Middle Eastern and Muslim Americans after 9/11, it is hardly surprising that some leaders described their experience in the early months afterward as an "emotional roller-coaster" and "shell shock." The targeted populations experienced the whole gamut of stressful emotional responses. But if one word best describes the atmosphere in the Arab/Muslim communities in the months following the terrorists' attacks, it is fear. Respondents mentioned their constituents' anxiety about becoming victims of the backlash. Large immigrant communities such as Brooklyn (New York), Paterson (New Jersey), Dearborn (Michigan), and southwestern Chicago felt most intimately the effects of the detentions, deportations, voluntary interviews, and special registration. Stories of FBI searches, wiretaps, arrests, and secrecy circulated in the targeted communities. At least eighteen films have documented the repercussions of the post-9/11 backlash for the lives of Arab and Muslim immigrants.[17]

One respondent explained: "This 9/11 created lots of fear within community members, which is 'I am guilty by association or affiliation, because I am an Arab or because my parents look like an Arab or my name sounds like an Arab, or because I came from that country, from Arabia or the Arabic [sic] world.' This, to be honest with you, is scary, and unfortunately what we hear lately about things done in the Congress, new laws and new rules and regulations." The director of a social service agency told us, "I remember a very particular story that one of my counselors came to me with. He said, 'I lost my clients.' I said, 'What do you mean, you lost your clients?' He said, 'They just disappeared.' I asked him, 'They are not at home?' He said, 'No, they left home. Nobody knows where they are.' Well, ultimately we found this family, but this family had kind of run away because they thought that what happened to them in [Iraq] would happen to them again."

In her ethnographic study of Jersey City, Jennifer Bryan argues that the Muslim immigrant population was "reluctant to report hate crimes because they were afraid of 'causing trouble'" (2005, 143). People were self-censoring their behavior, afraid to speak Arabic in public. The chairman of a compatriotic society explained that no meetings were scheduled because of the "fear factor." He continued, "We don't want them to think we have meetings because we speak in our language and they think we are terrorist[s] and all that." Another respondent commented,

> Certainly, people were on edge. . . . Our community was put under the microscope. . . . You lead a life that is painted [sic] with anxiety and uncertainty for what is coming the next day. . . . You start hearing rumors that the people who owned businesses are being harassed by government agencies. They are after them. People who donated money to charities now are worried: "What did I do? Did any of the money go somewhere where the government is going to consider it not so appropriate?" We all give money to orphanages in the Middle East. Well, if the orphanage is really linked to a group like Hamas, or Jihad, or Hezbollah, you start worrying about what they are going to say.

Given episodes of backlash in American history, Middle Eastern and Muslim communities were understandably apprehensive. One respondent asked rhetorically, "You remember people were talking about . . . [what] happened to the Japanese Americans? Could that kind of internment situation occur? Could we all be shipped out? Is it relevant that you have an American passport if your last name is [an Arab name]?" Another said, "The biggest concern I had, that all of a sudden, people would be behaving like they used to during the Iranian crisis. . . . See, I was in Oklahoma at that time, and I had a lot of Iranian friends, and all of the sudden, they left. . . . So I felt that we may be asked to leave the country or they'll quarantine us."

Some argued that at the dawn of the twenty-first century it would no longer be necessary to physically round up immigrant populations en masse and put them in camps in isolated areas of the country.[18] Modern technology has made World War II measures obsolete. The government no longer needs to house, feed, and guard a suspect population. Eavesdropping techniques and the powers the government appropriated in the PATRIOT Act make it possible for the administration to monitor their movement and actions. A respondent elaborated:

> I almost feel like there is a sort of internment . . . that's not physical. I mean, we have the technology now where you can intern people without putting them physically within a camp. You can make it so that they can't leave the country because if they leave the country they're afraid they won't be able to come back. . . . You're watching them in their home and they're . . . tapping their lines . . . e-mail. . . . They can't contribute to charities. . . .

People are terrified! They . . . take away from people the ability and the freedom to live their lives in a normal way.

Some people were so apprehensive that they left the country. A lawyer in our sample said,

> I was at a hearing, representing a client. I was waiting for our turn. The case before me was an Egyptian man who had applied for asylum. His lawyer was there, but it seemed there was no communication between them. He told the judge, "I want to go to Egypt." When the judge asked him, "Aren't you afraid of what will happen to you when you return to Egypt?" He replied, "I'm more afraid of my life here at this point than what might happen to me in Egypt. . . . I know of several people who left or are planning to leave the country. People are very scared."

Fear was particularly high among immigrant women, especially older homemakers who donned the *hijab*. One psychologist told us: "Our research indicates that fear among women is more than double the fear among men."

Understandably, individuals who were out of legal immigration status were also especially terrified. After a Pakistani immigrant family of seven died when their home caught fire in Brooklyn in 2002, some said they had been too frightened to call firefighters.[19] The data sharing between INS and the FBI aggravated the fears of noncitizens that they could be jailed or deported. As a respondent said: "I know of somebody who is a waitress. She used to drive before September 11th. She's out of status. And since then, her car is [parked] in front of her place." Another leader testified: "They're the ones who are targeted. They don't speak English, they don't understand the system, they're very insecure. . . . They are afraid to lose their job, or they're working under the table—which is even worse at this time because everybody's being watched. So even the Arabs that are employing them don't want to employ them anymore. . . . So they're the most vulnerable!" Still another concurred that new immigrants were more likely to "keep a low profile and not get too involved. . . . Those who have been here the longest have the least to fear. It's those who have no real immigrant status here or naturalization that face the detentions and possible removal from this country." Indeed the American born were the least afraid of backlash, though, as this volume demonstrates, they were not immune from being profiled and discriminated against after 9/11.

Compounding the fear among Middle Eastern and Muslim Americans was depression, sadness, and shock over the attacks themselves and a feeling of being excluded from the grieving process. Some of our respondents expressed sadness that they were not allowed to grieve and mourn the tragedy like their fellow citizens.[20] The president of a home-land association said, "We're just like anybody else who lives in New York City. We were shocked. We were afraid. We were sad. It's a tragedy that struck all of us. And for us as Arabs we suffered twice, or double the suffering [of] any other Americans. We suffered because we're living here as Americans. . . . That's number one. Number two, we were targeted . . . as Arabs." In Chicago, another Arab American echoed: "It's a crime; it's against me, you, him, her. I do not think about anything positive coming out of a tragedy . . . because it did target innocent people. . . . We suffered twice from it. We suffered as Americans; we suffered as Arab Americans." Still another respondent told us he had worked in the World Trade Center and had been there on the day of the attack. This man, who had managed to walk out of the North Tower before it col-lapsed, went on to say, "Actually, and truthfully, we felt the pain like double pain. Because first of all, I lost my very close co-workers [forty of them], whom I considered over the years part of my family. I spent more time with them than my own family at home. That's one. The other pain is for being part of Arab Americans, because no matter what the author-ities are saying . . . indirectly, they are telling the people that the Arabs [and Muslims] are responsible . . . for what happened."

Yet another response was bewilderment. The affected populations found the backlash confusing and incomprehensible. Why us? they asked; we are Americans, after all. The respondent who had escaped the World Trade Center told us that his children were asking him this. He admitted,

> The question was very difficult to answer actually because we all chose this country to be our home, and I came here when I was a young man, and my kids were born here. Also, my older son is a career sergeant marine, and he served in Afghanistan. And even though I'm a survivor of the World Trade Center, I have all these long memories in that beautiful building, which I was proud of, and being involved in politics and in social affairs, and being a father of a U.S. marine, but we felt in danger of being discriminated against. Thank God I did not feel so from my co-workers or from where I worked, because I've been with them for a long time. We know each other very close[ly]. But I was worried about my kids.

These compounded feelings produced what some clinicians described to us as widespread trauma in Middle Eastern and Muslim American communities. Mental health professionals measure trauma on a twelve-point scale that includes nightmares, continuous crying, depression, and lack of sleep. One researcher reported from a study conducted in October 2001 that "28 percent of this community had actually been traumatized by September 11th backlash. When I say traumatized . . . that indicates that if you score four or more symptoms that have been classified according to a mental health scale then you are traumatized 100 percent." A mental health expert in our sample confirmed: "The unique situation with Arab Americans is that they have been traumatized and retraumatized. . . . Grieving is a solution to somebody who is really traumatized, but the fact is that Arab Americans were not allowed to grieve. . . . We did notice that our clients had quadrupled their visits to us in the months after September 11th, meaning that those clients that we saw once a month we had to see almost every week."

Although for most Americans feelings of crisis surrounding 9/11 eventually began to recede, continuing harassment and discrimination, governmental or otherwise, and wars in the Middle East have meant that the crisis continues for Middle Eastern and Muslim Americans, and even more for Middle Eastern and Muslim noncitizens.[21] A year after 9/11, the director of an Arab American social service agency whom we interviewed assessed the situation as follows: "This is really what I would call the mental health status of the community. I observed, from our current counseling and treatment program, a continuous fear that is not going away. That fear is still valid and that fear is still enhanced by what I would call the war environment that we are still living, whether it is the war against Afghanistan or the recent statements related to the war with Iraq. Iraqi refugees, in particular, are very afraid." The conclusions of Victor Navasky (1980, 342) on the impact of McCarthyism seem appropriate here: "Few people actually died as a result of being informed against, but the pain was no less."

What degree of stress is debilitating and likely to manifest itself in psychosomatic symptoms? What degree of fear and anxiety qualifies as trauma and consequently is likely to produce post-traumatic stress syndrome? What is the legacy of heightened fear on family and communal life? What is the short- and long-term impact of these emotions on people's overall well-being? These questions need research attention, and we hope that studies by psychologists will address them. Admittedly, as sociologists we cannot do justice to psychological issues such as fear and anxiety. However, these psychological factors have sociological implications insofar as they constrain and restrict people's daily activities and lives. An environment of intimidation and fear forces individuals to keep a low profile and prevents them from leading normal lives.

## MISTRUST OF THE U.S. GOVERNMENT

The government initiatives led many Middle Eastern and Muslim Americans to be less trusting of the government. Their experiences contradicted everything they cherished about America. The principle that an individual is innocent until proven guilty was forgotten. One person complained that the "community felt criminalized." He believed that the government's actions had "created a lot of opposition within the Muslim community." Much as they wanted to believe President Bush's message to the American people that Islam was a religion of peace and his reassurances to Arab and Muslim Americans that they would be protected, the government's actions spoke volumes to the contrary.

Organizational leaders recognized the importance of President Bush's visit to the mosque immediately after the terrorist attacks and his public announcements. The representative of a major national Arab American advocacy organization in Washington, D.C., told us, "President Bush's appearance at the mosque saved many people's lives." He added, "But the government doesn't have any idea how damaging the Justice Department's initiatives have been and the actions of an attorney general who considers that this is a war with Islam." Leaders were frustrated with the contradictions, the "double-talk." It all felt like a witch-hunt to this respondent: "There was and still is a discrepancy between the two aims of the government. One is to protect the rights of innocent people against hate crimes and bias crimes, which is still something that the Office of Civil Rights in the Department of Justice is concerned about, and [the other is] the war on terrorism. And the fact is that they are sometimes contradictory." Another concurred: "Many of our community members . . . appreciate this commitment from the government that there is no intention or policy to single out or target [them. Yet] the vast majority of our community believe that they are . . . being singled out and targeted. . . The magic question is then 'Why these selective procedures, and directives, and policies that we are witnessing, which totally contradict this good commitment?'"

Leaders were particularly distressed that the political climate after the terrorist attacks had deterred some politicians and officials from addressing the grievances of Middle Eastern and Muslim Americans. Some felt that they were being relegated to a pariah status. A respondent said, "In the post-9/11 climate we have seen that some politicians, for example, are reluctant . . . to meet with us publicly or work with us publicly because they are afraid of the effect that that could have. I don't know if you saw what happened when FBI Director Mueller spoke at the AMC [American Muslim Council] conference. I mean, there was a firestorm of criticism . . . for . . . addressing this organization." A knowledgeable source agreed:

> I don't think the burden should be just on the Arab and Muslim groups because they've tried so hard to be part of larger efforts, but they were just dissed. One example of that is: members of CAIR have gone to community meetings before September 11—have tried to work with politicians, have tried to work with labor, but whenever they did, Jewish groups put on the pressure not to work with them. So they would have a speaker confirmed to address a meeting that they were organizing, and [at the] last minute they would [be told]: "[He/she] can't go." So I feel like it's not just a unilateral [case of] "They have no track record, they've done nothing." I think there's been a concerted effort to discredit them.

Moreover, this discourse is actually detrimental to government's policy. Seconding the sentiments of the leaders in our study, David Cole notes that "when law enforcement and intelligence officials treat a wide cross-section of the Arab and Muslim community as suspect largely by virtue of their ethnicity or religion, Arabs and Muslims will be less likely to cooperate with authorities and provide needed information" (2003, 183). This is something the country cannot afford, for the double standard leads the targeted communities to question the legitimacy of the government.

Given that many Middle Eastern and Muslim immigrants come from countries where people who speak out against the regime are punished, the post-9/11 initiatives were counterproductive in instilling democratic principles in America's new citizens. A respondent stated:

> The concept of the Middle East is [that] the government, the dictator, makes the law, and if you break the law you are helping the people against the dictator. So these two concepts [are oppositional]. [W]hen someone comes here, they can't accept the concept that the government cannot control your life. So by the time they have gotten to know that America is different . . . [that] a stop sign is not put there by the government, [but] by the neighborhood, [that] the government [only] enforces the law. You train people. You teach them. And once you have got them to a level to participate, to become more involved, to respect the law, to become active, to understand what is going, September 11th happened. The government came in and proved the opposite, put them in jail, searched them, didn't give them any rights.

## EROSION OF CIVIL RIGHTS

The Middle Eastern and Muslim American advocacy and grassroots leaders shared an agenda with the civil rights groups: they believed that the government initiatives, which targeted mostly working-age Arab and Muslim immigrant men, were eroding the civil rights of all Americans. As David Cole has argued (chapter 2), the Bush administration has been sacrificing Americans' hard-won civil liberties in the name of national security. More specifically, it has denied the rights of noncitizens. Cole writes, "This is a politically tempting way to mediate the tension between liberty and security. Citizens need not forgo *their* rights, and the targeted noncitizens have no direct voice in the democratic process by which to register their objections. No one has been voted out of office for targeting foreign nationals in times of crisis; to the contrary, crises often inspire the demonization of 'aliens' as the nation seeks unity by emphasizing differences between 'us' and 'them'" (2003, 4–5; D. Cole and Lobel 2007).

Concern over the erosion of democracy was common. A leader reflected: "It's to the advantage of our country to look internally in terms of how we are building our country. I mean what's happened with the USA PATRIOT Act, this is a big issue that impacts not only on Arabs. Right now we are the center because we are the most vulnerable and they are able to pass this kind of legislation, this kind of policy under the guise of the fear of the Arab and the Muslim, but this has a big impact on civil liberties for all Americans." Another respondent said, "We have a damaged democracy. Our democracy's being chipped away." Still another respondent commented, "Our country is right now at a crossroads. We are very close to taking a turn to a dictatorship unless we stand up. . . . Without our freedom, this country is worth nothing." Paradoxically, the U.S. government, while allegedly exporting democracy to the Middle East, was denying Middle Eastern Americans their civil rights.

Some leaders were more concerned that the civil rights agenda, particularly secret evidence, had been placed on the back burner. A leader noted, "I think what's changed is that domestic civil liberties issues are much more difficult now. Because before 9/11, as you probably know, President Bush had come out against the secret evidence. We . . . were on track to, I think, revising immigration legislation so it would be more positive. We had some very good discussions with the Justice Department on civil liberties for green card holders and people like that. So all of that's been put on hold."

Advocates remain concerned because they realize that if some of the civil rights Americans enjoy are removed at this juncture, it may be very difficult to reinstitute them. A second-generation Arab American immigration attorney told us:

What happened on 9/11 affected all Americans, including Arab and Muslims. . . . We understand the need to protect our citizens, but there are also fundamental rights that . . . our country is built on. . . . Acts that curtail people's civil liberties and rights are not proper. And that's not what our country is made of and I think it shows a lack of respect for the court system and for our congressional leaders, and our people who can make decisions. And in that sense we are very concerned, because once those civil rights are gone it's very difficult to get it back.

Constitutional scholars sounded the alarm; they endorsed the law enforcement system but advocated safeguards and built-in measures designed to protect civil liberties. Chishti et al. (2003) are concerned about "the character of the nation." The saying *E pluribus unum,* or "From many, one," is a fundamental component of American identity. They write: "We believe that an effort to include Muslim communities in a more positive way in the fight against terrorism would not only serve this American value but help break the impasse between security and liberty, strengthening both" (2003, 6). The authors further point to the negative ramifications of civil rights violations (8):

Domestic immigration policy reverberates in foreign policy through the perceptions it conveys about America and the character of our society. When we intimidate Arab and Muslim communities in the United States, there is an echo effect that deepens the perception abroad that America is anti-Muslim and that its principles are hypocritical. This reinforces fears in the Arab and Muslim worlds of persecution and exclusion by the West. It strengthens the voices of radicals and other detractors in their drive to recruit followers and expand influence, at the expense of moderate and other actors more sympathetic or intellectually aligned with Western philosophies and goals.

Thus, in the name of buttressing domestic security, current immigration policy may be contributing to forces that potentially make us more vulnerable. In the post-September 11 era, immigration policy and actions must be part of a new security system in which the measures we take to protect ourselves domestically can also win over hearts and minds abroad.

In summary, a nationally prominent respondent succinctly explains the outcome of the backlash:

I think that a newfound aura of fear and suspicion about Arab Americans and Muslims has become prevalent. I think the notion that Arab Americans are a fifth column, potentially disloyal, potentially dangerous—particularly when it comes to air travel—is quite widespread, more widespread than sometimes we'd like to admit. . . . But in particular since 9/11, a lot of people who harbor what I would regard as blatantly racist sentiments about Arabs and Muslims, commentators especially on the political right, seem to feel licensed now to say exactly what they think and even use hostile and abusive language, sometimes even epithets, sometimes even obscenities.

In the last two chapters we have analyzed the impact of different types of backlash on Middle Eastern and Muslim Americans. Deconstructing the backlash further by specific components, we started with hate crimes, profiling, bias incidents, and employment discrimination and then examined detentions, the PATRIOT Act, voluntary interviews, the absconder initiative, and NSEERS. We then examined the consequences of the backlash. We paid particular attention to the widespread fear in the communities under siege. They suffered a cumulative effect from the backlash. Undoubtedly, the biggest effect to date has been emotional turmoil. Psychological distress has had a deleterious effect on the victims' physical well-being and has permeated almost every aspect of their lives. The affected communities are more mistrustful of the government. Additionally, leaders are apprehensive that civil rights laws are being dismantled.

# 7

# Mobilization

The 9/11 terrorist attacks and the subsequent backlash experienced by Middle Eastern and Muslim American populations resulted in a few months of paralysis, isolation, and retrenchment. "People were in shock and they were hiding. They didn't know how to react or what to do," said a respondent in Brooklyn. "People are tending to isolate themselves and insulate themselves in their compacted ghetto areas," noted another in Dearborn. When we asked a respondent how she had handled the crisis, she replied: "We're just like anybody else who lives in New York City. We were shocked. We were afraid. We were sad. It's a tragedy that struck all of us." Nonetheless, the events of September 11 had changed irrevocably their status from invisible minorities to notorious suspects of terrorism. Given the pressing and serious challenges facing their communities, the leaders realized that the onus was on them; immediate decisions and actions were warranted.

"We have had to step back, trying to regroup and rethink our strategy," said a respondent, summing up the process. Another charted the tasks ahead: "I think we have to . . . take responsibility for certain things and get the American public to know us." They had to convince immigrants to believe in the American way of activism, advocacy, and mobilization, as one of them argued: "Our people are immigrants who bring with them the complexes of the East, they are afraid to confront authority and challenge them. But with time, as they settle here, they learn the ways of American society." The leaders delved into the process of defining goals and plans, which entailed airing opinions, debating conflicting perspectives, and reaching resolutions after negotiations and compromise.

Rather than inflate their constituents' fears, the leaders found it more expedient to channel their energies toward civic and political integration. Their behavior was contrary to commonly attributed characteristics of CBO elites: "engendering ethnic insecurity through highly selective and often distorted narratives and representations, the deliberate planning of rumors, and so on" (Brubaker 2004, 110). Indeed, our respondents were not "entrepreneurs of fear" (110).

Middle Eastern and Muslim American leaders seized the momentum of political opportunity and proactively claimed the rightful place of their constituents in American society. They declared that no one was going to scare them away; they were in the United States to stay. They framed their demands in civil rights and civil liberties language and historical precedents. They chose nonviolent, legal methods as their repertoire of collective action, such as rallies, press conferences and releases, letter-writing campaigns, other public relations techniques, and lawsuits, to make claims to state and societal actors. They openly critiqued the government initiatives and profiling being instituted against their constituents as illegal and un-American. They also built bridges with other ethnic/racial organizations, as well as civil rights and immigrant advocacy agencies. These coalitions contributed significantly to their resource mobilization. The end purpose of the mobilization was integration and political empowerment (see chapter 8).

While recruiting new members into their organizations, they told stories of brave victims of hate crimes who had collaborated with law enforcement and had been vindicated when the abuser was convicted. They challenged their constituents to call their representatives in Congress, as well as state and local council representatives, to influence their vote on pending bills. They also made numerous appeals for donations. The financial and educational resources of the targeted groups were particularly beneficial in the effort. They fought administrative excesses with their coalition partners.

In this chapter, we explore in detail the mobilization of Middle Eastern and Muslim American organizations in the wake of the 9/11 backlash. We illustrate empirically our model of mobilization (see chapter 1) with our interviews and the public output of CBOs (e.g., press releases). We begin with examples of claims making. Then we briefly reiterate the political opportunities pertinent to our case study. We follow up with an exploration of the variety of frames that were used to define group identity and goals and with a sampling of the repertoires used by the CBOs. The last section of this chapter is devoted to networking and coalitions as a form of resource mobilization. We should emphasize that the concepts we highlight—resource mobilization, frames, repertoires, political opportunity structure—are not hierarchical constructs. Mobilization is by nature a process that is circular, dynamic, and unpredictable rather than linear, discrete, and concrete.

## CLAIMS-MAKING ACTIVITIES

The terms *claims making* and *mobilization,* as explained in chapter 1, imply groups of actors engaged in social movements to make calculated political claims in the public sphere. Their demands are in the name of the collectivity on behalf of whose interests they speak, and their achievements are for the benefit of the group. In this section, we examine the pre- and post-9/11 claims making of Middle Eastern and Muslim Americans.

## REPEALING SECRET EVIDENCE

Secret evidence was a troubling issue for Arab and Muslim American advocacy groups with the passing of the 1996 Antiterrorism and Effective Death Penalty Act (see chapter 2). It became a campaign issue in the 2000 presidential elections. Both Republican and Democratic nominees voiced their opposition to secret evidence, but the Bush campaign was willing to take action. We were fortunate to interview a respondent who was involved in high-level negotiations with the Republican Party. We heard the following account in January 2002:

> I went to [name of high-ranking Bush advisor] three years ago and gave him a proposal that said, "If you want the Muslim votes, I'll help you get them. This is how you get them." I said, "I'll help you in my own time. I'll volunteer. I'll take unpaid leave. . . ." Politicians usually ignore Muslims because they don't want to upset Jewish voters. Yet actually Muslims vote [Republican] . . . I brought him *USA Today* and MPAC and AMC studies [showing that] Muslims voted two to one for Bush in [1992, but in 1996, two to one for Clinton]. So this is a swing vote. You will get them on your side if you give them respect.

The Bush advisor asked our respondent how this could be achieved.

I said, "The president has to visit a mosque. You have to say 'churches, synagogues, and mosques.' When they say 'Judeo-Christian,' you should say, 'Christians, Muslims, and Jews.'" So, if you noticed, Bush started that tradition. One time he forgot and I e-mailed [name], and the next day he used it.

This respondent next met with Muslim leaders and asked them what they wanted in return for delivering the Muslim vote for Bush. He argued that they had to ask for something attainable. The United States was unlikely to change its position on Jerusalem or Kashmir. The Muslim community perceived the secret evidence bill as specifically targeting their community. At a meeting in Austin, Texas, a fourteen-member Muslim group told George W. Bush that if he would state publicly his intention of abolishing secret evidence they would vote for him. Soon thereafter, during the second televised debate, candidate Bush called secret evidence an abusive practice, particularly damaging to Arab and Muslim Americans. Keeping their promise, Muslim groups announced their endorsement of Bush at the National Press Club.

Given the close vote count in Florida in 2000, Muslim Americans, among others, took credit for putting George W. Bush in the White House. The respondent who allegedly orchestrated the "Muslim vote" boasted that the president recognized that Muslims had overwhelmingly voted in his favor. As payback, a White House meeting of Muslim leaders was scheduled for September 11, 2001. Our respondent continued, "The day of September 11, we hosted a meeting . . . in our office. . . . There was a ten o'clock meeting before the lunch with Muslim groups. . . . We were meeting with the president at 3:00 to talk about secret evidence." Several leaders in our sample confirmed the White House appointment. Needless to say, however, the meeting never took place.

In the aftermath of 9/11, the goal of repealing the use of secret evidence became unattainable. More seriously, the Bush administration radically changed its policies vis-à-vis Middle Easterners and Muslims, at home and abroad. A Muslim leader who had met with the Bush 2000 campaign committee as part of the American Muslim Political Coordinating Council corroborated this: "We were almost successful in getting it [repealed]. . . . We had more than one hundred members of Congress signing for it—in three or four months. So it was really a successful campaign. Then 9/11 came." A knowledgeable source added: "We were working with other organizations to help get rid of secret evidence. . . .

Now, in addition to that, you have the PATRIOT Act, which incorporates it, and now, not only do we have it, it's being used. So ironically
things went backward."

## PROTESTING PROFILING AND GOVERNMENT INITIATIVES AFTER 9/11

The blow inflicted by the terrorist attacks to the aspirations of the
affected communities was temporary. The leaders guided their constituents in claims making: stop the hate crimes and profiling and stop the
detentions, deportations, and other government initiatives against immigrants. A leader we interviewed in October 2002 confided: "I would say,
quite honestly, the Arab American community in the Detroit area, before
September 11th, was seeing itself playing a central role in the future of the
state of Michigan, and maybe a role that is similar to the Jewish American community in New York or the Cuban American community in
Miami. . . . I think that there has been a bit of a setback. . . . But at the
same time, I am talking to people and no one is giving up. . . . People in
the end did not lose hope in the sense of fairness here in this country."

Community activists applauded President Bush's leadership when he
publicly condemned hate crimes, bias incidents, and discrimination.
They also appreciated the FBI's efforts to hunt down the vigilante patriots. A respondent said: "I have to give credit to [the FBI] Hate Crimes
Unit, [which] has done a lot of outreach." The Civil Rights Division of
the Department of Justice and the EEOC received praise for prosecuting
hate-mongers (AAI 2002, 7). Yet the leaders were highly critical of the
administration on the issue of detentions, deportations, the PATRIOT
Act, and NSEERS. "It's a real mixed message," a respondent told us,
and our entire sample would have agreed. The government was assuming guilt, breaking American law and tradition. A lawyer we interviewed argued, "Due process doesn't apply when you are a Muslim or
an Arab. What kind of justice is that?"

The civil rights community and the Middle Eastern and Muslim
groups mobilized to protest the detentions. In New York, they staged
rallies in front of the Metropolitan Detention Center with the blessing of
the New York Immigration Coalition and Norman Siegel, former director of New York Civil Liberties Union. An Arab American leader
recounted: "I was very frustrated. So Norman came up with this idea:
Why don't we start demonstrating every Saturday in front of the detention center in Brooklyn, asking for the names of the detainees? We're not
saying, "Release them." We're not saying who should be released or who

shouldn't be released. . . . But tell us who they are, at least . . . so we know what to do [and] how to help them." Given the secrecy surrounding the detentions, the CBOs disseminated information about their plight. Another respondent elaborated: "We tried to speak to our elected officials about this. Every Saturday we are holding the demonstrations at 29th Street and 3rd Avenue, from 12:00 to 1:00. And we are demanding two things. Release the names of those who are being detained, and release the charges. I got the information, I faxed and sent it to every mosque I know in the area and encouraged the Muslim community to go out and to demonstrate." Throughout the country, there were similar rallies, demonstrations, vigils, petitions, and other forms of protest.

Arab and Muslim organizations also used legal action in claims making. The government's watch list comprised a large number of Arab and Muslim names erroneously. Investigations by the Government Accountability Office in September 2006 declared that out of thousands who had requested that their names be removed only thirty-one had been successful. In response to numerous complaints, DHS has developed the Traveler Redress Inquiry Program (TRIP) for individuals whose names are erroneously on government lists. Between February and April 2007, TRIP received between six hundred and eight hundred requests per week. Arab and Muslim organizations partnered with the ACLU in legal proceedings against DHS and the FBI for abusing citizens' civil rights while crossing borders.[1]

On April 29, 2008, ADC issued a press release welcoming a new DHS and TSA program—to go into effect in early 2009—that reduces the problems faced by travelers whose names are mistaken for those of terrorists on the government's watch lists. By using passengers' date of birth, airlines will be able to verify their identities and reduce their inconvenience. The press release declared:

> ADC has been at the forefront of advocating for constructive changes in the "watch list program," as it has been greatly impacted the Arab-American and Muslim-American communities. In the past five years, ADC has worked with the DHS Office of Civil Rights and Civil Liberties (CRCL) and the TSA to address the continuing challenges of "false positive" identifications due to name confusion. Over the years, ADC has provided both DHS CRCL and TSA with numerous cases where innocent travelers were falsely identified as a result of having a name similar to one on a government watch list.[2]

SALDEF also issued a press release on the same occasion, noting: "While the Muslim and Arab American communities have suffered the greatest over similar sounding and spelled names, SALDEF has been involved with over 25 cases involving Sikh Americans who had to endure additional security checks."[3]

In another case, ADC and a number of civil rights organizations filed an amicus brief against the National Security Agency for violating the U.S. Constitution in wiretapping telephone communications. The case shows a "history of warrantless wiretapping and surveillance and its crippling effect on civil rights." Moreover, it argues that "appropriate judicial oversight must remain in place to require intelligence agencies to be regulated in their surveillance activities."[4]

## POLITICAL OPPORTUNITY STRUCTURES

The political opportunity structure model downplays the significance of individual grievances and attributes the emergence of collective movements to new political opportunities that make it possible for disaffected people to engage in claims making (Tarrow 1994). When political opportunity structures are "open" for claimants, it becomes feasible to reach the attention of those in power. Conversely, at times the political structure is so repressive that it becomes too costly to challenge the system. Therefore, the fate of any given collective movement depends, in part, on the larger context in that society (see McAdam and Snow 1997).

In chapter 2, we established that the 9/11 backlash was different from its historical predecessors. We attributed this difference to (1) the civil right laws enacted in 1964 and 1965, (2) the emergence of oversight organizations that monitor the government's actions and call foul when it violates the laws, (3) the success of the Japanese redress movement, and (4) the increasingly multicultural nature of American society in the last quarter of the twentieth century. In our estimation, these issues explain the difference between the treatment of Middle Eastern and Muslim noncitizens after 9/11 and the internment of native-born and naturalized Japanese Americans during World War II. In the language of mobilization theory, the above-listed factors cumulatively created political opportunity structures in the 9/11 case that were not available in the past. Without the civil rights laws and the ideological climate they fostered, persons of Middle Eastern descent and Muslim faith, whether born in the United States or naturalized, might have been subjected to more severe discriminatory measures. Additionally, new political opportunities emerged after the 9/11 backlash for Middle Eastern and Muslim CBOs in the form of coalition partners, as we shall see later in this chapter. These collaborations brought indispensable resources to the overwhelmed and beleaguered organizations, another important component of mobilization.

## FRAMING MECHANISMS

Scholars of social movements have noted that framing is an essential component of mobilization. When there is contention between different groups of actors, the claimants—those demanding, opposing, contesting—use framing processes to communicate their message more effectively. That is, they couch their message in culturally resonant symbols and language. Susan Olzak confirms that "ideological frames legitimate powerful claims against injustice and provide strong motivation for activating local group identities" (2006, 9). In the post-9/11 case, Middle Eastern and Muslim American leaders shepherded their organizations by distancing and condemning terrorists, demonstrating allegiance to the United States though outreach, and calling for the inclusion of Islam in America's mosaic. Their efforts to reach the American public have focused on spelling out the fundamentals of Islam and denouncing the ways in which Al Qaeda has misappropriated the true meaning of the Qu'ran and the teachings of the Prophet Mohammed. Additionally, the CBOs have jockeyed to serve as consultants to government agencies.

## DISTANCING FROM AND CONDEMNING TERRORISM

Right after the terrorist attacks, the Middle Eastern and Muslim CBOs had to examine the situation dispassionately and come to terms with the fact that the hijackers shared their ethnicity and religion. Many were relieved when all the terrorists were identified as foreigners. One respondent declared, "The good thing about it, after this 9/11 deal, there was no Arab American involved in this thing. That shows you how loyal Arab Americans are to this country, the United States." Another noted, "We are not going to have collective guilt. We are not responsible for this. This is not us. These people do not represent us." It was imperative that they condemn the heinous actions and distance themselves from the terrorists. "We are not terrorists" became their mantra.

A sensational news report aired on national television right after 9/11 showing Arabs in the Middle East cheering and celebrating the collapse of the Twin Towers. Howard Stern, the radio personality, announced on his show that Arabs and Muslims were celebrating in Paterson. This story was picked up by many right-wing radio talk shows and other media outlets around the country. Our respondents found the propaganda insulting. A respondent in Paterson vehemently denied the charges, saying it "was really a total fabrication and lie." Elsewhere in the country, another respondent alluded to the clip in the context of biased media reporting of the alleged silence of Middle Eastern and Muslim Americans to the attacks: "I denounced [the attacks] the first day it happened. When there was talk that it might be a Muslim or Arab, we denounced it. You don't hear that too much. You just see a lot of the images of people celebrating overseas or whatever, but every organization I have heard speak on the issue has condemned what took place."

Effectively, many respondents appeared in the media denouncing the terrorist acts. A leader told us, "After the president made his speech about not accepting hate and intimidation against Arabs, I appeared on TV, on all the stations, actually NBC, ABC, CBS, CNN, Fox. I made a plea to the American community that we are innocent like you. We have been victimized twice: once by the terrorists, and another time by those small-minded people who associate us with the terrorists."

Though many Middle Eastern and Muslim groups condemned outright the terrorist attacks, the chaos that ensued in the aftermath led to some internal miscommunication, as one national leader suggested: "A major hurdle Muslim organizations face in dealing with the American public is 'selective deafness.' In an op-ed piece in the *Los Angeles Times,* Khaled Abou El Fadl wrote that there should be a condemnation of terrorism by Muslim organizations. Muslims were very upset with Khaled's statement because it's coming from one of us now, whereas there have been numerous condemnations of the terrorist attacks."

In the years since 9/11, Arab and Muslim American organizations have become more organized in unequivocally condemning acts of terrorism around the world and the "We are not terrorists" catch-phrase has been used with their constituents, antagonists, and bystanders. Even the U.S. Institute of Peace agreed that "on the subject of terrorism and conflict resolution, clearly all American Muslim groups have denounced it emphatically, while some have gone beyond words by becoming involved with foreign policy, lobbying efforts, and mobilizing grassroots campaigns in the community" (Huda 2006, 17).[5]

Shortly before the first anniversary of 9/11, the Fiqh Council of North America, an organization concerned with Islamic jurisprudence, stated in a press release that it "reiterates its earlier, repeated, unequivocal and unqualified condemnation of the destruction and violence committed against innocent men and women on September 11, 2001."[6] After the London bombings, the Fiqh Council issued a *fatwa,* a nonbinding legal opinion, stating: "Islam strictly condemns religious extremism and the use of violence against innocent lives. There is no justification in Islam for extremism and terrorism. Targeting civilians' life and property through suicide bombings or any other method of attack is forbidden— and those who commit these barbaric acts are criminals, not martyrs."[7]

In 2005, Muslim American organizations publicized their antiterrorist stance by publishing a handbook entitled *Grassroots Campaign to Fight Terrorism* (MPAC 2005). It includes a section entitled "Recommended Mosque Guidelines" on maintaining financial records in good order, having all activities sanctioned by the leadership, not allowing guests to sleep overnight, and monitoring bags on Fridays and holidays, when mosques get crowded. There is also a section entitled "Mosque Etiquette for Law Enforcement."

The thwarted plot to bomb ten transatlantic airliners in Britain in August 2006 provided an opportunity for Arab and Muslim American organizations to further demonstrate their abhorrence of terrorism. This time, the FBI sent a representative to the press conference at the National Press Club in Washington, D.C., which was aired on C-SPAN throughout that day. Joseph Persichini, assistant director in charge of the Washington, D.C., field office, acknowledged the work of the organizers in combating extremism and called for stronger ties between law enforcement and the affected communities.[8] Shortly thereafter, a similar press conference in Los Angeles included law enforcement officials, indicating that perhaps Arabs and Muslims were finally being heard.[9]

The Danish cartoon incident in 2006 provided another framing occasion. When the cartoons instigated unrest, the consistent message of the Muslim American advocacy organizations to their brothers and sisters in Europe was: "You must stop the violence because the Prophet Muhammad would never have approved, and you are playing into the stereotype of Muslims as barbarians." Conversely, their message to foreign diplomats in Washington, D.C., was "We, too, value free speech, but your governments should condemn the cartoons as hateful and bigoted and work at better integrating your alienated Muslim minorities."[10]

The CBOs in our sample did not miss any opportunity to frame their position as bona fide Americans with views and values in synchrony with the majority population. When a Muslim man burst into the offices of the Jewish Federation of Greater Seattle, killing one and wounding five others in July 2006, Muslim American organizations were quick in their condemnation. Salam Al-Marayati, executive director of MPAC, declared: "Our fellow Jewish neighbors, and fellow Americans of all persuasions, should hear our loud and explicit condemnation of this murder and hate crime. No matter the differences in viewpoints on the Middle East crisis, we are all Americans, and disagreements should never go beyond the level of civil discourse we as a nation pride ourselves in. This act, although committed by someone seemingly mentally ill, is simply intolerable. We reiterate our prayers for loved ones affected by this tragic hate crime."[11]

The terms *good Muslim* and *bad Muslim* have gained significant currency since 9/11. Choosing these adjectives as the title of his book, Mamdani (2004) has argued that with the end of the Cold War Islam has come to replace communism as the "Other." The new global threat is interpreted as "the clash of civilizations," with the challenge coming from "bad" Muslims in the form of fundamentalism, Islamism, extremism, and jihad. The leader of a national Muslim organization further demonstrated this dichotomized view: "I came [out] very strongly against Bin Laden and his groups. . . . I have received many criticisms. And some of them told me, 'You are sold out to the administration' or 'You became like the Uncle Toms of the Americans.' In one interview for a satellite [channel], they told me, 'You['re] sold for the Americans.' I said, 'I'm not sold for the Americans. I'm an American! I thank you for telling me that.'"

Muslim American leaders also distanced themselves from Holocaust deniers who had convened at a conference in Tehran in December 2006. American Muslims distinguished themselves from their coreligionists overseas by acknowledging the Holocaust, denouncing those who question history, and agreeing that "denying the pain endured by millions of human beings only intensifies it."[12] As an "act of solidarity," they visited the U.S. Holocaust Memorial Museum, lit candles, and observed a moment of silence in memory of those who had perished in "one of the low points of history."[13] Furthermore, CAIR issued the following statement: "No legitimate cause or agenda can ever be advanced by denying or belittling the immense human suffering caused by the murder of millions of Jews and other minority groups by the Nazi regime and its allies during World War II. Cynical attempts to use Holocaust denial as a political tool in the Middle East conflict will only serve to deepen the level of mistrust and hostility already present in that troubled region."[14]

When six Muslims were arrested for plotting a terrorist attack at Fort Dix in New Jersey in May 2007, MPAC likewise deplored their actions with the following message: "MPAC is outraged by the religious justifications used by suspects, as revealed in the court documents yesterday. Their false and sinister understanding of 'jihad' in no way justifies their alleged plot. At the same time, it is crucial that public officials and federal law enforcement are strategic with their characterizations of the suspects. Any affirmation of the suspects' so-called Islamic motivations serves to isolate the majority of the Muslim American community rather than the criminal elements who mask their heinous and terrorist acts with Islam."[15] Additionally, MPAC stated that the indictment had been made possible because individuals from the local Muslim community had helped in the investigation. Seeking collaboration with law enforcement has been their goal since 9/11.

Almost all the public denouncements of terrorism issued by the Middle Eastern and Muslim CBOs since 9/11 fell on deaf ears, for the American public was not receptive to their perspective. In our own talks on the backlash around the country, audiences invariably asked us, "Why is it that the Arab/Muslim communities have not denounced terrorism?" One can blame the media's failure to disseminate the message consistently and continuously; the climate of fear, in which people seek a group to blame for the situation; the crystallization of anti-Arab and anti-Muslim stereotypes in American culture since 9/11; and the quagmire in Iraq and other political crises in the Middle East and the Muslim world, to name a few reasons. Indeed, it might take a long time to change the hearts and minds of the American people.

## DEMONSTRATING ALLEGIANCE

For most Middle Eastern and Muslim immigrants, the choice between their country of birth and the United States was clear, as one respondent poignantly declared: "Arab Americans are here to stay. . . . There are no other choices. . . . Even if we are immigrants, we have already made a conscious decision to come to the United States and become citizens. . . . So this is where we are going to die. This is where our kids are going to grow up and have their kids. So we are not going to go anywhere. So the only option we have is to fight for our rights and share the responsibility of providing security for the whole nation."

A young Afghan leader who had come to the United States as a child noted, "For a lot of us, this is home! Afghanistan, maybe we go there for a year of internship or something; not a lot of young people want to go back. Our lives are here. So we would like to be part of American society, American culture." Another respondent concurred, "I came to this country, many, many years [ago]—thirty-two, thirty-three years now. . . . I was born in Egypt, but I'm going to die in the United States. This is my home, and this is the home of my kids." A national leader asked rhetorically, "Where is home? Is it where the grandfather is buried or the grandson is brought up?" By declaring that "the former is roots," he readily indicated that the latter was home. A Muslim respondent believed the post-9/11 era was a watershed mark for American Muslims: "Is it being American or foreign? . . . This is our time to develop our American Muslim culture, and whatever it entails, because we cannot have dual loyalties." In short, leaders in our study were strongly committed to the United States, and they preached their ideology to their constituents.

While some immigrants concealed their Arabic- or Muslim-sounding names after 9/11, the majority deliberately emphasized their hyphenated identity. A respondent observed, "Before [9/11] I used to say I'm from Bangladesh. Now I want to make sure that people know that I am an American Bangladeshi. . . . This is my country too. Even though I happen to be a different color, and maybe I have [an] accent, . . . I have all the rights that the Constitution of this country [affords]."

Third-generation Arab Americans also mobilized to speak out on behalf of their newest co-ethnics. One respondent told us:

> I'm very proud of my Arab heritage. . . . They are dynamic people, hard-working. They put their shoulder to the wheel. . . . The fact that some of our families have been here longer than others, the American born have had to step up to the plate, because after 9/11 the foreign born were criticized in that if they wanted to voice their opinion, they were told, "Why don't you just go back where you came from?" Well, [name] is a veteran. I'm a veteran. My dad was a veteran. So we step up to the plate, because when they tell us to go back where we came from, we tell them, "Oh, you mean Dearborn, Michigan?"

## DISPLAYING THE FLAG

Immediately following the terrorist attacks, Americans of every class, race, religion, and region displayed the Stars and Stripes on their houses, cars, desks, and persons. A national opinion poll of 388 persons, conducted between January and February 2002 by the Brudnick Center on Violence and Conflict at Northeastern University, explored Americans' widespread flag display (Levin and Rabrenovic 2001b, 221–31). While only 21 percent of the sample had displayed a U.S. flag before 9/11, 60 percent did so at the time of the survey. Half of the sample (50 percent) flew the flag in their yard or from their apartment. But sizable numbers displayed the flag on their cars (30 percent) or their clothing (27 percent). When asked about their reasons for waving the flag, 92 percent said they did it "to symbolize America's strength and power," 85 percent said it was to "support our government," and 88 percent said they wanted "to show national unity against the enemy." However, the majority of survey respondents (95 percent) wanted to "support the victims of September 11th and their families." The authors found a positive correlation between displaying flags and having negative stereotypes of Arabs. Many flag-wavers believed they had to "keep an eye on Arabs in public places," some even saying, "I would exclude Arabs from my country." The study concluded that "the flag became an emotional symbol to a nation in mourning." In summary, exhibiting flags in public signified patriotism and "othered" Arabs and Muslims.

Despite this "othering," Middle Easterners and Muslims also followed the flag fad. Even the CBOs felt compelled to make sure that their loyalty and allegiance to the United States was unquestionable. In an analysis of fifty-two Arab American Web sites in Detroit, Los Angeles, San Francisco, and Washington, D.C., Nagel and Staeheli (2004) discovered that red, white, and blue were the colors of choice for Arab Americans and that "expressions of loyalty, patriotism and civic-mindedness were pronounced after the terrorist attacks" (15). Our respondents concurred: "Every Arab business in Detroit went out and bought the biggest American flag they could find. . . . Arab Americans do have a choice, but they feel safer by flying the flag." Sikhs too affixed patriotic stickers to prove their allegiance. "Yeah, definitely, they [put] . . . banners on the cars: 'Proud to be an American and a Sikh.' Even my wife put up one on our car," said one respondent.

## TEACHING ABOUT THE MIDDLE EAST AND ISLAM

The directors and board members of the CBOs in our study realized soon after the terrorist incidents that their primary objective was to enlighten the American public about their heritage because there was much ignorance on the subject. Congressional representatives, opinion leaders, journalists, policy makers, and even the educated segment of the U.S. population with graduate or professional degrees seemed uninformed or misinformed about Muslims, Arabs, and other Middle Easterners.[16] At the same time, there was a genuine desire on the part of the American public to learn more about the targeted groups. Accepting this challenge, the CBOs played an active role in disseminating information on these topics in a variety of media. This is a task that almost all the organizations took seriously irrespective of their mission. They waged a public relations campaign to educate mainstream America about Islam and the Middle East. The outreach took many forms, ranging from basic information about what Muslims believe in and where they come from to more sophisticated historical, theological, and other types of knowledge. As noted, some churches, synagogues, libraries, and universities sponsored talks on Middle Eastern history and culture. Such initiatives led to reciprocal invitations to mosque "open house" and interfaith events.

The director of a national Muslim advocacy group said: "The desire to know more about us as Muslims and about our faith . . . was important to us—that many bookstores have completely sold [out] copies of the translation of the Qu'ran, and many books about Islam." Another respondent in Washington, D.C., stated, "We've been overwhelmed by the media. We could not even respond to the needs of people who want speakers. . . . I went to colleges [across] the nation, . . . even to Helena, Montana." Another respondent noted that Arab Americans are "more present in the minds of other sections of American society now than ever. . . . And not only in a bad way, but also as a community that has a certain role to play and that needs to be taken into consideration."

In response to heightened Islamophobia or anti-Muslim racism, CAIR launched its print advertisement campaign "Islam in America," depicting a person's or family's story and photo. The first of the series appeared in the *New York Times* on February 16, 2003. In her analysis of post-9/11 nonprofit advertising, Evelyn Alsultany writes, "The ads attempt to redefine Islam and its relationship to America. . . . [They] assert that 'American' and 'Muslim' are compatible" (2007, 600). They impart three messages: (1) "delink Islam from Arabs"; (2) challenge the notion that Muslims are foreign or new, thus un-American; and (3) assert that Muslims are patriotic citizens. Only six ads were placed in the *Times* because of financial constraints (618).[17] CAIR also developed thirty- and sixty-second television and radio public service announcements featuring American Muslims of European, African American, Hispanic, and Native American backgrounds speaking about serving America and ending with "I am an American Muslim." These spots aired nationally.[18]

There was an increase in enrollment in college courses in the Arabic language and a surge in minors and majors in Middle Eastern and Islamic studies in undergraduate and graduate programs. Given the novelty and topicality of Arab Americans, some universities have created new lines and hired recent graduates. Islam has been an even more popular subject in academia and for funding agencies. Many new books on Islam were published, and new sites were developed and updated on the Internet to satisfy this heightened demand for knowledge. Institutions of higher education supplied the leadership, the knowledge, research, and the cultural products.

## SERVING AS CONSULTANTS TO GOVERNMENT AGENCIES

The Middle Eastern and Muslim American advocacy organizations were particularly upset that the government had not consulted them in the fight against terrorists. After all, they knew the culture, the language, and the population and would have been useful in providing feedback. A respondent noted: "We come from the community. We know what the feelings of the community [are] and what the problems are in the community, . . . [whereas] you are actually sitting there in Washington just giving these strategies, which sometimes actually do not really reflect what is really taking place in the field. . . . And my feeling is: go back to the community and get your marching orders from the community, not the other way around."

Middle Eastern and Muslim advocacy organizations have written numerous position papers and posted many of them on their Web sites. MPAC has published several documents in response to specific issues. For instance, there was one on terrorism and Islamophobia to critique the government's policies for not including a Muslim perspective; this framed the problem of radicalization of the youth and offered recommendations to the government and Muslim American institutions. Yet another paper criticized the lucrative counterterrorism "experts" such as Steve Emerson, author of *American Jihad,* who spread fear and hatred and scapegoat Muslims while not improving the security of Americans.[19] There is some evidence that the government has begun to listen to Muslim American and Middle Eastern American input. For example, speaking at a briefing on September 25, 2006, Congresswoman Jane Harman (D-CA) declared: "Since September 11th, the federal government and the Muslim community have been working together to combat terrorism. . . . MPAC's National Grassroots Campaign to Fight Terrorism is an excellent tool and demonstrates a love for this country. . . . The Muslim community is a valuable partner for the war on terror and because of this relationship, America is safer."[20] Additionally, the DHS Incident Management Team includes ADC, MPAC, and other groups.[21] The advocacy organizations' primary aim is to become advisors, ambassadors, and a resource base for the U.S. government in its relations with the Middle East and the Muslim world.[22]

The CBOs proactively negotiated with various government agencies to develop models and guidelines that would spare their constituents painful experiences. The executive director of ADC in Michigan worked with local law enforcement to develop BRIDGES, a national model for community-police relations (see chapter 5). Others worked with the Transportation Security Administration (TSA) to develop guidelines for security officers at airports and border crossings for Muslims returning from Mecca, Saudi Arabia, for the annual hajj (pilgrimage). Since an estimated twenty thousand American Muslims make this journey every year, it was deemed necessary to educate the more than forty-three thousand screeners at U.S. airports. In December 2006, DHS provided guidelines to thousands of employees of TSA and Customs and Border Protection regarding hajj. Likewise, TSA advised travelers wishing to bring *zamzam* (sacred water) to remember that larger than three-ounce containers were permitted only in checked baggage.[23]

ADC also collaborated with DHS's Office of Civil Rights and Civil Liberties in developing a fifty-minute training DVD entitled *Introduction to Arab American and Muslim American Cultures for DHS Personnel*. This documentary aimed to educate the more than two hundred thousand DHS employees across the nation.[24] It covers "the basic tenets of Islam; demographics; cultural norms and mores; and history of Arabs and Muslims, both abroad and in the United States." In its press release, ADC claims that "this project is another example of the Arab American community constructively working with government agencies to help in fulfilling the agencies' mandates more effectively and efficiently, while at the same time protecting the rights of all individuals who interact with agencies."[25]

Given the confusion and ignorance of many Americans, including DHS employees, about the Sikh turban and *kirpan* (ceremonial dagger), SALDEF has been particularly keen to work with government agencies to increase staff awareness. In January 2007, an audience of law enforcement in Washington, D.C., was shown a seventeen-minute video entitled, *On Common Ground—Sikh American Cultural Awareness for*

*Law Enforcement,* a co-production with the U.S. Department of Justice.[26] Prior to this, SALDEF developed a poster in collaboration with the U.S. Department of Justice entitled "Common Sikh American Head Coverings,"[27] and another poster in partnership with DHS entitled "Sikh Americans and the *Kirpan.*"[28]

Governmental plans to thwart radicalism have also incorporated the influence of Middle Eastern and Muslim organizations. In light of the London bombings, Michael Chertoff, secretary of DHS, initiated a conversation with four prominent Muslim American activists to brainstorm solutions for preventing homegrown radicalism in May 2007. In contrast to past discriminatory measures adopted by DHS, such as NSEERS and the planting of FBI informants in mosques, this inaugural meeting was interpreted as a positive step toward greater trust and respect. In particular, the experts recommended that the government replace the terms *Islamofascists,*[29] *Islamist terrorists,* and *Muslim terrorists* with *Jihadists.* Though *jihad* implies an inner struggle, its use to describe external struggles has become widespread in the Arab world.[30] Muslim groups have even been able to affect already proposed initiatives, as evidenced by the outcome of a controversy regarding the mapping of Muslims in Los Angeles. On November 9, 2007, journalists announced the Los Angeles Police Department's intention to map the Los Angeles Muslim community in an effort to prevent radicalization.[31] However, Muslim groups were quick to condemn the proposal as racial profiling, and by November 15 the police chief had publicly abandoned the plan, calling it "'dead on arrival.'"[32]

## REPERTOIRES OF COLLECTIVE ACTION

The word *repertoire* denotes the varieties of actions undertaken by organizations and coalitions in claims making (see chapter 1). Repertoires are also called strategies and tactics in the collective action literature (McCarthy and Zald 1977). They include demonstrations, rallies, vigils, petition drives, press conferences, and press releases. For the most part, these are scripted routines, learned cultural creations, that are repeated by actors in a given place and historical period. Yet innovations emerge as actors adapt to new situations such as new adversaries, repression by authorities, and challenges from allies. Here we discuss tactics used by the CBOs of the affected populations, then highlight the creative responses of the second generation.

The organizations in our sample have mostly solicited from their constituents electronic petitions and phone calls to elected officials for pending legislation or condemnation of terrorist acts or endorsement of an action by a government agency. Given the demographic profile of the affected populations—foreign born, of high socioeconomic status, geographically dispersed—these seem appropriate methods. With their coalition partners, the CBOs in our sample staged demonstrations, rallies, and vigils. Again, this makes sense because attracting large numbers of participants requires more than one organization or ethnic group to draw a crowd. Four days after the crisis, an interfaith group in Washington, D.C., organized a prayer meeting at Georgetown University: "Then we had a town hall meeting with the local TV station where the mayor and South Asian leaders participated." The "Day of Action to Restore Law and Justice" aimed to reinstate habeas corpus and due process and to end torture. It was called by the ACLU, Amnesty International, the Leadership Conference for Civil Rights, and ADC. Buses were arranged to bring participants to the rally in Upper Senate Park in Washington, D.C., on June 26, 2007.[33] The next day, the Arab American Family Support Center, a social service agency, organized a candlelight march from Atlantic Avenue to the Brooklyn Promenade. In addition to Christian and Muslim clergy from the Arab American community, other groups participated.[34]

An unanticipated outcome of the post-9/11 backlash was the empowerment of young people, who emerged as leaders and claimants in their own right. They demonstrated pride in their dual identities and courage to speak out. They applied their skills and talents, sophisticated analysis, and astute strategies to organization building. One leader commented, "I see young Arab or Middle Eastern students who became now actively involved because of the backlash." Another respondent lavished praise on young people, saying that they had "become more visible and known to the community than before. Younger generations have done a wonderful job—within existing organizations." An educator in our sample commented that young people had more confidence than their parents, adding: "Nobody is going to deny their identity for the sake of being accepted. . . . I am not as strong in my identity as my own children are. . . . They learned to be free from Day One."

Several in the one-and-a-half (born abroad but came to the United States as a child) and second generations started new organizations in the aftermath of the terrorist attacks (see chapter 4). Others joined forces to jump-start existing organizations out of their dormant status. Many increased their activism with more frequent attendance at a variety of political events, becoming more politically informed. Thanks to modern communications technology, large numbers of individuals shared news and views and even debated complicated issues in virtual space.

The second generation were particularly innovative in their claims making. They used arts, literature, and cultural products in their advocacy. Accompanying a thirty-minute DVD entitle, *Flying while Muslim,* merchandise such as T-shirts and magnets with the logo "FLYING WHILE MUSLIM—It's not a crime" have been marketed to increase public awareness of the problem.[35] Likewise, Dalia Ghanem designed T-shirts that address Arab American identity politics, such as a boy's T-shirt that reads "Future Palestinian Activist Inside."[36]

Performers found their one-person shows particularly effective in humanizing Arabs and Muslims to wider audiences.[37] Betty Shamieh's play *Roar* and Heather Raffo's *Nine Parts of Desire* had long Off Broadway runs.[38] Dean Obeidallah gave up a career in law for comedy with the mission to change stereotypes of Arabs and Muslims "one laugh at a time."[39] His "The Watch List" was shown on Cable's Comedy Central in March 2007 to rave reviews and possible prime-time showings.[40] Iranian American Maz Jobrani has teamed up with Egyptian American Ahmed Ahmed and Palestinian American Aron Kader to launch "The Axis of Evil Comedy Tour."[41] Maysoun Zayid, the thirty-year-old "Palestinian-Muslim virgin with cerebral palsy from New Jersey," tours college campuses with her comedy routine with a political message.[42]

Others have used the visual arts to voice their messages as the post-9/11 era has become culturally and artistically vibrant for youth from Middle Eastern and South Asian backgrounds.[43] Emily Jacir's and Walid Raad's artwork has been shown at the prestigious Whitney Biennial and the Museum of Modern Art. Still others have found their medium in photography, film, music, or fiction. Alwan for the Arts has used its space in downtown New York to promote the arts and culture of the region through film festivals, concerts, lectures, and social mixers, bringing together heritage youth and mainstream Americans curious about the Middle East.[44]

Suheir Hammad, a Palestinian-born, Brooklyn-raised poet and artist, earned media recognition for her appearance at Def Poetry Jam.[45] Her poem "First Writing Since" on 9/11 portrays accurately and eloquently the sentiments of her peers:

> fire in the city air and i feared for my sister's life in a way never before. and then, and now, i fear for the rest of us.
>
> first, please god, let it be a mistake, the pilot's heart failed, the plane's engine died.

then please god, let it be a nightmare, wake me now.
please god, after the second plane, please, don't let it be anyone
who looks like my brothers.

i do not know how bad a life has to break in order to kill.
i have never been so hungry that i willed hunger
i have never been so angry as to want to control a gun over a pen.
not really.
even as a woman, as a palestinian, as a broken human being.
never this broken.

more than ever, i believe there is no difference.
the most privileged nation, most americans do not know the difference
between indians, afghanis, syrians, muslims, sikhs, hindus.
more than ever, there is no difference.
                              . . .
one more person ask me if i knew the hijackers.
one more motherfucker ask me what navy my brother is in.
one more person assume no arabs or muslims were killed.
one more person assume they know me, or that i represent a people.
or that a people represent an evil. or that evil is as simple as a
flag and words on a page.

we did not vilify all white men when mcveigh bombed oklahoma.
america did not give out his family's addresses or where he went to
church. or blame the bible or pat robertson.

and when the networks air footage of palestinians dancing in the
street, there is no apology that hungry children are bribed with
sweets that turn their teeth brown. that correspondents edit images.
that archives are there to facilitate lazy and inaccurate
journalism.

and when we talk about holy books and hooded men and death,
     why do we
never mention the kkk?[46]


## RESOURCE MOBILIZATION

Resource mobilization draws attention to the importance of organizations and the ability to utilize their resources to coordinate collective
action for a political goal (chapter 1). Resources include the organization's membership base and ability to attract recruits; degree of internal
solidarity and cohesion; preexisting coalitions with outside actors and
groups; access to networks, free or affordable space, financial assets,
and high levels of affluence among members and supporters; lobbying
"know-how" and expertise in using the media; and capable and articulate leaders. As demonstrated in chapter 3, Middle Eastern and Muslim

American populations are fortunate to have fairly high levels of human capital. We also saw in chapter 4 that on the eve of 9/11 Arab and Muslim Americans already had several national and grassroots advocacy organizations. Though these CBOs were overwhelmed with the increased demands on their resources, their pre-9/11 infrastructure and coalitions were a springboard for jump-starting collective action. When Iranian immigrants were arrested under NSEERS in December 2002, the Iranian American Bar Association accelerated its activities and the National Iranian American Council and IAPAC were established; nonetheless, this ethnic group still does not have a civil rights organization equivalent to ADC and CAIR.[47] Here we begin with an analysis of coalitions, exploring their characteristics, their types and bases, reasons for coalition work, and possible conflicts within coalitions; then we explore political socialization. The remainder of the chapter examines resource mobilization.

## BUILDING COALITIONS

Given Middle Eastern Americans' newcomer status and inadequate linkages with the political elite, coalitions with other organizations and communities were indispensable. On the basis of her study of Arab and Muslim immigrant groups in New York City, Minnite concludes that when these groups found themselves politically "outside the circle" in the aftermath of 9/11 they were prompted to expand their organizational and "coalition-building efforts" (2005, 181). At the same time, as the backlash increased the visibility of Middle Eastern and Muslim Americans, their conspicuous absence from most networks, coalitions, and cooperative alliances became noticeable. Immigrant and civil rights organizations were first to include Arab and Muslim representatives at citywide and countywide forums, seeking their "insider" expertise to add value to their deliberations on the government initiatives.[48]

### HOW COLLABORATION WORKS

In the immigration and social movement literatures, coalitions imply alliances among ethnic and other groups for the purpose of joint action. The alliance may be temporary or a matter of convenience, but it is in the interest of each participant group. We asked the executive of a prominent umbrella group for immigrant rights about how a coalition was formed. At the time, she was starting a detention and racial profiling coalition. Here is her description: "First, people agree to make an official coalition. And then you pass a mission [statement], which I think for this group is going to be very general: civil liberties, constitutional rights, no discrimination. And then you get people to join it officially. So maybe we'll get fifteen groups initially and have a lot more groups join [later]. And you either do a couple of campaigns that everybody could participate in . . . a campaign to free all detainees."

Any serious advocacy work, especially at the national level, is accomplished through coalitions. When we asked a prominent leader in Washington, D.C., "Have you worked with other Middle Eastern, Muslim, or Muslim communities or organizations?" He replied, "Of course, all the time. Most of what we do is in coalition. . . . We're not large enough to do much of the stuff we do alone." The leader of a Muslim organization bragged, "No one spends 80 percent of their resources on coalition building like we do. We're part of so many coalitions that never heard of Muslims before."

In practical terms, coalitions depend on ties between the leaders or high-ranking staff. At one end of the continuum, it means that the two or more individuals have known each other for many years as professional colleagues, even friends. At the other end, it implies that these persons know each other's name and affiliation but little else. Coalition linkages fluctuate in their composition, purpose, tenure, and frequency of contact. We learned that ADC and SMART were part of a task force on hate crimes in Washington, D.C.,[49] but it is not clear to what extent their voices are shaping the outcome of the debates. Generally, coalitions are initiated by more established organizations; their national headquarters or a local chapter may orchestrate the claims making. The leader of a pan-ethnic affiliate confirmed, "The . . . D.C. office has not been as involved in this issue [of profiling] as the ACLU. . . . On the local level some of our chapters have worked very closely with the NAACP."

Organizational capacity, including staff size, budget, and structural complexity, is significant for the organization's ability to engage in collaborative networks. There is a threshold below which organizations are unable to participate in such efforts. If they are too small in terms of full-time employees, space, telephone lines, and Internet connections, they are unable to spare staff time and energy to attend meetings, demonstrations, or other activities that are called for by coalitions, as the following quote from a grassroots leader shows: "We've definitely been thinking about what more can be done with Arab American groups and Muslim groups. And we have not found the right avenue . . . or the right opportunity. . . . Most of those organizations have full-time staff, and, for us . . . we're at a disadvantage, because we're not there yet." Small organizations and those dependent on volunteer labor have no choice but to rely on professionally staffed pan-ethnic, supranational, or pan-religious institutions to advocate on their behalf. The representative of one such group said, "First of all, the Druze community is not a large community, it's a small community, and it is part of the Arab American community." This respondent mentioned ties with AAI and ADC.

After the terrorist attacks, organizations established ties according to the specific expertise of their partners: "On political action, of course we try to work with ADC. But when we get a case, if the case comes to us, if we feel that it is useful to involve ADC or ACCESS, then we will." Understandably, coalition work entails a certain amount of task sharing, as one respondent observed: "I think there is a division of labor. . . . We're called to do more of the kinds of things ADC normally would do simply because of the volume, and vice versa." AMC used to have a legal division, but it was discontinued in 1995 because CAIR had been established the previous year with the specific agenda of handling civil rights cases of Muslim Americans. AMC continues to espouse civil rights as an issue but no longer handles individual cases. One leader told us, "CAIR is doing good work when it comes to racial profiling. So we do not want to put resources in areas where other Muslim organizations are working."

Community members likewise learn very quickly where they should go if they want to report a case of profiling or discrimination, or which organization will have resources on voter registration or background information on political candidates. One respondent said of his organization: "When it comes to Muslim issues, they almost always come to us. They might go to their mosques, but the mosque will refer [them] to us." Similarly, the director of a CBO argued, "I don't need to have those [social] services if other South Asians are providing this. So I would like to actually refer them back to other groups." Likewise, it makes no sense to have "know your rights" pamphlets translated into an ethnic language if some other organization has already done it.

## TYPES AND BASES OF COALITIONS

Umbrella organizations and coalitions can be classified in a number of ways. According to Sonenshein (1993), the criteria for a successful coalition include: (1) common interests, (2) similar ideology, and (3) strong personal ties among the leaders, such as experience, trust, and memories. Jones-Correa (2001) notes that participants in a coalition must consider their ties to be (1) pragmatic, (2) mutually beneficial, (3) ideologically in tune with their mission, and (4) morally right. Coalitions emerge on the basis of at least three binding elements: identity politics, which produces intraethnic and pan-ethnic/religious coalitions; particular situations or needs, which produce interethnic coalitions, as well as localized ties with professional groups and institutions; and aims of social justice and civil rights, which produce "rainbow coalitions." Coalitions are even more fluid than "ethnic boundaries." Therefore, there is much overlap among these categories and coalitions.

Coalitions Based on Identity Politics   The number of umbrella organizations among Middle Easterners has increased since the backlash crisis. ACCESS, the oldest and largest Arab American CBO, has taken the lead in mentoring grassroots supranational organizations through NNAAC (see chapter 4). It was inspired by a "feeling of urgency" and the need for a "national response" and "a national agenda." With grants from the Kellogg Foundation and Americorps among others, an inaugural conference was convened in November 2002. By the fourth annual convention in 2006, thirteen CBOs from across the United States had joined as full members and a handful of others had submitted their applications.[50]

The Congress of Arab American Organizations was being formed before 9/11 but took on new significance after the attacks. Muslims have several pan-ethnic organizations, including the American Muslim Alliance, which coordinates efforts within the Muslim community and speaks with one voice. The Arab American Christian Coalition emerged after 9/11; one of its founders explained to us, "The reason I thought of this was that all the time we're being addressed as Arabs and Muslims, and all the time they're speaking about how much the Muslim community is suffering because of September 11. Well, that is not true. The Christian community is suffering as much."[51]

Even though the role of religion remains complicated and ambiguous in American politics because of the constitutional separation of church and state, Islam has been used as a mobilizing agent since 9/11. Mature ethnic organizations develop ties with co-ethnic, co-religious grassroots organizations and form pan-ethnic, pan-religious, or supranational umbrella organizations based on identity politics.[52] A respondent commented:

The last couple of months . . . [we have] been tightening up our relationship with South Asian organizations. We actually have been doing that, namely with the Taxi Workers' Alliance, which is an organizing legal assistance group for New York taxicab drivers. A majority of those taxicab drivers are actually South Asian Muslim immigrants. So we've actually been working with them on [some] issues. We're currently working with DRUM [Desis Rising Up and Moving], which does a lot of immigration-detention [work].

Multiple, overlapping identities of Middle Eastern and Muslim Americans can at times be conflicting. Building "Arab American" versus "Muslim American" coalitions is a dilemma in the affected populations, as a respondent explained:

[Our organization is] very careful to maintain a secular, broad, ethnic identifier of "Arab American" . . . [mainly] because you have to have some boundaries. . . . It doesn't mean we don't have coalitions, relationships, with other Middle Eastern groups and Muslim groups. . . . [Yet] there is still a critical mass of secular Muslim Arabs who . . . don't want to affiliate and don't want to see their primary identity as their religion but feel that their ethnic identity, cultural identity, is more important.

Identity has consequences for organizational membership, philanthropic contributions, and leadership roles. Nonetheless, as the representative of a Muslim organization reminds us, practicality may trump other considerations: "Do you identify yourself as Arab first, or do you identify yourself as Muslim first? . . . Even if they don't identify themselves as Muslim first, if they are Muslim they . . . will come to us [because] there is no other . . . community service organization." Some organizations have tried to bridge the religious divide: "Muslims organizations have been successful in many ways: to kind of get their name out and have their identity shaped and framed. And yet we are very committed to retaining the ability [to shape constituents' identity] in a secular way. Because what we do not want to see happen is a segregation of Arab Muslims and Arab Christians."

Situational Alliances    Situational alliances emerge as several organizations respond to a common crisis or need. New awareness of shared aims drives them to work together. These coalitions tend to be either interethnic or broader umbrella organizations, but they also include politicians and government representatives with the goal of addressing local concerns. Sikhs mobilized quickly after the first 9/11 hate crime victim in Arizona and became indispensable in coalition networks. Muslims' situational coalitions with Arab Americans are another example of this form of linkage. A representative told us that before 9/11 they "didn't have a lot of deep relationships with Arab American organizations."

Most coalition work in the post-9/11 era has included representatives from Arab, Muslim, South Asian, and Sikh organizations. It has become commonplace to see representatives of these groups at public events such as "know your rights" meetings and solidarity rallies. Undoubtedly, establishing commonality across ethnic, religious, national-origin, and racial differences has forced many new immigrant groups out of their isolation. One leader observed, "In terms of our relationship with South Asian groups, it's stayed the same. We've always had tight connections to relationships with them. But this is actually the first time our organization and Asian Americans have actually worked with Arab Americans." The leaders felt solidarity with their new allies: "I remember being on the phone with . . . [name] and they're saying, 'Oh, this happened to me, and that happened to me too!'"

Another example of situational alliances is neighborhood or local interest coalitions, such as the Unity Task Force in Bay Ridge, Brooklyn. The task force was formed in the late 1990s when Bay Ridge experienced a number of bias incidents in response to the Second Intifada. Unfamiliar with the situation, the police captain sought help. Father Khader El-Yateem, pastor of the Salam Arabic Lutheran Church, took the initiative to convene local politicians, religious/ethnic leaders and government officials for a meeting. About twenty-five guests attended the breakfast that launched the Unity Task Force. As the pastor articulated its aims, "We want to bring respect and understanding to our community." He added, "We're not blaming each other but learning to sympathize with each other.'"[53]

Several community members credited the Unity Task Force with the near-absence of hate crimes in Bay Ridge immediately after 9/11. One of them told us:

> The Wednesday after the attack on the World Trade Center, I called the Unity Task Force, the Christians, the Muslims, and the Jews came to the church, we held a meeting at night, and about 150 people attended. This was just for the leaders plus the media and the police department and the elected officials, the city council's Marty Golden came. We issued a resolution to condemn the attack and to commit ourselves that we will continue to work together towards unity, peace, and understanding, and we will not allow anything to happen to any specific ethnic group in our community.

An article by a student at the Columbia School of Journalism similarly reported that "the Unity Task Force, a group of Muslim, Jewish, and Christian clerics as well as politicians and community leaders in Bay Ridge, released a letter yesterday reading in part: 'We are a diversified community and cannot condemn or place the blame on a whole group for the actions of a few.' The letter was signed by 17 leaders and authored by Barry Levine, 59, who is the executive director of the Bay Ridge Jewish Center on Fourth Avenue. 'I hope people use a little thought before they take action,' Levine said. 'We don't need vigilantes running around.'"[54]

The Unity Task Force continues to promote interfaith and intercultural understanding after 9/11 through its active involvement in the entire community's issues and concerns. In May 2002 it sponsored a prayer meeting focused on ending conflict abroad and promoting tranquillity within the local community. This marked the first joint service for all community members, for previous joint prayer sessions had been held with only Unity Task Force leaders. The executive director of the Bay Ridge Jewish Center highlighted the power of this event for his particular congregation. He explained: "To sit and see how other people pray and to have them be witness to our prayers was a revelation. Afterwards, I talked to many of the people who heard the *imam* pray and they were mesmerized because they had not had exposure to this before." The president of the Islamic Society of Bay Ridge noted the broader implication of this prayer meeting, stating that "doing our prayers in a church and listening to other people say their prayers made you feel that human beings are all the same. . . . By having these services, we demonstrate that we can sit together. We can talk. We can agree."[55]

Social Justice Alliances    Social justice alliances are based on the recognition that collective bargaining is more effective in achieving policy changes at the local and federal level. We found two kinds of social justice alliances formed in response to the 9/11 backlash. The first was with civil rights groups that could provide legal expertise and had a history of monitoring government policies on human rights issues, such as the Leadership Conference for Civil Rights, the National Jewish Community Relations Advisory Council, and the NAACP.[56] Because of the need to monitor the post-9/11 government initiatives and help people caught in the dragnet, the Middle Eastern and Muslim American organizations were impelled to forge alliances with the ACLU and other such organizations.[57] An Arab American respondent explained. "I don't see [the collaboration] . . . as being able to exert more pressure [on the government], but I certainly see them as more skilled in the meat of the issue. . . . These are lawyers and legal scholars experienced in civil liberties issues, and those of us in ethnic advocacy organizations don't have as much experience in those issues. So they're our natural allies."

The second kind of social justice alliance was formed with organizations specializing in immigration and refugee rights, such as the New York Immigration Coalition. The coalition was founded in 1987 "to mobilize the leadership of New York's immigrant communities in response to the Immigration Reform and Control Act of 1986." Its objectives include policy analysis and advocacy, civic participation and voter education, and community education in health, housing, and language access.[58] It has since grown to include over 150 grassroots organizations representing a cross section of New York's mix of religious and ethnic communities, including Arab and Muslim CBOs. Membership in such collectives not only is prestigious but opens doors to other opportunities for the CBO and its leadership. As one respondent told us: "One of the first [groups] that I also got connected with was the New York Immigration Coalition, of which I'm a board member now. I've been connected with them almost ever since we opened. They also have a lot of connections with many different immigrant groups and ethnic groups, so I've been very actively involved with them. We collaborate with a lot of other service providers—legal services, domestic violence services, health services."

In other words, if ethnic/religious CBOs want to reach their mobilization goals, they must participate in a variety of coalitions. These interactions ebb and flow with the urgency of a crisis.

## REASONS FOR COALITION WORK

The crisis increased the scope and frequency of coalition participation; it also expanded organizational ties with more specialized and diverse partners. One respondent stated, "I think overall Muslim organizations in the U.S. felt a greater need that we should work closely. Before this, probably once a year or once every other year we used to meet, but after this in four months we have met five or six times already." Another knowledgeable source similarly commented that "with September 11th it became a whole host of issues that we were working on, and the meetings became much more frequent, and we were oftentimes really working hand in hand . . . on issues, especially from my perspective on legislation, trying to . . . repeal or at least modify the PATRIOT Act and trying to change the customs immunity provision that was in . . . a massive bill, trying to get civil rights protections into the Homeland Security Act."

The detentions in fall 2001 caught the CBOs by surprise; they were largely unprepared to handle the crisis. Civil liberties organizations—the ACLU, the American Friends Committee, the Lawyers Committee for Human Rights, the National Asian Pacific American Legal Consortium, and the Asian American Legal Defense and Education Fund—were indispensable as coalition partners at this crucial juncture. As one respondent told us, "The detainee issue has brought about some coalition building between civil liberty groups, Muslim community groups, and activist groups in general." Another stated that before 9/11 "you would run into ACLU every once in a while, but everyone had their own organization. But because [9/11] was covering an entire group of people, this forced everyone to make contact and know what the other one was doing." The crisis also created new political opportunities for coalition building. For example, the Arab-American Bar Association was invited to speak to the Chicago Bar Association on September 26, 2001.[59]

Secret evidence was a major impetus to galvanize the national Arab and Muslim American advocacy organizations to seek partners outside their ethnic and religious networks. As Muslim leader noted, the sowing of "the seed" of coalition work before 9/11 paid off when 9/11 happened. Another told us, "CAIR, AMC, MPAC, and AMA [American Muslim Alliance] are the founding members of the AMPCC—the American Muslim Political Coordinating Council. . . . We've been working with the national coalition for five years against secret evidence. . . . We have learned in our work against the secret evidence how to really work with the coalitions. We have developed a very good rapport with the civil rights groups, with the . . . interfaith community, with the ethnic communities, . . . pluralistic America." Still another reported that "before September 11th we had worked with groups like the ACLU and the National Lawyers Guild on the issue of secret evidence."

The government initiatives forced the CBOs in our sample to solicit the help of immigration specialists, constitutional lawyers, and experienced advocates and activists. Such professional experts were accessible through coalition membership. A leader said, "We felt a much stronger need that we should develop coalitions with other ethnic organizations and non-Muslim organizations: human rights organizations, civil liberties organizations, groups like that. . . . We also saw that there is a lot more support when it comes to open-minded . . . churches [and] religious organizations."

Another reason for building coalitions can be the new opportunities opened up at the local level. For example, as Chicago's Arab American community started participating in the city's annual Humanities Festival they developed ties with the administration and other communities. The availability of funds at the city level was instrumental in engaging community involvement. In another instance, a leader in a predominantly Middle Eastern immigrant region explained that their coalition was established "as a result of some clashes which took place between some Arab students at [name] High School and some Latino students at the same school. . . . We thought it would be a good idea for us to start some kind of an organization which defends the rights of Arab Americans and actually enlightens them to their responsibilities and so on and so forth." Thanks to coalition work, Arab Americans now serve on the school board of this town and are involved in elections for representatives to state and federal office.

Finally, coalitions can be initiated for ideological reasons. One respondent told us, "We have to start standing next to those who are also being faced by unjust policies in this country and standing up for their causes too. . . . We're not a monolithic community and do not necessarily have a progressive political agenda."

The crisis provided clear evidence of the benefits of coalition formation, summed up by one of our respondents: "We've had unprecedented levels of interest in Arab Americans and the Muslim community. There has been more coverage in the media. It's been encouraging to find allies. We've had solidarity and support from many organizations. We've begun to develop coalitions; 9/11 has kick-started us into advocacy work. We're now working with civil rights organizations on many fronts." Ultimately, coalitions were essential for procuring resources, expertise, and informational material and for mentoring newer or smaller groups.

## CONFLICT WITHIN COALITIONS: FOREIGN VERSUS DOMESTIC POLICY

Needless to say, relations within organizations and coalitions are not always harmonious. Conflict can occur within and between organizations that are or are not in coalitions. An inherent tension in Middle Eastern and Muslim American organizations is their dual role as advocates of both domestic and foreign policy. We asked our respondents to comment on how they juggled these often-opposing interests. There was a consensus that both were important:

> Both, domestic and foreign, it has to be both. Yes. And I'll tell you why it has to be both. Because, in terms of civil liberties, in terms of civil rights, it's our analysis, and I think we're absolutely right that you cannot separate the discrimination Arab Americans face from the consequence of U.S. foreign policy and attitudes towards the Middle East. That, in fact, were the relationship between the United States and the Middle East very different, we'd not see much of the discrimination that we do see. So much of it is politically tinged; the defamation from Hollywood, the civil liberties violations, much of the way in which the hatred and discrimination is structured, is rationalized in the minds of people, has to do directly with foreign policy. We cannot address one without the other.

Notwithstanding the symbiotic relationship between foreign and domestic policy, after 9/11 there was a more concerted effort to devote more weight to domestic policy.[60] A respondent said, "Yes, that is an interesting shift. At [name], we try to stay away from too many foreign policy issues. I will tell you that we are very focused on domestic issues—the situation of Muslims in America. And if Muslims are being affected for their foreign views in America, then we focus on that. . . . We tell [our members], if you are not recognized on domestic issues, you will not be effective on foreign issues—domestic policy first."

Sometimes alliances are made with traditional foes, leaving many wondering about such unlikely bedfellows. A representative of the ADL chairs a coalition of rights-oriented agencies that monitors hate crimes. This Jewish American organization has come to the defense of not only Jews, who have some of the highest levels of hate crimes, but also Arabs and Muslims. ADL and ADC have been active participants in this coalition. A knowledgeable source explained:

> The Jewish community in the United States, they are some of the staunchest defenders of the rights of houses of worship, and I know of a number of cases . . . where local synagogues have come together to help a local mosque establish itself because they recognize very easily that as a religious minority in the United States this stuff can kind of quickly turn against them. . . . I mean, they've faced this kind of discrimination before. And I think that this also is . . . a lesson . . . to Muslims, especially, . . . newer immigrants, who maybe have not seen this side of interfaith relations before, to see that we're partners in these kinds of issues when it comes to zoning and parking and cemeteries and mosques.[61]

This person elucidated: "We have a relationship with ADL. . . . They've never been in an immigrants' rights group. . . . To be really honest and blunt, . . . we don't invite them." Yet ADL is the sought-after member in hate crime–related business. "The ADL has been around a lot longer than the Sikh Media Watch and Resource Task Force has been around. So we benefit from sitting around the table and having a premeeting."

Because Arabs and Jews vehemently disagree on foreign policy, it is difficult for them to be on coalitions. "It's clearly an issue, because most Jewish organizations do have a policy for Israel, and most of the Arab organizations do too. . . . If we are supportive of an organization that might have a policy in the Middle East that would be counter to other issues that we're dealing with, that makes it very tricky. So . . . we don't do any . . . foreign policy at all, period."

More specifically, Arab and Jewish organizations have agreed that legislation regarding secret evidence must be changed, but they cannot agree on the details. A respondent who is on the board of an immigration coalition explained: "[Arab/Muslim organizations] are saying, 'Look, this is just fundamentally wrong. Secret evidence needs to be repealed.' . . . [Jewish groups] say they agree that there is a problem . . . in the way this law is being applied, but . . . they take a different position. . . . They're willing to support a lot more protections in the law, but not necessarily throwing out the law outright." A knowledgeable source confirmed that in "1996 [when] the antiterrorist legislation [was] enshrined, the secret evidence provision . . . was the first time we were in a vastly different place, where the Jewish groups frankly had strong feelings one way and everybody else had strong feelings in another way, and those were institutional issues. . . . The Jewish community so far has pretty much stepped back and allowed the civil rights community to address the secret evidence question, but . . . they're expressing concerns."

Before 9/11, Arab American organizations' focus on foreign policy kept them from entering a number of coalitions. Here is one perspective from a knowledgeable source: "I think the principal reason why the Arab American groups have not been central in the immigrants' rights debate [is] because we don't do foreign policy. We . . . focus on a domestic constituency. I think the inverse of that was true [of 9/11] . . . for obvious reasons. Folks in those communities have been forced to . . . look domestically because that's where some of the biggest crisis is." This person continued, "In a room where there were no Arab American or Muslim leaders, . . . it sort of feels like part of our job. . . . We know what it is and how to deal with using immigration laws aggressively and in a selective way. We have expertise in that area." These professional advocates with years of experience in the trenches have a strong ideological commitment to immigration and civil rights no matter who the specific ethnic or religious groups may be. Nonetheless, we were warned that the conflict could hinder progress: "I think we need as many institutions as possible working on the domestic stuff, and we just need them to leave their foreign policy—whatever disputes they have . . . at the door. . . . On domestic policy we need people to be unified."

## POLITICAL SOCIALIZATION

September 11 "was a wake-up call because it showed a couple of things. Unity did not matter. Participation was the key," one respondent observed. This implied political engagement and educational campaigns among the affected populations. "You just have to do the education. Arabs and Muslims do not understand the system," said a leader. We also heard that many immigrants shy away from "politics" because of their lack of knowledge and native-country experience.[62] An Afghan respondent elaborated: "Wanting your rights is not politics. Well, it is politics, but you're not joining a political party; you are speaking for yourself. . . . So we would like to teach them how to be involved in the community, how to be active citizens." The representative of a national advocacy group similarly asserted: "One [goal] is a civic—citizenship—organization to help Arab Americans become more involved in the electoral process in the United States. Everything from joining parties, to registering to vote, to working on elections, to running for elections, to raising money for candidates at all levels—local school boards, city council, judges, state officials, and federal officials. The second part of it, of course, is once you have people involved in the electoral process, you have to build a policy platform for them [and engage in] . . . policy and research."

Middle Eastern and Muslim American organizations taught their constituents the ABCs of political engagement. Their objectives included encouraging and enabling their constituents to (1) keep abreast of news relevant to their communities at home and abroad as well as domestic and foreign policy issues; (2) register to vote and voting at elections; (3) e-mail and phone political representatives to protest or support specific legislation or other issues; (4) support political candidates and representatives through cash donations and volunteering; (5) run for office; (6) volunteer on school boards or for other honorific positions in one's community; (7) intern with CBOs, reputable policy, immigration, or civil rights institutes, or offices of elected officials and government agencies; (8) collaborate with law enforcement in cases of hate crimes or other pertinent circumstances; and (9) learn a "citizenship curriculum," which one respondent defined as standing up to injustice and voicing one's rights.

The organizations disseminated information in a variety of ways, including town hall meetings, "know your rights" workshops, bilingual pamphlets, listservs, and Web sites. They also used more traditional methods. One respondent told us, "I published [articles] in three newspapers here [on] how to file a complaint." Door-to-door canvassing was another approach: "We went out to the communities [after 9/11]. We went out to Richmond, . . . Jackson Heights, . . . Corona, . . . Coney Island. We posted fliers everywhere, but on top of that we were talking to people about what was going on." Thanks to the Internet, organizations are able to communicate with their constituents relatively cheaply and frequently. National advocacy organizations such as AAI, ADC, CAIR, and MPAC have large listservs and send messages on average once a day. Even some grassroots organizations send electronic newsletters to their membership, and almost all CBOs have Web sites.

Most leaders mentioned the importance of voting in our interviews. One man said, "If you are a citizen, if you hold the passport, well, you should vote, and think who to vote for." But immigrants needed persuasion. A Muslim leader observed, "I know many people who are citizens but are not registered voters. So this is one area [we want to emphasize] by pushing people to go and register. Even if you do not like any candidate, go and register to vote." Another seconded, "Even if you do not like any candidate, . . . give [your vote] to the Green Party." A Bangladeshi respondent echoed: "After September 11 . . . people realize[d] that they need to . . . become voters and participate in the election process to . . . influence some of the people in terms [of] . . . policies that hurt the immigrant American, and also the civil rights. . . . The only way you can speak about it is if you . . . become a voter." The president of a grassroots Arab American organization summed up the rationale of political empowerment:

> I want people to get involved in politics and to get registered and to vote for what they believe is the right person to represent them from the local government, to the state, and the nation. However, we understand that it will take our community so many years to be politically active, noting that people came from the Middle East, where rulers can rule for a long time, and whether they go for voting or not, they know that they have no say. . . .

So the United States is different. If you don't vote, if you don't have a vote, you don't exist! . . . But if you have a voice and you prove that you are part of this country and you are active, it's not by just making money but to get involved in the politics, then people will listen to you.

Voter registration drives have been frequent since 9/11. Since its founding in early 2002, NAAP-NY (see chapter 4) has organized at least sixty-seven voting related events, according to its Web site.[63] "Yalla Vote" in 2002 consisted of twenty-one meetings, including "Election Day Outreach" in New York and New Jersey the weekend before election Tuesday, to address questions asked frequently during registration drives, such as "Who should I vote for?"[64] NAAP attested: "While we will not be promoting for any specific candidates, the information on our fact sheets will provide candidates' history regarding both bread/butter issues and Arab/Muslim issues."[65] NAAP's goal was to "organize a visible community effort that let political leaders know that Arab Americans are serious about their civic participation and that their interests need to be recognized. By empowering the community, we have a chance to give back to the community abroad by influencing policies that affect our people."[66]

In 2003 the campaign "Vote! Our Voices MUST Be Heard" scheduled twenty-two meetings in several locations. In February 2004, a "community forum" was organized to address the questions: "How does the electoral system work? Why should Arab Americans vote? How will my vote make a difference?" Additionally, during the fall, there were calls for volunteers to visit Arab neighborhoods and distribute candidate information; conduct "phone banking" (calling registered Arab American voters in swing states); and forward candidate information electronically to friends and family. Voter registration was scheduled on most Saturdays between July and October in 2004. The "Voting Caravan" in 2005 distributed flyers in Bay Ridge, Atlantic Avenue, Astoria, and Yonkers in New York City, as well as Paterson, Jersey City, Newark, Holmdell, Woodbridge, and Little Falls in New Jersey. As in previous years, "Vote 2006 YA ARAB" registered voters on at least six occasions in several neighborhoods, and its "Election Caravan" distributed flyers. NAAP relied on AAI for accurate research and analysis on candidates and issues,[67] and it referred members to its Web site, "Arabs Vote."[68]

Voicing an opinion on political candidates or elected officials at local, state, and federal levels and pending legislation is the next step of political empowerment. The specialists in this area are the national advocacy organizations such as AAI, ADC, MPAC, CAIR, and IAPAC in Washington, DC. Their staff are responsible for breaking down the news into easily understood, coherent content and then communicating it clearly and concisely when requesting constituents to take action. A respondent explained:

> Through our Web site we have the ability to put individuals in direct contact with their congressional members or any other type of decision maker. We've prepared letters on issues that we have alerts on. . . . We always have two letters at a minimum, sometimes even three, and we let people choose whichever letter that already fits with their viewpoints. We're not telling them what to think. We're helping them say what they already think. But we also get statistics: How many people are sending letter 1 and how many people are sending letters 2 and 3?

In January 2007, people on ADC's listserv received an e-mail entitled "ADC Action Alert: Contact the New 110th Congress, Let Them Know They Have Arab American Constituents." Members were to congratulate their congressional representatives on their electoral victory, frame themselves as Arab Americans who were "proud, patriotic Americans" who, "like all Americans, . . . want the best for our country," and express the hope that the congressional representatives would "uphold and protect civil rights and civil liberties" and "pursue a fair and balanced foreign policy."[69] Another action alert was in support of comprehensive immigration reform. In this case, ADC provided phone numbers, talking points, and every detail members needed to make the call to congressional offices.[70] ADC also sent out action alerts in support of civil rights and liberties. It advocated against an amendment proposed by Senator John Cornyn (R-TX) that would have denied green card holders the opportunity to become citizens on the basis of secret evidence.[71] ADC favored legislation (HR 1592, the Local Enforcement Enhancement Act of 2007) that would increase protection for victims of hate crimes.[72]

The political process requires money. Candidates, whether running for office for the first time or for reelection, require funds for their campaigns. Although advocacy organizations are not cheap to operate, our respondents were well aware of the stakes. Many leaders agreed that resources should be pooled, especially campaign financing and outreach, to maximize the outcome: "There is a certain group of Arab Americans who have a long history of political contributions who are quite wealthy and influential. I think [they] are starting to get more ready to be Arab Americans in how they engage in some of their political relations." Connections are also valuable resources in the political process. A Pakistani respondent bragged that the board members of his organization networked with their senators and congressmen from around the state. Another respondent stated that community power "revolves around the political process and evolves around money and using it wisely, using it in successful ways and intelligently."

Significant political representation at all levels is a major goal. "We say that Muslims in America are anywhere between, let's say, five, six, seven million. But our representation in the Congress or Senate, even at the local levels, city levels, our representation is nil. These are the areas that we see the need because these are the decision-making bodies, policy-making bodies of this country, and our voice is not there," observed a respondent. For many of the affected communities, however, this goal has remained elusive. One respondent stated, "I would like to see Afghans being elected officials. . . . Lobbying would be maybe a five- to ten-year plan." A Pakistani leader similarly told us, "We are encouraging our youngsters who just got their law degrees, or any other professional degrees, to get into the system."

Relations between the affected populations and law enforcement or government authorities were not always smooth. Yet the various agencies and the Arab and Muslim leaders did not miss any opportunities to advertise the importance of reporting hate crimes and the benefits of collaborating. In a case handled with the Department of Justice's Civil Rights Division and the FBI, a Philadelphia woman was charged in October 2007 for committing a hate crime against her Arab American boss.[73] She had sent her boss a letter that included such statements as "Remember 9/11," "You and your kids will die like dogs," and "I strategically planned death." A press conference was convened at the conclusion of the seven-month investigation. The verdict was announced by the special agent in charge from the FBI Philadelphia Field Office, the U.S. attorney prosecutor for eastern Pennsylvania, and MPAC. There were also press releases from the Civil Rights Division and ADC. Here are the remarks of Sireen Sawaf, MPAC's government relations director in Southern California: "The expedient, diligent and aggressive investigation and arrest of the suspect in this chilling hate crime calls for the recognition of the involved government agencies. . . . When individuals who are fearful and distrustful of the authorities witness first-hand the fruits of direct engagement, it contributes to the restoration of the trust and confidence the public have in government."[74] In a similar case ending in November 2007, the Delaware Department of Labor ruled in favor of an Arab Muslim former Exxon employee who brought charges against ExxonMobil Corporation for discrimination and harassment. When the court concluded that he had been "'continually subjected to harassment by his supervisor in regards to his religious beliefs and national origin,'" ADC circulated a press release announcing the verdict.[75]

CAIR has taken the lead within the Muslim American community in educating its members about how to combat stereotypes and prejudiced speech.[76] An illustration of its "Citizenship Curriculum" is the April 15, 2004, memo sent to CAIR's extensive listserv. This civil rights organization launched a "Hate Hurts America" radio campaign targeting the Islamophobia of Michael Graham, a radio talk host on 630 WMAL in Washington, D.C. Michael Graham had strongly supported banning an American Muslim security guard from working in a Washington, D.C., hotel because he was "Muslim and Arab." Graham had said: "Oh, you're a Muslim, oh, you're an Arab Muslim, oh, you have a gun around Jewish people." Incidentally, the Muslim guard was a U.S. citizen who had been born in Ethiopia. Graham had also said: "Would you hire an Arab Muslim group for a friend's daughter's Bat Mitzvah, I wouldn't, if you would you're a dope, that's not bigotry, that's completely reasonable smart discrimination." CAIR's message stated that "the increasing attacks on Islam by conservative talk show hosts nationwide is [sic] not only offensive to Muslims and other people of conscience, but also harms the United States by creating a downward spiral of interfaith mistrust and hostility." It requested that members contact the radio station to express their concerns about Michael Graham's Islamophobic rhetoric. Members were reminded: "As always, be POLITE." Moreover, they were given "step-by-step instructions on how to monitor local and syndicated radio programs, report anti-Muslim hate, file FCC complaints, and contact advertisers to register their concerns."[77] CAIR has also attempted to tackle this issue through preventative measures by requesting Muslims' financial support to distribute a journalists' educational guide to Islam.[78]

"Truth over Fear: Countering Islamophobia" is another example of the "civic curriculum" that MPAC aims to inculcate among Muslim Americans. The four-pronged campaign relies on MPAC's Hollywood Bureau to consult "the news and entertainment industries to promote accurate media portrayals of Islam and Muslims and counter distortions." It has since served as a consultant on a prime-time sitcom about a Muslim exchange student dealing with life in Wisconsin.[79] MPAC staff offer training seminars and workshops to media, government, civic, religious, and academic groups. They are developing an activist handbook. MPAC has released a report analyzing in detail examples of Islamophobia (MPAC 2007), and the organization has planned for its site to become a clearinghouse for statistics, action plans, talking points, and resources.[80]

Political socialization was taken seriously by all CBOs because all segments of our sample, irrespective of ethnic/religious affiliation, generational status, educational attainment, or organizational representation, believed that political participation was essential to becoming American and having clout as a collectivity. African American and Jewish American mobilization efforts were held up as successful models to emulate.[81] A national Muslim leader summed up these arguments with his "Dream to Mainstream":

> We may have businesses, we may have schools, we have mosques, we may have charity organizations, but without building our political base . . . [we] will always be liable to be taken in a storm of hate. . . . 9/11 has shown that our political work has paid [off] a little bit. . . . We are not at the table yet to really become a player, but we have started to knock on the door. . . . We tell our community, "It's from PTA to Pennsylvania Avenue." If you do not start with the Parent-Teacher Association of your neighborhood school, you're not in the American system. . . . If you are not part of the process, you will not be effective. If you are voteless, you are worthless in America, period. . . . Vote and you will be counted.

In summary, we have used empirical evidence in this chapter to show that mobilization followed the backlash. The bulk of this chapter illustrates the four components of claims making: First, the *political opportunity structure* after the civil rights era made it possible for the affected populations to mobilize almost immediately after the backlash, unlike the Japanese Americans, whose reparations movement took several decades. Second, the CBOs used a variety of *framing mechanisms* to couch their demands in a socially acceptable manner. They distanced their communities from the terrorists, denouncing terrorism at each outbreak around the world. They demonstrated their allegiance to the United States, joining their fellow Americans in "flag patriotism." Outreach about Islam and the Middle East was another strategy for enabling persons in the mainstream to understand their history, culture, and beliefs and to realize that Muslims and Middle Easterners are not inherently terrorists. Third, the CBOs used a variety of *repertoires* in their collective action. The second generation was particularly creative in using comedy, theater, film, music, poetry, and the arts to humanize the plight of Middle Easterners and Muslims. Fourth, *coalition building* was essential for resource mobilization. In fights for or against governmental policy, there is more strength in numbers. The leaders in our sample participated in three types of coalitions: identity politics coalitions, situational alliances, and social justice alliances. When Middle Easterners and Muslims worked in coalitions with Jewish groups, they often came into conflict over foreign policy. But the CBOs continued to collaborate on hate crimes and other areas where there was agreement. CBOs engaged in political socialization of their constituents, teaching them the ABCs of voting and civic citizenship.

# 8

# Religious Accommodation, Civic Engagement, and Political Integration

espite the painful outcomes of the terrorist attacks, new opportunities opened up for Middle Easterners and Muslims, allowing them to emerge as a distinct, visible category in American society. In this respect, their ordeal was transformative and empowering. In this chapter we first examine the Americanization of Islam, looking in particular at institutional changes and their limitations and exploring interfaith relations. Next, we discuss the leaders' visions of integration into American society, including getting out of the ghetto, gaining English fluency, and being politically active. As the saying goes, the leaders not only talked the talk but walked the walk; we present some of their stories of hobnobbing with political power brokers and being in the media limelight. The chapter ends with a summary of and conclusions to the entire book.

Since African American Muslims and converts to Islam in the United States have not been the main targets of the government initiatives after 9/11, our focus in this book has been on the immigrants. African American Muslims, who make up about one-third of all American Muslims (Pew 2007),[1] have a contentious relationship with their immigrant counterparts. We suggest three factors to explain the social distance between the two communities. First, because of the self-selection pattern of immigration, foreign-born Muslims tend to have higher human and social capital resources than the generally economically disadvantaged African American converts to Islam. Furthermore, the immigrants speak their native languages and try to maintain their cultural heritage, aesthetic sensibilities, and norms regarding hospitality and communal behavior; they also endorse endogamy. Second, these immigrants either arrive in the United States with racist ideas or quickly adopt the racism of the white majority. It is understandable that African Americans resent newcomers who assert not only their socioeconomic superiority but also their Islamic authenticity because of their direct ties to the Middle East and their knowledge of Arabic (Ebaugh and Chafetz 2000). Third, immigrants' interest in U.S. foreign policy in the Middle East and South Asia sets them apart from their African American co-religionists, who favor more public programs in the United States. A respondent concurred that there was "discomfort between African American Muslims—preoccupied with domestic issues—and immigrant Muslims—preoccupied with foreign affairs" (see also Mazrui 2004).

It is probable that all three factors are conflated as both populations act on their stereotypes of each other (see Schmidt 2004, 26–29). The leader of one national Muslim organization told us:

> Many immigrants . . . come [with] . . . racist attitudes towards African Americans. . . . [But] I think it's mutual. . . . Many African Americans look at their history here in the United States, their involvement in the civil rights struggle, and suddenly you've got these new people coming in and kind of telling them how things are and how they ought to act and how they ought to believe and how they ought to practice and what issues ought to concern them, and they're kind of like, "Take a hike. We've been here. We . . . know this place a lot better than you do."

Most respondents in our sample would have agreed that efforts to "bridge the gap . . . [are] happening at a somewhat slow rate." Nonetheless, some leaders are genuinely trying.[2]

## NOT JUST MUSLIMS IN AMERICA BUT AMERICAN ISLAM

The post-9/11 era has been aptly called the "Muslim moment" by Muzaffar Chishti, defined as "a period of rising Muslim self-consciousness, new alliances outside their own communities, and a generational change. . . . The notion of a distinct 'American Muslim' identity has gained new currency. It is an identity that seeks to assert its independence from forces abroad, one that combines the essential elements of Islam and the values of American constitutional democracy" (Chishti et al. 2003, 7).[3] In many ways, the accommodation of Muslim immigrants at the turn of the twenty-first century mirrors that of their Catholic, Greek/Russian/Syrian Orthodox, and Jewish predecessors a century earlier (e.g., Bodnar 1985; Conzen et al. 1992; Dolan 1975; Glazer 1957).

According to Timothy Smith (1978), religion was a major organizational principle for the mobilization of immigrants at the end of the nineteenth century. "The appeal of common language, national feeling, and belief in a common descent was sufficient in only a few minor cases to outweigh the attraction of religious affiliation as an organizing impulse" (1169). Moreover, these immigrants reconfigured their boundaries along religious lines—Protestant, Catholic, Jew, as the title of Herberg's classic study indicates (1960). Yang and Ebaugh (2001) state that the religions of the post-1965 immigrants differ from those of previous waves in three ways. First, they are "de-Europeanizing" American Christianity. Second, the new religious traditions—Islam, Buddhism, Hinduism, Zoroastrianism, Sikhism, Jainism—are becoming more inclusive in their membership, and even those that did not proselytize are accepting converts (e.g., spouses of the intermarried). Finally, given their resource-rich endowments in the U.S. diaspora, they are in a position to be influential transnationally and globally (see also Levitt 2007).

Joanna Pfaff-Czarnecka and Aristide Zolberg note the distinctiveness of religion in the assimilation process when compared to other immigrant characteristics such as language.

> Paradoxically, whereas the process of incorporation usually takes it for granted that immigrants will assimilate into the linguistic culture of the host country, the concept of religious freedom, which is now hegemonic throughout the West, fosters a very different social contract, whereby immigrants can maintain their faith and religious culture. Religious diversity differs fundamentally from linguistic diversity in that, whereas languages are cumulative (learning a new one does not necessitate abandoning the previous one), religions tend to be mutually exclusive. This is especially the case of monotheistic faiths. While syncretistic arrangements are possible at the level of individual conscience, this is not practical in the public domain. Under these conditions, it is likely that this culture will serve as a major vehicle of identity maintenance.[4]

In their authoritative book on immigrant religions, Ebaugh and Chafetz explain that immigrant religions adapt to American society by incorporating elements of the "congregational structure and a community center model of secular service delivery to members" (2000, 347; see also Yang and Ebaugh 2001). They define congregational structure as an ideal typical construct that "1) has a formal list or roster of members who elect 2) a local governing body (board or council) composed of lay members that makes policy for, and administers the affairs of, the institution; 3) has committees/ministries composed of lay members who conduct the work of the institution; 4) has clergy who are selected by the local organization; and 5) raises most of its operating funds from its own local members" (Ebaugh and Chafetz 2000, 347).

Diana Eck offers a legal rationale for the "congregational structure" of the new immigrant religions:

> Creating visible landmarks of one's presence in the U.S. is a part of the process of becoming American. Religious life in the U.S., while separate from the sphere of government, has one important governmental component: the establishing of tax-exempt nonprofit status with the Internal Revenue Service. One of the requirements is having a "membership," although being a "member" of a particular "congregation" is alien to many immigrant traditions. . . . As a nonprofit corporation in America, however, the community needs to have members. In addition, because there is no government funding for religious establishments, the community must raise money, necessitating mailing lists, e-mail solicitations, and fundraisers. . . . Indeed, the shape of "religion" in the U.S. has been molded by the exigencies of becoming a nonprofit voluntary organization and the necessity of competing as such for adherents and support. (2007, 220)

Ebaugh and Chafetz also contend that the immigrant status of new congregations propels them to adopt the "community center model," which implies, "1) the communal celebration of secular holidays; 2) the provision of secular classes (e.g., in native culture and language, GED, ESL, citizenship); 3) the formal provision of mundane services for members (e.g., financial planning, job listings, health services, emergency financial, food and/or housing aid, psychological/addition counseling/self-help groups, immigration status help/information); 4) the presence of recreational facilities; and 5) the existence of a community hall in which social activities occur" (2000, 354).

Irrespective of generation, religiosity, and national origins, the events of 9/11 put the onus on Muslims to reassess their collective presence in the United States. As Garbi Schmidt aptly observes: "Although faith can be practiced at home, institutions are the key when it comes to describing how people practice faith together and how faith becomes a visible element in society" (2004, 10). The leaders in our study would have agreed with the following respondent: "We found that there is a need to establish an American Muslim culture, a need to develop American Muslim [institutions] . . . that will address issues of Muslims here—not to import answers and edicts and rulings from the Muslim world because it does not respond to the realities of our environment here."

America's Judeo-Christian laws and customs have been inadequate in dealing with Muslims' religious obligations of daily prayer, burial rites, dietary prohibitions, and financial transactions, as well as recognition of Muslim holidays and the practice of polygamy, to name a few.[5] Mosque space and rituals have required accommodations to American values, sensibilities, geography, and the workweek. Women's roles within the mosque and the community have been contested.[6] In congregations where the faithful have hailed from many nations and backgrounds, negotiations have been necessary to distinguish cultural traditions from religious canons. Islamic schools (full time and part time),[7] social service and mental health institutions,[8] shelters for battered women, Islamic lending agencies, and philanthropies have been in short supply. There have also been theological matters to be resolved, even a new *fiqh* (Islamic jurisprudence) for Muslim populations in countries where they are a minority (see Al-Alwani 2004; Khalidi 2004; Khan 2004). In summary, as Schmidt reminds us, "Islam as practiced in America has become, and continues to become, American" (2004, 190).

## INSTITUTIONAL CHANGES

A number of modifications in Muslim space and Islamic practices have already been made in the United States. The founding of an Islamic center is an exercise in "Americanization." Leaders have to interact "with planning commissions, county commissioners, zoning boards, and skeptical neighbors" (Eck 2007, 221). The Islamic center is itself an innovation, as is the Sunday service, which attracts entire families, affording those who live at a distance the time and leisure to travel. Moreover, both the center and the service serve "inspirational, communal, social, and educational needs" (Jamal 2005a, 61).

Even the architecture of American Islamic centers has already adapted to local conditions. The Al-Noor Mosque in Houston, for instance, consists of a prayer hall accommodating about five hundred men during the *juma* (Friday) prayer and on *eid* (feast days), an auxiliary room for about two hundred female worshipers, a *wudu* (ablution) area, classrooms, a banquet hall, a kitchen, a fenced playground, a basketball court, an outdoor hall for functions when weather permits, a funeral home, and the imam's residence (Badr 2000, 194–95).[9] The community hall is ubiquitous in American religious architecture. Its main function is the socialization and bonding of the congregation and the "informal reproduction of ethnicity" (Ebaugh and Chafetz 2000, 357; see also Schmidt 2004). Islamic centers are no exception. Badr reports that "the attention to providing spaces where Muslims can not only pray but congregate socially illustrates the expanded role of mosques in the United States compared to their strictly religious functions in Muslim countries" (2000, 195).

While Arabic will always be the *lingua sacra* of prayers and ritual in Islam (e.g., Wolfe 2003), English is becoming the *lingua franca* in Islamic centers (see Y. Haddad and Lummis 1987; Ebaugh and Chafetz 2000; Yang and Ebaugh 2001, 277). This is evident in formal communications (newsletters, listservs, announcements, etc.), as well as informal communications, study groups, and even *khutba* (sermons), and is most prominent among the second generation. The hegemony of English will not come about without conflict between native speakers of Arabic, other immigrants, and converts. In Chicago, for instance, Schmidt found that Muslims from the Arab world "received religious authority simply on the basis of their national origin" (2004, 170). Creative solutions are certainly preferable. Wise elders at a mosque in Houston avoided potential disagreements among their members by hiring an Egyptian imam who was fluent in Arabic and Urdu (Badr 2000).

Another issue of possible contention among American Muslims is the celebration of American holidays. While many have been celebrating Thanksgiving, Mother's Day, Memorial Day, and Independence Day to assert their belonging in America's mosaic (Y. Haddad and Smith 1996), some maintain their difference.[10] For example, Al-Noor School in Brooklyn considers non-Muslim holidays *haram* (unlawful, prohibited). On Thanksgiving Day, the school is open and students are encouraged by their principal to shun festivities. "If your uncle's family or other relatives invite you over for Thanksgiving dinner, say, 'No, I don't do that. I'm a Muslim.' If someone invites me to their home for turkey dinner: No. I am Muslim. I am different. I don't do Thanksgiving" (Cristillo 2004, 184).

Mosques and Islamic centers in the United States are financially self-sufficient. They have to raise funds to cover their expenses such as rent, utilities, and salaries for an imam and custodians, and they have to be accountable to their membership. Generally, a board of trustees manages the affairs of a center, including financial transactions. The board may even dictate the center's theological choices, tipping the balance of power in favor of the lay leaders.[11] This in turn offers the flock in large metropolitan regions the opportunity to "shop around" for a mosque they feel comfortable with. Individual preferences may focus on the ethnic or class background of the faithful; whether the mosque is Sunni or Shiʿa or Sufi; and the degree of conservatism and Americanization (English speaking).

Women have gained a bigger presence and voice in the affairs of their religious communities in America. Nonetheless, gender roles remain sex-typed (see also Abdo 2006, ch. 6). Men tend to monopolize the positions that concern the spiritual and administrative aspects of a mosque, allowing only a token number of women in such status-enhancing positions. Women therefore focus on the mosque's school and social services as well as social activities such as potlucks and community *iftar* dinners.

An imam's duties in the United States are more likely to resemble those of an American rabbi, priest, or clergyman than those of an imam in the Middle East or South Asia (see Y. Haddad and Lummis 1987, 59). In addition to leading the call to prayer and handling all rites of passage from birth to death, even visiting and consoling the sick, an American imam has to be an educator, an administrator, and a fiscal officer for the affairs of the mosque, an ambassador receiving guests at the mosque and participating in interfaith encounters, a marriage and family counselor, and even a matchmaker.[12] Moreover, a well-educated congregation demands the equivalent in an imam. A respondent in Michigan was proud that his mosque had an imam with a PhD. Yet he also acknowledged that some imported imams may be simple-minded, conservative, or not the best trained because the profession has not been valued in the modern era as a vehicle of social mobility. He elucidated: "It was the last choice, in the sense that you were the runt of the family, couldn't make it to professional school, and therefore you were put in religious school. So you obviously already are not probably very capable, educationally, and maybe not intelligent either. . . . So these guys oftentimes were just brought from overseas, just put in places to lead prayer. Of course, they have to give sermons, and that is where the problem comes in. But they are just simplistic."

American-born imams who speak English fluently, know how to open a 401(k) account for *zakat,* are able to relate to the youth, and do not treat depression as lack of faith are in great demand.[13] In an attempt to solve the problem of foreign-born imams, two American converts founded the Zaytuna Institute, a full-time Islamic seminary in Hayward, California.[14] CAIR has publicly declared its policy of nurturing U.S.-born imams.[15] Such imams not only are faced with mundane congregational challenges but have the obligation "to lead the faithful in a faith under fire," as Andrea Elliott noted for the *New York Times* in her extensive coverage of one imam in Bay Ridge. An imam "must keep the trust of his congregants, who feel unfairly singled out by law enforcement," yet respond to the pressure to cooperate with the authorities. Elliott adds, "For American *imams*, no subject is more charged than terrorism. While under scrutiny themselves, *imams* are often called upon to usher the authorities past the barriers of fear that surround their communities. Many are reluctant. They worry that their assistance will backfire in unwarranted investigations, or a loss of credibility at the pulpit."[16]

The legacy of immigrant groups in U.S. history endures today with reputable institutions such as the Society of St. Vincent de Paul, the American Friends Service Committee, the Lutheran Medical Center, and Jewish Social Services, to name a few. Muslim Americans are likely to follow in their footsteps, though there may be a lag in some of the institutions. For example, nursing homes are still taboo for most immigrants and their children. Nonetheless, such institutions are likely to emerge in the future. Americanization, the lengthening of the life span, the ability of modern medicine to keep patients alive but not necessarily in good health, and changes in family patterns will affect American Muslims and necessitate communal responses.[17]

## MUSLIM IDENTITY AND THE SECOND GENERATION

Coming from countries where Islam is the majority religion, immigrants find their faith threatened and feel insecure. To counter these feelings, they often immerse themselves in the study of their religious traditions (see Ebaugh and Chafetz 2000, 336). The "Americanization" experience ignites their zeal to maintain their ancestral faith in the New World and, just as important, to incorporate religion as a prominent component of their identity. Since religious affiliation is a "recognized and meaningful social category in the U.S.," it allows immigrants to "secure their sense of identity and also gain acceptance in the wider society" (Eck 2007, 215).

Jennifer Bryan (2005) found that the Muslims in Jersey City reacted to the backlash by trying to "show America 'the true Islam.'" Their experience of "living in terror" induced more traditional practices. There was a "renewed and intensified interest in the Qu'ran" (Bryan 2005, 152; see also Cainkar 2004b); women donned the *hijab;* even wedding celebrations became less lavish and reverted to appointing separate halls for men and women. She writes, "The observation that most Arab Muslims in Jersey City did not attempt to blend in or downplay their Arab or Muslim appearance presents a challenge to the classic model of assimilation" (Bryan 2005, 151).

While growing up, the children of immigrant Muslims may feel that their religious affiliation is ascribed, but as adults they have a choice in whether to practice the faith they inherited because in the United States all religious institutions "are voluntary associations" (Ebaugh and Chafetz 2000, 447). Many Muslim leaders in our sample were well aware of these patterns; one stated that the "younger generation is challenging the Islam of the older generation. Young people want to know." Certainly, their faith is no longer taken for granted; they want to know about jihad, human rights in Muslim countries, and especially how Muslim countries treat non-Muslims. Our respondent added, "Whoever picks Islam must be serious, since it is not glamorous. . . . 9/11 came as a sobering event."

Some second-generation Muslims have chosen the academic route to pursue their investigations into the religion of their ancestors (e.g., Aslan 2005; Safi 2003). Given their native English proficiency and familiarity with the American media, they have become spokespersons for their communities whether or not they are observant or belong to a mosque. Some have dared to defy traditional strictures within Islamic communities in North America by advocating for greater equality for women and gay and lesbian Muslims (e.g., Abdul-Ghafur 2005; Husain 2006; Manji 2003), even creating organizations for stigmatized Muslims such as the Al-Fatiha Foundation for Lesbian, Gay, Bisexual, and Transgendered (LGBT) Muslims.[18]

## ACCOMMODATION CHALLENGES OF AMERICAN ISLAM

Muslim immigrants have made significant accommodations to practice their faith in the United States. These changes have generally been within the religious and Islamic institutional structures and at the individual level. Schmidt observes that "just as American society values individual choice, the central components of the formation of Islam and Islamic identities in America are personal choice, conviction, and dedication. Parents choose to send their children to weekend schools and Muslim full-time schools. Muslim students choose to enroll in the Muslim Students' Association. Young women choose the *hijab*. Muslim professionals choose to dedicate their spare time to publicizing and explaining Islam"

(2004, 190). At the institutional level, however, American society has been slow in making it possible for Muslims to practice their faith more easily. They are denied the accommodations allowed Christians and Jews.

In regions of the country where the population density of Muslims is high, community activists have been able to negotiate with local authorities for a number of accommodations. Dearborn public schools, for example, have come to recognize Muslim holidays, permit the wearing of the *hijab,* create prayer facilities on school property, and offer *halal* food in the cafeteria. In her ethnography of Cobb High School in Dearborn, where 40 percent of the student body was Muslim (mostly Yemeni), Loukia Sarroub (2005) chronicles how some of these accommodations were institutionalized. The principal of the school and district administrators were committed to honoring Eid-al-Fitr (the holiday marking the end of Ramadan) and Eid-al-Adha (the holiday celebrating Abraham's sacrifice), but they were afraid that low school attendance would cost them state funding on the basis of a Michigan law. Just before Eid-al-Adha in 1997, which was to begin on a Thursday, teachers received a memo stating: "Without being insensitive to the importance of this religious holiday, if there is a way for you to encourage your Muslim families to delay the holiday celebration till the weekend it would be beneficial to our district" (87). Understandably, the Arab community revolted and ADC was called in. Sarroub states that "Detroit area newspaper portrayals included descriptive phrases such as 'strife,' 'ethnic turmoil,' 'conflict,' 'understanding needed,' 'ethnic fighting,' 'cultural clash,' and 'unrest'" (89). Similar negotiations mirrored this case elsewhere in the country.[19]

The Workplace Religious Freedom Act illustrates an accommodation at the federal level. Introduced in Congress in March 2005, this bipartisan bill endorsed by Sikhs, Orthodox Jews, and Muslims will criminalize discrimination against the religious practice of employees. If it is passed, employers will have to make reasonable accommodations, including the Sikh beard and turban and Muslim *hijab;* prayer at work; breaking of the fast at sunset during Ramadan; and observance of holy days such as Eid-al-Adha.[20]

In tandem with state accommodations, the marketplace is slowly responding to Muslims as niche consumers. Entrepreneurs are courting them as investors;[21] designers and retailers are manufacturing fashionable but modest outfits to Muslim women;[22] advertisers are becoming more sensitive to Muslim Americans' needs.[23] Physicians and other professionals are also finding it expedient to serve their patients with cultural sensitivity. For example, administrators at a medical center in Portland, Maine, developed a two-piece exam gown after they discovered that Muslim Somali women were skipping appointments because they considered the traditional short gown shameful.[24] Even the U.S. military is reaching out to Muslim American recruits by engaging part-time and full-time imams as chaplains at academies and bases, designating space as prayer rooms, and encouraging non-Muslim high-ranking officers to celebrate Muslim holy days with their staff.[25]

## INTERFAITH RELATIONS

In *America and the Challenges of Religious Diversity,* the sociologist Robert Wuthnow (2005) argues that the immigration of non-Western religious groups in the last decades of the twentieth century has given rise to serious theological and social challenges. If Americans want to truly live in a pluralist society, there is much work to be done. Wuthnow explains that generally interfaith ventures tend to fail because of "opposition from other religious groups in the community, indifference, real or perceived concerns" (301). Opposition results from people who care about their own faith and are willing to fight over it. And generally people are too busy with their work, family, and other interests to dedicate unlimited time and energy to a new venture.

According to Wuthnow, the most successful interfaith projects have "concrete, task-specific objectives" such as "disaster relief, medical care, poverty assistance, aid for women and children"[26] (2005, 303). Indeed, as a respondent testifies, interfaith exchanges are part of a repertoire of mobilization for social justice and other humanitarian agendas:

> The interfaith organization, the one which I am part of, it's not only focused on religious issues. It does work on the critical issues facing the metropolitan area. We discuss the issues on AIDS. We discuss the issues on racial discrimination, violence in the society, drugs . . . many issues which are facing the entire area. I remember there were riots many years ago in the Latino community. . . . We also discussed the issues when Farrakhan held a rally in Washington . . . the Million Man March. And then we also were involved in the Million Mom March, which was the anti-gun coalition. So it has never been just limited to discussing theological issues and similarities and differences.

Rather than engage in debates about beliefs and the nature of God, it is best to build personal relationships among individuals from different religious groups.

All parties should "be willing to grant respect to the other traditions—respect that recognizes the sincerity and seriousness with which followers of other religions practice their faith" (Wuthnow 2005, 305). Interfaith dialogue promotes a "shared sense of humanity and spirituality" (Saeed 2002, 47), increases trust and respect, debunks negative stereotypes, fosters cohesion among Muslims, furthers their integration, and acknowledges that they belong in the United States (J. Smith 2004). By explaining that *Allah* is Arabic for "God," an Arab clergyman illustrates one of the objectives of interfaith projects.

> [Hate-mongers] think Muslims just believe in *Allah* so *Allah* is the God of the Muslims. When I hold the services here Sunday morning, I pray for *Allah! Allah* is not a Muslim word; it's an Arabic word. Friday night, the same week of the tragedy, I was invited to [name] Jewish Center to speak in their Friday night service. And I spoke about unity and peace and how we should work together and be united at this time, as New Yorkers, as Americans against anything that will divide us, and to make sure that those who are suffering in the community, that we respond to their needs and bring the message of hope and comfort to them.

Interfaith relations proliferated after 9/11. These exchanges mobilized Muslim Americans and contributed to the internal dialogue on American Islam. Much of this effort took place between individual congregations in neighborhoods across the country. It was part of a massive grassroots campaign to educate the American population about Arabs and Muslims (chapter 7). The National Council of Churches U.S.A., the Interfaith Conference of Metropolitan Washington, the North American Interfaith Network, the Interfaith Center of New York, and the American Sufi Muslim Association, among others, provided leadership and coordination in interfaith activities.[27]

Interfaith exchanges are particularly significant to immigrant religious groups in establishing connections and resources, as the following respondent describes: "I tried to establish relations . . . with JCRC [the Jewish Community Relations Council]. They were very helpful to us and have been supportive ever since. . . . So whenever I needed help . . . I would go to them. I must admit that this helped us a lot. This is New York. The Jewish community has their connections. They know the right people. If you have credibility with them, I think they will help you." A leader in Dearborn credited the city's ability to weather the 9/11 crisis to the religious leaders' investments in interfaith networks: "We had many activities across the community where people—Muslims, Christians, and other groups—were invited to participate in some kind of a peace event, a 'prayer for peace' type of event. The mayor was there. Community leaders were there. Priests from all religions were represented. Our Muslim imams in the community were very, very active and effective. They went to the Interfaith Roundtable, so they know other religious leaders."

Because interfaith activity is valued in a pluralist society such as the United States, mosques hosted "open house" events and invited Christian and Jewish neighbors to *iftar* dinners.[28] A respondent in Chicago illustrates: "During Ramadan . . . the Christians joined the Muslims for breaking the fast. There are people in this neighborhood who belong to the Christian peace team who live around here, they had newly moved here. They even fasted during Ramadan with the Muslims. So these were really important gestures that were happening in this society." There were also creative productions to demonstrate the commonality between Jews, Christians, and Muslims. We attended a performance staged by the American Sufi Muslim Association, entitled *Cordoba Bread Fest,* at St. Bartholomew's in New York City in June 2003. Harkening back to eleventh-century Moorish Spain, the play portrayed the Abrahamic faiths as living side by side in harmony.[29]

The next quote illustrates how a multireligious neighborhood in Chicago found common ground in the backlash crisis:

> Every Friday, the nuns from the Sisters of St. Kashmir and the other churches in the area came together and made a human chain around the mosque at the time of prayer. So they [the nuns] would come, the [Southwest] Collaborative would come, the Latino organization would come, the other organizations, the [Arab American] Action Network, and the pastors and preachers from the area would come, and we would make stops as we were coming, and they would read different passages that were prepared about living together and respecting one another, embracing our different religions, and different cultures and all of that. For the person that is going into the mosque, those older persons, seeing the nuns and the priests surrounding [the mosque] and saying, "We defend your right to pray," I'm telling you, I was in tears every week.

Sociologist Kai Erikson observes that every disaster brings "a stage of euphoria" and "post-disaster utopia," the formation of a "community of sufferers" and "rituals of gathering," what ordinary people call a silver lining (2005, 356). Indeed, hate-mongers were by far outnumbered by Americans, of various backgrounds, who went out of their way to show goodwill and understanding to their Arab, Muslim, and Sikh neighbors. When a social service agency sent out a call for volunteers to escort women and children to school and the supermarket, the response was enormous. The respondent said: "The outpouring of the support that we got from the volunteers, their concern and their wanting to help, I think, was very, very positive. Support that we've gotten from organizations and foundations and funders and people who believe in us and believe in our work . . . I think has been positive." Even members of Congress went out of their way to be charitable to victims of the backlash. Congressman Rush Holt (D-NJ) ushered a private relief bill through Congress to help the wife and four daughters of Waqar Hasan, a Pakistani immigrant who had been the victim of a hate crime in a convenience store in Dallas on September 15, 2001. Hasan's American citizenship was pending, and his family's status depended on his application. In October 2004, HR 867 was passed in the House of Representatives, granting the family permanent residency.[30]

A Muslim leader echoed, "Many groups came to us from the coalitions we work with and offered support. We received many e-mails and letters and phone calls saying, 'We hear reports of harassment. Are you okay? Is anyone bothering you?'" Another respondent noted, "We got a lot of support after 9/11. We got letters from the National Council of Churches. We got letters from so many people. I have not had the time to thank people." Many of the leaders would have agreed with the following respondent: "Institutionally the Arab, Muslim, Southeast Asian organizations are receiving much more support from other American organizations and institutions. . . . The religious community has responded extremely well, making invitations to mosques to attend their services and vice versa to attend services at the local mosque. On that level . . . there has been a very positive spin or result of post-9/11."

These personal experiences demonstrate the humanity and commonality that Wuthnow calls transformative. Agha Saeed (2002, 48) sums up the interfaith experience of Muslim Americans in the post-9/11 era: "Though there remains much to be desired about the quality of Christian-Muslim relations in the United States, and these relations cannot be totally separated from Christian-Muslim relations elsewhere in the world, the process has definitely progressed beyond tolerance and acceptance to fellowship and shared spiritual pursuits."

## THE MUSLIM/ARAB VOTE

As noted in the previous chapter, there is a consensus among Middle Eastern and Muslim American leaders that political participation is essential to becoming American and in having clout as a collectivity. Is there a "Muslim vote"? On the one hand, given the growing size of this population and its economic prospects, the immigrants' high educational attainment, and the fact that mosques and Islamic centers serve as centers for mobilizing voters across the country, the potential for developing a voting bloc is significant. On the other hand, mosque-affiliated Muslims are a relatively small percentage of the American Muslim population, and "personal aspects of religious identity, such as prayer and salience of religion in daily life, have little to no relationship to political involvement, while active participation in the mosque promotes political consciousness and activity" (Read 2006, 91).

No structural ties bind mosque congregations together because Islam has no hierarchical authority: a quorum of men in a given locality and financial resources are the only prerequisites for founding a mosque community (Cristillo and Minnite 2002), and the "community" is neither homogenous nor cohesive internally (see chapter 3), as a respondent reminds us: "People are talking about different interests, both immigrant Muslims and African American Muslims. National organizations in Washington represent primarily immigrant Muslims. . . . Endorsing Bush is an immigrant Muslim initiative rather than an African American Muslim initiative. . . . They will [probably] vote in one way on the issue of, say, Palestine, but they will not vote in one way as far as other issues. . . . So in addition to ethnic tensions, there will be social and political issues. There are Lexus-driving Muslims on Long Island with interests quite different from those in Harlem."

The "Arab vote" is equally problematic. Arab Americans are highly diverse (chapter 3), though they are passionate about safeguarding their image as good citizens and eager to contest their negative stereotypes of terrorists and to condemn the escalation of war and political stalemate in the Middle East. AAI's poll in 2007 found that Arab Americans are similar to other voters on domestic policy but that "the community's connection to the Iraq war makes it the most important issue in determining their pick for president in 2008." About 40 percent of respondents knew someone in Iraq, including U.S. service personnel. They also said they would vote for a candidate who promised to actively engage in a peace process between Israel and the Palestinians.[31]

Two American Muslim polls conducted by Project MAPS (Muslims in the American Public Square) and Zogby International (2001, 2004) suggest a swing vote in presidential elections. In November 2001, the polling firm conducted a phone survey of 1,781 individuals across the

United States, age eighteen and older, who identified as Muslim.[32] The methodology was replicated in August/September 2004 and yielded 1,845 responses. In 2001, 79 percent of Muslims polled were registered to vote; 40 percent were Democrats and 28 percent Republicans. Over half of Arabs and Pakistanis voted for Bush (54 percent and 56 percent, respectively). Four years later, 82 percent of the respondents were registered to vote and 88 percent said they were very likely to vote; 50 percent considered themselves Democrats and 12 percent Republicans. Only 7 percent wanted to vote for Bush/Cheney in contrast to 76 percent for Kerry/Edwards. Comparing the 2001 and 2004 polls, the MAPS/Zogby report concludes that there was "a massive migration away from the Republican Party by Muslim voters. It also shows huge movement away from President Bush's re-election effort." The Pew Research Center's poll of Muslim Americans (2007) confirms these results. Of the 1,050 randomly surveyed Muslims, 63 percent were registered to vote (compared to 76 percent of the general population), 58 percent of whom had voted in the 2004 presidential election (compared to 74 percent of the general population). Muslims voted overwhelmingly for Kerry (71 percent vs. 14 percent for Bush), and those sampled were more likely to be Democrats (63 percent vs. 11 percent Republican).

Sociologist Jen'nan Ghazal Read (2006) has analyzed the 2001 and 2004 American Muslim Polls on political engagement, noting that both Muslim men and women have high levels of political consciousness and political participation in part because of their higher socioeconomic status. Additionally, Jamal (2005a, 61) attests that Islamic centers act as "collectivizing forums" that nurture and develop "common fate" attitudes among participants as they share their struggles in becoming Americans. The "mosqued" are linked with sympathizers in other faith communities as well as with local politicians and government officials, resulting in higher levels of mobilization. DAAS data also affirmed that people who are active in mosques tend to be "joiners" in other organizations and are more likely to be registered to vote and to cast their vote during elections. Most importantly, Stockton notes that these "participation patterns are the normal ones typical of the American polity" (2006, 73; see also Jamal 2005b; Howell and Jamal 2008).

According to AAI's analysis of the 2006 elections, Arab American voters played a "critical role" in "too close to call" races, as evidenced by the number of candidates who courted them. The report announced that 100 percent of the "12 U.S. House members who voted correctly on Lebanon resolution (HR 921) . . . won re-election"[33] and that "100 percent of the 35 U.S. House members who voted correctly on the bill to cut Palestinian aid (HR 4681) . . . won re-election." AAI and its local chapters sponsored sixteen "candidates' nights, rallies and civic education workshops"; 82 percent of "candidates endorsed by Arab American community leaders" won. Of the fifty-four Arab American candidates nationwide, 44 percent won in the general election, including four in the U.S. House of Representatives, a governor (Maine), and Mayor Mohamed Khairallah, who won 62 percent of the votes in Prospect Park, New Jersey (AAI 2007).

We agree with Ismael Ahmed, co-founder and executive director of ACCESS, that 9/11 "created a sense of urgency about continuing on the path toward integration and reaffirming the community's validity and its loyalty to the nation. . . . [There was] unprecedented political vigor. . . . The shadow of suspicion that fell over the community [was] converted into commitment to the political issues of civil rights and immigration policy" (Ahmed 2006, 49).[34] Yet the political facts indicate that Arab Americans are still "new kids on the block." When Dearborn's longtime mayor died, several Arabs joined the race for the position. However, "despite the fact that roughly one in three Dearborn residents is of Arab origin, most of the Arab American candidates had dropped out by mid-January [2007]. Poll numbers showed that none of them could win." Internal conflicts among the Lebanese, Iraqi, and Yemeni communities did not help.[35]

Moushumi Khan, an activist and attorney of Bangladeshi descent, outlines this dilemma clearly: "Our growing numbers do not yet translate into commensurate influence; Muslim votes and issues are still taken for granted or ignored by leaders we elect. In the last presidential election when Muslim organizations requested a meeting with Kerry, he declined."[36] Khan's solution calls for more Muslim engagement in the United States but also an equal commitment on the part of American government and society vis-à-vis Muslims. Howell and Jamal likewise argue that there is a cost when governmental agencies do not take Arab Americans seriously. They write, "When Arab organizations are included in public diplomacy and community policing efforts but are not treated as full partners with a voice in setting agendas and negotiating strategies, then they risk weakening their grassroots strength and eroding Arab confidence in American public institutions and government" (2008, 71).

In conclusion, Muslim Americans have taken steps since 9/11 to claim that the United States is indeed their home country and has their political allegiance. Perhaps the most powerful symbolic action in this era was the election of Ingrid Mattson as president of the Islamic Society of North America, a twenty-thousand-member umbrella organization, in September 2006. Mattson is a Canadian-born white female convert and professor of Islamic Studies at Hartford Seminary. Writing in the *New York Times,* Neil MacFarquhar states that "to her supporters, Professor Mattson's selection comes as a significant breakthrough, a chance for North American Muslims to show that they are a diverse, enlightened community with real roots here—and not alien, sexist extremists bent on the destruction of Western civilization. Some grumble that a woman should not head any Muslim organization because the faith bars women from leading men in congregational prayers, but they are a distinct minority."[37] Equally persuasive is the report on American Muslims by the United States Institute of Peace:

> [The] activities [of Muslim American organizations] display a conscious effort to make for themselves in American society, while contributing as bridge builders to the Muslim world. Their activities have already established a definite American Muslim model of inclusion and participation that differs from Muslim communities in Europe where communities are less involved in law enforcement and civic participation.
>
> The participation of American Muslims in mainstream politics is to empower the community in many different levels of public life. American Muslim advocacy groups have tackled stereotyping of Muslims as a matter of public debate, and they have aggressively worked toward resolving incidents of discrimination and civil rights abuses. These achievements have shifted political attitudes that have enabled American Muslims to integrate in American political institutions. (Huda 2006, 17–18)

## CIVIC AND POLITICAL INTEGRATION

### DEFINING INTEGRATION

Although the post-9/11 backlash against Middle Eastern and Muslim Americans spurred them to engage in claims making, the ultimate goal was integration. Here we explore how the CBOs pursued their integration goals. MPAC, in a policy paper about young Muslims, notes that "the very constitutional structure of our country yields the ability for diverse communities to fully engage and integrate the broader society" (MPAC 2007, 14). Thanks to multiculturalism, the "dominant group must 'make space' for the most palpable elements of the culture of the recent immigrant while asking her to strip those elements that just don't work in the West" (14).

In a report entitled *Strengthening America: The Civic and Political Integration of Muslim Americans,* a task force consisting of over thirty stakeholders and experts explored the integration of Muslims in America and offered a number of recommendations (Whitney 2007). The report addresses a societal perception that Muslim American institutions have not sufficiently acknowledged the probability of extremists in their midst and that Islam is not compatible with American values. Given this climate of mistrust and suspicion, the integration of Muslims is "an urgent national need": "While the integration of Muslim Americans could eventually be achieved on its own, the need to accelerate the process is urgent. The risks of inaction are substantial: further marginalization of Muslim Americans at best and serious alienation at worst. It is in the interest of the United States to ensure that this does not happen" (34).

*Strengthening America* recommends the following: expanding contributions to homeland security; fighting Islamophobia by working with the media; engaging in public education about Islam and Muslims; emphasizing the harmony between the teachings of the Qu'ran and American values; expanding partnerships with non-Muslim organizations such as Habitat for Humanity; building coalitions on policy initiatives; bridging religious divides through interfaith projects; making charitable donations to all Americans in crises; building stronger Muslim American institutions so they can be at the table with other ethnic and religious national advocacy organizations; and working with youth and prioritizing Muslim American integration. The group placed responsibility for accelerating the integration of Muslim immigrants on Muslim Americans, the government, "the policy establishment, the media, and other major American institutions" (Whitney 2007, 70).

The leaders in our sample delved into the challenges of both integration and assimilation.[38] They hoped to become fully incorporated into the political and civic life of their country while maintaining their faith and some of their ancestral values and traditions. Given the temptations in America's consumerist, individualistic culture, their biggest fears were that their children would be led astray and succumb to self-destructive and delinquent habits. "In order for Islam to survive in this country, it is very important that our second generation does not get influenced by the American culture. When I say American culture's influences, it is the negative part of it," said a respondent. Another elaborated: "Specifically, with the teenagers, maybe drinking, going out to clubs. We don't want our children to assimilate with that." Yet another said, "We lost a lot of young kids; they were dealing with the drugs. So we don't want that." These fears, however, echo common sentiments; Americans overwhelmingly worry about their children.

Middle Eastern and Muslim immigrants are emulating their fellow Americans in establishing after-school educational programs, summer camps, and other recreational programs to engage young people in productive pursuits, as one respondent notes: "We made a program for our kids, like art galleries, activities, parties, trips, to keep them close to the school system. We got involved with the Parent-Teacher Association. I was myself a president of the Parents' Advisory Council for thirteen years in a row in the city of [name]." Some believed that raising good Muslims meant raising good Americans: "We show [young people] the beauty in the values of Islam, and they will become eventually responsible individuals. They would be better not only to their families as a Muslim but also as an American citizen, because this is a person who knows how to control emotions and desires and work as a responsible person."

Yet however much Arab and Muslim Americans try to integrate, they are treated unequally. Leaders asked in exasperation: When does an Arab or Muslim become American? A respondent mused:

> I did an interview with the *New York Times,* with a journalist. She said, "What do you want to say to the American people?" I said, "My grandfather came here in 1896. My dad came in 1917 . . . and said, 'How do you become an American?' 'Well, we're fighting a war, a World War.' He joined the army, fought in Europe, and came back. I'm a veteran. The question is when do I become an American? That's the question. I am third generation. . . . You know the old saying, "Where are you from?" You know what they're really saying? "You don't belong here." . . . And you know what? That's the question we have always been asked. . . . Damn it, you get tired of hearing it.

This issue has been articulated eloquently by Arab American poets and writers. The refrain of "not being quite equal" has been persistent in their memoirs, poetry, essays, and plays (e.g., Kadi 1994; L. Joseph 2005; Shakir 1997; Shamieh 2004).

As social scientists have argued, identity can be imposed from outside objectively or determined from inside subjectively (Barth 1969; see also Eriksen 1993; Nagel and Staeheli 2005). During the civil rights movements in the 1960s, for example, African Americans reacted to racism by displaying symbols of their heritage, such as Afros and Adinkra cloth outfits—in a sense wearing their identity on their sleeve. Middle Easterners and Muslims are reacting similarly to stereotypes and Islamophobia. Most noticeable is the increase in women wearing the *hijab* (Bryan 2005; Cainkar 2004b; Peek 2003). As Arabs and Muslims embrace their unique identity, they also appropriate America's multiculturalism: "People say: 'Why do you keep hyphenating? Why do you keep calling yourselves Arab Americans?' I say: 'I don't do it. I'm an American. You keep calling me an Arab American. And so, I use 'Arab American' as a way to educate you about who I am, so you'll see that I'm not any different from anybody else who's come here before me.'"

In summary, the vast majority of Middle Easterners and Muslims are "good citizens" who pay their taxes and obey the law, work hard and generally succeed economically, and are patriots who are proud to be American. They are equally proud of their hyphenated identity. This vision of economic and political incorporation but cultural and leisure-time celebration of one's ethnic heritage has been widely accepted in post–civil rights multicultural America. Their major grievance, however, is lack of reciprocal respect.

The attempts of Middle Eastern and especially Muslim immigrants to both claim their own cultural heritage and enter the American mainstream after 9/11 parallel the attempts of other ethnic and religious groups in U.S. history. The conflicts with the second generation, the changing of ethnic traditions to "purer" religious ones, the development of voluntary associations, the creation of communal spaces to socialize, the provision of social, educational, and other services for newcomers, and the continuous efforts to raise funds are all reminiscent of the struggles of earlier waves of immigrants. However, the context is different: America is more accepting of diversity since the 1960s. Newcomers can integrate while maintaining their ancestral identity and faith and aspects of their cultural heritage. Assimilation is not forced as it was during the "100 percent American" period. There is an exception, however. As Pfaff-Czarnecka and Zolberg have argued, religious integration is different from ethnic integration because it takes place in public, during work or school time. New faith traditions such as Islam and Sikhism are advocating for institutional accommodations and demanding an expansion in the religious character of the United States.

## VISIONS OF INTEGRATION

We asked our respondents, "How does one become American?" For many of our respondents, the first step was to get out of the ghetto. Here is a passionate and eloquent declaration from an immigrant leader:

I believe that the moment we came here to this country, we came here to live. And we cannot live in small boxes, in small closed communities or cultures. We have to be open to the community. And that means we have to participate. We have to take an active role. We have to volunteer. We have to give money. We have to register. We have to vote. We have to run for office. We have to participate in the schools. I have to express my opinion. And I am pushing very hard for the people that they have to do this. You cannot come here and live for sixteen years and you don't speak English. . . . I think to be recognized, and to be protected, and to be given your constitutional rights, we have to participate. You can take, take, take, but if you don't give back, that doesn't mean anything.

There was consensus among our respondents that Middle Eastern and Muslim immigrants must learn English and become "good Americans," implying social mobility, civic engagement, and political integration.

Civic engagement meant "becoming vital" and visible in one's locality and nationally by volunteering on school boards and other committees and contributing hard-earned dollars to political campaigns. It also meant getting people of Middle Eastern and Muslim descent into the government at all levels, from police officers and firefighters to generals in the armed forces, governors, and appointed officials. A third-generation respondent in Dearborn cited the case of an immigrant family that lost a child in a fire because the police and firefighters who responded to the rescue call could not speak Arabic. In Washington, D.C., a respondent told us: "We think that Muslims should join the military, should join the FBI, [they] should work in all institutions. . . . There is a big vacuum, and when decisions are made, there is no Muslim input because there [are] no Muslims." Arab and Muslim organizations have begun to co-sponsor job fairs with government agencies. For example, MPAC organized a visit for young professional Muslims to the State Department in Washington, D.C., in July 2007. They met with Shirin Tahir-Kheli, the first Muslim to be appointed U.S. ambassador, and other Muslim officials.[39] Finally, civic engagement meant holding politicians accountable. When Los Angeles mayor Antonio Villaraigosa attended two pro-Israeli rallies during the Lebanon bombing but failed to attend an interfaith vigil organized by MPAC on July 16, 2006, the Muslim American community felt confident enough to challenge his partisanship and accepted his subsequent apology.[40]

A further indicator of belonging and legitimacy has been the grants that mainstream foundations have offered immigrant organizations. After 9/11, major philanthropies such as the Ford Foundation, the Rockefeller Foundation, the Four Freedoms Fund, and the Tides Foundation gave Arab and Muslim organizations unsolicited funds. For the most part, the recipients were first-time grantees. A respondent reflected on the significance of these offerings: "I think, for me, it was putting the community on the map. . . . By giving us funding, you're recognizing that we are a community and that we deserve services just like everybody else."

## POLITICAL EMPOWERMENT OF LEADERS

Middle Eastern and Muslim American CBOs have long felt excluded from business circles, political networks, boards of philanthropic associations, and other local and national circles of movers and shakers that affect the lives of their constituents. But 9/11 offered unexpected chances for the CBOs and their leaders, and our respondents were eager to display their newfound connections. One of them told us, "When I place a call to the U.S. Customs, to the Secret Service, to the FBI, to any agency, I receive the courtesy of a call within fifteen minutes to a half an hour with a clarification. . . . They are very responsive. Even the U.S. Attorney's office, Mr. Connell's office, is very responsive." Another leader bragged: "In October, I met with Norman Minetta with a large group of other interested groups to talk about what was going on. So we do have some federal attention." A Sikh respondent boasted, "I was invited on September 20th to meet with the president along with twenty-seven other religious leaders. And then, on the 26th of September, the president again invited a group of Sikhs to the White House and met with them, had a photo-op, to send the message that Sikhs are to be protected." Even a neighborhood imam we interviewed, a recent immigrant, was eager to show us the business card of his precinct's captain. He beamed: "After September 11, they give me their cellular phone [number]."

Success as an organization and as a community was interpreted as power by our respondents. When a U.S. president attends a minority group's annual dinner or the mayor of a city walks in their parade, these are par excellence the symbols of achievement. Yet another sign of power was delivering money and votes to a candidate. One respondent in Michigan showed off the clout of the Arab American community by saying: "We helped elect the Wayne County prosecutor. He had our support, our votes, and our money. We helped elect the mayor of Detroit and local congressmen. John Dingell is our congressman, the most powerful man in the House and the longest-serving member of the House. Detroit has three of those kinds of congressmen, Bonior, Conyers, and Dingell. They were huge. So all of that translates from the relationship.

Governor Engler was elected on a large Arab vote." One Dearborn respondent claimed that before 9/11 Arab Americans had been very close to reaching the inner circle of decision makers, at least in Michigan: "In this community, we had the first Arab American senator from Michigan. In the last national election, the Gore-Bush election, I had newspapers and reporters coming from all over the world to kind of gauge where Arab Americans were in this campaign. It was so close that these marginal communities became so powerful in their presence. So this community was really feeling that they are the future of the state of Michigan. We were counting what we could do."

All our respondents would have acknowledged with the above leader that "the political process resolves around, and evolves around money, and using it wisely, using it in successful ways and intelligently." This same leader told us, "We had ten thousand small business owned by Arab Americans in the Detroit metropolitan area. We are a very large tax base in the state of Michigan. We established the Arab American Chamber of Commerce. We were talking about trade with the Middle East and other countries."

Access to the media was deemed equally important. As already noted, Middle Eastern and Muslim Americans felt that the mainstream media was biased against them. Our respondents were vociferous in their criticism. It was therefore logical for them to believe that if more journalists and reporters were willing to listen to them and disseminate their "truth," the communities would be better served. The events of 9/11 directed the media's spotlight on the hitherto invisible Middle Eastern and Muslim communities. The attention of the media, politicians, and the leaders of other ethnic and religious groups in their locality disoriented a few of the leaders in our sample. They succumbed to their human foibles and came to believe in their own myth of fame and self-aggrandizement. Nonetheless, being in the public eye is a component of integration. It is not surprising that ADC's press release regarding its 2007 annual national convention reported on media coverage. The list of media outlets included C-SPAN, CNN, Al-Jazeera, Al-Arabiya, Agence France Press (AFP), and "numerous publication, television, and radio stations from American, Arab, and French news agencies."[41]

## PAN-RELIGIOUS (ISLAMIC) ORGANIZATIONS AND COALITIONS

In this section, we explore the structural and cultural factors that have allowed Muslim Americans to mobilize along pan-religious lines and

Arab Americans to mobilize as a supranational category but have hampered Middle Easterners' efforts. The role of religion in promoting supranational solidarity is missing in the literature, yet religious solidarity develops if religion is the classificatory principle in a political/ideological crisis. In the aftermath of 9/11 and the war on terrorism, Islam has emerged as a major classification category for governmental policy, and it has subsequently been adopted by the media and the rest of society. Muslim Americans have therefore forged pan-ethnic alliances across national origins. Even though South Asians have much more in common with Middle Easterners than they do with East Asians, there is clearly no effort to pull them together. On the contrary, South Asians have realized the benefits of being considered an official minority group under the pan-ethnic *Asian American* label.

Though American Muslims have a long way to go before they reach political parity with Christians and Jews in this country, they can no longer be ignored. CAIR, the Islamic Society of North America, and MPAC—quintessentially American in their mission, policies, scope, and funding[42]—have probably been the most prominent pan-religious organizations in the post-9/11 era. Their constituents are kept informed and engaged through their listservs and frequently updated Web sites. These organizations survey the media around the world on a daily basis and interpret the news. They cover a wide range of topics in their periodic news summaries—well beyond what one might consider of religious interest or even the interest of their immigrant populations. For example, when a powerful earthquake shook Pakistan in October 2005, it was to be expected that the Muslim organizations would raise funds for the victims because the majority of Pakistani nationals are Muslim; and MPAC, for instance, has also gathered donations for Katrina and other humanitarian concerns in the United States.[43] Islamic organizations also provide community outreach by advertising upcoming conferences and other events.

The American Muslim organizations' message is more coherent than most pan-ethnic messages. They want to make Islam one of the major religions of the United States, despite its sects (e.g., Sunni and Shiʿa), schools of law (Hanafi, Maliki, Shafiʿi, Hanbali), and other divisions (e.g., Sufi, Alevi, Ismaili) (see Gregorian 2003). Their demands tend to be concrete and attainable under universal principles of human rights and citizenship. Not being discriminated against for praying at work or wearing religious attire is a right that is being fought in the courts, and at times won, in various jurisdictions across the country. Dietary requirements—*halal* food and no pork—in school meals are being negotiated wherever Muslims are concentrated. Many other accommodations may be settled at state and federal levels in the future.

Structural conditions conducive to Middle Eastern mobilization include relatively high levels of discrimination and a proclivity for professional and entrepreneurial modes of economic incorporation into American society. Culturally, Arabs, Iranians, and Turks share the rich legacy of Islamic civilization. The region's peoples share cultural affinities and a set of common values. However, not everyone has been convinced of the benefits of pan-ethnic solidarity: for example, some Christians, notably Maronites, Chaldeans, and Copts tend to object to the label *Arab* (see chapter 3), though this does not preclude their ethno-religious or national affiliations. The factors impeding the development of pan-ethnicity include (1) linguistic, religious, generational, and class differences; (2) geographic dispersion across the United States, which makes mobilization more difficult; (3) classification as "white" (in census and other governmental forms), so that Middle Easterners are not externally grouped together and cannot use entitlement programs as an impetus for pan-ethnic formation; and (4) a preoccupation with Middle Eastern politics, which reproduces the conflicts in the region and contributes to divisiveness, though attenuated, in the diaspora.

Many Arabs are mobilized by the political situation in Israel/ Palestine and oppose a number of the policies of the U.S. government in the Middle East, including the war in Afghanistan, Iraq, and Lebanon. They share a language, culture, and history. Arab American umbrella organizations such as AAI and ADC stepped up their operations after 9/11 to advocate for their constituents and mobilize them toward great political integration into the American mainstream. Nonetheless, Arab American affiliation and identity are weakened by religious, generational, and class differences. Supranational "Arab American" ethnic identities and coalitions are different from those of, say, Hispanic Americans: as Portes and Rumbaut have noted, "Colombian immigrants certainly know that they are Colombian and Mexicans that they are Mexican; what they probably do not know when they arrive in the United States is that they belong to a larger ethnic category called Hispanics" (2006, 158). In contrast, Egyptians, Syrians, Lebanese, Yemenis, and other Arabic-speaking immigrants have known that they were Arabs since the 1950s, when pan-Arabism spread throughout the region. Thus "Arab American" is a supranational ethnic category, like "Chinese," and not a pan-ethnic category like "Asian American" or "Hispanic" (chapter 1).

Mobilization is easier when the demands are specific rather than amorphous political and ideological campaigns pertaining to foreign policy. Pan–Middle Eastern organizations do not have a unifying agenda; they are more likely to have a history of national and sectarian conflicts. Iranian Americans who are mostly political exiles have begun to develop separate advocacy organizations. They are politically fragmented and religiously diverse, with a long history of conflict with Arabs. For several reasons, the Turkish American community, under the sponsorship of the government of Turkey, is not yet mobilized for integration into the United States. Immigrants from Turkey are relatively new and principally economic migrants. Moreover, the post-9/11 backlash has largely spared this population, as it obviously has spared Israelis. In fact, the inclusion of Israelis under the "Middle Eastern" category is the principal reason why Arabs reject the label *Middle Eastern American*. Turks were spared by the backlash; they are also eager to represent their heritage in a modern and democratic light and actively debunk any account that could tarnish this image, such as that of the Armenian genocide. Exile/refugee populations such as Iranians and Iraqis do not endorse regimes in their home countries.

Muslim Americans and Arab Americans, in that order, were the most successful groups to mobilize after 9/11. Nadine Naber has observed that in the San Francisco Bay Area Muslim social movements and community activities have increased while those "organized around the category 'Arab' have decreased or remained stagnant" (2005, 482).[44] This has resulted in "Muslim first, Arab/ethnicity second" sentiment. In the past there were two types of mobilizations: (1) a single ethnic group (e.g., Japanese) or an ethno-religious group (e.g., Jews, Armenians, Greeks); or (2) a pan-ethnic group (e.g., Asian Americans), resulting from generational shifts and the sharing of similar phenotypes, racism, and entitlement programs. Both Muslim and Arab American mobilization are therefore atypical from a historical perspective because one (Muslim) is a religious category and the other (Arab) a supranational ethnic category. In this book, we problematize the ethnic aspect of mobilization and show how a government can generate a religion as a category in contradiction to its constitution. We have argued that American Islam was invented in the post-9/11 period.

## CONCLUSION

September 11, 2001, has become for most Americans the day when they realized that the security of their country could no longer be taken for granted. For Middle Eastern and Muslim Americans, 9/11 is remembered as the dawn of an era of "double" insecurity: one that they share with all Americans and another that they alone experience as targets of backlash. Hate crimes and bias incidents perpetrated by fellow Americans were front-page news immediately after the attacks. These included murders (four confirmed), arson, and violent assaults. The FBI reported that anti-Islamic hate crimes increased 1,600 percent between 2000 and 2001 (from 28 to 481 cases). Although the spike subsided in the following year, rates have remained higher than pre-9/11 levels (chapter 5). Many Sikhs were the targets of hate crimes, though they are neither Muslim nor Middle Eastern, because their turbans and beards erroneously linked them in people's minds with Osama Bin Laden.

The state appeared to have contradictory objectives vis-à-vis Middle Eastern and Muslim Americans. On the one hand, President Bush and other officials publicly condemned vigilante actions and hate crimes and declared that Islam was a religion of peace. The U.S. Department of Justice's Civil Rights Division has been prosecuting cases of hate crimes and has won convictions for heinous acts. The EEOC has been handling the increasing number of employment discrimination cases, especially against Muslims who have attempted to observe their faith at work—praying, breaking the fast during Ramadan, or, for women, wearing the *hijab*. On the other hand, the government's series of initiatives, including the USA PATRIOT Act, detentions, deportations, the absconder initiative, special registration, and NSEERS (see Appendix), affected noncitizen Arab and Muslim men. Many of these men had overstayed their nonimmigrant visas. Since they were often heads of households, their families, including U.S.-born children, suffered material deprivation and separation due to deportation (chapter 6). From the perspective of Middle Eastern and Muslim Americans, the government dragnet was more devastating than actions by vigilantes. The administration's actions spoke louder than official proclamations, singling out Arabs and Muslims (chapter 1). The neophyte status of these groups and their lack of political connections with the political elite increased their vulnerability.

The case of the post-9/11 backlash is neither new nor unique in American history. During World War I, Germans were closely supervised and forced to assimilate. The "Bolshevik menace," which sparked the Red Scare of 1919–20, led to the Palmer Raids, arrests, and deportation of some prominent leaders. The internment of 120,000 Japanese, including the U.S. born, in detention camps during World War II was the most deplorable case of scapegoating. Contrary to the opinion of military strategists at the time, racist elites on the West Coast pressured the government to retaliate after the bombing of Pearl Harbor in 1941. McCarthyism during the height of the Cold War penalized former Communist Party members and sympathizers. Iranian students faced mandatory registration and potential deportation during the Iranian hostage crisis (1979–81). Government excesses during these episodes caused many economic and social losses and much psychological trauma to large numbers of innocent people but yielded few culprits.

Our historical comparisons show that in times of war or political/ ideological crisis the state has overreacted and pursued policies targeting minorities or outgroups (chapter 2). By developing a typology of these cases (table 1) we examined (1) the cause of the crisis, (2) the ethnic minority or outgroup being targeted, (3) the legal status of the targeted population, (4) the U.S. government's policies, (5) the yield from government investigations, and (6) the response of the affected group(s). This approach allowed us to identify the unique characteristics of the post-9/11 case. With the exception of the Iranian hostage crisis, all historical precedents involved both citizens and noncitizens. In the current case, only noncitizens, who have the least constitutional protections, became the victims of the detentions, deportations, special interviews, and special registration. Moreover, the administration's actions were shrouded in secrecy, further violating due process and other constitutional procedures. Even years after the events, the final tally of the detentions and deportations is not known.

We have been researching the post-9/11 backlash against Middle Eastern and Muslim Americans as it has evolved from the time immediately after the terrorist attacks. We conducted sixty interviews with high-ranking representatives of Middle Eastern and Muslim American advocacy and community-based organizations (CBOs) and fifteen interviews with "knowledgeable sources" from civil rights and governmental agencies across the nation (chapters 1 and 4). This was a representative sample because we were able to include almost all the major national Middle Eastern and Muslim and some grassroots organizations. Leaders provide an institutional memory and a broader perspective on the community that cannot be replicated by the rank and file. In particular, we tapped their knowledge in the midst of the crisis. The in-person interview method offers other advantages such as feasibility and cost effectiveness. In addition to our formal interviews, we used participant observation of Middle Eastern communities and analyzed listserv messages and Web sites as well as the ethnic and mainstream media.

Given the confusion and misinformation about Middle Eastern and South Asian populations in the United States, we devoted chapter 3 to describing their immigration history and patterns, demographic and socioeconomic characteristics, and identity issues. Middle Easterners are classified as "white" by the Office of Management and Budget and the Census Bureau. The pioneers were mostly Christians who arrived from Ottoman-ruled Greater Syria in the late nineteenth century. Changes in U.S. immigration laws and political upheavals and economic changes were responsible for the second wave of immigrants, who were mostly Muslims from the Arab world and Iran. They arrived in large numbers as foreign students from oil-producing countries after the mid-1970s, and many stayed on. Muslims from Pakistan, India, and Bangladesh are newcomers. They are an official minority category subsumed under the larger category of "Asians." Ironically, they have more in common with Middle Easterners than they do with East Asians.

Middle Eastern populations are small in size: even the largest supranational ancestry group (Arab) makes up barely half the total population of all Middle Easterners. Yet these populations share (1) languages (Arabic, Persian, Turkish); (2) history (Islamic civilization, Ottoman Empire, French and British colonial rule, and the ongoing conflict in the region); (3) religion (Islam, Eastern Rite Christianity, Mizrahi Judaism); (4) cultural traits (privileging of the family unit over individuals; deference to elders; values of hospitality, generosity, and honor; cuisine; aesthetic sensibilities in music, poetry, and art); (5) a recent influx of immigrants; (6) similar socioeconomic characteristics (high educational achievement, self-employment, and professional specialty occupations); (7) concentration in a few urban areas (Detroit, New York, Chicago, and Los Angeles); and, last but not least, (8) past and present suffering from prejudice and negative stereotypes that have been ingrained in the American media and popular culture. The post-9/11 backlash has reinforced these biases, leading some scholars to posit that Arabs and Muslims in America are being racialized (chapter 3).

Despite these commonalities, Middle Eastern and Muslim groups vary significantly in some respects. Years after the terrorist attacks, much of the American public remains ignorant of the variation within these populations. The labels *Arab* and *Muslim* are confused; there is even less differentiation between, say, an Egyptian Copt, an Iranian Jew, an Iraqi Kurd, a Lebanese Shiʿa, a Syrian Orthodox Christian, and a Sunni Yemeni. The high rates of hate crimes against Sikhs attest to this misunderstanding. Debunking myths about Middle Easterners and Muslims has become a preoccupation of these communities.

In chapter 4 we analyzed the Middle Eastern and Muslim advocacy and grassroots organizations in our sample and documented their transformation as a result of the crisis. While many of the CBOs were established prior to the terrorist attacks, a new urgency in the wake of 9/11 stimulated these populations to mobilize. Irrespective of their function and characteristics, almost all the organizations were impelled to engage in advocacy. Even leaders of compatriotic societies, who were out of their league given their limited resources and mission, joined in the massive mobilization efforts. The backlash catapulted many leaders and their organizations into national, even international, attention. It also led to the emergence of new leaders, especially among the second generation, who created new organizations to fill existing gaps.

The cumulative effect of the 9/11 backlash on Middle Eastern and Muslim Americans was widespread fear, anxiety, and a growing mistrust of the government. Even those in the third or later generations were shaken by the government's tendency to associate them with terrorism. They wondered whether they would be carted off to remote camps just like the Japanese during World War II, though some reasoned that in the age of electronic communications there would be no need for physical relocation (chapter 6). Japanese Americans were particularly attuned to the plight of Arabs and Muslims. Many demonstrated empathy and solidarity and even protested state policies (chapter 2).

Instead of caving in, the leaders of the Middle Eastern and Muslim American advocacy and grassroots organizations called for civic and political integration into American society. In this case, unlike historical precedents, the targeted groups were very quick to respond. It took Japanese Americans several decades after their internment to mobilize for redress. We attribute these differences to the codification and institutionalization of civil rights since the 1960s.

In the parlance of social movements, the political opportunity structure for fighting back and reclaiming rights was open in the 9/11 case. The civil rights and civil liberties organizations have been vocal watchdogs monitoring the government's actions and keeping it accountable; after all, hard-won civil rights require much vigilance and buttressing. For example, the ACLU and other civil rights organizations spurred the general public to defeat a proposed Bush administration measure, Operation TIPS. TIPS would have asked civilians such as mail carriers, electricians, and service delivery personnel who entered the homes of Middle Eastern and Muslim Americans to report to the federal government any suspicious evidence of terrorism (chapter 6).

Backlash gave rise to mobilization or claims making, which has four components: the political opportunity structure, framing mechanisms, repertoires of collective action, and resource mobilization. As noted above, the post–civil rights era presented opportunities to the Middle Eastern and Muslim American organizational leaders that had not been available to their predecessors. In chapter 7, we showed how the affected communities framed their message in a way that could be understood by the American people and the government. They distanced themselves from the terrorists and condemned their actions; they demonstrated their allegiance to the United States; and they engaged in outreach to educate the American public about the Middle East and the Muslim faith. The leaders in our sample used a wide range of repertoires of collective action, including press releases, letter-writing or e-mail campaigns to public officials, demonstrations, vigils, and lawsuits. These communities were also engaged in extensive political socialization. The organizations actively involved their constituents in voter registration efforts, know-your-rights forums, and civic and political integration. Immigrants were encouraged to become familiar with their local, state, and federal representatives, contribute to their campaigns, and voice their approval or disapproval of their policies. The second generation was particularly creative; they used comedy, theater, poems, and other art forms to get their message across. The Middle Eastern and Muslim American organizations also tried to persuade the government to consider them as a valuable resource in fighting terrorism at home and abroad.

Coalition building was a major tool of resource mobilization. The opportunities for entering a variety of networks multiplied exponentially, including coalitions based on identity politics, situational alliances, and social justice alliances. Pan-Islamic organizations, such CAIR and MPAC, have risen to regional and national prominence. They have been successful because Islam, as a new religion in America, forms the basis for their group identity and solidarity. Also structurally, mosques and Islamic centers provide space for meetings, the dissemination of information, and networks of activism and fundraising, at least among the observant Muslims (chapter 8). In contrast, Middle Eastern Americans have had difficulty building pan-ethnic coalitions after 9/11. Their differences have proved to be more powerful than their similarities. These include national and sectarian conflicts; linguistic, generational, and class differences; and political infighting over regimes in their native countries. But because Middle Easterners are not an official minority, according to the Office of Management and Budget, grouping them under one umbrella category has little structural basis.

Specifically, the post-9/11 era ushered in the "Muslim moment." The faithful engaged in consciousness-raising as distinct "American Muslims," blending elements of their religion with American civil rights and constitutional democracy. Mosques and Islamic centers have been adapting physically and socially to life in the United States, taking on elements from congregational and social service models (chapter 8). But 9/11 politicized American Muslims rapidly, spurring pan-religious organizations to seek new alliances outside their communities through interfaith exchanges. While in the nineteenth century ethnicity became a legitimate factor in American politics, in the current epoch, where the ideology of "the clash of civilizations" seems to reign, American Islam has become crystallized as a distinct new category in the nation's classificatory system. It has been claimed that the "Muslim/Arab vote" was the decisive vote in the 2000 presidential elections, cast in favor of candidate George W. Bush because he had promised to repeal secret evidence if elected. In the aftermath of 9/11, however, there is evidence that Arab/Muslim voters overwhelmingly favored his opponent in the 2004 election.

The repressive role of the state has been largely ignored in the literature on immigration and ethnic minorities in the United States and in the hate crimes and advocacy literatures generally. Theories of intergroup conflict do not address the role of the state as an active agent. Generally, the focus is on competition and violence between two or more minority groups or between a majority and one or more minorities. When the state is included in American immigration research, it is treated as a gatekeeper. Our major theoretical contribution in this book is our model of backlash and mobilization (see figures 1 to 3). We argue that during periods of war or political/ideological crises the state tends to target a minority population or "outgroup" that happens to share the same immigrant/ethnic or religious background as the "enemy." Such repressive measures rarely happen in a vacuum. The targeted group(s) generally suffer from widespread scapegoating and stereotypes. Thus there is a feedback loop between the hate crimes and bias incidents perpetrated by common people and the repressive policies of the state; both are mediated and reinforced through deep-seated prejudice. We therefore define backlash as a combination of stereotyping, scapegoating, hate crimes, and government initiatives. We also argue that backlash gives rise to mobilization or claims making. In the 9/11 case, the mobilization of the Middle Eastern and Muslim populations was very quick, thanks to the existence of civil rights laws, the political opportunity infrastructure, and a culture of pluralism and religious diversity.

We hope we have accurately told the story of the post-9/11 backlash against Middle Eastern and Muslim Americans and their struggle for inclusion in American social and political life. Their experiences can tell us much about the challenges of inclusion and exclusion and about the ability of the United States to remain a country that welcomes immigrants. As Arab and Muslim immigrants have faced discrimination and hate crimes, and even later-generation descendants have been profiled by the expanding state security apparatus, their example reminds us that America's hard-won ideals of equality and equity will be at risk if civil rights are abused and lost.

# A Time Line of Government Initiatives and Actions

## GOVERNMENT INITIATIVES

September 17, 2001: INS changed the regulation regarding detentions. An alien could be detained without charge for forty-eight hours or "an additional reasonable period of time" if there was an "emergency or other extraordinary circumstance" (Ibish 2003, 141; Chishti et al. 2003, Appendix F, 1).

September 21, 2001: Chief Immigration Judge Michael Creppy issued a memorandum regarding "secure" hearings, meaning that in certain cases proceedings would be closed to the public (Ibish 2003, 141; Chishti et al. 2003, Appendix F, 1).

October 4, 2001: The FBI issued a comprehensive, generic "boilerplate" memo opposing bond in all post-9/11 detention cases because it was collecting information that might link the suspect to terrorism (Ibish 2003, 142; Chishti et al. 2003, Appendix F, 1).

October 25, 2001: U.S. Attorney General John Ashcroft announced: "To date, our antiterrorism offensive has arrested or detained nearly 1,000 individuals as part of the Sept. 11 terrorism investigation" (Chishti et al. 2003, Appendix F, 2).

October 25, 2001: Congress passed the sweeping USA PATRIOT Act, virtually without debate. The next day, President Bush signed it into law.

October 31, 2001: The U.S. Department of Justice's Bureau of Prisons issued an interim regulation permitting eavesdropping on attorney-client communications of detainees suspected of terrorism (Ibish 2003, 142).

October 31, 2001: Seven prominent members of Congress wrote to Attorney General Ashcroft requesting that the identities and charges against the detainees be revealed (Chishti et al. 2003, Appendix F, 2). Later, the government publicly acknowledged 1,182 detainees (Dan Eggen and Susan Schmidt, "Count of Released Detainees Is Hard to Pin Down," *Washington Post,* November 6, 2001, A10; Todd S. Purdum, "A Nation Challenged: The Attorney General; Ashcroft's About-Face on the Detainees," *New York Times,* November 28, 2001, B7; Amy Goldstein and Dan Eggen, "U.S. to Stop Issuing Detention Tallies," *Washington Post,* November 9, 2001, A16).

October 31, 2001: The attorney general sent a letter to Secretary of State Powell, asking him to designate forty-six new groups as terrorist under the new PATRIOT Act (Ibish 2003, 141; Chishti et al. 2003, Appendix F, 2).

November 7, 2001: President Bush held "the first formal meeting of the full Homeland Security Council, and announced the creation of a 'Foreign Terrorist Tracking Task Force' which will deny entry, locate, detain, prosecute and deport anyone suspected of terrorist activity" (Ibish 2003, 142).

November 9, 2001: The "Attorney General issued a memo directing voluntary interviews of a list of 5,000 men, ages 18–33, who entered the U.S. since Jan. 2000 and who came from countries where Al Qaeda has a 'terrorist presence or activity.'" Those found in violation of immigration laws were to be arrested and kept without bail (Ibish 2003, 142; see also Chishti et al. 2003, Appendix F, 3).

November 9, 2001: The visa-granting process for men aged sixteen to forty-five from a number of Arab and Muslim countries was slowed by about twenty days (Hing 2006).

November 13, 2001: "President Bush issue[d] an Executive Order authorizing [the] creation of military tribunals to try noncitizens alleged to be involved in international terrorism" (Ibish 2003, 142).

November 15, 2001: The State Department declared that it would require twenty days to process visa applications of men, ages sixteen to forty-five, from a number of Arab and Muslim countries (Ibish 2003, 142).

November 16, 2001: Congress received a letter addressed to Senator Feingold from the Department of Justice. It noted that information on the detainees was not forthcoming (Ibish 2003, 142).

November 19, 2003: President Bush signed into law the Aviation and Transportation Security Act, which established the TSA. The law empowered the TSA "'to use information from government agencies to identify individuals on passenger lists who may be a threat to civil or national security' and to 'prevent the identified individual[s] from boarding an aircraft'" (Chishti et al. 2003, Appendix F, 3).

November 23, 2001: INS directed its agents, who were conducting interviews with the five thousand aliens (see above, November 9), to respond to state and local authorities involved in the process (Ibish 2003, 143; Chishti et al. 2003, Appendix F, 3).

November 26, 2001: U.S. attorneys in Detroit stated in a letter that the "voluntary" interviews of five thousand men (see above, November 9) were not voluntary when recipients were mandated to comply (Ibish 2003, 143; Chishti et al. 2003, Appendix F, 3).

November 28, 2001: The U.S. attorney general provided the names of ninety-three individuals who had been criminally charged in the 9/11 investigation. However, their violations tended to involve credit card fraud and lying in passport applications. He also released information on 548 persons who remained in detention because of immigration charges. No names were made public, but nationality, date of birth, and charges were (Chishti et al. 2003, Appendix F, 3).

December 4, 2001: Senator Feingold, chair of the Subcommittee on the Constitution, held hearings on 9/11. Attorney General Ashcroft argued that those who questioned his policies were "abiding and abating terrorism" (Ibish 2003, 143).

December 6, 2001: James Ziglar, commissioner of INS, declared that there were more than three hundred thousand aliens in the United States who had stayed beyond their deportation orders. The Absconders Apprehension Initiative aimed to deport them (Chishti et al. 2003, Appendix F, 4).

December 19, 2001: According to the U.S. Department of Justice, 460 individuals associated with the 9/11 investigation were still in detention (Chishti et al. 2003, Appendix F, 4).

January 8, 2002: The "Department of Justice add[ed] to the FBI's National Crime Information Center database the names of approximately 6,000 men from countries believed to be harboring al-Qaeda members who . . . ignored deportation or removal orders. The department use[d] country, age, and gender criteria to identify these 6,000 'absconders' for removal" (Chishti et al. 2003, Appendix F, 4).

February 19, 2002: The attorney general publicized reforms for the Board of Immigration Appeals (BIA). Procedures were simplified: there was a one-judge review; board membership was reduced from twenty-one to eleven members (Ibish 2003, 143; Chishti et al. 2003, Appendix F, 4).

February 26, 2002: The *Final Report on Interview Project* was released. It said that out of 5,000 Arab and/or Muslim men on the list, 2,261 had been interviewed and fewer than 20 had been taken into custody (three on criminal violations and the rest on immigration charges (Ibish 2003, 143; Chishti et al. 2003, Appendix F, 6).

March 2002: The Operation TIPS program was announced as part of the Citizen Corps initiative whose intent was to allow the general American public to help combat terrorism. Operation TIPS was proposed as "a nationwide program to help thousands of American truck drivers, letter carriers, train conductors, ship captains, and utility workers report potential terrorist activity" (DHS 2002, 12). This program was quickly criticized as a violation of civil liberties (Ellen Sorokin, "Planned Volunteer-Informant Corps Elicit '1984' Fears; Accessing Private Homes Is Objective of 'Operation TIPS,'" *Washington Times*, July 16, 2002, A03).

March 19, 2002: The Department of Justice revealed that it would conduct an additional three thousand interviews (Ibish 2003, 143; Chishti et al. 2003, Appendix F, 7).

March 20, 2002: The U.S. Customs Service, the IRS, other agencies, and local police used a sealed search warrant to "raid about 14 homes and businesses in northern Virginia seeking information about possible money laundering and financial links between those entities and terrorist groups" (Chishti et al. 2003, Appendix F, 7).

March 27, 2002: The "State Department updated its list of terrorists and terrorist organizations whose property interests [were] blocked following an initial order by President Bush on Sept. 26, 2001" (Chishti et al. 2003, Appendix F, 7).

April 12, 2002: INS established a new limitation for visitors to the United States of thirty days, or a "fair and reasonable period," depending on their rationale for staying. Visitors could not change their status to "student" or attend a school while their status was pending (Ibish 2003, 143; Chishti et al. 2003, Appendix F, 8).

April 22, 2002: Attorney General Ashcroft initiated an interim rule prohibiting state and county jails from sharing information about INS detainees in their facilities. This invalidated New Jersey State Judge D'Italia's order on March 26, 2002, ordering the contrary (Ibish 2003, 44; Chishti et al. 2003, Appendix F, 8).

May 9, 2002: The attorney general "require[d] that aliens subject to final orders of removal surrender to INS within 30 days of the final order or be barred forever from any discretionary relief from deportation, including asylum relief, while she/he remain[ed] in the U.S. or for ten years after departing from the U.S." (Ibish 2003, 144; Chishti et al. 2003, Appendix F, 9).

May 10, 2002: INS required "District Offices and Service Centers to run IBIS (Interagency Border Inspection System) security checks for all applicants and petitions, including naturalization. The checks [were] to be run not only on foreign nationals, but also on every name on the application, including U.S. citizen petitions and attorneys" (Ibish 2003, 144; Chishti et al. 2003, Appendix F, 9).

May 14, 2002: President Bush signed into law the Enhanced Border Security and Visa Entry Reform Act. In addition to increasing funding for consular services, this law authorized information sharing between the CIA, INS, and the State Department (Chishti et al. 2003, Appendix F, 9).

May 16, 2002: The attorney general introduced the Student and Exchange Visitor System (SEVIS), which became law on January 30, 2003. This system tracked student enrollment, start date of each semester, failure to enroll, dropping below nine credits per term, disciplinary action by the institution, early graduation, etc. (Ibish 2003, 144; Chishti et al. 2003, Appendix F, 9).

June 6, 2002: The attorney general announced a new entry-exit system: the National Security Entry-Exit Registration System (NSEERS). It compelled aliens from designated countries to "(1) register, submit to fingerprints and photographs upon their arrival in the United States; (2) report to INS field offices within 30 days, and then re-report annually, and (3) notify an INS agent of their departure, with possible criminal prosecution for those who fail to comply" (Chishti et al. 2003, Appendix F, 10). While the government initially noted that NSEERS would apply to twenty-six countries, the documentation available (*Fed. Reg.* 67 [155], http://judiciary.house.gov/OversightTestimony .aspx?ID=428) lists only twenty-five: Afghanistan, Algeria, Bahrain, Djibouti, Egypt, Eritrea, Indonesia, Iran, Iraq, Jordan, Kuwait, Lebanon, Libya, Malaysia, Morocco, Oman, Pakistan, Qatar, Saudi Arabia, Somalia, Sudan, Syria, Tunisia, United Arab Emirates, and Yemen. It is likely that the original list included the Republic of Armenia as the twenty-sixth country, for a later federal register (*Fed. Reg.* 67 [243], http://edocket.access.gpo.gov/2002/02–32045.htm) rescinds the inclusion of Armenia as one of the designated NSEERS countries. From the start, NSEERS encountered opposition such as an ADC press release that stated: "Since the inception of the program, ADC, several members of Congress, including . . . members of the Senate Judiciary committee, and . . . civil libertarian and immigrant rights advocates, have taken issue with the constitutional legality of NSEERS discrimination based on national origin" (ADC, "When Will the 'Shame of NSEERs' End?" press release, July 26, 2007, http://archives 2007.ghazali.net/html/adc_reiterates.html).

June 18, 2002: Homeland Security Director Tom Ridge delivered to Congress the Homeland Security Act of 2002. This bill established the Department of Homeland Security and defined its mission and responsibilities (Chishti et al. 2003, Appendix F, 10).

June 26, 2002: The Department of Justice deported 131 Pakistani nationals who had been detained for months at various INS facilities. Most were arrested for ignoring previous deportation orders (Chishti et al. 2003, Appendix F, 11). Another 100 men were deported on August 21, 2002 (Chishti et al. 2003, Appendix F, 13).

July 11, 2002: The Department of Justice declared that a majority of the 9/11 detainees had been released and that many of them had been deported (Chishti et al. 2003, Appendix F, 11).

July 15, 2002: The Department of Justice announced Operation TIPS, a surveillance program allowing U.S. citizens to report "'suspicious activity'" (Hing 2006). Strong criticism by the American public killed the TIPS program (see chapter 6).

July 24, 2002: The Department of Justice issued a final rule allowing "the Attorney General to authorize any state or local law enforcement officer, with the consent of the head of the department whose geographic boundary the officer is serving, to exercise and enforce immigration laws during the period of a declared 'mass influx of aliens'" (Ibish 2003, 145; Chishti et al. 2003, Appendix F, 11).

July 24, 2002: The U.S. Commission on Civil Rights reaffirmed its commitment to protect the rights of Arab and Muslim Americans (Chishti et al. 2003, Appendix F, 12).

September 14, 2002: Five men of Yemeni descent were charged with operating an Al Qaeda cell in Lackawanna, New York (Chishti et al. 2003, Appendix F, 14).

September 16, 2002: Attorney General Ashcroft instructed INS to examine political asylum cases and identify immigrants who "admitted to accusations of terrorist activity or being members of any terrorist organization" (Hing 2006).

September 2002: Florida signed a Memorandum of Understanding with the FBI to deputize its state and local police to enforce immigration violators. Formalized agreements were later established with Alabama and Virginia (Henderson et al. 2006). Facing heavy criticism, Virginia backed off (Mary Beth Sheridan, "Virginia Police Back Off Immigration Enforcement," *Washington Post,* June 6, 2005, B1).

November 6, 2002: INS required male Iranian, Iraqi, Libyan, Sudanese, and Syrian citizens older than sixteen who had entered the United States before September 10, 2002, and intended to remain at least until December 16, 2002, to register with INS prior to this date. Failure to report was cause for deportation (Chishti et al. 2003, Appendix F, 16). On December 16, 2002, INS added other countries to the list. Armenia was included but was immediately removed, apparently because the "Armenians complained sufficiently loudly" (D. Cole 2003, 197). The list in August 2007 stood at twenty countries, mostly from the Middle East (Chishti et al. 2003, Appendix F, 17).

November 18, 2002: The Court of Review of the Foreign Intelligence Surveillance Act (FISA) declared that under the PATRIOT Act the Department of Justice can use wiretaps and other surveillance methods on terrorism suspects in the United States (Hing 2006).

November 25, 2002: President Bush signed into law the Department of Homeland Security. This new cabinet-level department merged twenty-two federal agencies, employing about 170,000 people (Chishti et al. 2003, Appendix F, 16). President Bush also proposed the Justice Department's Operation TIPS, which was intended to enlist thousands of truck drivers, mail carriers, and bus drivers as "citizen observers" (Chishti et al. 2003, Appendix F, 17). Widespread opposition to TIPS eventually killed the project.

January 16, 2003: INS extended the date of deadlines for special registration. Statistics were released stating that almost 1,200 were detained during the NSEERS special registration program (Chishti et al. 2003, Appendix F, 19).

February 2003: Draft legislation for "Domestic Security Enhancement Act of 2003" was proposed. About seventy civil liberties groups critiqued it as "PATRIOT II," arguing that it would seriously threaten the fundamental freedoms of citizens (AAI Alert, vol. 4, no. 12, March 21, 2003). The proposed legislation even alarmed representatives from the right such as James Sensenbrenner (R-WI), chairman of the House Judiciary Committee (AAI Alert, vol. 4, no. 7, April 23, 2003).

March 17, 2003: The government announced Operation Liberty Shield. Its goals were to promote national security and preparedness in the event of terrorist attacks through increased patrolling of borders and security in airports and transportation. Additionally, asylum seekers from "nations where al-Qaeda, [and] al-Qaeda sympathizers" had operated would be detained while their applications were being processed for monitoring. The program faced opposition by human rights groups and was in effect only for one month (White House, "Fact Sheet: Operation Liberty Shield," March 17, 2003, www .whitehouse.gov/news/releases/2003/03/20030317–9.html; Human Rights First, 2003, "Media Alert: Operation Liberty Shield Quietly Terminated," press release, www.humanrightsfirst.org/media/2003 _alerts/0515.htm; see also Hing 2006).

March 20, 2003: The attorney general disclosed that, starting December 18, 2002, FBI agents and U.S. marshals had been detaining foreign nationals for supposed immigration violations without sufficient evidence to hold them under criminal charges (Hing 2006).

May 27, 2003: The U.S. Senate passed SR 133, which condemned hate crimes against Arabs, Muslims, and Sikhs. Senator Dick Durban (D-IL) introduced the resolution. It was co-sponsored by John Sununu (R-NH) and Russell Feingold (D-WI) ("AAI Commends Senate for Passage of Hate Crimes Resolution," press release, May 27, 2003, www.aaiusa.org/press-room/911/pro52703a).

June 10, 2003: The BBC reported that out of the eighty-two thousand Arab and Muslim men who had responded to the government's special registration initiative, more than thirteen thousand risked deportation. They were charged with minor immigration irregularities. An official at DHS noted, "We need to focus our enforcement efforts on the biggest threats. If a loophole can be exploited by an immigrant, it can also be exploited by a terrorist." Critics have argued that

NSEERS had targeted Arabs and Muslims and had not found any real terrorists ("U.S. Threatens Mass Expulsions," *BBC News,* June 10, 2003, http://news.bbc.co.uk/1/hi/world/americas/2974882.stm).

July 9, 2003: Congressman Charles Norwood (R-GA) introduced HR 2671, the Clear Law Enforcement for Criminal Alien Removal Act (CLEAR). This act, if passed, would affirm the authority of state and local law enforcement to enforce immigration violations (Henderson et al. 2006). Civil rights organizations opposed its passage.

Early October 2003: The U.S. House of Representatives passed HR 234, condemning bigotry and violence against Arabs, Muslims, and Sikhs. The resolution was introduced by Arab American Congressman Darrell Issa (R-CA) and co-sponsored by Congressman Joe Wilson (R-SC) and Joseph Crowley (D-NY) (www.saldef.org/default .aspx?zone=article.view&a=948).

December 2, 2003: Effective on this date, DHS suspended the NSEERS program. It had required that males over age sixteen from twenty-five countries, mostly Arab and Muslim, be interviewed and registered within thirty days of entering the United States and annually thereafter (*Federal Register,* vol. 68, no. 231).

December, 2004: DHS suspended a few of the NSEER requirements. However, as of 2007, civil and criminal penalties are associated with failure to comply with NSEERS, including arrest, detention, monetary fines, and/or removal from the United States (ADC, "When Will the 'Shame of NSEERS' End?" press release, July 26, 2007, http://archives 2007.ghazali.net/html/adc_reiterates.html).

December 17, 2005: President Bush confirms having allowed the National Security Agency to wiretap U.S. citizens' international phone calls ("Bush Says He Signed NSA Wiretap Order," December 17, 2005, *CNN News,* www.cnn.com/2005/POLITICS/12/17/bush.nsa/).

December 25, 2005: About fifty Muslim Americans were returning from a conference, "Reviving the Islamic Spirit," in Toronto, when they were detained for more than four hours at the border, fingerprinted, and questioned, even though most were U.S. citizens with valid passports. The group sued DHS for degradation and humiliation. Some of those detained later sued the government for targeting American citizens for participation in religious conferences outside the United States (Andrea Elliott, "Five Muslims to Sue U.S. over Border Detentions," *New York Times,* April 20, 2005, B3). It has been suggested that Arabic or Muslim names are more likely to be flagged and subjected to surveillance by mechanisms such as the Violent Gang and Terrorist Organization File, which is used to monitor traffic at borders and airports and contains hundreds of names of alleged terrorists (Kevin Johnson, "Border Incident Angers Muslims," *USA Today*, February 8, 2005).

March 9, 2006: President George W. Bush signed into law HR 3199, the USA PATRIOT Improvement and Reauthorization Act of 2005, and S 2271, the USA PATRIOT Act Additional Reauthorizing Amendments Act of 2006. He declared: "The bills will help us continue to fight terrorism effectively and to combat the use of the illegal drug methamphetamine that is ruining too many lives." The renewal of the PATRIOT Act was made possible with 89 to 11 votes in the Senate and 280 to 138 votes in the House (White House, "President's Statement on H.R. 199, the 'USA PATRIOT Improvement and Reauthorization Act of 2005,'" www.whitehouse.gov/news/releases/2006/03/20060309–8.html). Included in the renewed legislation were "curbs" on its ability to impinge on civil liberties. For example, people who receive subpoenas granted under the Foreign Intelligence Surveillance Act for library, medical, computer, and other records can challenge gag orders in court (Nedra Pickler, "Bush Renews Patriot Act, Says It Helped Save Lives," *Washington Times*, March 10, 2006).

August 17, 2006: U.S. District Judge Anna Diggs Taylor declared that warrantless wiretapping violates the Constitution. This was one of several lawsuits against the government's domestic surveillance program that have been filed by civil rights organizations since September 11, 2001. However, the White House and the U.S. Department of Justice vowed to fight this ruling (David Stout, "Federal Judge Orders End to Warrantless Wiretapping," *New York Times*, August 17, 2006).

February 21, 2007: DHS launched TRIP to provide a way for "travelers to address situations where [they] . . . have been incorrectly delayed, denied boarding, identified for additional screening, or [have] . . . experienced difficulties . . . seeking entrance into the country" (DHS, "DHS Launches Traveler Redress Inquiry Program," press release, February 21, 2007, www.dhs.gov/xnews/releases/pr_1172073065966.shtm).

## GOVERNMENT ACTIONS

Since the 9/11 attacks, the U.S. Treasury has frozen the assets of several prominent Muslims charities, including the Holy Land Foundation, the Benevolence International Foundation, the Al Haramain Islamic Foundation, the Global Relief Foundation, the Islamic American Relief Agency, and KindHearts USA. These organizations have been accused of financing terrorism; however, none of these charities or any of their senior officers have been convicted of terrorism. Some of the charities have not even faced criminal charges, exacerbating Muslim American distrust of the federal government (Neil MacFarquhar, "Muslim Charity Sues Treasury Dept. and Seeks Dismissal of Charges of Terrorism," *New York Times,* December 12, 2006, A24).

August 22, 2003: Daniel Pipes officially became a member of the U.S. Institute of Peace. This recess appointment was highly controversial because of Pipe's anti-Muslim views. The *Guardian* wrote, "As a frequent commentator, he has warned that America's Muslims are the enemy within and called for unrestricted racial profiling and monitoring of Muslims in the military." Scholars find his position extreme. He has angered many in the academic community for the Web site Campus Watch, which "has initiated a witch-hunt against those he views as critics of Israel or lacking in patriotic zeal" ("Bush Appoints Anti-Muslim to Peace Role," *Guardian,* August 23, 2003, www.guardian.co.uk/usa/story/0,12271,1028113,00.html#articl).

July 30, 2004: The *New York Times* claimed that the Census Bureau had "provided specially tabulated population statistics on Arab Americans to the Department of Homeland Security, including detailed information on how many people of Arab backgrounds live in certain ZIP codes" (Lynette Clemetson, "Homeland Security Given Data on Arab Americans," A14). Arab American advocacy organizations were highly critical of the government for its breach of trust and insensitive behavior, especially after 9/11. AAI protested with a letter signed by over fifty organizations and persons. A month later, the bureau announced that it had changed its policy and would not share special tabulations on "sensitive populations" (Lynette Clemetson, "Census Policy on Providing Sensitive Data Is Revised," *New York Times,* August 31, 2004, A14).

Professor Tariq Ramadan, a prominent Swiss-born scholar of Islamic theology, was appointed to be the Henry R. Luce Chair of Religion, Conflict and Peace Building at the Joan B. Kroc Institute for International Peace Studies at the University of Notre Dame in fall 2004. The U.S. Embassy revoked his work visa without any explanation. Section 411 of the PATRIOT Act was used to deny him entry because he had allegedly "espoused or endorsed terrorist activity." In spite of protests,

Ramadan was not allowed into the country (Scott Smallwood, "U.S. Revokes Visa to Muslim Scholar," *Chronicle of Higher Education,* September 3, 2004, A14). A lawsuit filed by ACLU on behalf of three academic and writers' organizations (including PEN American Center) who had invited Ramadan to speak had a hearing in federal district court in Manhattan in April 2006. Contrary to its original position, the government no longer cited the PATRIOT Act's ban of foreigners' endorsement of terrorism as the reason for Ramadan's inability to obtain a visa for the United States. The government, however, did not reveal why Ramadan continued to be a national security risk (Julia Preston, "Hearing for Muslim Barred by U.S.," *New York Times,* April 14, 2006, A16). By the end of September 2006, the U.S. government had dropped charges against him, yet it continued to deny him a U.S. visa, pointing to donations Ramadan had made to a Swiss Palestinian-support group on the American "blacklist" because of its alleged ties with Hamas, even though Ramadan's donations had been made prior to the support group's being blacklisted, and even though the organization was officially recognized by the Swiss authorities (Tariq Ramadan, "What the West Can Learn from Islam," *Chronicle of Higher Education,* February 16, 2007, B6).

The 2005 CAIR report suggested that the government had caved to the influence of "certain right-wing pro-Israeli groups that 'waged a campaign' against moderate Muslim scholars and intellectuals whose views on Islam and the Middle East conflict with their own" (CAIR 2005], 31).

The press continued to feature human interest stories on individuals and families caught in the government's dragnet after 9/11. The case of Kamal, Hassan, and Housseine Essaheb appeared in the *New York Times.* These brothers from Queens, New York, all in graduate school, had come to the United States from Morocco with their parents in 1992. They obeyed the special registration requirements, only to realize that their immigration papers were not legal. They face deportation to an unknown country (Andrea Elliott, "Caught in the Net Thrown for Terrorists: A Family of Strivers Faces Deportation to a Country They Barely Recall," *New York Times,* May 24, 2005, B1).

After two years of imprisonment, Sami Al-Arian came to trial in Tampa, Florida, in June 2005 for his support of the Palestinian Islamic Jihad organization, which the U.S. government deemed a terrorist group. Until 2003, when he was fired, Al-Arian was a tenured professor of computer engineering at the University of South Florida. The evidence comes from over four million wiretaps to his phone and fax between 1994 and 2003, thanks to provisions in the PATRIOT Act and the Foreign Intelligence Surveillance Act (John Gravois, "Terrorism Trial of Ex-Professor Gets Started in Florida: Case Will Hinge on Nature of Al-Arian's Involvement with Palestinian Group," *Chronicle of Higher Education,* June 17, 2005, A1). In December 2005, the jury acquitted him of eight of seventeen charges but was deadlocked on the others. This was a defeat for the government because it had hailed this case as the centerpiece of its antiterrorism policies. In a plea-bargain agreement, Al-Arian agreed to a lesser charge and deportation (Mark Sherman, "Ex-Professor in Terror Case to Be Deported," *Associated Press,* April 14, 2006). However, Judge James S. Moody Jr. of the federal district court disregarded the agreement and sentenced Al-Arian to serve an additional one and a half years, the maximum allowed by the law. He also chastised Al-Arian by calling him a "master manipulator." Citing bombings in Israel, the judge noted, "Anyone with even the slightest bit of human compassion would be sickened. Not you. You saw it as an opportunity to solicit more money to carry out more bombings." He went on to say, "Your only connection to widows and orphans is that you create them" (Jennifer Steinhauer, "19 Months More in Prison for Professor in Terror Case," *New York Times* May 2, 2006, A14; John Gravois, "Judge Keeps Sami Al-Arian in Jail for an Additional 18 Months," *Chronicle of Higher Education,* May 12, 2006, A21).

In spite of the government's need for Arabic-speaking employees (John Diamond, "Terror War Still Short on Linguistics," *USA Today,* June 20, 2005), it has not utilized an obvious resource, namely Arab and Muslim Americans. A case in point is FBI agent Bassem Youssef, who has sued the agency for being passed over for counterterrorism promotions in spite of his skills (John Solomon, "AP Enterprises: FBI Managers Admit They Didn't Seek Out Terrorism Expertise after Sept. 11," Associated Press, June 19, 2005, http://ap.tbo.com/ap/breaking/MGBQ3ZUC5AE.html).

# Notes

## 1. BACKLASH

1. In 2001 the *New York Times* was quick to report this case of mistaken identity: "The nation's Sikhs, conspicuous in turbans that resemble the head wrap of suspected terrorist Osama bin Laden, have suddenly found themselves particularly vulnerable. By yesterday afternoon, more than 200 Sikhs had reported incidents to a Sikh anti-defamation group." Laurie Goodstein and Tamar Lewin, "A Nation Challenged, Violence and Harassment: Victims of Mistaken Identity, Sikhs Pay a Price for Turban," *New York Times,* September 19, 2001, A1.

2. Ibid.

3. Though this new term originates from the Qu'ran, designating the three monotheistic religions it considers sacred—Judaism, Christianity, and Islam—it is more inclusive and factual to call the United States a religiously pluralistic society.

4. Also, for sixty-eight interviews with Muslim and Arab Americans on the 9/11 backlash, see September 11 Digital Archive (2002–3).

5. See White House, "'Islam Is Peace' Says President," press release, September 17, 2001, www.whitehouse.gov/news/releases/2001/09/20010917-11.html.

6. This guilty verdict was applauded by the Sikh Mediawatch and Resource Task Force (SMART; now SALDEF—Sikh American Legal Defense and Education Fund) for clearly establishing the fact that crimes motivated by hatred and bias will be prosecuted. SMART has been advocating for the civil rights of Sikhs since 1996. See "Guilty Verdict Reached in First Post-9/11 Hate Crime Fatality,"

October 1, 2003, Sikh American Legal Defense and Education Fund, www.saldef.org/content.aspx?a=921.

7. White House, "Press Briefing by Ari Fleischer," press release, June 20, 2002, www.whitehouse.gov/news/releases/2002/06/20020620-12.html.

8. Heather MacDonald, "Straighten Up and Fly Right," *Wall Street Journal,* December 2, 2004, www.manhattan-institute.org/html_wsj-straighten_up.htm; "Delta Settles Discrimination Case," Business Briefs section, *Honolulu Star Bulletin,* June 22, 2004, http://starbulletin.com/2004/06/22/business/bizbriefs.html.

9. There are also Web site data sources on 9/11. For instance, we have collaborated with a Web-based archive whose objective was to save memories and memorabilia for future historians in digital form. See the September 11 Digital Archive's Web site at www.september11digitalarchive.org.

10. For other titles, see Ethan Bronner, "Collateral Damage: The Effects of the War on Terrorism on American Freedom and Privacy Are Not Easy to Assess," *New York Times Book Review,* February 22, 2004, 10–11.

11. For example, see Lee Clarke's edited volume *Terrorism and Disaster: New Threats, New Ideas,* which showed that people did not panic after 9/11. Contrary to popular belief, "altruism and cohesion, not self-interest and panic, are the central tendencies in response to extreme events" (Clarke 2003, 132; see also Clarke 2002). After waking up from their "cognitive blindness," Americans realized that airports and other infrastructure were vulnerable and that the country could not be safe. The contributors to the volume focus on fear, myths of disasters, the long-term recovery of survivors, and emergency management response. Other edited volumes (Ursano, Fullerton, and Norwood 2003; Moser and Frantz 2003) focus on mental health, specifically on what interventions have been successful; how to deal with traumatic death, stress, violence, and relocation; and how the impact of a disaster varies for different segments of the population.

12. See, e.g., the home page of Kathleen Tierney, a professor of sociology at the University of Colorado and director of the National Hazards Research and Applications Information Center in Boulder, http://socsci.colorado.edu/SOC/People/Faculty/tierney.html. See also Claudia Dreifus, "A Sociologist with an Advanced Degree in Calamity," *New York Times,* September 7, 2004; Tierney et al. (2006). Scholars have debunked the "panic myth" by proving that "people act to help those in danger who are physically near them, and they are willing to put themselves in danger to help others"; examples are not only "first responders" but also "unofficial first responders." Sociologists have discovered that disasters have a greater impact on vulnerable populations such as children, the elderly, the poor, and the disabled. The American Sociological Association invited members who specialize in disaster studies to address a congressional briefing on the human dimension of disasters in October 2003. See Lee Herring, "ASA Congressional Briefing Examines Policy Implications Regarding Disasters," *Footnotes,* December 2003, 1, 9.

13. See Detroit Arab American Study, 2003, www.icpsr.umich.edu/cocoon/ICPSR/STUDY/04413.xml#skipto.

14. The American public seems oblivious to the extent and pervasiveness of the backlash. We have learned from conversations with Arab and Muslim com-

munity leaders that even the FBI does not realize the impact that the government initiatives have had on these populations. This lack of understanding can be detected in the media as well. For example, in a review of the Arab American National Museum in Dearborn, a *New York Times* art critic wrote: "The museum comments that after 9/11 'Arab Americans were unfairly held responsible, yet not a single Arab American was found guilty of any connection to September 11th.' But how were Arab Americans 'unfairly held responsible' for 9/11, except by bigots? Some unfairness undoubtedly manifested itself in the quest for information, but who held Arab Americans responsible as a group? The second assertion is also phrased so narrowly that it misses the point: some Arab Americans have indeed been found guilty of financing terrorism, and reasonable doubts have been raised about some others" (Edward Rothstein, "A Mosaic of Arab Culture at Home in America," *New York Times,* October 24, 2005, E1, E7).

15. Syrian Arabs, mostly Christian, and Armenians from the Ottoman Empire were part of the early cohorts arriving from the Middle East (see chapter 3).

16. The ethnoracial pentagon consists of the following five classifications: (1) white, (2) black or African American, (3) Hispanic or Latino, (4) Asian and other Pacific Islander, and (5) Native American Indian or Alaska Native.

17. Even a book whose title includes the term *backlash* does not offer a definition (Ellen Reese, *Backlash against Welfare Mothers: Past and Present* [Berkeley: University of California Press, 2005]). Michael Omi and Howard Winant's seminal book *Racial Formation in the United States* also uses the word *backlash* without defining it. Its use implies racial reaction: "Issues of race have once again been dramatically revived in the 1980s, this time in the form of a 'backlash' to the political gains of racial minority movements of the past" (1994, 2). We surmise that *backlash* is used more as a colloquial term than as a conceptual tool.

18. According to the *Oxford English Dictionary,* backlash is "an excessive or violent reaction, reactionary attitudes or opinion" (*New Shorter Oxford English Dictionary,* ed. Lesley Brown [Oxford: Clarendon Press,1993]). The *American Heritage Dictionary of the English Language,* 4th ed. (Boston: Houghton Mifflin, 2000), defines backlash as "an antagonistic reaction to a trend, development, or event."

19. Evidence from Australia confirms that anti-Muslim/Arab hate crimes only intensified "existing, ongoing and everyday forms and patterns of vilification" (Poynting 2004, 3) following international incidents, including the Gulf War (1991), the Bali bombings (October 2002), and 9/11. See also Poynting (2002) and chapter 5 of this book.

20. Evidence shows that this election outcome was part of the terrorists' plan. Elliott reports that "a 42-page document . . . produced by an Islamic think tank of sorts . . . analyzed the political situation in Spain and argued that 'painful blows' were needed to force the Spanish government to withdraw its troops from Iraq. It also suggested making 'the utmost use' of the approaching elections." Andrea Elliott, "Where Boys Grow Up to Be Jihadists," *New York Times Magazine,* November 25, 2007, 77.

21. Renwick McLean, "Spain: Aznar Defends Actions after Madrid Bombings," *New York Times*, November 30, 2004, A6.

22. See, e.g., Lizette Alvarez, "Revenge Attacks and Vandalism Unnerve Muslims in Britain," *New York Times*, July 12, 2005, A8; "Schools Get Racial Tension Advice," *BBC News*, July 13, 2005; Lizette Vikram Dodd, "Attack on London: Murder, Islamophobia Blamed for Attack," *Guardian*, July 13, 2005, 5; "Special Report: Muslim Extremism in Europe: The Enemy Within," *Economist*, July 16, 2005, 24–25; Michael Holden, "UK Faith-Hate Crimes Rise after Bombs," *Reuters*, July 28, 2005; Hassan M. Fattah, "Britain's Muslims Take Tough Line on Militants," *New York Times*, August 11, 2005, A10; H. D. S. Greenway, "British Muslims Face New Hurdles," *Boston Globe*, October 18, 2005, A15; Aisha Labi, "McCarthyism in Britain? Muslim Students Question Call for University Leaders to Monitor Their Campuses," *Chronicle of Higher Education*, October 21, 2005, A49.

23. "Timeline: French Riots, a Chronology of Key Events," *BBC News*, November 14, 2005, http://news.bbc.co.uk/1/hi/world/europe/4413964.stm.

24. Other incidents involving Muslims in Europe include the September 2005 publication by the Danish daily *Jyllands-Posten* of a series of cartoons that riled Muslims around the globe, particularly one depicting the Prophet Muhammad's headdress shaped like a bomb with a burning fuse. When several European papers reprinted the cartoons in defense of a free press ("Newspapers Rerun Islamic Cartoons," *Washington Post*, February 2, 2006), there were violent demonstrations in Damascus, Beirut, and elsewhere, leading to deaths and damaged property and a successful boycott of Danish products in the Middle East (Rami G. Khouri, "The Danish Cartoons: A Neo-Colonial Slap," *Daily Star*, February 8, 2006; Hassan M. Fattah, "At Mecca Meeting, Cartoon Outrage Crystallized," *New York Times*, February 9, 2006, A1). Needless to say, this increased the amount of negative attention focused on Muslims in Europe.

25. See Alan Cowell and Dexter Filkins, "Britain Says Plan Was to Sneak Liquid Explosives on Planes," *New York Times*, August 11, 2006, A1, A7.

26. For example, Alan Cowell, "Top Police Spar in London over Muslims as 'Victims,'" *New York Times*, August 20, 2006, A4; Drake Bennett, "Hearts and Minds: Drawn to Ballots not Bombs, America's Muslim Community Shows Few Signs of the Radicalism Seen in Britain. But with Anger over U.S. Policies at Home and Abroad, a Younger Generation May be Up for Grabs," *Boston Globe*, August 20, 2006, D1.

27. Seven men loyal to Al Qaeda were arrested in Florida in June 2006 (John O'Neil, "Seven Are Charged with Plot to Blow Up Sears Tower," *New York Times*, June 23, 2006). We have not included them in our analysis because they are neither Muslim nor ethnically linked to the Middle East or South Asia.

28. Ian Austen and David Johnson, "17 Held in Plot to Bomb Sites across Ontario: Officials Say Men Trained and Bought Materials in Plan for Attacks," *New York Times*, June 4, 2006, A1, A24. See also Anthony DePalma, "Canada Saw Plot to Seize Officials," *New York Times*, June 7, 2006, A1, A14.

29. Lisa Miller, "American Dreamers: Muslim Americans Are One of This Country's Greatest Strengths. But They're Vulnerable as Never Before," *Newsweek*, July 30, 2007, 25–33.

30. The eight suspects in the foiled plot, which had called for the detonation of two car bombs in London's West End and an attack at the Glasgow airport (July 3, 2007), included Dr. Mohammed Asha, a twenty-six-year-old neurosurgeon born in Saudi Arabia and trained in Jordan; Dr. Bilal Abdullah, a British-born Iraqi doctor who had studied at Cambridge; and Kafeel Ahmed, an Indian aeronautical engineer. See Jane Perlez, "Doctor Born in Saudi Arabia Is 4th Charged in Bomb Plot," *New York Times,* July 20 2007, A8; Mark Landler and Sarah Lyall, "All 8 Suspects in British Attacks Are Expatriate Medical Professionals," *New York Times,* A6.

31. David Rieff, "Policing Terrorism: The Case for the British Way of Fighting Violent Islamists," *New York Times Magazine,* July 22, 2007, 13–14.

32. Our own identities, research interests, and affiliations are squarely Middle Eastern American. Bozorgmehr is co-director and Bakalian is associate director of MEMEAC. Bakalian was born in Lebanon to Armenian parents, attended the American University of Beirut, and received her PhD in sociology from Columbia University; her dissertation was on Armenian Americans. Bozorgmehr, son of a Muslim father and a Christian Assyrian mother, was born and raised in Iran. He received his PhD in sociology from UCLA, and his dissertation was on Iranians in Los Angeles. Together we are proficient in Arabic, Armenian, Turkish, and Persian. Therefore, as researchers we have had no problems accessing spokespersons representing Middle Eastern and Muslim community-based organizations.

33. The September 11 Digital Archive was initiated by the American Social History Project/Center for Media and Learning at the Graduate Center, City University of New York, and the Center for History and the Media at George Mason University. See http://911digitalarchive.org.

34. We thank Michael Lichter, the workshop co-organizer, for arranging meetings with local officials.

35. See, e.g., Michelle Garcia, "Muslims Detained at Border Sue U.S. Homeland Security," *Washington Post,* April 21, 2005, A08; Kevin Johnson, "Border Incident Angers Muslims," *USA Today,* February 9, 2005, 3A.

36. Matthew Purdy and Lowell Bergman, "Unclear Danger: Inside the Lackawanna Terror Case," *New York Times,* October 12, 2003, A1, A35–36.

37. For example, *Aramica,* a biweekly newspaper, published in Arabic and English, that was established shortly after 9/11 has kept us informed of the activities of the Arab American community in metropolitan New York. For a write-up about *Aramica,* see Samantha Henry and Michael Karas, "Copies of Aramica on Display at the Arab American Festival in New York City. There Was a Scarcity of Arab American Voices in the Mainstream Media before September 11, 2001," *Herald News,* July 30, 2007.

38. N-Vivo is a product of QSR International Pty. Ltd. in Melbourne, Australia. N-Vivo provides three systems for managing data: documents (in our case the transcribed interviews), nodes (codes we created to categorize the various concepts and issues), and attributes (characteristics of the organization, such as year founded, size of board, and budget, and characteristics of the respondents, such as gender, age, level of education, and religion). Attributes have values (e.g., gender is male or female). The software allows the researcher

to search for linkages between two concepts—two or more nodes or a node and an attribute. The software also searches for words or string of words in the text.

39. All three interviewers were young women and present or former students at the City University of New York. One was born in Egypt and spoke Arabic; one was from Pakistan and spoke Urdu; and one was studying Arabic. The interviews were conducted in New York City, but one of the interviewers took the initiative to recruit respondents over the Internet. Thus several interviews were conducted over the phone with Arab and/or Muslim respondents across the United States.

## 2. COMPARATIVE AND HISTORICAL PERSPECTIVES

1. Teresa Watanabe, "Frustrated U.S. Muslims Feel Marginalized Again," *Washington Report on Middle Eastern Affairs,* December 2002, www.thefree library.com/Frustrated+U.S.+Muslims+feel+marginalized+again=a094769821.

2. Hanna Rosin, "Snapshot of an Immigrant's Dream Fading: A Legacy of September 11 Sweeps Pakistani to the Point of No Return," *Washington Post,* March 24, 2002, A1.

3. Scholars have weighed in on the definition of war. Edward Tiryakian argues that the present situation of the United States qualifies as "a new form of global conflict, and it is not inappropriate to view it as World War III" ("From the Welfare State to the Warfare State," *Contexts* 4, no. 2 [Spring 2005]: 23). Even neoconservative scholar Francis Fukuyama has parted ways with his intellectual heritage and denounced the foreign policy of the Bush administration: "We are fighting hot counter-insurgency wars in Afghanistan and Iraq and against the international *jihadist* movement, wars in which we need to prevail. But 'war' is the wrong metaphor for the broader struggle, since wars are fought at full intensity and have clear beginnings and endings" (Francis Fukuyama, "After Neoconservatism," *New York Times Magazine,* February 19, 2006, 67).

4. Roger Daniels, "Detaining Minority Citizens, Then and Now," *Chronicle of Higher Education,* February 15, 2002, B10. See also Gerstle (2004).

5. In 1920 Congress expanded grounds for deportation. Thus "aliens who believe in, advise, advocate, or teach, or who are members of or affiliated with any organization, association, society, or group, that believes in, advises, or teaches . . . the overthrow by force or violence of the Government of the United States or of all forms of law" could be deported (quoted in Motomura 2006, 42).

6. In 1870 the naturalization statute replaced the 1790 law that had restricted naturalization to "free white persons." The Fourteenth Amendment granted "white persons and persons of African descent" the right to naturalization. But Congress deliberately barred individuals of Chinese and Japanese descent from obtaining these rights (Daniels 1988, 139).

7. The public hearings were meant to humiliate and stigmatize. "The target becomes in the eyes of his condemners literally 'different,' 'a new person.' It is not that new attributes are added to the old identity. He is not changed; he is, rather, reconstituted, transformed" (Navasky 1980, 319). Some victims internalized the accusations with which they had been charged; they ended up believing something was wrong with them. Even children were implicated. "'Commie

kids' were taunted, beaten up, ostracized—just like their parents. The stigma was . . . pervasive" (Schrecker 1998, 367).

8. A fifty-minute documentary also entitled *Reel Bad Arabs* (dir. Sut Jhally, prod. Media Education Foundation) was released in November 2006. See also William Booth, "Cast of Villains: 'Reel Bad Arabs' Takes on Hollywood Stereotyping," *Washington Post,* June 23, 2007, C01.

9. Jonathan Friedlander of the Center for Near Eastern Studies at UCLA has been documenting examples of Orientalism in architecture, entertainment, consumerism, and pageantry across the country. See the home page for UCLA's Center for Near Eastern Studies, www.isop.ucla.edu/cnes/home/meus.asp#.

10. According to Ronald Stockton, Arabs are portrayed as sexually depraved, treating women as chattel in their harems; having savage leaders who order their subjects to sacrifice themselves in suicide bombings; being deceitful; and having peculiar genetic traits such as "thick lips, evil eyes, unkempt hair, scruffy beard, weak chin, crooked nose, vile look. . . . heavy brow, stupid expression, stooped shoulders" (1994, 135).

11. Garbi Schmidt (2004, 33) documents the discriminatory behavior in Chicago after the Pan American Airlines explosion over Lockerbie in 1988.

12. For many Americans, the 1973 Arab oil embargo clinched the negative association between their pocketbooks and the Middle East, reinforcing their already negative image of Middle Easterners. In response to the Arab defeat at the hands of Israel in the Yom Kippur War, the Organization of the Petroleum Exporting Countries (OPEC), led by Saudi Arabia, announced that the Arab countries were cutting production, placing an embargo on shipments of crude oil to Western countries, and enforcing a complete economic boycott of Israel. As a result, oil prices skyrocketed to four times their previous levels. Arab *sheiks* (princes) were perceived as enriching themselves at the expense of common people in the West. By early 1974, most of the world was hit by the worst economic slump since the Great Depression of 1932–40.

13. In the middle of the Lebanese civil war, President Reagan deployed 1,200 U.S. Marines as part of the U.S. Multi-National Forces (USMNF) contingent. Their role was to act as peacekeepers between the Lebanese Army and the Syrian-backed Shiᶜa militia for a sixty-day period. In April 1983, the U.S. Embassy in Beirut was destroyed, killing seventeen U.S. nationals and forty others. Again in October 1983, a suicide bomber drove his truck into the U.S. Marine barracks stationed near the Beirut International Airport. This time the toll was heavier; 241 marines died.

14. On June 14, 1985, Hezbollah fighters hijacked TWA flight 847 from Athens to Beirut, demanding the release of 766 Shiᶜa imprisoned in Israel. On board were 104 Americans, including five navy divers. One of them was shot in the head while the global media taped the scene. Four days into the crisis, the hostages were released except for thirty-nine Americans who were removed to a secure location. Complicated negotiations finally led to their release, but only after Israel began to let go of the Shiᶜa prisoners.

15. On October 7, 1985, four heavily armed Palestinians hijacked an Italian cruise ship, the *Achille Lauro,* carrying more than four hundred passengers and crew, off the Egyptian coast. The hijackers demanded that Israel free fifty

Palestinian prisoners. Leon Klinghoffer, a sixty-nine-year-old disabled American tourist, was killed, and his body was thrown overboard in his wheelchair.

16. In February 1993, six persons were killed and over a thousand injured in the bombing of the World Trade Center in New York City. Six Muslims of Arab descent, including Sheikh Omar Abdel Rahman, were convicted for masterminding the explosion.

17. These sentiments are perhaps best portrayed by the headline "Jumping to Conclusions: Many in the Press and Public Were Quick to Assume the Crime Had Mideast Origins. But 'John Doe' Is One of Us," *Newsweek,* May 1, 1995, 55. See also Richard Roeper, "Media Stumble Badly in Rush to Judgment," *Chicago Sun-Times,* April 24, 1995, 11; Mary Abowd, "Arab Americans Suffer Hatred after Bombing," *Chicago Sun-Times,* May 13, 1995, 14; Penny Bender Fuchs, "Jumping to Conclusions in Oklahoma City?" *American Journalism Review,* June 1995, www.ajr.org/Article.asp?id=1980.

18. Lydia Saad, "Anti-Muslim Feelings Fairly Commonplace," August 10, 2006,www.gallup.com/poll/24073/AntiMuslim-Sentiments-Fairly-Common place.aspx.

19. Juan Cole (2007) explains that the term *Islamophobia* was coined in the last decades of the twentieth century. He quotes United Nations Secretary General Kofi Annan, who sounded the alarm on Muslims' fears about their well-being and the erosion of their civil rights.

20. In 2005 the *Los Angeles Times* questioned the accuracy of the evidence against the L.A. 8. It described how FBI Special Agent Frank H. Knight, without any knowledge of Arabic language or culture, followed a group of Palestinians and then reported them to the INS. On February 15, 1986, he observed 1,200 Palestinians at the Glendale Civic Auditorium who had gathered to raise funds for the PFLP and other "homeland" causes, including medical care and schooling in the camps. There were speeches, an amateur dance troupe, flags and pamphlets, and a procession of youth in khaki shirts and camouflage trousers. Hiding in the engineering booth, Knight reported that the "general mood" was "militaristic" and found the khaki outfits not "normal attire for obtaining cash for orphans." There was also an inadvertent incident during the rehearsal when a dancer took the American flag from its standard and leaned it against a wall. Knight interpreted this as an anti-American message: "They treat the flag the way they would treat the enemy. And, so, it wouldn't be part of their event." Peter H. King, "18 Years Waiting for a Gavel to Fall: A Group of Palestinians Have Been in Legal Limbo for Nearly Two Decades as the U.S. Has Sought to Deport Them. Their Case Foreshadowed Post-9/11 Policy," *Los Angeles Times,* June 29, 2005.

21. Henry Weinstein, "Final Two L.A. 8 Defendants Cleared," *New York Times,* October 31, 2007, B1.

22. While the AAI press release on secret evidence insinuates that the Omnibus Counter-Terrorism Bill of 1995 was triggered by a backlash against illegal immigrants, our respondents suggested otherwise. One leader was convinced that the bill followed the crash of TWA 800. When the plane exploded on July 17, 1996, over Long Island, New York, it was widely speculated that Arab/Muslim terrorists had shot it down by a missile. This cannot be true because the bill was

introduced in February 1995 and signed by President Clinton on April 24, 1996. Another respondent noted that the Counter-Terrorism Bill was instigated after the Oklahoma bombing in 1995, a more plausible explanation.

23. ADC, Action Alert, November 2, 1999, www.adc.org/action/1999/2nov99.htm.

24. We have removed all references that might identify this respondent.

25. Mann uses a wide range of case studies, starting with the Assyrians in the second millennium and ending with Rwanda, but is careful to analyze how each case fits or does not fit his thesis. See Scott McLemee, "Delving into Democracy's Shadow: The Sociologist Michael Mann Took a Detour from His Epic Study of Power in Human History. It Led Him Straight to the Horrors at the Center of Modern Life," *Chronicle of Higher Education,* September 17, 2004, A10.

26. Gerstle (2004, 95) puts the number of Germans on the eve of World War I at four million. If one were to add German-speaking immigrants from the Austro-Hungarian Empire, their numbers would certainly reach eight million, a population size that might frighten most governments at war.

27. Neil Lewis, "Prosecutor Urges Death for Concealing Sept. 11 Plot," *New York Times,* March 7, 2006, A14; Neil Lewis, "Moussaoui Given Life Term by Jury over Link to 9/11," *New York Times,* May 4, 2006, A1; "Timeline: The Zacarias Moussaoui Case," *CNN.com,* March 14, 2006, http://edition.cnn.com/interactive/us/0207/moussoui.timeline/frameset.exclude.html.

28. Robert Inlow, "Padilla's Ordeal," *USA Today,* March 8, 2007, A10; D. Cole and Lobel (2007, 95).

29. Peter Whoriskey, "Jury Convicts Jose Padilla of Terror Charges," *Washington Post,* August 17, 2007, A1.

30. Zachary Coile and Bob Egelko, "Justices Affirm Rights of Detainees: Terror Suspects Must Be Given Access to U.S. Court," *San Francisco Chronicle,* June 29, 2004; Michael Isikoff and Mark Hosenball, "Out of the Brig: 'Enemy Combatant' Yaser Hamdi Will Soon Be Released from a Military Prison without Facing Any Charges," *Newsweek Online,* September 15, 2004.

31. Carolyn Marshall, "24-Year Term for Californian in Terrorism Training Case," *New York Times,* September 11, 2007, A20.

32. Mathew Purdy and Lowell Bergman, "Unclear Danger: Inside the Lackawanna Terror Case," *New York Times,* October 12, 2003, A1, A35–37.

33. The London bombings on July 7, 2005, were also executed by homegrown terrorists.

34. We acknowledge Michael Mann for bringing this important issue to our attention.

35. Jim Garamone, "Search Continues for Taliban, Al Qaeda Terrorists," *American Forces Press Service,* December 27, 2001.

36. For example, the Military Commissions Act "strips the U.S. courts of the jurisdiction to hear habeas corpus appeals challenging the lawfulness or conditions of detention of any non-U.S. citizen held in U.S. custody as an 'enemy combatant,' . . . permits the use of classified information as 'evidence' against a defendant, without affording the defendant the right to challenge the information, particularly the 'sources, methods or activities' by which the

government acquired it, . . . permits the use of classified information as 'evidence' against a defendant, without affording the defendant the right to challenge the information, particularly the 'sources, methods or activities' by which the government acquired it." See Amnesty International (2006).

37. "UN Calls for Guantánamo Closure," *BBC News*, February 16, 2007.

38. William Glaberson, "New Detainee Rights Weighed in Plans to Close Guantánamo," *New York Times*, November 4, 2007, A1.

39. Martin Asser, "Abu Ghraib: Dark Stain on Iraq's Past," *BBC News*, May 25, 2004.

40. Seymour Hersh, "Torture at Abu Ghraib," *New Yorker*, May 10, 2004.

41. Robert Worth, "U.S. Military Plans to Move Detainees Out of Abu Ghraib," *New York Times*, March 9, 2006.

42. "[The U.S. federal war crimes statute] defines a war crime as a violation of the existing international laws of war, including the Geneva Conventions. To be enforced, that law depends on the existence of a Geneva Convention violation; similarly, the Uniform Code of Military Justice prohibits war crimes, but without a Geneva Convention violation, there was no war crime." Phillip Carter, "The Road to Abu Ghraib: The Biggest Scandal of the Bush Administration Began at the Top," *Washington Monthly*, November 2004.

43. Ibid.

44. Craig Whitlock, "Testimony Helps Detail CIA's Post-9/11 Reach: Europeans Told of Plans for Abductions," Washington Post Foreign Service, December 16, 2006, A01.

45. Absconders are illegal immigrants who have been issued deportation orders but remain in the United States.

46. In Detroit, six Arab Americans were charged with supporting terrorism, but all had connections to Hezbollah, not Al Qaeda (Howell and Jamal 2008). In May 2007, the FBI and Immigration and Customs Enforcement officers arrested six men in a plot to fire grenades and kill soldiers at Fort Dix, New Jersey, a training base for soldiers before heading to Iraq and Afghanistan. Although three of the suspects were ethnic Albanians who had entered the United States illegally, the other suspects included a Jordan-born U.S. citizen and legal U.S. residents from Turkey and Yugoslavia (David Kocieniewski, "Six Men Arrested in a Terror Plot against Ft. Dix," *New York Times*, May 9, 2007, A1, B6). A month later, four Muslim men were accused of scheming to attack New York's John F. Kennedy International Airport by blowing up the major jet-fuel tanks and supply pipeline. One of these was a U.S. citizen from Guyana (Greg Miller and Erika Hayasaki, "Arrests Made in Alleged Plot against JFK Airport," *Los Angeles Times*, June 3 2007, A1).

47. JACL, established in 1930, was the most prominent national *Nisei* (second-generation) organization; it barred the *Issei* (first generation) from joining. Unlike other Japanese American organizations of that period, it did not stress "the study of Japanese culture" (Daniels 1988, 180). Rather, it was concerned with civil rights. Sucheng Chan concurs that since they were "concerned with economic success and social status, JACL members believed that the best way for them to prove their worthiness in the eyes of the Euro-Americans was to be totally loyal to American ideals, which they understood to be individualism,

free enterprise, and the ownership of private property. As loyal Americans, they never criticized racism, although they worked hard to challenge discriminatory laws" (1991, 117).

48. The most effective opposition to the JACL's cooperation came from the *Kibei,* American-born Japanese who were sent back to Japan for education and employment (Daniels 1972). Daniels estimates that there were some eleven thousand *Kibei* by the 1940s, probably about 20 percent of the second-generation *Nisei.* Considering their experiences in Japan, it might be assumed that the *Kibei* would be more loyal to that country. However, Daniels stresses their marginality in relation to both American and Japanese cultures and argues that many were uncomfortable in both (1988, 176–77).

49. See JACL, "History of the Japanese American Citizens League," 2008, www.jacl.org/about/jacl-history.htm.

50. Todd Bensman, "FBI Contacts Iraqi Immigrants in Area," *Dallas Morning News,* December 15, 2002.

51. Jill Serjeant, "Hundreds of Muslim Immigrants Rounded up in California," Reuters, December 19, 2002; "Mass Arrests of Muslims in LA," *BBC News,* December 19, 2002, http://news.bbc.co.uk/1/hi/world/americas/2589317.stm.

52. See "Mass Arrests of Muslims."

53. For example, Robert R. Hosokawa, "We Knew We Weren't the Enemy: A Familiar Knot of Anxiety over Post-9/11 Civil Liberties Issues Shows a *Nisei* How Far America Has Come—And Still Has to Go," *Christian Science Monitor,* July 28, 2004. The author references an article he wrote sixty-one years earlier: Robert Hosokawa, "An American with a Japanese Face," *Christian Science Monitor,* May 22, 1943.

54. Available from Lina Hoshino, c/o Institute for Equity, Ecology, Humor and Art, 150 Albion Street, San Francisco, CA 94110, e-mail: lina@ieeha.org, www.caughtinbetween.org.

55. Teresa Watanabe, "Frustrated U.S. Muslims Feel Marginalized Again," *Washington Report on Middle Eastern Affairs,* December 2002. In New York, the Japanese Peace Organization met with representatives of the Arab American Family Support Center, ADC, and other Arab/Muslim community leaders. See Alyssa Misner, "Brooklyn Arab Americans Share Their Post-9/11 Experience with Peace Boaters," *Brooklyn Daily Eagle,* June 16, 2006.

56. Nina Bernstein, "Echoes of '40s Internment Are Seen in Muslim Detainees' Suit," *New York Times,* April 3, 2007, B1.

57. Nikkei for Civil Rights and Redress, "Break the Fast, November 15, 2003," n.d., www.ncrr-la.org/news/12_14_03/2.html.

58. Daniels, "Detaining Minority Citizens," B10.

59. A survey by the *New York Times* concurred that Americans endorsed such views. See Robin Toner and Janet Elder, "A Nation Challenged: Attitudes; Public Is Wary but Supportive on Rights Curbs," *New York Times,* December 12, 2001, A1.

60. Lawsuits involving warrants, wiretapping, and data mining of telephone records have been filed since the early days of the backlash (see Appendix).

61. See Nina Bernstein, "Judge Rules That U.S. Has Broad Powers to Detain Noncitizens Indefinitely," *New York Times,* June 15, 2006.

62. Yossi Shain argues that Americans have been more cautious in making charges of disloyalty in the post–civil rights era. He cites the Oklahoma City bombing, when President Clinton warned "the American public not to draw hasty, race-based conclusions about the identity of the perpetrators" (1999, 20).

## 3. IMMIGRATION PATTERNS

1. Although Cyprus is near Turkey, Syria, and Lebanon and shares a historical and cultural background with these countries, it is not part of the Middle East.

2. South Asia consists of Bangladesh, Burma, India, Nepal, Pakistan, and Sri Lanka—a very heterogeneous group of countries and peoples divided by language, religion, national origin, caste, and race.

3. Publications on Middle Eastern Americans include Bozorgmehr and Feldman (1996); Bozorgmehr, Der-Martirosian, and Sabagh (1996); Bozorgmehr and Baron (2001); Marvasti and McKinney (2004); and Tehranian (2008).

4. The "top-down" mobilization of Indian political elites after 1974 was not necessarily welcomed by the rank-and-file members of this population. Some challenged "the very idea of being raced" (Kibria 2006, 215).

5. See AAI's home page at www.aaiusa.org. The collaboration between AAI and the Census Bureau has produced two special reports that summarize demographic data on Arab Americans in the 2000 census: de la Cruz and Brittingham (2003) and Brittingham and de la Cruz (2005). These were the first-ever publications on any Middle Eastern group by the bureau.

6. The authors of this book serve on the board of AAI's Census Information Center. Helen Samhan, the executive director in charge of the center, shared this information during a board meeting in Washington, D.C., on November 22, 2002.

7. See AAI, "Coalition of American Ethnic Organizations Call on U.S. Census to Include Question on Ancestry in 2010," press release, April 6, 2007.

8. Data are based on table 2, "Immigration by Region and Selected Country of Last Residence, Fiscal Years 1820–1998," from the *1998 Statistical Yearbook of the Immigration and Naturalization Service* (U.S. DHS 1998). We examined data under "region and country of last residence" and checked "Turkey," assuming that it stood for the Ottoman Empire.

9. Industrialization and the need for cheap labor resulted in the "Great Migrations" that brought masses of eastern and southern Europeans to the United States (see, e.g., Handlin 1973). The various ethnic and religious groups that made up the peoples of the Ottoman Empire were also part of that movement, particularly Arabic-speaking Christians from Greater Syria and Armenians from the Turkish mainland. The ports of Beirut, Alexandretta, Smyrna, and Constantinople were accessible to many of the minority populations who wanted to emigrate.

10. Under the charismatic leadership of Egypt's Gamal abd al Nasser, pan-Arabism flourished. This was a secular, socialist movement that opposed Western intervention in local politics and traditional elites. The principal instrument of pan-Arabism was the Baʿath Party, which was active in Syria, Iraq, Jordan,

and Yemen. For a personal interpretation of Arabism and Arab identity, see L. Ahmed (1999, ch. 11, "On Becoming an Arab").

11. In his memoir *Out of Egypt* (1994), André Aciman, a Jewish scholar who grew up in Alexandria in a diverse ethnic and religious community, describes the financial difficulties that gave his family little option but to leave (see also Alhadeff 1998). Leila Ahmed's autobiography (1999) complements Aciman's. Her account of growing up in Egypt takes the perspective of a woman from an upper-class Muslim family. For a modern history of Jews in Egypt and their dispersion, see Beinin (1998) and Kramer (1989).

12. In the decades that followed, many university-educated professionals, "frustrated and dismayed by the instability and the lack of opportunities for advancement back home," also emigrated (Suleiman 1994, 46).

13. Religion is not coded by the census, and few other minorities (e.g., Armenians) are left in today's Israel/Palestine.

14. Punjabi immigrants were peasants whose lands could no longer sustain their families because of population increase and subdivision. The independence of Pakistan in 1947 created conflict between Muslims and Sikhs in California. The Sikhs erected their *gurdwaras* and the Muslims built mosques, further dividing the community (Leonard 1992).

15. These numbers indicate not only new arrivals but those who have obtained legal resident status either through adjustment of status or as new arrivals. The data were compiled from several U.S. federal agencies that have regulated immigration, including INS and DHS.

16. Spencer S. Hsu and Robin Wright, "Crocker Blasts Refugee Process: Iraqis Could Wait 2 Years for Entry, Ambassador Says," *Washington Post*, September 17, 2007, A1, A15.

17. Morton Abramowitz et al., "A 'Surge' for Refugees," *New York Times*, April 22, 2008, A27.

18. The numbers for the country of Jordan include Arab Palestine from 1965 to 2003, after which they are placed under "unknown" in the *Statistical Yearbooks of the Immigration and Naturalization Service*.

19. The numbers for employee-based preferences include the spouses and children of those admitted under this category.

20. Some Arab Americans have tried a variety of measures to gain a minority status, but so far their efforts have not borne fruit. According to one respondent, during the tenure of Mayor Washington there was an attempt to make Arab Americans a legal minority in Chicago. The process proved impossible. We also learned from respondents that some individuals (those from Egypt) had tried to pass as Asian or African American but had failed.

21. As sociologist C. Wright Mills (1959) would have predicted, identity is historically specific. The notion that ethnic identity is socially constructed is now well accepted (Berger and Luckman 1966).

22. After the 1920s, as the Republic of Lebanon was emerging, Naoum and his brother Salloum A. Mokarzel, editors of *Al-Hoda* (The Guidance), an Arabic language weekly established in New York in 1898, spearheaded the unsuccessful adoption of the new title *Lebanese* (Suleiman 1999, 7). Alixa Naff argues that when homeland politics during the French mandate (1914–41) pitted "kin

against kin and friend against friend, clubs [in the United States] hotly debated whether to call themselves Syrian or Lebanese American. Maronites formed Phoenician clubs in an effort to tie themselves to that ancient civilization and to distance themselves and Lebanon from Arab Syria and from Muslims, whose larger population threatened Maronite domination" (1994, 33).

23. Armenians pride themselves on belonging to the first Christian nation and are divided into Apostolic/Orthodox, Catholic, and Protestant denominations. They started to emigrate from the Ottoman Empire at the turn of the twentieth century because of economic crisis and political unrest. They were later almost completely chased out by a series of massacres culminating in the 1915 genocide and deportations. While some emigrated straight to America, others first settled in adjoining countries, namely Syria, Lebanon, Iran, Iraq, and Egypt. By the second half of the twentieth century, the social, economic, and political turmoil that ensued in their adopted countries led them to emigrate again (Bakalian 1993). By the 1970s, the first wave had successfully integrated into American society. The new wave of immigrants arrived primarily from Iran and Lebanon; there was also a huge influx in the 1990s after the collapse of the Soviet Union. The "new" second generation—that is, the children of the post-1965 immigrants—are, like their predecessors, rapidly achieving the American dream. However, Armenian language and endogamy are more likely to be maintained than before. This is because of the greater tolerance of identity and leisure-time celebration of ethnicity in the United States after the civil rights movement and the development of an extensive institutional infrastructure in the Armenian community (such as all-day Armenian schools). On Armenian history in the United States, see Alexander 2005; Bakalian 1993, 2007; Bulbulian 2000; Mesrobian 2000; Mirak 1980, 1983; Kooshian 2002.

24. Yvonne Haddad (1994) explains that Eastern Rite churches believe they were founded by the apostles: St. Paul established the Antiochian Church, St. Thomas the Assyrian Church, and St. Mark the Coptic Church. Their differences can be traced to the Council of Chalcedon in 451 A.D., when the church elders decided that Christ was fully human and fully divine. The Antiochian and Melkite Churches are Chalcedonian in their Christology. The others—Coptic Orthodox, Syrian Orthodox, Chaldean, Assyrian, and Armenian Churches—are called Monophysites because of their belief that the divinity of Christ came before his humanity. The Uniate churches, Melkite/Greek Catholic and Chaldean, came under the suzerainty of Rome after they were influenced by Roman Catholic religious orders who offered educational and other missions in the Near East. The Maronite Church is named after the fifth century St. Maron of Mount Lebanon, who preached monothelitism, that is, the one will of Christ, a compromise position between Chalcedonians and Monophysites. Maronites were recognized fully by the Vatican in 1736. Arab Protestant congregations were the result of American and British missionary proselytizing after 1839. Maronites hail mostly from Lebanon (Ahdab-Yehia 1974, 1983); Melkites (also called Greek Catholics) emigrated predominantly from Egypt, Palestine, and Lebanon (see Kayal 1974); and the origins of Chaldeans are in present-day Iraq (see Sengstock 1974, 1982, 1983; David 2000). The adherents of Orthodox

Christianity follow a number of ecclesiastic jurisdictions. Immigrants from Lebanon, Palestine, and Syria tend to follow the Syrian or Antiochian Orthodox Church. Those who come from Iraq follow the Assyrian, Chaldean/Nestorian, or Syrian Orthodox Church. Others may follow the Orthodox Patriarchate in Istanbul or Athens. Most Egyptian Christians are Copts (see Jones 2000). For Protestant Arabs, see also Kayyali (2006). The Antiochian Orthodox Church established an archdiocese in North America in 1975, the Syrian Orthodox had a patriarchate in 1958 and an archdiocese in 1968, the Maronites had an exarchate in 1966 and a diocese in 1972, the Chaldeans established their exarchate in Detroit in 1982, and the Melkites established theirs in 1966 (Y. Haddad 1994, 65–70).

25. Most of the Muslim world is Sunni. The Shiʿa are a majority in Iran and Iraq and are the largest sect in Lebanon. Several minority sects are offshoots of Islam, such as the Alevi in Turkey, the Alawi in Syria, and the Druze, who originate from the mountains of Lebanon and modern-day northern Israel and southern Syria *(Jabal el Druze)*.

26. Middle Eastern Jews came from Iraq, Yemen, Syria, Lebanon, Egypt, and Morocco after the middle of the twentieth century (see Younis 1995, 182–83; Dahbany-Miraglia 1987, 1988; Zenner 1983, 2000, 2002). These communities are steeped in the music, cuisine, and other cultural norms of the Arab world.

27. Iranian immigrants include Muslims, Jews, Christians (mostly Armenians but also Assyrians), Bahais, and Zoroastrians. The mother tongue of Muslim, Bahai, and Jewish Iranian immigrants is Persian. Although Armenian and Assyrian Iranian immigrants have their respective languages, they also speak Persian (Bozorgmehr 1998). Most but not all Israeli-born immigrants are Hebrew-speaking Jews. Some Muslim and Christian Arabs also come from Israel.

28. In re Najour, 174 F. 735 (N.D. Ga. 1909).

29. In re Halladjian, 174 F. 834 (C.C.D. Mass. 1909); United States v. Cartozian, 6 F.2d 919 (D. Or. 1925).

30. Some Maronites in the United States (as well as Lebanon) have been denying their "Arab" identity, preferring to be called Lebanese, Phoenicians, or even Middle Easterners. During the civil war in Lebanon (1975–92), their resistance to being called Arab intensified after their militia clashed with Palestinian forces (Walbridge 1997). Iraqi Chaldeans, who have settled mostly in the Detroit area, follow a similar pattern. After 9/11, many Maronites and Iraqi Chaldeans have gone as far as the Census Bureau in an effort to dissociate themselves from Arab Americans. Some have even started calling themselves "Antiochian and Babylonian Christians." However, a leader we interviewed noted that the people who object to the Arab American identity are a minority. See also Raja G. Mattar, "Arab Christians Are Arabs," 2005, Al-Hewar Center, www.alhewar.com/arab_christians_are_arabs.htm; Frederick Aprim, "'Arab Christians'? Not in My View," *Baltimore Chronicle,* September 1, 2005, www.christiansofiraq.com/fred8315.htm. Another example is the e-mail we received while composing a press release about an event we were hosting at our center, MEMEAC: "To be clear on this, none of the four artists showing is an Arab. You can send PR to all

Arab American associations, but we need to make sure that none of the artists is described as Arab American or Arab Lebanese etc."

31. According to the American Community Survey, a total of 85,821 persons of Arab ancestry resided in the five boroughs of New York City in 2005. The 2000 census, on the other hand, reported 69,985 such persons. Egyptians are the most numerous (17,223 persons), followed by those declaring "Arab" background (14,572), Lebanese (11,419), Syrians (10,985), Moroccans (5,116), Palestinians (3,184), Iraqis (957), Jordanians (897), and individuals of other Arab ancestry (6,612). The total is 70,965 persons. It is possible that there has been an increase between 2000 and 2005 of 18 percent. See Jerome Krase, Suzanne Nicoletti-Krase, and Kathryn Krase, "Community Needs Assessment: New York City's Arab American Community," unpublished report, 2007, http://tamkeenny.org/.

32. After 9/11, the Pakistani immigrant community of Coney Island experienced backlash, and the large number of detentions and deportations resulted in business losses (ACLU 2004c, 10–11; see also Nguyen 2005). For Devon Avenue, see Neil MacFarquhar, "Pakistanis Find U.S. an Easier Fit Than Britain: Assimilation Is Rule—Siege Mentality Is Largely Absent," *New York Times*, August 21, 2006, A1, A15.

33. During our visit to Dearborn, we attended the opening session of the Second Annual Refugee Symposium, organized by ACCESS's Community Health and Research Center and Psychosocial Rehabilitation Center. Moreover, the *Detroit Free Press* carried the story of Iraqi refugees in its "Body & Mind" supplement: Patricia Anstett, "Weary Hearts, Troubled Minds: Depression, Fear and Post-9/11 Anxiety among Mental-Health Problems Facing Refugees," *Body & Mind*, October 1, 2002, 6–9H.

34. Because of the small Algerian population, Algerian immigration to the United States is probably highly selective.

35. Jodi Wilgoren, "Going by 'Joe,' Not 'Yussef,' but Still Feeling Like an Outcast," *New York Times*, September 11, 2002, A15. See graphic insert, "In Times of Crisis, More Choose to Be Americans."

36. See Leslie Casimir, "Arab-Sounding Immigrants? Wait 1,001 Nites," *Daily News* (New York), May 28, 2006, 29.

37. Julia Preston, "Sharp Rise Seen in Applications for Citizenship: Legal Immigrants Spurred by Drives, Fee Increase and Senate Debate," *New York Times*, July 5, 2007, A1–10.

38. Read (2004a, 72) writes: "Endogamous marriages are often accompanied by extended kinship networks that can add to [women's] demands, requiring greater commitment to labor-intensive ethnic practices, such as frequent family gatherings and obligations to prepare traditional meals for family members."

39. It was commissioned by the Center of Muslim-Christian Understanding at Georgetown University, Washington, D.C., and conducted by the polling/market research firm Zogby International. See Project MAPS and Zogby International (2001).

40. Andrea Elliott, "More Muslims Are Coming to U.S. after a Decline in Wake of 9/11," *New York Times*, September 10, 2006, A1 and A32.

## 4. ORGANIZATIONAL STRUCTURES

1. We are grateful to Philip Kasinitz for his comments on this topic as the discussant at two panels where we presented our preliminary findings on immigrant organizations: the Eastern Sociological Society meetings, February 20, 2004, and Baruch College, May 3, 2004.

2. Lee Herring, "ASA Congressional Briefing Examines Policy Implications Regarding Disasters," *Footnotes,* December 2003, 1, 9.

3. Claudia Dreifus, "A Sociologist with an Advanced Degree in Calamity," *New York Times,* September 7, 2004, F2.

4. The notable exceptions were poets and writers whose work revolutionized Arabic literature at the turn of the twentieth century. Among these, Gibran Khalil Gibran, author of *The Prophet,* is familiar to many Americans (see Younis 1995, ch. 10).

5. "As CFO today, Mrs. Freij oversees a budget of over $12 million." ACCESS, "Maha Freij, Deputy Executive Director & Chief Financial Officer," 2007, www.accesscommunity.org/site/PageServer?pagename=Maha_Freij_Biography.

6. See "MPAC Calls for Meeting of National Council of American Muslim Non-profits on Kindhearts Closure," *MPACnews,* March 3, 2006; "National Council of Muslim Non-profits to Meet in DC on Mar. 16," *MPACnews,* March 7, 2006.

7. See, e.g., John K. Clemens and Douglas F. Mayer, *The Classic Touch: Lessons in Leadership from Homer to Hemingway* (Chicago: Contemporary Books, 1999); Peter F. Drucker, *The Essential Drucker: The Best Sixty Years of Peter Drucker's Essential Writings on Management* (New York: HarperCollins, 2001; Edgar H. Schein, *Organizational Culture and Leadership,* 3rd ed. (San Francisco: Jossey-Bass, 2004).

8. An example is Resource Associates Corporation's Rising Stars program, which Anny Bakalian helped develop in the 1990s. See its Web site at www.americasrisingstars.cc/.

9. Since 1981, ADC has offered over four hundred college students eleven-week summer internships in Washington, D.C. Additionally, ADC has a leadership training program for Arab American young professionals. ADC's ultimate goal is to nurture effective advocates for Arab American causes. See the Web site of the Hala Foundation, established by the late Arab American leader and ADC President Hala Salaam Maksoud, at www.halafoundation.org/psp.php. MPAC offers part-time and full-time internships to students in two locations: Washington, D.C., and Los Angeles. MPAC offers summer internships in Washington, D.C., and Los Angeles. They seek applicants who are "interested in working for the Muslim American community, bridging the gap between Muslim Americans and decision makers, understanding how policy gets shaped, and gaining experience in the non-profit sector" ("Announcing MPAC's 2007 Summer Internship Program," *MPACnews,* April 6, 2007). Desis Rising Up and Moving (DRUM) has received funding for its Youth Power Internship Program: for six or eight weeks in the summer, it offers low-income South Asian youth the opportunity to learn community-organizing skills. The very purpose of SAALT

is to build leadership and foster civic engagement in the Indian American community, especially among young people. SALDEF's "National Leadership and Empowerment Conference is dedicated to the development and fostering of the future generation of Sikh American leaders" ("SALDEF's 10th Anniversary Banquet," press release, June 9, 2006, www.saldef.org/content.aspx?&a=1447 &z=1&title=SALDEF.

10. Ian Wilhelm, "New Membership Group Will Set Standards for Islamic Charities," *Chronicle of Philanthropy,* March 31, 2005. Since 9/11, the nonprofit sector has become more vigilant in monitoring its constituents. GuideStar.org, JustGive.org, and NetworkforGood.org, among others, monitor the Treasury's Office of Foreign Assets Control for sanctions against organizations with a tax-exempt 501(c)3 designatio–sanctions that range from "blocking assets temporarily to declaring a person or company a Specially Designated National (SDN) or Specially Designated Global Terrorist (SDGT), thereby freezing all assets permanently." Christine Aube, "The PATRIOT Act and the Nonprofit Sector: Charitable Organizations after 9/11," September 2006, www.guidestar.org/news/features/patriot_act.jsp. Further, over forty nonprofits led by the Council on Foundations have established the Treasury Guidelines Working Group to keep an eye on new policies and laws with the goal of ensuring that costly and unfair burdens are not imposed on charities in the name of security.

11. Neil MacFarquhar, "Fears of Inquiry Dampen Giving by U.S. Muslims," *New York Times,* October 30, 2006, A23. See also Jay Tokasz, "Intent on Holy Season Charity, Muslims Feel a Probing Chill," *Buffalo News,* October 26, 2005, B1; Jessi Hempel, "Taking the Taint Out of Giving: Islamic Charities Are Trying to Win Back Donors Spooked by Fears of Fed Scrutiny," *Business Week,* September 26, 2005.

12. The case of Arab and Muslim American organizations is not unique. For example, after the 1992 Los Angeles civil unrest, which inflicted serious damage on Koreatown, nonprofit organizations received funding. Moreover, these CBOs "became the most politically visible entities within the community" (Chung 2005, 918).

13. See their Web site at www.patrioticapaam.org/.

14. See their Web site at www.naaponline.org/.

15. Six NAAP chapters have been formed since 9/11—Baltimore, Boston, Bay Area/California, New York, Philadelphia, and Washington, D.C. See their Web site at www.naaponline.org/.

16. The following are a sample of events sponsored by NAAP-NY and covered in *Aramica*: (1) a picnic ("Grilling and Chilling," *Aramica,* July 22–August 5, 2002, 24–25); (2) networking at a restaurant ("NAAP Networks Downtown," *Aramica,* January 20–February 5, 2003, 30); (3) a conference ("Uniting Tomorrow's Leaders Today—NAAP's 1st Annual Conference," *Aramica,* February 13–28, 2003, 27); (4) a party ("Summer J'nun! [madness]," *Aramica,* July 30–August 14, 2003, p. 43); (5) a banquet ("NAAP-NY Presents *Aramica* with Its 2004 Community Achievement Award," *Aramica,* March 2–17, 2004, 12–13); (6) another picnic ("NAAP 3rd Annual Picnic," *Aramica,* June 30–July 15, 2004, 36); (7) a get-together ("NAAP Rocks Out at Medina," *Aramica,*

September 2–16, 2004); (8) a banquet ("NAAP-NY Celebrates 3rd Anniversary," *Aramica,* March 5–16, 2005, 24); (9) a fashion show ("The 2005 NAAP Cultural Fashion Show," *Aramica,* June 14–29, 2005, 12–13). One can suggest that *Aramica* was rewarded for its coverage with the "Community Achievement Award" (*Aramica,* March 2–17, 2004, 12–13).

17. These include fundraisers such as the Multiple Sclerosis Walk, the Revlon Run/Walk for Breast and Ovarian Cancer, voter registration drives, seminars on "how to be an effective leader in an election year," and participation in antiwar demonstration and rallies. NAAP event attendees tend to be young first- and second-generation Arab Americans, both Christian and Muslim, some of whom wear the *hijab.*

18. The high approval ratings in DAAS may be explained by the exceptional status of the Dearborn-based ACCESS among Arab American CBOs.

## 5. HATE CRIMES AND BIAS INCIDENTS

1. Hate Crime Statistics Act of 1990, 28 U.S.C. 534.

2. Roger Mac Ginty observes that "a violent act may have multiple motivations and interpretations; the perpetrator and victim may variously interpret an action as criminal, political, or random or as motivated by religion, ethnicity, race or identity. The key point is that violence in ethno-national conflict is a complex phenomenon. It may vary in scale, complexity, intensity, longevity, number of actors, degree of external involvement, and military sophistication of the combatants" (2001, 640).

3. See, e.g., ACLU (2004a, 2004b, 2004c); Ibish (2003); CAIR (2002a, 2002b, 2004, 2005, 2006b); Human Rights Watch (2002b); New York City Commission on Human Rights (2003).

4. Alan Cooperman, "September 11 Backlash Murders and the State of 'Hate': Between Families and Police, a Gulf of Victim Count," *Washington Post,* January 20, 2002, A3, A14.

5. In New York City, the most hate crimes in a single day took place between September 15 and 17, 2001, according to the twenty-three-member Hate Crimes Task Force, which has been investigating such crimes since 2000, when the Hate Crimes Act came into effect. Jo Craven McGinty, "Breaking Down Hate Crime," *New York Times,* July 24, 2005, N 25.

6. Using the Quarterly Hate Crime Report Form, law enforcement agencies at city, county, and state levels enter data with the National Incident-Based Reporting System. Each bias-motivated incident is summarized and transmitted to the Uniform Crime Reporting (UCR) program. The law mandates the UCR program, which has been the clearinghouse for crime statistics since 1929, to collect information about bias-motivated crimes. As each incident can involve more than one offense, victim, and/or offender, "one offense is counted for each victim of a crime against person. One offense is counted for each distinct incident of crime against property and crime against society, regardless of the number of victims. The total number of victims in a given incident is the sum of victims associated with each offense that took place within the incident" (FBI 1999, 3).

7. See U.S. Department of Justice, "Civil Rights Division Employees Honored for Outstanding Achievements," press release, October 25, 2007, www.usdoj.gov/opa/pr/2007/October/07_crt_855.html; and FBI, Philadelphia Field Division, "Philadelphia Woman Pleads Guilty to Federal Hate Crime," press release, June 22, 2007, http://philadelphia.fbi.gov/doj/pressrel/2007/pho62207.htm.

8. See U.S. Department of Justice, Civil Rights Division, "Initiative to Combat Post-9/11 Discriminatory Backlash," February 18, 2004, www.usdoj.gov/crt/legalinfo/nordwg_mission.html. When Muslim and Arab leaders met with Attorney General Alberto Gonzales on January 30, 2006, they asked him "to make permanent the position of Post-9/11 Special Counsel for National Origin Discrimination within the Department of Justice, because of the great successes that have been made in the arena of combating hate crimes against Arab, Muslim and Sikh communities. The position is responsible for investigating and prosecuting federal hate crimes, and has been responsible for several federal convictions against hate crime perpetrators." "Muslim and Arab Leaders Meet with Attorney General Gonzales," *MPACnews,* January 31, 2006.

9. See methodology in Pew Research Center (2007).

10. The SAALT (2001) tally of the hate crimes that took place in the first week of 9/11 supports this conclusion. Of the 645 hate crimes reported nationally, only 38 took place in the New York metropolitan area, despite the massive loss of lives and destruction in New York City.

11. We were unable to substantiate accurately whether this death was indeed a hate crime.

12. Dearborn's total population is about ninety-eight thousand; thus Arabs make up a sizable 35 percent of the city (data in Howell and Jamal 2008).

13. There are corroborative data from the United Kingdom. Racist incidents—ranging from verbal abuse to vicious assaults—increased from 48,000 to 52,700 between 2000 and 2004. Incidentally, "it was the sparsely populated areas, home to the smallest, most isolated minority communities, that witnessed the significant increases." In London, which has about 1.9 million ethnic minorities, there was a decrease in hate crimes—from twenty-three thousand cases in 2000 to over fifteen thousand. Jay Rayner, "Racist Attacks on the Rise in Rural Britain," *Observer,* March 27, 2005. Another report notes that "racist incidents are diminishing fastest where immigrants and their families are most established, while it is the parts of Britain with least experience of immigration—the rural areas, on the whole—that are the most hostile." Leo Benedictus, "The World in One Country: Multicultural Britain," *Guardian,* January 23, 2006, special supplement, 3.

14. This information was shared with participants at the conference of the National Network for Arab American Communities in Dearborn, January 19–22, 2006, which Bakalian attended (see also AAI 2002, 9). The Philadelphia case mirrors what happened in Dearborn. Howell and Jamal quote Ron Amen, who was Wayne County Deputy Sheriff during the 9/11 crisis, as saying: "Ficano [the sheriff] offered to set up protection for the mosques for the prayer that was coming up on Friday, the next day, it was agreed. What we did is we

went out and sought volunteers from the sheriff's department who would work a few hours every Friday, beside their regular shift, at the various mosques. We did that and we were able to put at least 2 police officers at every mosque in Dearborn for the Friday prayer" (2008, n.p.).

15. Data on Arab Americans for the Vera Institute report was generated from telephone interviews in twenty municipal jurisdictions that represent approximately 25 percent of the total Arab American population but offer diversity in geographic region, size, and demographic makeup. Next, four sites were chosen as "case studies" for additional one-on-one interviews, focus groups, and participant observation. For the law enforcement data, 107 telephone interviews were conducted with police, FBI, and community leaders in sixteen of the twenty jurisdictions because of refusal to participate. There were also in-person interviews with twenty-two officers and community leaders and with focus groups (which comprised thirty-five police officers and forty-five community leaders) across the four case study sites. The total law enforcement sample adds up to 209 contacts (Henderson et al. 2006, ch. 4, "Research Design").

16. We disagree with the analysis in the Vera Institute report on the response of the affected communities: "lower membership rolls and decreases in charitable giving" (Henderson et al. 2006, 66). We have argued in chapter 6 that retrenchment was an initial, temporary reaction to the backlash. We also question the high percentage (80) of Arab American respondents who reported incidents of hate-related victimization (Henderson et al. 2006, 53). We believe more specific questions would have garnered more accurate results. Our results concur with the major DAAS survey conducted in the Detroit area.

17. See also Dan Eggen, "FBI Agents Still Lacking Arabic Skills: 33 of 12,000 Have Some Proficiency," *Washington Post,* October 11, 2006, 1.

18. New York City Police Commissioner Raymond W. Kelly "frequently visits mosques now, padding around in his stocking feet." He has also expanded the number of officers in the Community Affairs Bureau (Cara Buckley, "New York City Police Seek Trust among Immigrants," *New York Times,* May 31, 2007). Kelly also hired Khalid Latif to be the Muslim chaplain for his workforce (Rima Abdelkader, "NYPD's New Muslim Chaplain," *Arabisto.com,* April 4, 2007, www.arabisto.com/p_blogEntry.cfm?blogID=31&blogEntryID=443). Successful collaboration between Arab American activists and the police in Detroit resulted in Building Respect in Diverse Groups to Enhance Sensitivity (BRIDGES), a national model (Howell and Jamal 2008).

19. The Pew Research Center's national poll of American Muslims asked whether respondents had been singled out by airport security in the previous year because they were Muslims. Among those who had flown, 30 percent had experienced profiling (2007, 39).

20. "Arab American Heritage Park Festival," *Aramica,* August 1–15, 2005, 14–15.

21. Quoted in Moustafa Bayoumi, "Arab America's September 11," *Nation,* September 25, 2006. Dean Obeidallah is reported to say, "Arabs are the new blacks" in his comedy routine (Lorraine Ali, "Television: Mideast Humor. Seriously—'The Watch List,' Comedy Central's New Online Show,

Features (Very Funny) Americans of Middle-East Descent," *Newsweek*, January 19, 2007).

22. This respondent had a green card, but it made little difference. He was very upset that his fellow passengers did not get the same treatment.

23. Brad Foss, "Arab-Looking Passengers Expect Scrutiny Now, and Try to Lessen the Embarrassment," Associated Press, August, 28, 2002.

24. Salam Al-Marayati, "Guilty of 'Flying While Muslim'?" *Los Angeles Times,* December 11, 2004.

25. See Neil MacFarquhar, "U.S. Muslims Say Terror Fears Hamper Their Right to Travel," *New York Times,* June 1, 2006, A1, A22; Jean Merl, "Muslims, Others Air Grievances to FBI: At the Agency's Town Hall Meeting, Speakers Tell of Their Frustration and Embarrassment at Being Singled Out," *Los Angeles Times,* April 9, 2006. In November 2006, six imams were asked to disembark from a U.S. Airways flight leaving Minneapolis for "unsettling" behavior, such as praying at the gate and uttering the word "Allah" on boarding the plane, reported by passengers and crew. They were returning home from a conference of North American Imams Federation (Libby Sander, "6 Imams Removed from Flight for Behavior Deemed Suspicious," *New York Times,* November 22, 2006, A18.

26. The Associated Press, "Airline Passenger Told to Conceal Arabic T-Shirt: Human Rights Activist Was Briefly Barred from JetBlue Flight to Oakland," August 30, 2006, www.msnbc.msn.com/id/14591252/from/ET/.

27. CAIR, "Hearings on Profiling Sought after Imams Removed from MN Flight," press release, November 21, 2006, RedOrbit, www.redorbit.com/news/business/739944/hearings_on_profiling_sought_after_imams_removed_from_mn_flight/index.html; Sander, "6 Imams Removed"; Alexandra Marks, "In Imams' Airline Case, a Clash of Rights, Prejudice, Security," *Christian Science Monitor,* May 1, 2007, 1.

28. Type II errors are false positives, as when an African American is found guilty without evidence because of his or her race.

29. For example, on January 17, 2007, SALDEF and the Community Relations Service of the Department of Justice released a police training video. It aims to educate law enforcement officials about the cultural norms of Sikh Americans, as Sikhs have been the subject of more hate crimes since 9/11. SALDEF, "Department of Justice and SALDEF Release New Law Enforcement Roll Call Training Video," press release, January 19, 2007, www.saldef.org/content.aspx?a=1633. See also SMART, "Recommendations for Law Enforcement when Interacting with Sikh Americans," 2003, www.sikhmediawatch.org/pubs/LawEnforcementRefrCard.PDF. On November 21, 2006, SALDEF issued a press release announcing that its cooperation with DHS had resulted in a poster on the Sikh *kirpan* that would be distributed to 8,700 federal facilities (SALDEF, "SALDEF Asks for Community's Support to Continue Awareness, Empowerment Efforts," press release, November 21, 2006, http://saldef.org/content.aspx?a=1609). See also Michelle Boorstein, "A Pointed Reminder for Security Screeners: Disputes over Sikhs' Required Daggers Prompt a Federal Poster on Respectful Procedures," *Washington Post,* November 21, 2006, A6.

30. See also Jodi Wilgoren, "Going by 'Joe,' Not 'Yussef,' but Still Feeling Like an Outcast," *New York Times*, September 11, 2002, A15.

31. Chris Reiter, "New York Is Hell for Young Osama," Reuters, June 8, 2007, www.reuters.com/article/latestCrisis/idUSN06394027.

32. Sherien Sultan, "Subway Negotiations," *Muslim Perspectives*, Summer 2003, 10–11. She was awarded the prize "Women's Voices in War Zones" by Women's WORLD, a global free speech network of feminist writers, in June 2003. This paper has since been published in an edited volume by Sarah Husain (2006).

33. Reports by ADC (Ibish 2003) and CAIR (2002a, 2002b, 2004), and others have documented the increase in such incidents.

34. Neil MacFarquhar, "A Simple Scarf, but Meaning Much More Than Faith," *New York Times*, September 8, 2006, A22.

35. Like the *hijab*, Sikh men's turban has led to many discrimination cases. SALDEF and other Sikh advocacy groups have been fighting bias in and out of the courts, and often winning. See SALDEF, "Georgia Court Apologizes for Denying Sikh American Man Entrance to Court: Incident Forces County to Implement New Policies Permitting Religious Head Covering," press release, April 20, 2006, www.saldef.org/content.aspx?a=1391; "National Park Service Apologizes and Learns," *SikhNN*, June 16, 2006, www.sikhnn.com/modules .php?op=modload&name=News&file=article&sid=501&mode=thread&order =0&thold=0.

36. U.S. EEOC, San Francisco Office, "Albion River Inn Sued for Retaliation and Race/National Origin Discrimination," *EEOC News*, August 31, 2006, www.lccr.com/8%2031%2006%20Press%20Release.pdf.

37. U.S. EEOC, "EEOC To Receive 'Friend in Government Award' from American-Arab Anti-Discrimination Committee," press release, October 1, 2004, www.eeoc.gov/press/10-1-04.html.

38. ADC, "ADC Welcomes Jury Award of Muslim Woman," press release, ADCNYC@yahoogroups.com, June 4, 2007.

39. Rick Hampson, "Fear 'as Bad as after 9/11,'" *USA Today*, December 12, 2006, www.usatoday.com/news/nation/2006-12-12-arab-americans-cover _x.htm; Salam Al-Marayati and Safiya Ghori, "Islamophobia: Bigotry toward Muslims Is Growing in the United States," *San Diego Union-Tribune*, December 15, 2006.

40. See Huntington (1993, 22–28; 1996); Peter Ford, "Crusade: A Freudian Slip? Europe Cringes at President Bush's 'Crusade' against Terrorists," *Christian Science Monitor*, September 19, 2001; "White House Apologizes for Using 'Crusade' to Describe War on Terrorism," Associated Press, September 8, 2001. In August 2006, President Bush called Hezbollah and the plotters of the transatlantic airline bombing in Britain "Islamic fascists." This new epithet was inflammatory. CAIR and MPAC reacted immediately arguing that it is incorrect to assume that the actions of extremist Muslims are caused by their religion (Richard Allen Greene, "Bush's Language Angers U.S. Muslims," *BBC News*, August 12, 2006, http://news.bbc.co.uk/2/hi/americas/4785065.stm). See also Frederic J. Frommer, "Feingold to Bush: Stop Calling Them 'Islamic Fascists,'"

*Capital Times,* September 12, A3; Alia Malek, "What's in a Name?" *Columbia Journalism Review,* September 6, 2006, www.cjrdaily.org; "Islamic Fascism," *Chronicle of Higher Education,* September 22, 2006, http://chronicle.com/weekly/v53/i05/05b00401.htm.

41. We should add to the list the anthrax scare. Coming on the heels of 9/11, letters containing anthrax bacteria were sent to two senators and a number of news agencies. Five persons died as a result. Understandably, the incidents shook the U.S. public.

42. Mahdis Keshavarz, vice president of the New York–based public relations firm Riptide Communications, "Public Relations and the Media in the Aftermath of 9/11," lecture given at MEMEAC, at the Graduate Center, City University of New York, October 29, 2004.

43. Coverage of the detention situation was extensive in the *Washington Post.* See, e.g., Hanna Rosin, "Snapshot of an Immigrant's Dream Fading," *Washington Post,* March 24, 2002, A01.

44. See, e.g., Megan Garvey et al., "Hundreds Are Detained after Visits to INS," *Los Angeles Times,* December 19, 2002, A1.

45. See Matthew Purdy and Lowell Bergman, "Unclear Danger: Inside the Lackawanna Terror Case," *New York Times,* October 12, 2003, A1, A35–37.

46. Mrinalini Reddy, "Muslims on TV, No Terror in Sight," *New York Times,* November 11, 2007, E30.

47. CAIR, "Franklin Graham Smears Islam Again," press release, August 6, 2002, www.cair.com/ArticleDetails.aspx?mid1=777&&ArticleID=15105&&name=n&&currPage=113.

48. Elissa Gootman, "A New School Plans to Teach Half of Classes Using Arabic," *New York Times,* February 13, 2007.

49. Though *madrassa* means school in Arabic, the word has been used in the Western media to mean conservative Islamic schools, allegedly those that teach students to become terrorists.

50. Mary Frost, "'Jihad School' or 'School for Everyone?'" *Brooklyn Daily Eagle,* May 9, 2007.

51. Alexandra Marks, "Arabic School in N.Y.C. Creates a Stir," *Christian Science Monitor,* June 1, 2007, www.csmonitor.com/2007/0601/p03s01-ussc. See Sarah Garland, "New Brooklyn School to Offer Middle East Studies," *New York Sun,* March 7, 2007; Julie Bosman, "Plan for Arabic School in Brooklyn Arouses Protests," *New York Times,* May 4, 2007; Jonathan Zimmerman, "Arabic School's Critics Are the True Zealots," *New York Daily News,* May 9, 2007; Debbie Almontaser, "Arabic Public School Will Unite, Not Divide, Us," *New York Daily News,* May 20, 2007. See also Beila Rabinowitz and William Mayer, "Hamas Sympathizers Tied To Khalil Gibran International Academy?" *PipelineNews.org,* July 17, 2007, www.pipelinenews.org/index.cfm?page=kgiahamas71807.htm.

52. Julie Bosman, "Head of City's Arabic School Steps Down under Pressure," *New York Times,* August 11, 2007, B1; Samuel G. Freeman, "Critics Ignored the Record of a Muslim Principal," *New York Times,* August 29, 2007; Jennifer Medina, "Arabic School Ex-Principal Fights to Get Her Job Back," *New York Times,* October 17, 2007, B3.

53. Andrea Elliott, "Battle in Brooklyn: A Principal's Rise and Fall, Critics Cost Muslim Educator Her Dream School," *New York Times*, April 28, 2008, A1, A16–17.

54. For an example of the anti-Islamic/Arab opposition, see Jane Kramer, "The Petition," *New Yorker*, April 14, 2008, 50–59.

55. Neil MacFarquhar, "Scrutiny Increases for a Group Advocating for Muslims in the U.S." *New York Times*, March 14, 2007, A1, A17. See also Jim Abrams, "House GOP Try to Halt Muslim Seminar," *Washingtonpost.com*, March 12, 2007, www.washingtonpost.com/wp-dyn/content/article/2007/03/12/AR2007031200856_p.

56. Zachary A. Goldfarb, "Va. Lawmaker's Remarks on Muslims Criticized: Republican Had Decried the Use of the Koran for Congressman's Oath of Office," *Washington Post*, December 21, 2006, A11.

57. Amy Argetsinger and Roxanne Roberts, "But It's Thomas Jefferson's Koran!" *Washington Post*, January 3, 2007, C03; see also Jane Lampman, "At Swearing In, Congressman Wants to Carry Koran, and He's Already under Fire," *Christian Science Monitor*, December 7, 2006, www.csmonitor.com/2006/1207/p01s03-uspo.

58. AAI, "A Regular Update from the Arab American Institute: 42 Days until Election 2007!" *AAI Countdown*, September 28, 2007.

59. When six young men were arrested for plotting to bomb Fort Dix, CAIR reported at least two backlash incidents: "A man allegedly yelled racial slurs at a Muslim woman headed to a laundromat; in another, a Jordanian woman was punched in the face by a man who threatened to kill Muslims" (Kareem Fahim, "Open House at Mosque of Suspects Proves Tense," *New York Times*, May 19, 2007, B5).

## 6. GOVERNMENT INITIATIVES AND IMPACT

1. Personal communication, October 3, 2002.

2. See Adam Liptak, "Tips, Please: A Nation of Informers—or Alert Citizens," *New York Times*, September 22, 2002, sec. 4, 1.

3. See "Man in Terror Scare Says Woman Is Lying," *CNN News*, September 13, 2002, http://archives.cnn.com/2002/US/09/13/alligator.alley/.

4. Hank Williams, "Reem Released," *Messenger*, Summer 2002, 10. Professors, administrators, and students advocated for her release. She was eventually released.

5. The ACLU relied on a survey by the Council of Pakistan Organizations to tally the impact of 9/11 on Little Pakistan.

6. While the American public supports the PATRIOT Act, most people are unaware of its contents. A random sample of eight hundred American adults conducted by the Center for Survey Research and Analysis at the University of Connecticut between August 4 and 22, 2005 (margin of error 3.5 percent) found that 64 percent of the sample supported the PATRIOT Act (85 percent of Republicans, 50 percent of Democrats). While 57 percent of those polled said they were "familiar" with the provisions of the act, only 31 percent passed the quiz on specifics (University of Connecticut, Center for Survey Research and

Analysis, "University of Connecticut Releases New National Poll on the USA PATRIOT ACT," press release, August 26, 2005, www.csra.uconn.edu/pdf/PATRIOTACTPRESSRELEASE.pdf). The PATRIOT Act was reauthorized in March 2006. See Nedra Pickler, "Bush Renews PATRIOT Act, Says It Helped Save Lives," *Washington Post*, March 10, 2006. The ACLU issued a press release noting that the minor amendments were not sufficient to protect the liberty and privacy of Americans ("ACLU Says Cosmetic Changes to the Patriot Act Hollow, Measures Approved by the House Fail to Protect American Liberty and Privacy," March 7, 2006, www.aclu.org/safefree/general/24417prs20060307.html).

7. Net worth includes cash on hand and in bank accounts, refundable deposits, loans, tax refunds, gold and silver certificates, shares, stocks, bonds, IRA plans, and net income. See Zakat Center, "Zakat Calculator," 2008, www.thezakat.org/zakat-calculator.aspx.

8. ADC, "ADC, MPAC, and Muslim Advocates Welcome Ramadan and Provide Guidance on Charitable Giving," press release, September 12, 2007, www.adc.org/index.php?id=3180.

9. Andrew Stern, "U.S. Jury Acquits Two Men of Hamas Conspiracy," Reuters, February 1, 2007, http://today.reuters.com/misc/PrinterFriendlyPopup .aspx?type=topNews&storyID=2007–02–01; Rudolph Bush and Jeff Coen, "Jury Acquits Men of Funneling Money to Hamas," *Chicago Tribune*, February 1, 2007.

10. Greg Krikorian, "Questions Arise over Case against Islamic Charity: Federal Prosecutors Rely Heavily on Israeli Intelligence," *Los Angeles Times*, June 18, 2006.

11. Neil MacFarquhar, "As Muslim Group Goes on Trial, Other Charities Watch Warily," *New York Times*, July 17, 2007, A14.

12. "U.S. Prosecution of Muslim Group Ends in Mistrial," *New York Times*, October 23, 2007, A1.

13. Visa overstayers stay in the United States beyond the date of their visa. Absconders are those who not only have overstayed their visa but were issued deportation orders, yet remained in the United States.

14. Megan Garvey, Martin Groves, and Henry Weinstein, "Hundreds Are Detained after Visits to INS: Thousands Protest Arrests of Mideast Boys and Men Who Complied with Order to Register," *Los Angeles Times*, December 19, 2002, A1.

15. See Diane Cardwell, "The Immigrant Muslims Face Deportation, but Say U.S. Is Their Home," *New York Times*, June 13, 2003, A22.

16. In 2003 the actor and playwright Kayhan Irani produced a one-woman show entitled *We've Come Undone*. Five female characters provide a perspective on the post-9/11 backlash, including an INS agent who rants about the long hours she is required to work: "I can't take this job anymore, it's getting to me. All these new rules, new regulations, this whole registration business got me twisted. . . . This whole place can't even keep up with the numbers that are coming in, look at that line—there's no way we're processing all those guys today, no way. I guess no one counted on them obeying the law huh? You know what I say, I say we just do like they did in L.A. and lock 'em all up and deal with them when we can. . . . Those poor jerks, they all want to do the 'right thing'

but they're just gonna get deported. . . . I feel like going up to them and saying if you ain't got papers, no evidence of coming in, get off the line, go home, and let me go home. Save us all the trouble. . . . You think any of them are really terrorists? Gimme a break. What terrorist, lemme ask you, what terrorist is going to wait in line for ten hours to register?" Though this narrative is fictional, it is inspired by interviews that Kayhan Irani conducted with victims of backlash and INS employees. See her Web page "Kayhan Irani," 2005, www.thehouse thatwebuilt.com/kayhan.htm.

17. Examples of documentaries on the 9/11 backlash include *Raising Our Voices: South Asian Americans Address Hate,* dir. and prod. SAALT (2002); *Caught in the Crossfire: Arab Americans in Wartime,* dir. and prod. David Van Taylor and Brad Lichenstein, First Run Icarus Films (2002); *Caught in Between: What to Call Home in Times of War,* dir. and prod. Lina Hoshino (2004); *Brothers and Others: The Impact of September 11 on Arabs, Muslims and South Asians in America,* dir. Nicolas Rossier, Arab Film Distribution (2002); *Persons of Interest,* dir. Alison Maclean and Tobias Perse, First Run/Icarus Films (2004); and *Everything Is Gonna Be Alright,* dir. Tamer Ezzat, Myth and Semat Productions (2004).

18. Schrecker would agree. At the end of her book *Many Are the Crimes: McCarthyism in America,* she asks: "Can it happen again?" She answers: "The process through which McCarthyism came to dominate American politics is infinitely replicable. The demonization of politically marginalized groups and the use of state power to repress them goes on all the time, as does the willingness of so many important individuals to collaborate with the process. Only now, under the impact of a globalized, yet atomized, capitalist system, political repression may have become so diffuse that we do not recognize it when it occurs" (1998, 415).

19. Elizza Gootman and Thomas J. Luek, "Fire Engulfs Brooklyn Building Killing Seven People in One Family," *New York Times,* June 24, 2002, A1; see also Elizabeth Hays and Bill Hutchinson, "Deadly Brooklyn Fire Haunts Survivor," *Daily News,* June 24, 2003, 10.

20. The communal processing of shock and grief resembled the normal stages of mourning and recovery that individuals experience when they suffer a loss (e.g., Kubler-Ross 1969).

21. For example, the Israeli bombing of Lebanon in July 2006 raised fears among the Arab Americans. See Tal Abbady, "South Florida Arabs Afraid to Speak Out on Crisis in Middle East," *Sun-Sentinel.com,* July 25, 2006, www .sun-sentinel.com/news/local/southflorida/sfl-cfear24jl24,0,7163421,print.story.

## 7. MOBILIZATION

1. Neil MacFarquhar, "Borders Spell Trouble for Arab-Americans," *New York Times,* April 29, 2007. The same article reports that the ACLU forced the government to release documents showing that "the Customs and Border Patrol agency has received more than 11,000 queries about border issues since September 11, 2001 . . . while Immigration and Customs Enforcement has received 4,855" and that the Electronic Privacy Information Center, an oversight group,

has faulted watch lists for compiling information that cannot be challenged. The *Times* article recounts the experiences of a thirty-nine-year-old U.S. citizen of Palestinian background who was harassed on each of his fourteen trips to visit family in Canada across the Ambassador Bridge, Michigan, during a calendar year. His fingerprints were taken fourteen times, he endured nine body searches, and he was handcuffed four times and detained in an isolation room thirteen times. Ironically, he had no problems when he was traveling on his Canadian passport and green card between 2001 and 2006.

2. ADC, "ADC Welcomes New TSA Aviation Security and Traveler Screening Enhancements," press release, April 29, 2008, www.adc.org/index.php ?id=3304.

3. SALDEF, "TSA to Allow for Flexibility in Traveler Identity: SALDEF Welcomes New Procedure Affecting Millions of Travelers," press release, May 5, 2008, www.saldef.org/content.aspx?&a=3572&z=1&title=TSA%20to%20 Allow%20for%20Flexibility%20in%20Traveler%20Identity.

4. ADC, "ADC Joins New Amicus Brief Opposing Illegal NSA Wiretapping," press release, ADCNYC@yahoogroups.com, May 4, 2007. In this case, ADC joined the National Association for the Advancement of Colored People, JACL, the League of United Latin American Citizens, and United for Peace and Justice. See also ADC "Stop Spying on Americans! Ask Congress to Roll Back Executive Powers Allowing Warrantless Wiretapping," press release, ADCNY@yahoo.com, October 16, 2007.

5. "The United States Institute of Peace is an independent, nonpartisan, national institution established and funded by Congress. Its goals are to help prevent and resolve violent conflicts, promote post-conflict stability and development, and increase peacebuilding capacity, tools, and intellectual capital worldwide. The Institute does this by empowering others with knowledge, skills, and resources, as well as by directly engaging in peacebuilding efforts around the globe." U.S. Institute of Peace home page, April 10, 2008, www.usip.org/.

6. See Fiqh Council of North America, "Statement of the Fiqh Council of North America on the Day of Remembrance of the Tragic Events of September 11, 2001," August 29, 2002, www.alhewar.org/SEPTEMBER%2011/statement _of_the_fiqh_council.htm.

7. Jason DeRose, "U.S. Muslim Scholars Issue Edict against Terrorism," *All Things Considered,* National Public Radio, July 28, 2005, www.npr.org/ templates/story/story.php?storyId=4775588.

8. See "MPAC Hosts Press Conference with FBI-DC to React to UK Terror Plot," *MPACnews,* August 11, 2006; see also "MPAC Expresses Relief on Foiled Terror Plot," *MPACnews,* August 10, 2006.

9. See "MPAC, British Consul, Law Enforcement Officials Discuss Importance of Partnership at Press Conference," *MPACnews,* August 14, 2006.

10. Laurie Goostein, "U.S. Muslims Try to Ease Europe's Discord," *New York Times,* February 13, 2006, A6; See also "MPAC Condemns Beirut Riots, Calls for 'Calm and Restraint,'" *MPACnews,* February 6, 2006. American Muslims also want to be consulted in dealing with crises in the Middle East. See MPAC, "MPAC Calls for American Muslim Advisor for Secretary Rice's Trip to Middle East," press release, July 21, 2006.

11. See "MPAC Unequivocally Condemns Seattle Murder," *MPACnews*, July 29, 2006; also AAI, "AAI Condemns Shooting in Seattle Targeting Jewish Center," press release, July 29, 2006.

12. "MPAC Visits U.S. Holocaust Museum with DC-Area Muslim Delegation," *MPACnews*, December 21, 2006.

13. Mary Beth Sheridan, "Muslims Remember Holocaust Victims at Memorial Museum," *Washington Post*, December 21, 2006.

14. "CAIR Condemns Iranian Holocaust Denial Conference," CAIR listserv, December 13, 2006.

15. "MPAC Commends FBI for Foiling Alleged Fort Dix Terror Plot," *MPACnews*, May 9, 2007; David Kocieniewski, "6 Men Arrested in a Terror Plot against Ft. Dix," *New York Times*, May 8, 2007, A1, B6.

16. See Neela Banerjee, "Muslim Staff Members on Mission to Educate Congress," *New York Times*, June 3, 2006, A11.

17. It is estimated that about one million readers saw the *New York Times* ads. Alsultany (2007) correctly concludes that their effectiveness cannot be evaluated given the limited circulation. Undoubtedly, financial resources and access to mainstream media are crucial resources in getting the message across.

18. CAIR, "CAIR's Anti-terrorism Campaigns," n.d. (accessed May 8, 2008), www.cair.com/AmericanMuslims/PublicServiceAnnouncements.aspx.

19. See Steven Emerson, *American Jihad: The Terrorists Living among Us* (New York: Free Press, 2002), and MPAC (2003, 2004, 2007).

20. "MPAC Participates in Harman's Briefing on 'Post-9/11: Muslim Americans as Partners in the Fight against Terrorism,'" *MPACnews*, September 27, 2006. This news e-mail also quoted Dan Sutherland, officer for civil rights and civil liberties at DHS as saying, "Muslim Americans should know that the executive branch is listening and incorporating their ideas." Moreover, Brett Hovington, chief of the Community Relations Unit at the FBI, noted, "Engagement with the Muslim American community means a level of inclusion, and issues being addressed before they become a problem."

21. ADC, "DHS Incident Management Discusses U.K. Terror Incidents," press release, ADCNYC@yahoogroups.com, July 2, 2007; "DHS and FBI Discuss National Intelligence Estimate with Muslim, Arab and South Asian Groups," *MPACnews*, July 17, 2007.

22. When Secretary of State Condoleezza Rice was preparing to visit the Middle East after the Israeli bombing of Lebanon in July 2006, MPAC addressed a letter to her encouraging her to take with her an American Muslim advisor. "Since their perspectives and points of views are invaluable in helping you to understand the sentiment on the streets of the Arab and Muslim worlds, we urge you to include an American Muslim advisor with you during your trip. We . . . believe that our contributions will complement and contextualize the perspectives offered by government officials you meet with in the region." The letter, signed by Salam Al-Marayati, executive director of MPAC, concludes: "The role of American Muslims in policy discourse is critical." See "MPAC Calls for American Muslim Advisor for Secretary Rice's Trip to Middle East," *MPACnews*, July 21, 2006.

23. Alexandra Marks, "For Airport Screeners, More Training about Muslims," *Christian Science Monitor*, January 9, 2007, 2; David Shelby, "U.S.

Airport Security Officers Briefed on Hajj Traditions," U.S. Department of State, December 26, 2006, www.usinfo.gov/xarchives/display.html?p=washfile-english&y=2006&m=December&x=2006122617215 5ndyblehso.4967768. See also "DHS Issues Hajj Travel Guidance," *ADC Update,* December 26, 2006, www.adc.org/index.php?id=3031; TSA, "Hajj Travel Information," November 27, 2007,www.tsa.gov/travelers/airtravel/assistant/hajj.shtm.

24. Staff from the TSA, Customs and Border Protection, Immigration and Customs Enforcement, the Federal Air Marshal Service, the Federal Emergency Management Agency, the U.S. Coast Guard, the U.S. Secret Service, and the U.S. Citizenship and Immigration Services will be educated with this tool.

25. ADC, "ADC and DHS Announce Release of Training DVD," press release, January 25, 2007.

26. SALDEF, "Department of Justice and SALDEF Release New Law Enforcement Training Video," press release, January 19, 2007.

27. See U.S. Department of Justice, Civil Rights Division, "Common Sikh Head Coverings," poster, 2004, www.usdoj.gov/crt/legalinfo/sikh_poster.pdf.

28. See SALDEF, "Sikh Americans and the Kirpan," 2006, www.saldef.org/anm/articlefiles/1604-SALDEF_DHS_Kirpan_Poster.jpg. In October 2007, the Sikh Coalition produced the document "Airport Screening Procedures for Sikh Travelers and Sikh Air Travelers' Bill of Rights," www.sikhcoalition.org/documents/SikhAirTravelersGuideandBillofRights.pdf.

29. President Bush used the term *Islamofascism* on October 6, 2005, in his address to the National Endowment for Democracy: "Islamic terrorist attacks serve a clear and focused ideology, a set of beliefs and goals that are evil, but not insane. Some call this evil Islamic radicalism; others, militant *Jihadism;* still others, Islamo-fascism. Whatever it's called, this ideology is very different from the religion of Islam. This form of radicalism exploits Islam to serve a violent, political vision: the establishment, by terrorism and subversion and insurgency, of a totalitarian empire that denies all political and religious freedom." White House, "President Discusses War on Terror at National Endowment for Democracy," press release, October 6, 2005, www.whitehouse.gov/news/releases/2005/10/20051006-3.html.

30. Matthai Chakko Kurvila, "Security Agency Enlisting Muslims to Rebut Radicals: Idea to Engage Young Minds in Ideological Battle," *San Francisco Chronicle,* June 5, 2007, A4.

31. See Neil MacFarquhar, "Protests Greet Police Plan to Map Muslim Angelenos," *New York Times,* November 9, 2007.

32. "Muslims Welcome Removal of LAPD's Mapping Program," *MPAC-news,* November 15, 2007.

33. ADC, "ADC Joins ACLU, Amnesty International, and LCCR in 'Day of Action to Restore Law and Justice,'" press release, ADCNYC@yahoogroups, June 19, 2007.

34. See "Voices: Brooklyn Arab-Americans Remember September 11," interviews by Jessica DuLong and photos by Joseph Rodriguez, *Saudi Aramco World,* November/December 2001, 2–5.

35. The shirt is for sale on CafePress at www.cafepress.com/media4hr/2817783.

36. The shirt is for sale at www.t-shirtat.com/home.asp. See also Samantha Henry, "T-Shirts Display Arab American Pride," *Herald News* (New Jersey), July 15, 2007.

37. See Liesl Schillinger, "The New 'Arab' Playwrights: They're Female, They're Organized and They're . . . Not All Arab," *New York Times,* April 4, 2004, E7. We should also note that Dalia Basiouny (2005), a PhD candidate in theater at the Graduate Center, City University of New York, is writing her dissertation on these young women of Middle Eastern descent who have emerged in the public sphere in the aftermath of 9/11. The Graduate Center's Segal Theater showcased many of these artists/activists—Nora Armani, Leila Buck, Betty Shamieh, Heather Raffo, Kayhan Irani, Elmas Abi Nader, Suha Al Jurf, and Rania Khalil. Interestingly, women outnumber men in this form of theater. Ismail Khalidi, who wrote *Truth Serum Blues,* is one of the exceptions. See MEMEAC, "MEMEAC Event Pictures Academic Year 2005_2006," 2006, http://web.gc.cuny.edu/memeac/gallery/Spring2006/59.htm, and "Past Events: *Truth Serum Blues,* Ismail Khalidi," flyer, 2006, http://web.gc.cuny.edu/memeac/flyers/ikhalidi.pdf.

38. On Shamieh, see Margo Jefferson, "'Roar': A Palestinian Blues Singer in Detroit? Her Father Thinks Not," *New York Times,* April 8, 2004, E3. On Raffo, see Lauren Sandler, "An American and Her Nine Iraqi Sisters: Trying to Understand Her Arab Roots Better, A Writer-Actress Gets under the Skin of Very Different Characters," *New York Times,* October 17, 2004; Heather Raffo, "Heather Raffo's Aha Moment," *O—The Oprah Magazine,* September 2006, 100, 102.

39. Clyde Haberman, "An Arab Who Wields a Rapier Wit," *New York Times,* July 19, 2006, B1. Obeidallah's six-part series, "The Watch List," was aired on Comedy Central, a cable station (Lorraine Ali, "Television: Mideast Humor. Seriously_'The Watch List,' Comedy Central's New Online Show, Features (Very Funny) Americans of Middle-East Descent," *Newsweek,* January 19, 2007, Web exclusive, www.msnbc.msn.com/id/16694508/site/newsweek.

40. For reviews, see Felicia R. Lee, "Comedians as Activists, Challenging Prejudice," *New York Times,* March 10, 2007, B7; James Poniewozik, "Stand-up Diplomacy," *Time,* March 8, 2007, www.time.com/time/printout/0,8816,1597524,00.html; David Zurawik, "Just a Little Innocent Comedy: In a New Television Special, These American Performers Are Taking on Middle Eastern Stereotypes," *Baltimore Sun,* March 4, 2007, 1E; Mike Duffy, "Middle East-American Comics Tackle Stereotypes," *Detroit Free Press,* March 9, 2007. On the possibility of prime-time showings, see Comedy Central Press Release, "Comedy Central Looks Ahead and Continues the Laughs with 2007/2008 Talent and Development Slate," May 29, 2007, www.comedycentral.com/press/press_releases/2007/ccdevelopment07–08.jhtml.

41. Nick Zaino, "On the Road with the Axis of Evil," *Boston Globe,* April 13, 2007, E3.

42. Joya Heydarpour, "The Comic Is Palestinian, the Jokes Bawdy," *New York Times,* November 21, 2006, B2. See also "Muslim Comedians at Kinder Event," *Washington Report on Middle East Affairs,* July 2006, 58.

43. Maysoun Freij, a PhD candidate in anthropology at Emory University, has devoted her dissertation to the artistic and cultural activism of Arab Americans in New York City after 9/11 (see Freij 2008).

44. See their Web site at www.alwanforthearts.org/.

45. See Lynda Richardson, "From Amman, Jordan, to Broadway, Via Brooklyn," *New York Times*, February 19, 2003, B2; Dinitia Smith, "Arab American Writers, Uneasy in Two Worlds: Immigrant Authors Feel Added Burdens since 9/11," *New York Times*, March 14, 2003, Arts Section, 1, 9.

46. Reprinted here with permission of the author. The entire poem is at www.teachingforchange.org/News%20Items/first_writing_since.htm.

47. The Public Affairs Alliance of Iranian Americans (PAAIA) was launched as this book went to press. See its Web site at www.paaia.org.

48. See, e.g., Lynette Clemetson, "Coalition Seeks Action on Shared Data on Arab Americans," *New York Times*, August 13, 2004, A14.

49. SMART was renamed SALDEF after 9/11. SALDEF celebrated its tenth anniversary of advocacy, empowerment, and outreach for the Sikh Americans in June 2006. During the commemoration gathering in Washington, D.C., the 2006 Dorothy Height Coalition Building Award was presented to ADC "for their efforts to build and sustain coalitions within the civil rights community." Mary Rose Oakar, president of ADC, accepted the award, saying, "The great thing about our country is its diversity, its cultural and religious diversity" (SALDEF Announcements, June 10, 2006). As a good coalition partner with Arab and Muslim American organizations, SALDEF issued a press release after the foiled terrorist plot in the U.K. endorsing collective efforts; see "SALDEF Works with Federal Agencies in Wake of Foiled UK Terrorist Plot to Ensure Safety of Sikh Community," August 15, 2006.

50. Anny Bakalian attended this January 2006 convention in Dearborn, Michigan.

51. In October 2003 the Arab American Christian Coalition held its inaugural dinner and invited FBI agents Joseph Billy and Jack Liao to speak about the post-9/11 vulnerability of the community. "AACC Dinner Held at Salam Arabic Church," *Aramica*, October 6–20, 2003, 42–43.

52. Examples of pan-ethnic and pan-religious coalitions include the American Muslim Political Coordinating Council, the Arab American Christian Coalition, the Congress of Arab American Organizations, the New York Arab American Leadership Council, ADC, AMC, AAI, CAIR, MPAC, and NNAAC.

53. Greg Meyer, "Anger and Amity Mix in Bay Ridge," September 2001, Columbia University, School of Journalism, student work online (no longer accessible, retrieved June 13, 2005); "Peace Grows in Brooklyn," *The Lutheran*, February 2001, www.thelutheran.org/article/article.cfm?article_id=200.

54. Meyer, "Anger and Amity Mix."

55. Shelby Davis, "An Interfaith Assembly Takes a Prayerful Stance," *Daily News*, May 26, 2002, www.nydailynews.com/archives/ny_local/2002/05/26/2002-05-26_an_interfaith_assembly_takes.html. The Unity Task Force remains active in Bay Ridge. A picnic was organized at Owl's Head Park to strengthen ties among the various groups in the community. See "Unity Task Force Holds Breakfast Gathering," *Aramica*, July 10–25, 2003, 33.

56. See the home page for civilrights.org, which calls itself "the Civil Rights Coalition for the 21st Century," at www.civilrights.org.

57. In March 2006, MPAC joined the Liberty Coalition, whose goal is to coordinate public policy initiatives focusing on civil liberties and human rights. The ACLU, the American Conservative Union, Common Cause, MoveOn.org Political Action, and Amnesty International are some of the members of the Liberty Coalition. See "MPAC Joins Liberty Coalition to Address Civil and Human Rights," *MPACnews*, March 6, 2006.

58. See the coalition's home page at www.thenyic.org.

59. Arab-American Bar Association of Illinois, "White Paper: Preliminary Report on Hate Crimes against Arabs and Muslims in the United States," paper presented at the News Conference of the Chicago Bar Association, September 26, 2001, www.arabbar.org/art-report.asp.

60. Muqtedar Khan, author of *American Muslims: Bridging Faith and Freedom* (Amana Press, 2002), has stressed the importance of this. At a panel entitled "American Muslim Communities: Security Risk or Source of Hope?" at New York University (March 22, 2006), he argued that after 9/11, foreign-born Muslims in the United States needed to choose between voting for candidate X because he is good for Pakistan and voting for candidate Y because he promises to improve civil liberties for American Muslims. For Khan, the choice was clear. He advised his coreligionists to vote for their children's future rather than in support of the interests of family in Pakistan.

61. Muslim American organizations have advocated for other religious groups. For example, MPAC came to the aid of rural churches, black and white, that had been burned in Alabama ("MPAC Mobilizes Muslims to Support Congregations of Burned Alabama Churches," *MPACnews*, February 8, 2006).

62. See also Christine Hauser, "Getting Out the Muslim Vote: Advocates Battle Cynicism in Community," *New York Times*, March 1, 2004, B1, B4.

63. This is likely to be an undercount due to omission in later years.

64. Yalla Vote is an initiative developed by AAI. During each election cycle, Yalla Vote is operated with the collaboration of CBOs across the country.

65. NAAP, "Election Day Outreach, 11/2/02 and 11/3/02," November 2, 2002, www.naaponline.org/ny/events/voteoutreach_11-02-02.htm.

66. NAAP, "Call for Volunteers," September 2003, www.naaponline.org/ny/vote.asp.

67. AAI's research and analysis is both published and posted on its Web site at www.aaiusa.org.

68. The Web site www.arabsvote.org has been inactive since summer 2007, but has promised to be up and running for the 2008 presidential elections.

69. "ADC Action Alert: Contact the 110th Congress, Let Them Know They Have Arab-American Constituents,"ADCNYC@yahoogroups.com, January 10, 2007 (expired on site but copy of e-mailed text available at http://annies-letters.blogspot.com/2007_01_05_archive.html).

70. "ADC Action Alert: Call-In Days to the Senate in Support of Comprehensive Immigration Reform," ADCNYC@yahoogroups.com, May 2, 2007. "NATIONWIDE CALL-IN DAYS, Tuesday, Wednesday, Thursday May 1–3, 2007. Keep the momentum for immigration reform surging ahead—call this

number and follow the instructions to connect to the offices of both your Senators: 1–800–417–7666. On Monday through Wednesday, call the toll-free number above between 9:00 a.m. and 5.00 p.m. Eastern time to have a better chance of connecting with the Senate offices. When you call, you will hear a recording: 1) The system will scan your phone number (or ask you to enter it) to verify your Senators. 2) The system will ask, to which Senator you would like to be connected. 3) Before connecting, you will hear a brief message about immigration reform to deliver. 4) After the message, you will be connected to your Senator. 5) After you are done, be sure to call again and connect to your other Senator's office. TALKING POINTS—ACT NOW IN FAVOR OF A COMPREHENSIVE IMMIGRATION PACKAGE THAT: *restores due process; *provides a path to citizenship; *reunites families; protects workers. Together we can make it happen—thank you for your effort" (caps in original).

71. "ADC Action Alert: Cornyn Amendment Would Allow Use of Secret Evidence," ADCNY@yahoogroups.com, May 24, 2007.

72. Center for Vigilant Freedom, "Department of Justice First Freedom Project," March 2007, http://chromatism.net/current/images/cvf/kansascity.pdf; see also the ADC's current "Action Alerts" page at http://capwiz.com/adc/home/. The Matthew Shepard Local Law Enforcement Hate Crimes Prevention Act passed the U.S. Senate in September 2007. See ADC, "ADC Welcomes Passage of Hate Crime Prevention Legislation," press release, September 27, 2007, adcma-news@yahoogroups.come; SALDEF, "SALEDF Applauds Passage of Hate Crime Prevention Act: Senate Bill Will Help Prevent Victims of Hate Crimes," press release, September 27, 2007.

73. The perpetrator received two years' probation, including incarceration for the first eight months. "She was also sentenced to 200 hours of community service which must be completed at a mosque. Additionally, she was mandated to take anger management and diversity training classes. In handing down the sentence, Judge Gene Pratter said, 'Our society cannot afford to dismiss this type of conduct'" ("Woman Charged with Hate Crime against Muslim American Sentenced Today," *MPACnews*, October 14, 2007).

74. John Shiffman, "Threat to Boss Results in Charge: A Woman's Note Referencing the 9/11 Attacks to an Arab American Supervisor Could Result in a Jail Term," *Philadelphia Inquirer,* May 2, 2007; "U.S. Attorney Issues Indictment in Hate Crime against Philadelphia Muslim Woman," *MPACnews,* May 1, 2007; "MPAC, U.S. Attorney, FBI, Hold Press Conference Announcing Indictment in Philly Hate Crime Case," *MPACnews,* May 3, 2007; "Feds File Charges against Philadelphia Woman Who Threatened Muslim Woman," *MPACnews,* May 4, 2007; ADC, "Federal Charges in Hate Crime Targeting Arab American Woman," press release, ADCNYC@yahoogroups.com, May 4, 2007; U.S. Department of Justice, "Philadelphia Woman Pleads Guilty to Federal Hate Crime," press release, June 22, 2007, www.usdoj.gov/opa/pr/2007/June/07_crt_446.html.

75. ADC, "Former Exxon Employees Challenge Discrimination Against Arabs and Muslims," press release, November 6, 2007, ADCNYC@yahoogroups.com.

76. Other organizations also routinely send messages encouraging their constituents to engage in the political process. AAI sent a memo to its listserv on May 30, 2006, requesting members to "send letters to the editor of the Plain Dealer newspaper in Cleveland, Ohio, in praise of their editorial board for taking a responsible stand on HR 4681 and informing them about how damaging this legislation is to U.S. interests in the Middle East."

77. The CAIR guidelines "How to Challenge Anti-Muslim Rhetoric on the Radio" (April 15, 2004) are:

1. Force yourself to listen. It may be distasteful and upsetting, but unless people of conscience listen to these programs, the bigotry they spew will go unchallenged.

2. Document the program's anti-Muslim content. Without exact quotes from the program, any response will be ineffective. Record the show. Label and date your tapes, and indicate the time on the tape of the most offensive quotes. You can record programs that are broadcast on the Internet using sound recording software such as Audacity. See: http://audacity.sourceforge.net/.

3. Set up a quick-response list of people in your area who can be contacted quickly by phone or e-mail to call in to the program.

4. Transcribe the most offensive comments. Distribute these transcripts to those on your action list.

5. Call in to the show. If several people call in, it can change the entire direction of the program. REMEMBER—On radio, the first person to get angry loses the debate.

6. Write letters to station managers or owners and ask others to write letters. Station officials need to hear your views. Even a few letters can have an impact.

7. Request a meeting between station officials and local Muslim leaders and activists. Bring interfaith and minority coalition partners along to the meeting.

8. Notify local media of your efforts. Send a press release about any action, such as protests or letter-writing campaigns to advertisers that you initiate.

9. Organize a demonstration. A demonstration can draw attention to the problem. Large signs or placards and a one-page flyer with some of the worst on-air statements by the host and your coalition's demands will educate the public.

10. Put pressure on advertisers. Make note of the advertisers on the offensive program. Contact each one and ask that others in your action list contact them as well. Ask that they drop their commercials from the offensive programs. BE POLITE and PROFESSIONAL in all your communications.

11. File a complaint with the FCC, particularly if the host uses indecent or obscene language.

78. CAIR, "Help Improve Coverage of Islam in the U.S. Media: Sponsor 'A Journalist's Guide to Understanding Islam and Muslims,'" listserv, November 13, 2007.

79. "'Aliens in America' to Premiere Tonight," *MPACnews*, October 1, 2007.

80. "Support MPAC's Efforts to Promote 'Truth over Fear: Countering Islamophobia,'" *MPACnews*, April 13, 2007.

81. Michael Suleiman disagrees that Arab Americans should emulate the political mobilization of Jewish Americans. He writes: "Arab Americans and their political activity are primarily and almost invariably compared to Jewish-American communities and their political activism, especially because of the relatively equal size of the two communities and their concern over similar but

competing interests in the Palestine/Israel question. This is not a useful exercise. It may be more productive to compare the political involvement of the Arab-American community with that of Latino Americans as, even given the differences in size, the two communities share such characteristics as diversity and the concomitant difficulty of identifying major common objectives and articulating them as a focused political program, marginalization by the larger society, and the failure of pluralism to address adequately their concerns as communities" (2006, 16).

## 8. RELIGIOUS ACCOMMODATION

1. Prison *Dawah* (proselytizing) and other types of *Dawah* among African Americans and Latinos are a significant method of conversion to Islam (see, e.g., Abdo 2006; Anway 2000; Dannin 2002; Ebaugh and Chafetz 2000, 332; Leonard 2003; Schmidt 2004; J. Smith 1999).

2. Andrea Elliott, "Between Black and Immigrant Muslims, an Uneasy Alliance," *New York Times*, March 11, 2007, A1, A30–31.

3. Since the terrorist attacks, journalists have been writing about the personal experiences of Muslim Americans. See, e.g., Tara Bahrampour, "Young U.S. Muslims Strive for Harmony: 9/11 Spurred Action, Helped Define Beliefs," *Washington Post*, September 4, 2006, A1; Abdo (2006, ch. 1).

4. Quoted with permission of the authors from notes for the Bielefeld University and Center for German and European Studies of the University of St. Petersburg Conference on Accommodating Religious Diversity, St. Petersburg, Russia, September 26–28, 2007.

5. In Muslim countries, the *azaan* (call to prayer) is electronically amplified five times a day. Attempts to use loudspeakers in the United States, even occasionally, are facing opposition. See Paul Brubaker, "Prayer or Public 'Nuisance'?" *Herald News* (North Jersey), June 13, 2007. Ablutions are required before prayer, but the installation of two footbaths at the University of Michigan, Dearborn, at a cost of $25,000 faced opposition from conservative blogs and radio programs that criticized the public expenditure for religious needs. See Tamar Lewin, "Universities Install Footbaths to Benefit Muslims, and Not Everyone Is Pleased," *New York Times*, August 7, 2007, A10. However, the ACLU argued, after reviewing the case, that the university was making "reasonable accommodation" for the sake of "safety and cleanliness" because students were using the public sinks and messing up the bathroom floors. The ACLU representative noted that footbaths "deal with a problem, not an attempt to make it easier for Muslims to pray" (Karen Bouffard, "Muslims Won't Fund Footbaths: Leaders Cite ACLU's Decision Not to Oppose Use of Public Money for UM-Dearborn," *Detroit News*, June 18, 2007). On burial rites, see Alia Malek, "For Muslim New Yorkers, Final Rites That Fit," *New York Times*, January 6, 2006, sec. 14, 8; Roja Heydarpour, "At Muslim Resting Place, 5 New Child-Size Graves," *New York Times*, March 18, 2007, 30 (Metro section). On financial transactions, see, e.g., Terry Pristin, "When the Landlord Is Muslim: For Believers, Property Investments Are Freighted with Dos and Don'ts," *New York Times*, September 21, 2005, C7. On recognition of Muslim holidays, see the U.S. Postal Service's news release in 2001 about issuing a thirty-four-cent stamp

to celebrate the Muslim Eid (see "U.S. Postage Stamp Celebrating Muslim Holiday to Be Issued by United States Postal Service," August 1, 2001, www.usps .com/news/2001/philatelic/sr01_054.htm). This was a token gesture acknowledging the presence of a growing Muslim American community. On polygamy, see Nina Bernstein, "Polygamy, Practiced in Secrecy, Follows Africans to New York," *New York Times*, March 23, 2007, A1, B6.

6. See, e.g., Thomas Bartlett, "The Quiet Heretic: A Controversial Prayer Upsets a Professor's Life," *Chronicle of Higher Education*, August 12, 2005, A10–12; Laurie Goodstein, "Muslim Women Seeking a Place in the Mosque," *New York Times*, July 22, 2004, A1. In San Francisco, the wall separating men and women in the Darussalam mosque was torn down, but this created controversy. Neil MacFarquhar, "As Barrier Comes Down, A Muslim Split Remains: Congregation Is Torn by a Wall's Removal," *New York Times*, June 25, 2006, A14.

7. Schmidt (2004) describes a variety of Muslim educational institutions in Chicago in the 1990s. These range from weekend schools, to full-time Muslim schools, to the Hafiz School, where about twenty-five boys, ages seven through fifteen, learn to recite the Qu'ran, to universities, even after-school programs.

8. For example, in 2008 the *Journal of Muslim Mental Health* published its third volume. See its Web page at www.muslimmentalhealth.com/Association _Docs/contribute.asp.

9. For a history of the establishment of Al-Noor Mosque in Houston, Texas, in the 1970s, see Ebaugh and Chafetz (2000, 351). Schmidt notes that the mosque built in 1995 in the Villa Park suburb of Chicago included a funeral building within the complex (2004, 163); see also Metcaff (1996) on issues of space.

10. Many observant Muslims do not recognize Halloween or Valentine's Day.

11. Some lay leaders have gained national prominence for their advocacy on behalf of Muslims after 9/11. Maher Hathout, a cardiologist originally from Egypt, is an example. His activism at the Islamic Center of Southern California and MPAC, his participation in a variety of interfaith coalitions, his proactive negotiations with law enforcement, his liberal views on gender, and his unequivocal endorsement of American Islam in the United States have made him popular with the press and have won him the prestigious John Allen Buggs Award for excellence in human relations from the Los Angeles County Commission on Human Relations. See Mehammed Mack, "An American Muslim: Maher Hathout and His Philosophy of Radical Openness," *Los Angeles Weekly*, January 3, 2007, www.laweekly.com/general/features/an-American-Muslim/15329.

12. See Andrea Elliott, "Tending to Muslim Hearts and Islam's Future," *New York Times*, March 7, 2006, A1, A10–11. This is one of three lengthy articles that Elliott wrote after shadowing Reda Shata, the imam of the Islamic Center for Bay Ridge, for six months. See also "To Lead the Faithful in a Faith under Fire," *New York Times*, March 6, 2006, A1, A12–13; and "A Muslim Leader in Brooklyn, Reconciling 2 Worlds," *New York Times*, March 5, 2006, A1, A26–27. On the topic of matchmaking, it is perhaps more cost effective (in terms of time spent and resultant marriage) to create new institutions that address the population's needs, such as the "matrimonial banquet," which is the

Muslim equivalent of speed-dating. See Neil MacFarquhar, "It's Muslim Boy Meets Girl, Yes, but Please Don't Call It Dating," *New York Times,* September 19, 2006, A1, A19.

13. Neil MacFarquhar, "A Growing Demand for the Rare American Imam," *New York Times,* June 1, 2007, A1.

14. See Laurie Goodstein, "American Muslim Clerics Seek a Modern Middle Ground," *New York Times,* June 18, 2006, A1, A22. For an interview with Sheikh Hamza Yusuf, see Abdo (2006, ch. 1).

15. Nihad Awad, executive director of CAIR, is reported as saying, "Imams who come from overseas, sometimes they bring a different mentality. They come from Muslim-majority places. They have different cultures, norms and traditions. . . . I think it's important that we develop our own." See Theresa Vargas, "After Homework, Duty as an Imam: With Cleric's Visa Denied, VA Center Enlists Its Most Learned: Two Teens," *Washington Post,* October 1, 2006, A01.

16. Elliott, "To Lead the Faithful." The Arab/Muslim community of Bay Ridge was impressed with the coverage and honored the reporter and the photographer at a banquet where Bay Ridge's religious groups were represented as well as the commander of the 68th Precinct. See Antoine Faisal and Virginia Sherwood, "On 'An Imam in America': A Timely Story of Needs Fulfilling Destiny," *Aramica,* March 9–23, 2006, 36–37.

17. See Lynette Clemetson, "U.S. Muslims Confront Taboo on Nursing Homes: Desire to Honor Koran Clashes with Reality of Modern Life," *New York Times,* A1, A20.

18. "Mirroring the feminist school of Islam, gay advocates pursue a holistic interpretation that emphasizes accepting everyone as equally God's creation," writes Neil MacFarquhar in "Gay Muslims Find Freedom, of a Sort, in the U.S.," *New York Times,* November 7, 2007, A20. In her edited volume *Voices of Resistance: Muslim Women on War, Faith and Sexuality,* Sarah Husain includes a large section entitled "Re-claiming Our Bodies/Re-claiming Our Sexualities," in which fifteen writers, poets, and artists from the United States explore new frontiers of sexuality and body politics. Those who have transgressed the bounds of traditional Islam have been criticized severely. Some, like Irshad Manji, who became a television pundit as an expert on everything Islamic, have been accused of making Islam a commodity and have been called "professional Muslims" (see Abdo 2006, 120–21). See the home page of the Al Fatiha Foundation at www.al-fatiha.org.

19. An initiative to include Eid-al-Fitr and Eid-al-Adha in the official holidays of the New York City Department of Education is underway, spearheaded by attorney Omar T. Mohammedi, the New York Civic Participation Project (NYCPP), ADC, and the Asian American Legal Defense and Education Fund (Eid School Holiday Bill (S3142), sponsored by State Senator John Sabini). A bill prohibiting testing on Eid-al-Adha and Eid-al-Fitr (Sabini's bill) passed the New York State Senate and State Assembly in June 2006 (ADC-NYC listserv, June 29, 2006; see also John Freeman Gill, "New York Up Close: Wrestling with Faith While Making the Grade," *New York Times,* February 19, 2006, sec. 14, 5; Emily Brady, "For Muslim Students, a Drive to Deem Holy Days as Holidays," *New York Times,* April 29, 2007, 5, City Section). It is worth noting that local

politicians have begun to respond to the advocacy of their constituents. New York City Council members John Liu and Robert Jackson and Speaker Christine Quinn celebrated the Eid-al-Fitr on October 22, 2007, in City Hall, highlighting "contributions made by Muslim Americans to New York City." The invitation was sent via to John Liu's group: JohnLiuNYCCouncil@googlegroups.com. In Baltimore County, Bash Pharaon has been waging a campaign to have schools closed on Eid-al-Fitr and Eid-al-Adha as a form of fairness to local Muslims. See Gina Davis, "Muslims Protest Shift by School Board," *Baltimore Sun,* January 9, 2007; Gina Davis, "An Unwavering Push for Muslim School Holidays: Man's Decade of Work Faces Obstacles, Including Law," *Baltimore Sun,* April 23, 2007, 14.

20. A bipartisan bill advocating workplace religious freedom was introduced in Congress in March 2005. If passed, it will allow employers to make reasonable accommodation for employees to practice their religion. Religious attire such as a beard and turban for Sikhs and *hijab* for Muslim women; observances such as fasting at Ramadan and praying at work; and holy days such as Eid-Al-Adha will be more tolerated. The coalition supporting the Workplace Religious Freedom Act includes the Union of Orthodox Jewish Congregations, the National Council of Churches, the North American Council of Muslim Women, and SALDEF. See Institute for Public Affairs, "The Workplace Religious Freedom Act: Background. Critical Legislation for the American Community," IPA Public Policy Library, www.ou.org/public/statements/bg/wrfa.htm.

21. Joshua Freed, "Companies Courting Muslims with Money—Growing Number of Firms Attract Believers by Following Islamic Law," *Charlotte Observer,* October 13, 2006.

22. Ruth LaFerla, "We, Myself and I," *New York Times,* April 5, 2007, G1, G7.

23. Louise Story, "Advertisers Rewrite the Rules for Reaching Muslims," *New York Times,* April 26, 2007, C1.

24. Katie Zezima, "The Muslim Patient Will See You Now, Doctor," *New York Times,* September 1, 2004, A17.

25. Richard Whittle, "Uncle Sam Wants U.S. Muslims to Serve," *Christian Science Monitor,* December 30, 2006.

26. One project concerns clergy from various faiths building a house for a low-income family in Charlotte, North Carolina. Some fifty clergy, including an imam, will partner with Habitat for Humanity to complete this goal. Tim Funk, "Clergy to Build House as Walls Torn Down," *Charlotte Observer,* June 12, 2007.

27. Robert Wuthnow (2005, ch. 7) mentions several others, such as the United Religions Initiative, which was established in San Francisco in 1995; the Kansas Interfaith Council, founded in 1989; the Thanks-Giving Square Foundation in Dallas; the Interfaith Alliance of Lehigh Valley in Allentown, Pennsylvania; and the defunct Madison Area Interfaith Network (MAIN).

28. CAIR has published a pamphlet ("Tips on Mosque Open House Projects," n.d., www.themodernreligion.com/basic/mosque/open-house.html) with guidelines on how to organize an open house. The pamphlet depicts the process step by step. Tips are offered on how to (1) prepare for the event, (2) invite community leaders and others, (3) publicize the event, (4) inform the guests about

mosque etiquette before their arrival, (5) clean up the mosque, (6) set up a reception area for guests with refreshments, (7) make literature on Islam available, and finally, (8) assign outgoing individuals to become greeters and hosts. The brochure adds, "Make sure all the guests are warmly received and given name tags. Special attention should be given to female guests because they may not be sure where they 'fit in.' Have sisters assigned as hosts for the female guests. In the event of an *iftar* open house, make sure Muslims and non-Muslims are seated together for the meal."

29. See also "Breaking Bread Together—ASMA Society Hosts Interfaith Event," *Aramica,* June 23–July 7, 2003, 30–31.

30. Congressman Holt's efforts were highlighted in the weekly electronic newsletter of AAI (January 24, 2003; July 9, 2004; and October 15, 2004).

31. AAI, "Zogby/AAI Poll Results: Arab American Voters to Decide on 2008 Presidential Candidates by Stance on Iraq War," press release, June 28, 2007.

32. "The telephone list was created by matching the zip codes of 300 randomly selected Islamic centers, against their respective local telephone exchanges. Listings of common Muslim surnames were then identified from the local telephone exchanges and called" (Project MAPS and Zogby 2001, 3).

33. Here *correctly* indicates that the vote was in favor of AAI's constituents.

34. Founded in 1971, ACCESS, in Dearborn, Michigan, is the oldest and largest Arab American community-based organization. In August 2007, after working with ACCESS for over three decades, Ismael Ahmed was appointed as the director of the Michigan Department of Human Services by Governor Jennifer M. Granholm. See "ACCESS Leader Appointed to Lead State DHHS," ACCESS, August 13, 2007; see also "Biography of Ismael Ahmed," 2007, www.michigan.gov/dhs/0,1607,7-124-5459_7097-174062-,00.html.

35. Neil MacFarquhar, "In Arab Capital of U.S., Ethnic Divide Remains," *New York Times,* January 23, 2007, A12.

36. Moushumi Khan, "Muslims in America: Integration or Isolation?" *Daily Star* (Bangladesh), January 25, 2006.

37. Neil MacFarquhar, "Putting a Different Face on Islam in America," *New York Times,* September 20, 2006, B1, B7.

38. It is important to note that lay persons who used the term *assimilation* in this study (almost all our respondents) did not necessarily use it in the same sense as scholars of immigration do (see Alba and Nee 2003). Often the concepts of assimilation and integration are confused.

39. Jane Morse, "Young American Muslims Encouraged to Seek Public-Service Careers: Group Meets with U.S. Officials, Elected Representatives in Washington," U.S. State Department press release, July 17, 2007, http://usinfo .state.gov/xarchives/display.html?p=washfile-english&y=2007&m=july&x= 20070717102301ajesroMo.8706629.

40. See Louis Sahagun, "Muslim Leaders Demand Inclusion: The Officials Say Schwarzenegger and Villaraigosa Should Represent All Residents on the Lebanon Conflict, Not Just Israel Backers," *Los Angeles Times,* August 5, 2006, B3; Ralph Frammolino, "Mayor Meets with Muslim Leaders: Villaraigosa Had Been Criticized for Visiting a Jewish Rally but Not with Local Islamic Groups," *Los Angeles Times,* August 7, 2006, B4.

41. ADC, "Over 2400 People Participate in ADC Annual National Convention," press release, June 14, 2007.

42. MPAC's e-mail messages to its listserv always end with the following lines: "How Does MPAC Help Muslims & Islam in America? As a matter of policy, MPAC DOES NOT accept any funding from foreign governments. The political and financial independence of MPAC will sustain the future of Islam in America. MPAC relies on your financial support to sustain its activities and represent the sentiments and interests of American Muslims not foreign governments" (emphasis in original).

43. Several Muslim organizations collected donations for Hurricane Katrina victims in September 2005. Muslim organizations also sent out press releases on the immigration debates ("Muslim Americans to Join 5/1 Immigration Marches Nationwide," *MPACnews,* April 20, 2006); the genocide in Darfur ("CAIR Asks Why No Muslim Groups to Speak at Darfur Rally," *CAIRNet,* April 30, 2006); and the Virginia Tech shootings ("MPAC Offers Condolences to Families of Virginia Tech Shooting Victims," *MPACnews,* April 16, 2007).

44. Naber (2005, 490) suggests that the "Muslim First" label is ideologically more amenable to developing a "politics of race" than the Arab label that U.S.-born youth inherit from their parents. Our evidence suggests that mobilizing to ensure that the faithful fulfill their religious obligations makes for clearer goals than maintaining an umbrella identity (Arab American).

# References

AAI. 2002. *Healing the Nation: The Arab American Experience after September 11.* Washington, DC: AAI. http://aai.3cdn.net/64de7330dc475fe470_h1m6boyk4.pdf.

———. 2007. *Election 2006: Arab Americans on the Move.* Washington, DC: AAI. www.aaiusa.org/resources/400/campaigns-elections-pdf.

Abdo, Geneive. 2006. *Mecca and Main Street: Muslim Life in America after 9/11.* New York: Oxford University Press.

Abdul-Ghafur, Saleemah, ed. 2005. *Living Islam Out Loud: American Muslim Women Speak.* Boston: Beacon Press.

Abraham, Nabeel. 1983. "The Yemeni Immigrant Community of Detroit: Background, Emigration, and Community Life." In *Arabs in the New World: Studies on Arab-American Communities,* edited by Sameer Y. Abraham and Nabeel Abraham, 109–34. Detroit: Wayne State University, Center for Urban Studies.

———. 1994. "Anti-Arab Racism and Violence in the United States." In *The Development of Arab American Identity,* edited by Ernest McCarus, 155–214. Ann Arbor: University of Michigan Press.

Abraham, Nabeel, and Andrew Shryock, eds. 2000. *Arab Detroit: From Margin to Mainstream.* Detroit: Wayne State University Press.

Abraham, Sameer, Nabeel Abraham, and Barbara Aswad. 1983. "The Southend: An Arab Muslim Working-Class Community." In *Arabs in the New World: Studies on Arab-American Communities,* edited by Sameer Y.

Abraham and Nabeel Abraham, 163–85. Detroit: Wayne State University, Center for Urban Studies.

Aciman, André. 1994. *Out of Egypt: A Memoir.* New York: Penguin Putman.

ACLU. 2002. *Civil Liberties after 9/11: A Historical Perspective on Protecting Liberty in Times of Crisis.* New York: ACLU. www.aclu.org/FilesPDFs/911_report.pdf.

———. 2004a. *America's Disappeared: Seeking International Justice for Immigrants Detained after September 11.* January. New York: ACLU. www.aclu.org/FilesPDFs/un%20report.pdf.

———. 2004b. *Sanctioned Bias: Racial Profiling since 9/11.* February. New York: ACLU. www.aclu.org/FilesPDFs/racial%20profiling%20report.pdf.

———. 2004c. *Worlds Apart: How Deporting Immigrants after 9/11 Tore Families Apart and Shattered Communities.* December. New York: ACLU. www.aclu.org/FilesPDFs/worldsapart.pdf.

———. 2005. "Fact Sheet: Extraordinary Rendition." December 6. www.aclu.org/safefree/extraordinaryrendition/22203res20051206.html.

Ahdab-Yehia, May. 1974. "The Detroit Maronite Community." In *Arabic Speaking Communities in American Cities,* edited by Barbara Aswad, 137–55. Staten Island, NY: Center for Migration Studies.

———. 1983. "The Lebanese Maronites: Patterns of Continuity and Change." In *Arabs in the New World: Studies on Arab-American Communities,* edited by Sameer Y. Abraham and Nabeel Abraham, 147–62. Detroit: Wayne State University, Center for Urban Studies.

Ahmed, Ismael. 2006. "Michigan Arab Americans: A Case Study of Electoral and Non-electoral Empowerment." In *American Arabs and Political Participation,* edited by Philippa Strum, 41–51. Washington, DC: Woodrow Wilson International Center for Scholars.

Ahmed, Leila. 1999. *A Border Passage: From Cairo to America—A Woman's Journey.* New York: Penguin.

Akram, Susan, and Kevin Johnson. 2004. "Race and Civil Rights Pre-September 11, 2001: The Targeting of Arabs and Muslims." In *Civil Rights in Peril: The Targeting of Arabs and Muslims,* edited by Elaine Hagopian, 9–25. Chicago: Haymarket Books.

Akram, Susan, and Maritza Karmely. 2005. "Immigration and Constitutional Consequences of Post-9/11 Policies Involving Arabs and Muslims in the United States: Is Alienage a Distinction without a Difference?" *University of California Davis Law Review* 38 (3): 609–99.

Al-Alwani, Taha Jabir. 2004. "Toward a *Fiqh* for Minorities: Some Reflections." In *Muslims' Place in the American Public Square,* edited by Zahid H. Bukhari, Sulayman S. Nyang, Mumtaz Ahmed, and John L. Esposito, 3–37. Walnut Creek, CA: Altamira Press.

Alba, Richard, and Victor Nee. 2003. *Remaking the American Mainstream.* Cambridge, MA: Harvard University Press.

Alexander, Benjamin F. 2005. "Armenian and American: The Changing Face of Ethnic Identity and Diasporic Nationalism, 1915–1955." PhD diss., City University of New York.

Alhadeff, Gini, 1998. *The Sun at Midday: Tales of Mediterranean Family.* New York: EuroPress.

Alsultany, Evelyn Azeeza. 2005. "The Changing Profile of Race in the United States: Media Representations of Racialization of Arab and Muslim Americans Post-9/11." PhD diss., Stanford University.

—————. 2007. "Selling American Diversity and Muslim American Identity through Nonprofit Advertising Post-9/11." *American Quarterly* 59 (3): 593–622.

Amnesty International. 2004. *Threat and Humiliation: Racial Profiling, Domestic Security, and Human Rights in the United States.* New York: Amnesty International U.S.A. www.amnestyusa.org/racial_profiling/report/rp_report.pdf.

—————. 2005. *USA: Guantánamo: Trusting the Executive, Prolonging the Injustice.* Report, AMR 51/030/2005. January 26. New York: Amnesty International. http://web.amnesty.org/library/index/engamr510302005.

—————. 2006. *USA: Guantánamo's Military Commissions: A Travesty of Justice.* Report, AMR 51/184/2006. December 8. http://asiapacific.amnesty.org/library/Index/ENGAMR511842006?open&of=ENG-2AM

Anway, Carol L. 2000. "American Women Choosing Islam." In *Muslims on the Americanization Path?* edited by Yvonne Yazbech Haddad and John L. Esposito, 145–60. New York: Oxford University Press.

Aslan, Reza. 2005. *No God but God: The Origins, Evolution, and Future of Islam.* New York: Random House.

Aswad, Barbara, ed. 1974. *Arabic Speaking Communities in American Cities.* Staten Island, NY: Center for Migration Studies.

Badr, Hoda. 2000. "Al-Noor Mosque: Strength through Unity." In *Religion and the New Immigrants: Continuities and Adaptations in Immigrant Congregations,* edited by Helen Rose Ebaugh and Janet Saltzman Chafetz, 193–237. Walnut Creek, CA: Altamira Press.

Bakalian, Anny. 1993. *Armenian Americans: From Being to Feeling Armenian.* New Brunswick, NJ: Transaction Books.

—————. 2007. "Armenian Identity in the United States among Second Generation Cohorts." In *Arméniens et Grecs en diaspora: approches comparatives,* edited by Michel Bruneau, Ioannis Hassiotis, Martine Hovanessian, and Claire Mouradian, 309–32. Athens: École française d'Athènes.

Bakalian, Anny, and Mehdi Bozorgmehr. 2005. "Muslim American Mobilization." *Diaspora: A Journal of Transnational Studies* 14 (1): 7–43.

Barth, Fredrick. 1969. "Introduction." In *Ethnic Groups and Boundaries: The Social Organization of Cultural Difference,* edited by Fredrik Barth, 9–38. Boston: Little, Brown.

Basiouny, Dalia. 2005. "Beyond Baklava: Arab American Women Do Political Theater." Paper presented at the conference "Middle Eastern Diasporas: (In)visible Minorities," March 18–20, Yale University.

Bawardi, Hani. 2008. "The Early Syrian/Arab Immigrant Organizations: Transnational Political Consciousness and the Development of Arab American Identity (1912–1967)." PhD diss., Wayne State University.

Ba-Yunus, Ilyas, and Kassim Kone. 2004. "Muslim Americans: A Demographic Report." In *Muslims' Place in the American Public Square,* edited by Zahid H. Bukhari, Sulayman S. Nyang, Mumtaz Ahmed, and John L. Esposito, 299–322. Walnut Creek, CA: Altamira Press.

Beinin, Joel. 1998. *The Dispersion of Egyptian Jewry: Culture, Politics, and the Formation of a Modern Diaspora.* Berkeley: University of California Press.

Belanger, Sarah and Maurice Pinard. 1991. "Ethnic Movements and the Competition Model: Some Missing Links." *American Sociological Review* 56 (4): 446–57.

Benford, Robert D. 1992. "Social Movements." In *Encyclopedia of Sociology,* edited by Edgar F. Borgatta, 1,880–1,887. New York: Macmillan.

Benford, Robert D., and David A. Snow. 2000. "Framing Processes and Social Movements: An Overview and Assessment." *Annual Review of Sociology* 26:611–39.

Benson, Kathleen, and Philip M. Kayal, eds. 2002. *A Community of Many Worlds: Arab-Americans in New York City.* Syracuse: Syracuse University Press.

Berger, L. Peter, and Thomas Luckmann. 1966. *The Social Construction of Reality: A Treatise in the Sociology of Knowledge.* New York: Anchor Books.

Bodnar, John. 1985. *The Transplanted: A History of Immigrants in Urban America.* Bloomington: Indiana University Press.

Bonacich, Edna, and John Modell. 1980. *The Economic Basis of Ethnic Solidarity: Small Business in the Japanese American Community.* Berkeley: University of California Press.

Bonilla-Silva, Eduardo. 2006. *Racism without Racists: Color-Blind Racism and the Persistence of Racial Inequality in the United States.* 2nd ed. Lanham, MD: Rowman and Littlefield.

Bozorgmehr, Mehdi. 1998. "From Iranian Studies to Studies of Iranians in the United States." *Iranian Studies* 31:5–30.

———. 2000. "Does Host Hostility Create Ethnic Solidarity? The Experience of Iranians in the United States." *Bulletin of the Royal Institute for Inter-Faith Studies* 2:159–78.

———. 2007. "Iran." In *The New Americans: A Handbook to Immigration since 1965,* edited by Mary Waters, Reed Ueda, and Helen Marrow, 469–78. Cambridge, MA: Harvard University Press.

Bozorgmehr, Mehdi, and Anny Bakalian. 2005a. "Discriminatory Reactions to September 11, 2001 Terrorism." In *Encyclopedia of Racism in the United States,* edited by Pyong Gap Min, 557–64. Westport, CT: Greenwood Press.

———. 2005b. "Muslim Philanthropic Organizations, Closure of after September 11, 2001." In *Encyclopedia of Racism in the United States,* edited by Pyong Gap Min, 418–19. Westport, CT: Greenwood Press.

———. 2005c. "Responding to the Backlash by Arab/Muslim American Advocacy Organizations." In *Encyclopedia of Racism in the United States,* edited by Pyong Gap Min, 43–45. Westport, Conn.: Greenwood Press.

———. 2008. "Post-9/11 Government Initiatives in Comparative and Historical Perspectives." In *From Arrival to Incorporation: Migrants to the U.S. in a Global Era,* edited by Elliott R. Barkan, Hasia Diner, and Alan M. Kraut, 246–66. New York: New York University Press.

Bozorgmehr, Mehdi, and Beth Baron, eds. 2001. *Philanthropy among Middle Eastern Americans and Their Historical Traditions of Giving.* Curriculum Guide No. 14. New York: Center for the Study of Philanthropy, Graduate Center, City University of New York.

Bozorgmehr, Mehdi, and Alison Feldman, eds. 1996. *Middle Eastern Diaspora Communities in America.* New York: Kevorkian Center for Near Eastern Studies, New York University.

Bozorgmehr, Mehdi, Claudia Der-Martirosian, and Georges Sabagh. 1996. "Middle Easterners: A New Kind of Immigrant." In *Ethnic Los Angeles,* edited by Roger Waldinger and Mehdi Bozorgmehr, 345–78. New York: Russell Sage Foundation.

Breton, Raymond. 1964. "Institutional Completeness of Ethnic Communities and the Personal Relations of Immigrants." *American Journal of Sociology* 70 (2):193–205.

Brittingham, Angela, and G. Patricia de la Cruz. 2005. *We the People of Arab Ancestry in the United States: 2000 Census Special Reports.* Washington, DC: U.S. Bureau of the Census.

Brown, Cynthia, ed. 2003. *Lost Liberties: Ashcroft and the Assault on Personal Freedom.* New York: New Press.

Brubaker, Rogers. 2004. *Ethnicity without Groups.* Cambridge, MA: Harvard University Press.

Bryan, Jennifer. 2005. "Constructing 'The True Islam' in Hostile Times: The Impact of 9/11 on Arab Muslims in Jersey City." In *Wounded City: The Social Impact of 9/11,* edited by Nancy Foner, 133–63. New York: Russell Sage Foundation.

Buechler, Steven. 2000. *Social Movements in Advanced Capitalism.* New York: Oxford University Press.

Bulbulian, Berge. 2000. *The Fresno Armenians: History of a Diaspora Community.* Fresno: Press at California State University.

Cahnman, Werner. 1944. "Religion and Nationality." *American Journal of Sociology* 49 (6): 524–29.

Cainkar, Louise. 2004a. "The Impact of the September 11 Attacks on Arab and Muslim Communities in the United States." In *The Maze of Fear: Security and Migration after 9/11,* edited by John Tirman, 215–39. New York: New Press.

———. 2004b. "Islamic Revival among Second-Generation Arab American Muslims: The American Experience and Globalization." *Bulletin of the Royal Institute for Inter-Faith Studies* 6 (2): 99–122.

———. 2006. "The Social Construction of Difference and the Arab American Experience." *Journal of American Ethnic History* 25 (2/3):243–78.

———. 2008. "Thinking Outside the Box: Arabs and Race in the United States." In *Race and Arab Americans before and after 9/11: From Invisible Citizens to Visible Subjects,* edited by Amaney Jamal and Nadine Naber, 46–80. Syracuse: Syracuse University Press.

Cainkar, Louise, and Sunaina Maira. 2005. "Targeting Arab/Muslim/South Asian Americans: Criminalization and Cultural Citizenship." *Amerasia Journal* 31 (3): 1–27.

CAIR. 2002a. *American Muslims: One Year after 9-11.* Washington, DC: CAIR.

———. 2002b. "The Status of Muslims in the United States: Stereotypes and Civil Liberties." Civil Rights Report, May. www.cair.com/CivilRights/Civil RightsReports/2002Report.aspx.

———. 2004. "Unpatriotic Acts: The Status of Muslim Civil Rights in the United States."www.cair.com/CivilRights/CivilRightsReports/2004Report.aspx.

———. 2005. "Unequal Protection: The Status of Muslim Civil Rights in the United States." Civil Rights Report. www.cair.com/CivilRights/CivilRights Reports/2005Report.aspx.

———. 2006a. *American Public Opinion about Islam and Muslims.* Washington, DC: CAIR. www.cair.com/Portals/0/pdf/american_public_opinion_on_ muslims_islam_2006.pdf.

———. 2006b. "The Status of Muslim Civil Rights in the United States: The Struggle for Equality." Civil Rights Report. www.arabvoices.net/2006-cair-civil-rights-report.pdf.

———. 2007. "The Status of Muslim Civil Rights in the United States: Presumption of Guilt." Civil Rights Report. www.cair.com/pdf/2007-Civil-Rights-Report.pdf.

Camp, Helen C. 1995. *Iron in Her Soul: Elizabeth Gurley Flynn and the American Left.* Pullman: Washington State University Press.

Chan, Sucheng. 1991. *Asian Americans: An Interpretive History.* Boston: Twayne.

Checkoway, Barry, Karen Rignall, and Aparna Ramakrishnan. 2005. *Arab Americans Arising: Case Studies of Community Based Organizations in Three American Cities.* Dearborn, MI: ACCESS-NNAAC. www.nnaac.org/ publications/ACCESS%20Case%20Study.indd.pdf.

Chishti, Muzaffar A., Doris Meissner, Demetrios G. Papademetriou, Jay Peterzell, Michael J. Wishnie, and Stephen W. Yale-Loehr. 2003. *America's Challenge: Domestic Security, Civil Liberties, and National Unity after September 11. Washington, DC: Migration Policy Institute.* www.migration policy.org/pubs/Americas_Challenges.pdf.

Chung, Angie Y. 2005. "'Politics without Politics': The Evolving Political Culture of Ethnic Non-profits in Koreatown, Los Angeles." *Journal of Ethnic and Migration Studies* 31 (5): 911–29.

Clarke, Lee. 2002. "Panic: Myth or Reality?" *Contexts* 1 (3): 21–26.

———. 2003. "Conceptualizing Responses to Extreme Events: The Problem of Panic and Failing Gracefully." In *Terrorism and Disaster: New Threats, New Ideas,* edited by Lee Clarke, 123–41. Amsterdam: Elsevier.

Cohen, Stanley. 2002. *Folk Devils and Moral Panics.* 3rd ed. London: Routledge.

Cole, David. 2003. *Enemy Aliens.* New York: New Press.

Cole, David, and James Dempsey. 2002. *Terrorism and the Constitution: Sacrificing Civil Liberties in the Name of National Security.* New York: New Press.

Cole, David, and Jules Lobel. 2007. *Less Safe, Less Free: Why America Is Losing the War on Terror.* New York: New Press.

Cole, Juan. 2007. "Islamophobia as a Social Problem: 2006 Presidential Address." *Middle East Studies Association Bulletin* 41 (1): 3–7.

Conzen, Kathleen Neils. 1980. "Germans." In *Harvard Encyclopedia of American Ethnic Groups,* edited by Stephan Thernstrom, Ann Orlov, and Oscar Handlin. Cambridge, MA: Harvard University Press.

Conzen, Kathleen Neils, David A. Gerber, Ewa Morawska, George E. Pozzetta, and Rudolph J. Vecoli. 1992. "The Invention of Ethnicity: A Perspective from the U.S.A." *Journal of American Ethnic History* 12 (1): 3–42.

Cordero-Guzman, Hector. 2001a. Immigrant Aid Societies and Organizations." In *Encyclopedia of American Immigration,* edited by James Ciment, 334–40. Armonk, NY: M. E. Sharpe.

———. 2001b. "Social Services." In *Encyclopedia of American Immigration,* edited by James Ciment, 730–36. Armonk, NY: M. E. Sharpe.

———. 2005. "Community Based Organizations and Migration in New York City." *Journal of Ethnic and Migration Studies* 31 (5): 889–909.

Coser, Lewis. 1956. *The Functions of Social Conflict.* New York: Free Press.

Cress, David, and David Snow. 1996. "Mobilization at the Margins: Resources, Benefactors, and Viability of Homeless Social Movement Organizations." *American Sociological Review* 61 (6): 1089–1109.

Cristillo, Louis Abdellatif, and Lorraine Minnite. 2002. "The Changing Arab New York Community." In *A Community of Many Worlds: Arab Americans in New York City,* edited by Kathleen Benson and Philip Kayal, 124–39. Syracuse: Syracuse University Press.

Cristillo, Louis Frances. 2004. "'God Has Willed It': Religiosity and Social Reproduction at a Private Muslim School in New York City." PhD diss., Columbia University.

Dahbany-Miraglia, Dina. 1987. "Yemenite Jewish Immigration and Adaptation to the United States, 1905–1941." In *Crossing the Waters: Arabic-Speaking Immigrants to the United States before 1940,* edited by Eric J. Hooglund, 119–31. Washington, DC: Smithsonian Institution Press.

———. 1988. "American Yemenite Jews: Interethnic Strategies." In *Persistence and Flexibility: Anthropological Perspectives on the American Jewish Experience,* edited by Walter P. Zenner, 63–78. Albany: State University of New York Press.

Daniels, Roger. 1972. *Concentration Camps U.S.A.: Japanese Americans and World War II.* New York: Holt, Rinehart and Winston.

———. 1988. *Asian Americans: Chinese and Japanese in the United States since 1850.* Seattle: University of Washington Press.

———. 1993. *Prisoners without Trial.* New York: Hill and Wang.

Dannin, Robert. 2002. *Black Pilgrimage to Islam.* New York: Oxford University Press.

Das Gupta, Monisha. 2005. "Of Hardship and Hostility: The Impact of 9/11 on New York City Taxi Drivers." In *Wounded City: The Social Impact of 9/11,* edited by Nancy Foner, 208–42. New York: Russell Sage Foundation.

David, Gary C. 2000. "Behind the Bulletproof Glass: Iraqi Chaldean Store Ownership in Metropolitan Detroit." In *Arab Detroit: From Margin to Mainstream,* edited by Nabeel Abraham and Andrew Shryock, 151–78. Detroit: Wayne State University Press.

De La Cruz, G. Patricia, and Angela Brittingham. 2003. *The Arab Population: 2000 Census Special Reports*. Washington, DC: U.S. Bureau of the Census.

De Tocqueville, Alexis. 1945. *Democracy in America*. Vol. 2. New York: Random House.

Dolan, Jay P. 1975. *The Immigrant Church: New York's Irish and German Catholics, 1815–1865*. Baltimore: Johns Hopkins University Press.

Ebaugh, Helen Rose, and Janet Saltzman Chafetz. 2000. *Religion and the New Immigrants: Continuities and Adaptations in Immigrant Congregations*. Walnut Creek, CA: Altamira Press.

Eck, Diana L. 2007. "Religion." In *The New Americans: A Handbook to Immigration since 1965,* edited by Mary Waters, Reed Ueda, and Helen Marrow, 214–27. Cambridge, MA: Harvard University Press.

Eickelman, Dale F. 2002. *The Middle East and Central Asia: An Anthropological Approach*. 4th ed. Saddle River, NJ: Prentice Hall.

Elkholy, Abdo A. 1966. *The Arab Moslems in the United States: Religion and Assimilation*. New Haven, CT: College and University Press.

Ennis, James G. 1987. "Fields of Action: Structure in Movements' Tactical Repertoires." *Sociological Forum* 2 (3): 520–33.

Eriksen, Thomas Hylland. 1993. *Ethnicity and Nationalism: Anthropological Perspectives*. London: Pluto Press.

Erikson, Kai. 2005. "Epilogue: The Geography of Disaster." In *Wounded City: The Social Impact of 9/11,* edited by Nancy Foner, 351–62. New York: Russell Sage Foundation.

Espiritu, Yen Le. 1992. *Asian American Panethnicity: Bridging Institutions and Identities*. Philadelphia: Temple University Press.

Etzioni, Amitai. 2004. *How Patriotic Is the Patriot Act? Freedom versus Security in the Age of Terrorism*. New York: Routledge.

FBI. 1999–2006. *Hate Crime Statistics*. Washington, DC: U.S. Department of Justice.

Freij, Maysoun. 2008. "Gender-based Performances of Arab American Artists in New York." Paper presented at the annual meeting of the Eastern Sociological Society, February 23, New York.

Friedlander, Jonathan. ed. 1988. *Sojourners and Settlers: The Yemeni Immigrant Experience*. Salt Lake City: University of Utah Press.

Gerstle, Gary. 2004. "The Immigrant as Threat to American Security: A Historical Perspective." In *The Maze of Fear: Security and Migration after 9/11,* edited by John Tirman, 87–108. New York: New Press.

Glazer, Nathan. 1957. *American Judaism*. Chicago: University of Chicago Press.

Glazer, Nathan, and Daniel P. Moynihan. 1970. *Beyond the Melting Pot: The Negroes, Puerto Ricans, Jews, Italians, and Irish of New York City*. 2nd ed. Cambridge, MA: MIT Press.

Goffman, Erving. 1974. *Frame Analysis: An Essay on the Organization of Experience*. New York: Harper and Row.

Gold, Steven J. 2002. *The Israeli Diaspora*. Seattle: University of Washington Press.

Gold, Steven J., and Mehdi Bozorgmehr. 2007. "Middle East and North Africa." In *The New Americans: A Handbook to Immigration since 1965,* edited by Mary Waters, Reed Ueda, and Helen Marrow, 518–33. Cambridge, MA: Harvard University Press.

Gregorian, Vartan. 2003. *Islam: A Mosaic, Not a Monolith.* Washington, DC: Brookings Institution Press.

Gualtieri, Sarah. 2001. "Becoming 'White': Race, Religion and the Foundations of Syrian/Lebanese Ethnicity in the United States." *Journal of American Ethnic History* 20 (4): 29–58.

———. 2004. "Gendering the Chain Migration Thesis: Women and Syrian Transatlantic Migration, 1878–1924." *Comparative Studies of South Asia, Africa and the Middle East* 24 (1): 67–78.

Haddad, William J. 2002. "Impact of the September 11th Attacks on the Freedoms of Arabs and Muslims." Paper presented at the American Immigration Law Foundation, Immigration Policy Center Forum.

Haddad, Yvonne Yazbeck. 1983. "Arab Muslims and Islamic Institutions in America: Adaptation and Reform." In *Arabs in the New World: Studies on Arab-American Communities,* edited by Sameer Y. Abraham and Nabeel Abraham, 64–81. Detroit: Wayne State University, Center for Urban Studies.

———. 1994. "Maintaining the Faith of the Fathers: Dilemmas of Religious Identity in the Christian and Muslim Arab American Communities." In *The Development of Arab American Identity,* edited by Ernest McCarus, 61–84. Ann Arbor: University of Michigan Press.

———. 2000. "The Dynamics of Islamic Identity in North America." In *Muslims on the Americanization Path?* edited by Yvonne Yazbech Haddad and John L. Esposito, 19–47. New York: Oxford University Press.

———. 2004. *Not Quite American? The Shaping of Arab and Muslim Identity in the United States.* Waco, TX: Baylor University Press.

Haddad, Yvonne Yazbeck, and Adair T. Lummis. 1987. *Islamic Values in the United States: A Comparative Study.* New York: Oxford University Press.

Haddad, Yvonne Yazbeck, and Jane I. Smith. 1996. "Islamic Values among American Muslims." In *Family and Gender among American Muslims: Issues Facing Middle Eastern Immigrants and their Descendants,* edited by Barbara C. Aswad and Barbara Bilgé, 19–40. Philadelphia: Temple University Press.

Hagan, Jaqueline, and Gonzalez Baker. 1993. "Implementing the U.S. Legalization Program: The Influence of Immigrant Communities and Local Agencies on Immigration Policy Reform." *International Migration Review* 27:513–35.

Hagopian, Elaine C., ed. 2004. *Civil Rights in Peril: The Targeting of Arabs and Muslims.* Chicago: Haymarket Books.

Handlin, Oscar. 1973. *The Uprooted: The Epic Story of the Great Migrations That Made the American People.* 2nd ed. Boston: Little, Brown.

Henderson, Nicole J., Christopher W. Ortiz, Naomi F. Sugie, and Joel Miller. 2006. *Law Enforcement and Arab American Community Relations after September 11, 2001.* Technical Report, June. New York: Vera Institute of Justice. www.vera.org/publication_pdf/353_636.pdf.

Herberg, Will. 1960. *Protestant, Catholic, Jew.* 2nd ed. Garden City, NY: Anchor Books.

Higham, John. 1988. *Strangers in the Land*. 2nd ed. New Brunswick: Rutgers University Press.

Hing, Bill Ong. 2006. *Deporting Our Souls: Values, Morality, and Immigration Policy*. Cambridge: Cambridge University Press.

Hitti, Philip Khuri. 1924. *The Syrians in America*. New York: George H. Doran.

Hooglund, Eric J. ed. 1987a. *Crossing the Waters: Arabic-Speaking Immigrants to the United States before 1940*. Washington, DC: Smithsonian Institution Press.

———. 1987b. "From the Near East to Down East: Ethnic Arabs in Waterville, Maine." In *Crossing the Waters: Arabic-Speaking Immigrants to the United States before 1940*, edited by Eric J. Hooglund, 85–103. Washington, DC: Smithsonian Institution Press.

Hopkins Burke, Roger, and Ed Pollock. 2004. "A Tale of Two Anomies: Some Observations on the Contribution of (Sociological) Criminology Theory to Explaining Hate Crime Motivation." *Internet Journal of Criminology*. www.internetjournalofcriminology.com/Hopkins%20Burke%20&%20 Pollock%20-%20A%20Tale%20of%20Two%20Anomies.pdf.

Howell, Sally, and Amaney Jamal. 2008. "The Aftermath of the 9/11 Attacks among Arab Americans: Detroit Exceptionalism and the Limits of Political Incorporation." In *Being and Belonging: Muslims in the United States since 9/11*, edited by Katherine Ewing. New York: Russell Sage Foundation.

Huda, Qamar-ul. 2006. "The Diversity of Muslims in the United States: Views as Americans." United States Institute for Peace, Special Report 159, February. www.usip.org/pubs/specialreports/sr159.html.

Human Rights Watch. 2002a. "Presumption of Guilt: Human Rights Abuses of Post-September 11 Detainees." *Human Rights Watch* 14 (4).

———. 2002b. "We Are Not the Enemy: Hate Crimes against Arabs, Muslims, and Those Perceived to Be Arab or Muslim after September 11." *Human Rights Watch* 14 (6).

———. 2006. "Pre 9/11 Renditions." Backgrounder. hrw.org/backgrounder/ eca/canada/arar/2.htm.

Huntington, Samuel P. 1993. "The Clash of Civilizations?" *Foreign Affairs* 72 (Summer): 22–28.

———. 1996. *The Clash of Civilizations and the Remaking of World Order*. New York: Simon and Schuster.

Husain, Sarah, ed. 2006. *Voices of Resistance: Muslim Women on War, Faith and Sexuality*. Emeryville, CA: Seal Press.

Ibish, Hussein, ed. 2003. *Report on Hate Crimes and Discrimination against Arab Americans: The Post–September 11 Backlash, September 11, 2001–October 11, 2002*. Washington, DC: ADC.

Ignatieff, Michael. 1995. *Blood and Belonging: Journeys into the New Nationalism*. New York: Farrar, Strauss and Giroux.

Illinois Advisory Committee to the U.S. Commission on Civil Rights. 2003. "Arab and Muslim Civil Rights Issues in the Chicago Metropolitan Area post-September 11." Report to the U.S. Commission on Civil Rights. May. www.usccr.gov/pubs/sac/il0503/main.htm.

Jacobs, James, and Kimberly Potter. 1998. *Hate Crimes: Criminal Law and Identity Politics*. New York: Oxford University Press.

Jamal, Amaney. 2005a. "Mosques, Collective Identity, and Gender Differences among Arab American Muslims." *Journal of Middle East Women's Studies* 1 (1): 51–78.

———. 2005b. "The Political Participation and Engagement of Muslim Americans: Mosque Involvement and Group Consciousness." *American Politics Research* 33 (4): 521–44.

———. 2005c. "Religious Identity, Discrimination and 9/11: The Determinants of Arab American Levels of Political Confidence in Mainstream and Ethnic Institutions." Paper presented at the conference "Middle Eastern Diasporas: (In)visible Minorities," March 18–20, Yale University.

———. 2008. "Civil Liberties and the Otherization of Arab and Muslim Americans." In *Race and Arab Americans before and after 9/11: From Invisible Citizens to Visible Subjects*, edited by Amaney Jamal and Nadine Naber, 114–30. Syracuse: Syracuse University Press.

Jamal, Amaney, and Nadine Naber, eds. 2008. *Race and Arab Americans before and after 9/11: From Invisible Citizens to Visible Subjects*. Syracuse: Syracuse University Press.

Jones, Richard. 2000. "Egyptian Copts in Detroit: Ethnic Community and Long Distance Nationalism." In *Arab Detroit: From Margins to Mainstream*, edited by Nabeel Abraham and Andrew Shryock, 219–41. Detroit: Wayne State University Press.

Jones-Correa, Michael. 2001. "Structural Shifts and Institutional Capacity: Possibilities for Ethnic Cooperation and Conflict in Urban Settings." In *Governing American Cities: Interethnic Coalitions, Competition and Conflict*, edited by Michael Jones-Correa, 183–209. New York: Russell Sage Foundation.

Joseph, Lawrence. 2005. *Codes, Precepts, Biases, and Taboos: Poems, 1973–1993*. New York: Farrar, Straus and Giroux.

Joseph, Suad. 1999. "Against the Grain of the Nation—The Arab." In *Arabs in America: Building a New Future*, edited by Michael W. Suleiman, 257–71. Philadelphia: Temple University Press.

Kadi, Joanna, ed. 1994. *Food for Our Grandmothers: Writings by Arab American and Arab Canadian Feminists*. Boston: South End Press.

Kasinitz, Philip. 1992. *Caribbean New York: Black Immigrants and the Politics of Race*. Ithaca: Cornell University Press.

Kasinitz, Philip, John Mollenkopf, and Mary C. Waters. 2002. "Becoming American/Becoming New Yorkers: The Experience of Assimilation in a Majority Minority City." *International Migration Review* 36 (4): 1020–36.

Kaushal, Neeraj, Robert Kaestner, and Cordelia Reimers. 2007. "Labor Market Effects of September 11th on Arab and Muslim Residents of the U.S." *Journal of Human Resources* 42 (2): 275–308.

Kayal, Philip M. 1983. "Arab Christians in the United States." In *Arabs in the New World: Studies on Arab-American Communities*, edited by Sameer Y. Abraham and Nabeel Abraham, 44–63. Detroit: Wayne State University Press.

————. 1995. "Epilogue." In *The Coming of the Arabic-Speaking People to the United States,* by Adele L. Younis, edited by Philip M. Kayal, 249–65. Staten Island, NY: Center for Migration Studies.

Kayyali, Randa A. 2006. *The Arab Americans.* Westport, CT: Greenwood Press.

Kennedy, David M. 1980. *Over Here: The First World War and American Society.* New York: Oxford University Press.

Khalidi, Omar. 2004. "Living as a Muslim in a Pluralistic Society and State: Theory and Experience." In *Muslims' Place in the American Public Square,* edited by Zahid H. Bukhari, Sulayman S. Nyang, Mumtaz Ahmed, and John L. Esposito, 38–72. Walnut Creek, CA: Altamira Press.

Khan, M. A. Muqtedar. 2004. "Living on Borderlines: Islam beyond the Clash and Dialogue of Civilizations." In *Muslims' Place in the American Public Square,* edited by Zahid H. Bukhari, Sulayman S. Nyang, Mumtaz Ahmed, and John L. Esposito, 84–113. Walnut Creek, CA: Altamira Press.

Khater, Akram. 2001. *Inventing Home: Emigration, Gender, and the Middle Class in Lebanon, 1870–1920.* Berkeley: University of California Press.

Kibria, Nazli. 2006. "South Asian Americans." In *Asian-Americans: Contemporary Trends and Issues,* edited by Pyong Gap Min, 206–27. Thousand Oaks, CA: Pine Forge Press.

Kimmel, Michael S. 2003. "Globalization and Its Mal(e)contents: The Gendered Moral and Political Economy of Terrorism." *International Sociology* 18 (3): 603–20.

Kitano, Harry H. L. 1980. "Japanese." In *Harvard Encyclopedia of American Ethnic Groups,* edited by Stephan Thernstrom, Ann Orlov, and Oscar Handlin. Cambridge, MA: Harvard University Press.

Koopmans, Ruud, Paul Statham, Marco Giugni, and Florence Passy. 2005. *Contested Citizenship: Immigration and Cultural Diversity in Europe.* Minneapolis: University of Minnesota Press.

Kooshian, George B., Jr. 2002. "The Armenian Immigrant Community of California: 1880–1935." PhD diss., University of California, Los Angeles.

Kosmin, Barry A., Egon Mayer, and Ariela Keysar. 2001. "American Religious Identification Survey." Unpublished report, Graduate Center, City University of New York.

Kramer, Gudrun. 1989. *The Jews in Modern Egypt, 1914–1952.* Seattle: University of Washington Press.

Kubler-Ross, Elisabeth. 1969. *On Death and Dying.* New York: Touchstone.

Kulczycki, Andrzej, and Arun Peter Lobo. 2001. "Deepening the Melting Pot: Arab Americans at the Turn of the Century." *Middle East Journal* 55 (3): 459–73.

————. 2002. "Patterns, Determinants, and Implications of Intermarriage among Arab Americans." *Journal of Marriage and Family* 64 (1): 202–10.

Lawyers Committee for Human Rights. 2002. *A Year of Loss: Reexamining Civil Liberties since September 11.* New York: Lawyers Committee for Human Rights. www.humanrightsfirst.org/pubs/descriptions/loss_report.pdf.

Leonard, Karen Isaksen. 1992. *Making Ethnic Choices: California's Punjabi Mexican Americans.* Philadelphia: Temple University Press.

———. 2003. *Muslims in the United States: The State of Research*. New York: Russell Sage Foundation.

Levin, Jack, and Gordana Rabrenovic, eds. 2001a. "Hate Crimes." Special issue, *American Behavioral Scientist* 45 (4).

———. 2001b. "Hate Crimes and Ethnic Conflict: An Introduction." *American Behavioral Scientist* 45 (4): 574–87.

Levitt, Peggy. 2007. *God Needs No Passports: Immigrants and the Changing American Religious Landscape*. New York: New Press.

Lieberson, Stanley, and Mary C. Waters. 1988. *From Many Strands: Ethnic and Racial Groups in Contemporary America*. New York: Russell Sage Foundation.

Light, Ivan. 1972. *Ethnic Enterprise in America*. Berkeley: University of California Press.

Lissak, Shpak Rivka. 1989. *Pluralism and Progressives: Hull House and the New Immigrants, 1890–1919*. Chicago: University of Chicago Press.

Lopez, David, and Yen Espiritu. 1990. "Panethnicity in the United States: A Theoretical Framework." *Ethnic and Racial Studies* 13 (2): 198–224.

Luebke, Frederick. 1974. *Bonds of Loyalty: German Americans and World War I*. DeKalb: University of Northern Illinois Press.

Mac Ginty, Roger. 2001. "Ethno-National Conflict and Hate Crime." *American Behavioral Scientist* 45 (4): 639–53.

Mamdani, Mahmood. 2004. *Good Muslim, Bad Muslim: America, the Cold War, and the Roots of Terror*. New York: Pantheon Books.

Manji, Irshad. 2003. *The Trouble with Islam Today: A Muslim's Call for Reform in Her Faith*. New York: St. Martin's Press.

Mann, Michael. 2005. *The Dark Side of Democracy: Explaining Ethnic Cleansing*. Cambridge: Cambridge University Press.

Mark, Stanley, Suzette Brooks Masters, and Cyrus D. Metha. 2002. "Have We Learned the Lessons of History: World War II Japanese Internment and Today's Secret Detentions." *Immigration Policy Focus* 1 (3) (October).

Marquez, Benjamin. 2003. *Constructing Identities in Mexican American Political Organizations*. Austin: University of Texas Press.

Marvasti, Amir, and Karyn D. McKinney. 2004. *Middle Eastern Lives in America*. Lanham, MD: Rowman and Littlefield.

Marwell, Nicole. 2004. "Privatizing the Welfare State: Nonprofit Community-Based Organizations as Political Actors." *American Sociological Review* 69 (2): 265–91.

Marx, Gary T., and James L. Wood. 1995. "Strands of Theory and Research in Collective Behavior." *Annual Review of Sociology* 1:363–428.

Mascia-Lees, Fran, and Susan H. Lees, eds. 2002. "In Focus: September 11, 2001." Special issue, *American Anthropologist* 104 (3).

Mazrui, Ali A. 2004. "Muslims between the Jewish Example and the Black Experience: American Policy Implications." In *Muslims' Place in the American Public Square*, edited by Zahid H. Bukhari, Sulayman S. Nyang, Mumtaz Ahmad, and John L. Esposito, 117–44. Walnut Creek, CA: Altamira Press.

McAdam, Douglas, and David A. Snow, eds. 1997. *Social Movements: Readings on Their Emergence, Mobilization, and Dynamics*. California: Roxbury.

McAdam, Douglas, Sidney Tarrow, and Charles Tilly. 2001. *Dynamics of Contention.* Cambridge: Cambridge University Press.

McCarthy, John, and Mayer Zald. 1977. "Resource Mobilization and Social Movements: A Partial Theory." *American Journal of Sociology* 82 (6): 1212–41.

McDevitt, Jack, Jennifer Balboni, Luis Garcia, and Joann Gu. 2001. "Consequences for Victims: A Comparison of Bias- and Non-bias-motivated Assaults." *American Behavioral Scientist* 45 (4): 697–713.

Mesrobian, Arpena S. 2000. *"Like One Family": The Armenians of Syracuse.* Ann Arbor, MI: Gomidas Institute.

Metcaff, Barbara Daly, ed. 1996. *Making Muslim Space in North America and Europe.* Berkeley: University of California Press.

Mills, C. Wright. 1959. *The Sociological Imagination.* New York: Oxford University Press.

Min, Pyong Gap. 1996. *Caught in the Middle: Korean Communities in New York and Los Angeles.* Berkeley: University of California Press.

———. 1999. "Ethnicity: Concepts, Theories, and Trends." In *Struggles for Ethnic Identity,* edited by Pyong Gap Min and Rose Kim, 16–46. Walnut Creek, CA: Altamira Press.

———. 2002. *The Second Generation: Ethnic Identity among Asian Americans.* Walnut Creek, CA: Altamira Press.

———. 2008. *Ethnic Solidarity for Economic Survival: Korean Greengrocers in New York City.* New York: Russell Sage Foundation.

Minnite, Lorraine. 2005. "Outside the Circle: The Impact of Post-9/11 Responses on Immigrant Communities in New York." In *Contentious City: The Politics of Recovery In New York City,* edited by John Mollenkopf, 265–205. New York: Russell Sage Foundation.

Mirak, Robert. 1980. "Armenians." In *Harvard Encyclopedia of American Ethnic Groups,* edited by Stephan Thernstrom, Ann Orlov, and Oscar Handlin. Cambridge, MA: Harvard University Press.

———. 1983. *Torn between Two Lands: Armenians in America, 1890 to World War I,* 136–49. Cambridge, MA: Harvard University Press.

Mollenkopf, John. 2005. "How 9/11 Reshaped the Political Environment in New York." In *Contentious City: The Politics of Recovery in New York City,* edited by John Mollenkopf, 205–22. New York: Russell Sage Foundation.

Moore, Kathleen. 1999. "A Closer Look at Anti-terrorism Law: *American-Arab Anti-Discrimination Committee v. Reno* and the Construction of Aliens' Rights." In *Arabs in America: Building a New Future,* edited by Michael W. Suleiman, 84–100. Philadelphia: Temple University Press.

Moser, Rosemarie Scolaro, and Corinne E. Frantz, eds. 2003. *Shocking Violence II: Violent Disaster, War, and Terrorism Affecting Our Youth.* Springfield, IL: Charles C. Thomas.

Motomura, Hiroshi. 2006. *Americans in Waiting: The Lost Story of Immigration and Citizenship in the United States.* New York: Oxford University Press.

Moya, Jose C. 2005. "Immigrants and Associations: A Global and Historical Perspective." *Journal of Ethnic and Migration Studies* 31 (5): 833–64.

MPAC. 2003. *A Review of U.S. Counterterrorism Policy: American Muslim Critique & Recommendations.* 2nd ed. Los Angeles: MPAC. www.mpac.org/publications/counterterrorism-policy-paper/counterterrorism-policy-paper.pdf.

———. 2004. *Counterproductive Counterterrorism: How Anti-Islamic Rhetoric is Impeding America's Homeland Security.* Los Angeles: MPAC. www.mpac.org/publications/counterproductive-counterterrorism/counter productive-counterterrorism.pdf.

———. 2005. *Grassroots Campaign to Fight Terrorism Handbook.* Los Angeles: MPAC. www.mpac.org/publications/campaign-to-fight-terrorism/campaign-to-fight-terrorism-brochure.pdf.

———. 2007. "The Impact of 9/11 on Muslim American Young People: National and Religious Identity Formation in the Age of Terrorism and Islamophobia." June. MPAC Special Report. www.mpac.org/publications/youth-paper/MPAC-Special-Report—Muslim-Youth.pdf.

Muscati, Sina Ali. 2003. "Reconstructing 'Evil': A Critical Assessment of Post-September 11 Political Discourse." *Journal of Muslim Minority Affairs* 23 (2): 249–69.

Naber, Nadine. 2000. "Ambiguous Insiders: An Investigation of Arab American Visibility." *Ethnic and Racial Studies* 23 (1): 37–61.

———. 2002. "So Our History Doesn't Become Your Future: The Local and Global Politics of Coalition Building post September 11th." *Journal of Asian American Studies* 5 (3): 217–42.

———. 2005. "Muslim First, Arab Second: A Strategic Politics of Race and Gender." *Muslim World* 95 (5): 479–95.

Naff, Alixa. 1980. "Arabs." In *Harvard Encyclopedia of American Ethnic Groups,* edited by Stephan Thernstrom, Ann Orlov, and Oscar Handlin, 128–36. Cambridge, MA: Harvard University Press.

———. 1985. *Becoming American: The Early Arab Immigrant Experience.* Carbondale: Southern Illinois University Press.

———. 1994. "The Early Arab Immigration Experience." In *The Development of Arab American Identity,* edited by Ernest McCarus, 23–35. Ann Arbor: University of Michigan Press.

Nagel, Caroline R., and Lynn A. Staeheli. 2004. "Citizenship, Identity and Transnational Migration: Arab Immigrants to the United States." *Space and Polity* 2 (1): 3–23.

———. 2005. "'We're Just Like the Irish': Narratives of Assimilation, Belonging and Citizenship amongst Arab American Activists." *Citizenship Studies* 9 (5): 485–98.

National Asian Pacific American Legal Consortium. 2002. *Backlash: When America Turned on Its Own: A Preliminary Report on the 2002 Audit of Violence against Asian Pacific Americans.* Washington, DC: National Asian Pacific American Legal Consortium.

National Commission on Terrorist Attacks upon the United States. *The 9/11 Commission Report: Final Report of the National Commission on Terrorist Attacks upon the United States.* 2004. New York: W. W. Norton.

Navasky, Victor S. 1980. *Naming Names.* New York: Viking Press.

New York City Commission on Human Rights. 2003. "Discrimination against Muslims, Arabs, and South Asians in New York City since 9/11." Summer. Report. http://home2.nyc.gov/html/cchr/pdf/sur_report.pdf

Nguyen, Tram. 2005. *We Are All Suspects Now: Untold Stories from Immigrant Communities after 9/11*. Boston: Beacon Press.

Nisbet, Erik C., and James Shanahan. 2004. "MSRG Special Report: Restrictions on Civil Liberties, Views of Islam, and Muslim Americans." Media and Society Research Group, Cornell University, December, www.comm.cornell.edu/msrg/report1a.pdf.

Oberschall, Anthony. 1973. *Social Conflicts and Social Movements*. Englewood Cliffs, NJ: Prentice Hall.

O'Brien, David, and Fugita, Stephen. 1991. *The Japanese American Experience*. Bloomington: Indiana University Press.

Okamoto, Dina G. 2003. "Toward a Theory of Panethnicity: Explaining Asian American Collective Action." *American Sociological Review* 68 (6): 811–42.

———. 2005. "Practicing Panethnicity: Boundary Spanning among Asian American Organizations." Working paper, Russell Sage Foundation.

Olzak, Susan. 1983. "Contemporary Ethnic Mobilization." *Annual Review of Sociology* 9:355–74.

———. 1992. *The Dynamics of Ethnic Competition and Conflict*. Stanford: Stanford University Press.

———. 2006. *Global Dynamics of Racial and Ethnic Mobilization*. Stanford: Stanford University Press.

Olzak, Susan, and Joane Nagel. 1986. *Competitive Ethnic Relations*. New York: Academic Press.

Olzak, Susan, and Emily Ryo. 2004."Diversity in Black Civil Rights Movement Organizations, 1955–1988." Paper presented at the annual meeting of the American Sociological Association, San Francisco.

Olzak, Susan, S. Shanahan, and E. H. McEneaney. 1996. "Poverty, Segregation, and Race Riots: 1960 to 1993." *American Sociological Review* 61 (4): 590–613.

Omi, Michael, and Howard Winant. 1994. *Racial Formations in the United States: From the 1960s to the 1990s*. 2nd ed. New York: Routledge.

Opp, Karl-Dieter, and Wolfgang Roehl. 1990. "Repression, Micromobilization, and Political Protest." *Social Forces* 69 (2): 521–47.

Orfield, Gary. 2003. "One Nation Indivisible, under God, with Liberty and Justice for All: Civil Right for Arabs, Muslims, and South Asians." May. Civil Rights Project, Harvard University (now moved to University of California, Los Angeles). www.civilrightsproject.ucla.edu/research/articles/Arab_Muslim_South%20Asian_Rights.pdf.

Painter, Nell Irvin. 1987. *Standing at Armageddon: The United States, 1877–1919*. New York: W. W. Norton.

Park, Robert. 1950. *Race and Culture*. Glencoe, IL: Free Press.

Peek, Lori A. 2002. "Religious and Ethnic Issues after September 11, 2001: Examining Muslim University Student Experiences." Natural Hazards Research and Applications Information Center, University of Colorado,

Boulder. Quick Response Report no. 156. June 21. www.colorado.edu/hazards/research/qr/qr156/qr156.html.

———. 2003. "Reactions and Response: Muslim Students' Experiences on New York City Campuses Post 9/11." *Journal of Muslim Minority Affairs* 23 (2): 272–83.

Perry, Barbara. 2001. *In the Name of Hate.* New York: Routledge.

———. 2003. "Where Do We Go from Here? Researching Hate Crime." *Internet Journal of Criminology.* www.internetjournalofcriminology.com/Where%20Do%20We%20Go%20From%20Here.%20Researching%20Hate%20Crime.pdf.

Pew Research Center. 2007. *Muslim Americans: Middle Class and Mostly Mainstream.* May 22. Washington, DC: Pew Research Center. http://pewresearch.org/assets/pdf/muslim-americans.pdf.

Pew Research Center for the People and the Press and the Pew Forum on Religion and Public Life. 2005. *Views of Muslim Americans Hold Steady after London Bombings.* July 26. Washington, DC: Pew Research Center. http://pewforum.org/docs/index.php?DocID=89.

Portes, Alejandro, and Ruben Rumbaut. 2001. *Legacies: The Story of the Immigrant Second Generation.* Berkeley: University of California Press.

———. 2006. *Immigrant America: A Portrait.* 3rd updated ed. Berkeley: University of California Press.

Portes, Alejandro, and Min Zhou. 1993. "The New Second Generation: Segmented Assimilation and its Variants." *Annals of the American Academy of Political and Social Sciences* 530:74–97.

Poynting, Scott. 2002. "'Bin Laden in the Suburbs': Attacks on Arab and Muslim Australians before and after 11 September." *Current Issues in Criminal Justice* 14 (1): 43–64.

———. 2004. "'I Can't Go Out; I Don't Have My Freedom': Australian Arabs' and Muslims' Experiences of Post-September 11 Racism." Paper presented at the Second Annual Conference on Hate Crimes, Nottingham Trent University.

Project MAPS and Zogby International. 2001. *American Muslim Poll 2001.* Washington, DC: Center for Muslim-Christian Understanding, Georgetown University. www.projectmaps.com/AMP2001report.pdf.

———. 2004. *American Muslim Poll 2004: Muslims in the American Public Square. Shifting Political Winds and Fallout from 9/11, Afghanistan, and Iraq.* Washington, DC: Center for Muslim-Christian Understanding/Georgetown University. www.projectmaps.com/AMP2004report.pdf.

Pyszczynski, Tom, Jeff Greenberg, and Sheldon Solomon. 2003. *In the Wake of 9/11: The Psychology of Terror.* Washington, DC: American Psychological Association.

Read, Jen'nan Ghazal. 2004a. "Cultural Influences on Immigrant Women's Labor Force Participation: The Arab-American Case." *International Migration Review* 38 (1): 52–77.

———. 2004b. *Culture, Class and Work among Arab American Women.* New York: LFB Scholarly Publishing LLC.

————. 2006. "The Gender Gap in Arab American Political Engagement." In *American Arabs and Political Participation,* edited by Philippa Strum, 79–92. Washington, DC: Woodrow Wilson International Center for Scholars.

————. 2008. "Discrimination and Identity Formation in a Post-9/11 Era." In *Race and Arab Americans before and after 9/11: From Invisible Citizens to Visible Subjects,* edited by Amaney Jamal and Nadine Naber, 305–17. Syracuse: Syracuse University Press.

Read, Jen'nan Ghazal, and Sharon Oselin. 2008. "Gender and the Education-Employment Paradox in Ethnic and Religious Contexts: The Case of Arab Americans." *American Sociological Review* 73 (2): 296–313.

Redfield, Robert. 1939. "Culture Contact without Conflict." *American Anthropologist* 41 (3): 514–17.

Reimers, David. 1998. *Unwelcome Strangers: American Identity and the Turn against Immigration.* New York: Columbia University Press.

Rignall, Karen. 2000. "Building the Infrastructure of Arab American Identity in Detroit: A Short History of ACCESS and the Community It Serves." In *Arab Detroit: From Margin to Mainstream,* edited by Nabeel Abraham and Andrew Shryock, 49–59. Detroit: Wayne State University Press.

Rumbaut, Ruben. 1995. "The New Californians: Comparative Research Findings on the Educational Progress of Immigrant Children." In *California's Immigrant Children: Theory, Research, and Implications for Educational Policy,* edited by Ruben Rumbaut and Wayne A. Cornelius, 17–70. San Diego: Center for Mexican Studies, University of California, San Diego.

SAALT. 2001. *American Backlash: Terrorists Bring War Home in More Ways Than One.* Washington, DC: SAALT.

Saeed, Agha. 2002. "The Arab Muslim Paradox." In *Muslim Minorities in the West: Visible and Invisible,* edited by Yvonne Yazbeck Haddad and Jane I. Smith, 39–58. Walnut Creek, CA: Altamira Press.

Safi, Omid. 2003. *Progressive Muslims: On Justice, Gender and Pluralism.* Oxford: Oneworld Publications.

Salaita, Steven. 2006. *Anti-Arab Racism in the U.S.A.: Where It Comes from and What It Means for Politics Today.* Ann Arbor, MI: Pluto Press.

Saliba, Najib E. 1983. "Emigration from Syria." In *Arabs in the New World: Studies on Arab-American Communities,* edited by Sameer Y. Abraham and Nabeel Abraham, 31–43. Detroit: Wayne State University, Center for Urban Studies.

Samhan, Helen Hatab. 1999. "Not Quite White: Race Classification and the Arab-American Experience." In *Arabs in America: Building a New Future,* edited by Michael W. Suleiman, 209–26. Philadelphia: Temple University Press.

Sarroub, Loukia K. 2005. *All American Yemeni Girls: Being Muslim in a Public School.* Philadelphia: University of Pennsylvania Press.

Schauer, Frederick. 2003. *Profiles, Probabilities and Stereotypes.* Cambridge, MA: Harvard University Press.

Schmidt, Garbi. 2004. *Islam in Urban America: Sunni Muslims in Chicago.* Philadelphia: Temple University Press.

Schrecker, Ellen. 1998. *Many Are the Crimes: McCarthyism in America.* Princeton: Princeton University Press.

Schrover, Marlou, and Floris Vermeulen. 2005a. "Immigrant Organizations." *Journal of Ethnic and Migration Studies* 31 (5) 823–32.

———, eds. 2005b. "Immigrant Organizations." Special issue, *Journal of Ethnic and Migration Studies* 31 (5).

Senechal de la Roche, Roberta, ed. 2004. "Theories of Terrorism." Special issue, *Sociological Theory* 22 (1).

Sengstock, Mary. 1974. "Iraqi Christians in Detroit: An Analysis of an Ethnic Occupation." In *Arabic Speaking Communities in American Cities,* edited by Barbara Aswad, 21–39. Staten Island, NY: Center for Migration Studies.

———. 1982. *Chaldean-Americans: Changing Conceptions of Ethnic Identity.* Staten Island, NY: Center for Migration Studies.

———. 1983. "Detroit's Iraqi-Chaldeans: A Conflicting Conception of Identity." In *Arabs in the New World: Studies on Arab-American Communities,* edited by Sameer Y. Abraham and Nabeel Abraham, 135–46. Detroit: Wayne State University, Center for Urban Studies.

September 11 Digital Archive. 2002–3. "Middle East and Middle Eastern American Center Interviews." http://911digitalarchive.org/repository.php?collection_id=14.

Shaheen, Jack G. 1984. *The TV Arab.* Bowling Green: Bowling Green State University Press.

———. 1994. "Arab Images in American Comic Books." *Journal of Popular Culture* 28 (1): 123–33.

———. 2001. *Reel Bad Arabs: How Hollywood Vilifies a People.* New York: Olive Branch Press.

Shain, Yossi. 1999. *Marketing the American Creed Abroad: Diasporas in the U.S. and Their Homelands.* Cambridge: Cambridge University Press.

Shakir, Evelyn. 1997. *Bint Arab: Arab and Arab American Women in the United States.* Westport, CT: Praeger.

Shamieh, Betty. 2004. *Roar.* New York: Broadway Play Publishing.

Shryock, Andrew. 2008. "The Moral Analogies of Race: Arab American Identity, Color Politics, and the Limits of Racialized Citizenship." In *Race and Arab Americans before and after 9/11: From Invisible Citizens to Visible Subjects,* edited by Amaney Jamal and Nadine Naber, 81–113. Syracuse: Syracuse University Press.

Shryock, Andrew, and Nabeel Abraham. 2000. "On Margins and Mainstreams." In *Arab Detroit: From Margins to Mainstream,* edited by Nabeel Abraham and Andrew Shryock, 15–35. Detroit: Wayne State University Press.

Simmel, Georg. 1955. *Conflict and the Web of Group-Affiliations.* Translated by Kurt H. Wolff and Reinhard Bendix. New York: Free Press.

Smelser, Neil J. 2007. *The Faces of Terrorism: Social and Psychological Dimensions.* Princeton: Princeton University Press.

Smith, Jane I. 1999. *Islam in America.* New York: Columbia University Press.

———. 2004. "Muslims as Partners in Interfaith Encounter." In *Muslim's Place in the American Public Square,* edited by Zahid H. Bukhari, Sulayman S. Nyang, Mumtaz Ahmad, and John L. Esposito, 165–97. Walnut Creek, CA: Altamira Press.

Smith, Timothy L. 1978. "Religion and Ethnicity in America." *Historical Review* 83 (3): 1155–85.

Sonenshein, Raphael. 1993. *Politics in Black and White.* Princeton: Princeton University Press.

Sorkin, Michael, and Sharon Zukin, eds. 2002. *After the World Trade Center: Rethinking New York City.* New York: Routledge.

Soyer, Daniel. 1997. *Jewish Immigrant Associations and American Identity in New York, 1880–1939.* Cambridge, MA: Harvard University Press.

Statham, Paul. 1999. "Political Mobilization by Minorities in Britain: Negative Feedback of 'Race Relations'?" *Journal of Ethnic and Migration Studies* 25 (4): 597–626.

Steinberg, Stephen. 1989. *The Ethnic Myth: Race, Ethnicity and Class in America.* Updated and expanded ed. New York: Atheneum.

Stockton, Ronald. 1994. "Ethnic Archetypes and the Arab Image." In *The Development of Arab-American Identity,* edited by Ernest McCarus, 119–53. Ann Arbor: University of Michigan Press.

———. 2006. "Arab American Political Participation: Findings from the Detroit Arab American Study." In *American Arabs and Political Participation,* edited by Philippa Strum, 53–78. Washington, DC: Woodrow Wilson International Center for Scholars.

Strum, Philippa, ed. 2006. *American Arabs and Political Participation.* Washington, DC: Woodrow Wilson International Center for Scholars.

Suleiman, Michael W. 1987. "Early Arab Americans: The Search for Identity." In *Crossing the Waters: Arabic-Speaking Immigrants to the United States before 1940,* edited by Eric J. Hooglund, 37–54. Washington, DC: Smithsonian Institution Press.

———. 1994. "Arab-Americans and the Political Process." In *The Development of Arab-American Identity,* edited by Ernest McCarus, 37–609. Ann Arbor: University of Michigan Press.

———. 1999. "Introduction: The Arab Immigrant Experience." In *Arabs in America: Building a New Future,* edited by Michael W. Suleiman, 1–21. Philadelphia: Temple University Press.

———. 2006. "A History of Arab-American Political Participation." In *American Arabs and Political Participation,* edited by Philippa Strum, 2–25. Washington, DC: Woodrow Wilson International Center for Scholars.

Sultan, Sherien. 2006. "Subway Negotiations." In *Voices of Resistance: Muslim Women on War, Faith and Sexuality,* edited by Sarah Husain, 48–50. Emeryville, CA: Seal Press.

Tarrow, Sidney. 1994. *Power in Movement: Social Movements, Collective Action, and Politics.* New York: Cambridge University Press.

Tehranian, John. 2008. *Whitewashed: America's Invisible Middle Eastern Minority.* New York: New York University Press.

Thomas, William I., and Florian Znaniecki. 1918–20/1958. *The Polish Peasant in Europe and America.* New York: Dover Publications.

Tierney, Kathleen, et al. 2006. "A Symposium on Natural Disasters." *Contemporary Sociology: A Journal of Reviews* 35 (3): 207–27.

Tilly, Charles. 1978. *From Mobilization to Revolution*. Reading, MA: Addison-Wesley.

———. 1986. *The Contentious French: Four Centuries of Popular Struggle*. Cambridge, MA: Harvard University Press.

———. 1995. *Popular Contention in Great Britain*. Cambridge, MA: Harvard University Press.

Tilly, Charles, and Sidney Tarrow. 2006. *Contentious Politics*. Boulder, CO: Paradigm.

Tirman, John, ed. 2004. *The Maze of Fear: Security and Migration after 9/11*. New York: New Press.

Torpey, John. 2006. *Making Whole What Has Been Smashed: On Reparation Politics*. Cambridge, MA: Harvard University Press.

Traugott, Mark, ed. 1994. *Repertoires and Cycles of Collective Action*. Durham: Duke University Press.

Tuan, Mia. 1998. *Forever Foreigners or Honorary Whites: The Asian Ethnic Experience Today*. New Brunswick: Rutgers University Press.

Ursano, Robert J., Carlo S. Fullerton, and Ann E. Norwood, eds. 2003. *Terrorism and Disaster: Individual and Community Mental Health Interventions*. Cambridge: Cambridge University Press.

U.S. Bureau of the Census. 2000a. "5-Percent Public Use Microdata Sample (PUMS) Files." www.census.gov/Press-Release/www/2003/PUMS5.html.

———. 2000b. "Summary File 4." www.census.gov/Press-Release/www/2003/SF4.html.

U.S. Department of Justice, Community Relations Service. 2003. "Responding to Hate Crimes and Bias-Motivated Incidents on College/University Campuses." September. www.usdoj.gov/crs/pubs/university92003.htm#21.

U.S. Department of Justice, Office of the Inspector General. 2003. *The September 11 Detainees: A Review of the Treatment of Aliens Held on Immigration Charges in Connection with the Investigations of the September 11 Attacks*. June. Washington, DC: U.S. Department of Justice. www.usdoj.gov/oig/special/0306/index.htm.

U.S. DHS. 1996–2005. *Statistical Yearbooks of the Immigration and Naturalization Service*. Washington, DC: Government Printing Office, 1997–2006.

———. 2002. *National Strategy for Homeland Security*. July. Washington, DC: Government Printing Office. www.dhs.gov/xabout/history/publication_0005.shtm.

U.S. EEOC. 2003. "Fiscal Year 2003 Annual Report." www.eeoc.gov/litigation/03annrpt/index.html.

U.S. INS. 1969. *1968 Annual Report*. Washington, DC: Government Printing Office.

———. 1971. *1970 Annual Report*. Washington, DC: Government Printing Office.

———. 1980. *1979 Annual Report*. Washington, DC: Government Printing Office.

———. 1979. *1978 Statistical Yearbook*. Washington, DC: Government Printing Office.

————. 1980. *1979 Statistical Yearbook.* Washington, DC: Government Printing Office.

————. 1982. *1980–1981 Statistical Yearbooks.* Washington, DC: Government Printing Office.

————. 1983. *1982 Statistical Yearbook.* Washington, DC: Government Printing Office.

————. 1984. *1983 Statistical Yearbook.* Washington, DC: Government Printing Office.

————. 1985. *1984 Statistical Yearbook.* Washington, DC: Government Printing Office.

————. 1986. *1985 Statistical Yearbook.* Washington, DC: Government Printing Office.

————. 1987. *1986 Statistical Yearbook.* Washington, DC: Government Printing Office.

————. 1988. *1987 Statistical Yearbook.* Washington, DC: Government Printing Office.

Varisco, Daniel M. 2004. "Inventing Islamism: The Rhetoric of Representing Violence in Islam." Paper presented at the annual meeting of the Middle East Studies Association, San Francisco.

Vermeulen, Floris. 2005. "Institutional Opportunities and Community Dynamics: Migrant Organizations in Amsterdam, 1960–1990." *Journal of Ethnic and Migration Studies* 31 (5): 951–73.

Volpp, Leti. 2002. "The Citizen and the Terrorist." *UCLA Law Review* 49:1575–1600.

Walbridge, Linda S. 1999. "A Look at Differing Ideologies among Shiᶜa Muslims in the United States." In *Arabs in America: Building a New Future,* edited by Michael W. Suleiman, 53–64. Philadelphia: Temple University Press.

Waldinger, Roger, and David Fitzgerald. 2004. "Transnationalism in Question." *American Journal of Sociology* 109:1177–95.

Waters, Mary. 1990. *Ethnic Options: Choosing Identities in America.* Berkeley: University of California Press.

————. 1999. *Black Identities: Western Indian Immigrant Dreams and American Realities.* New York: Russell Sage Foundation.

Warner, Lloyd, ed. 1963. *Yankee City.* Abridged ed. New Haven: Yale University Press.

Weisser, Michael R. 1985. *A Brotherhood of Memory: Jewish Landsmanshaftn in the New World.* New York: Basic Books.

Whitney, Christopher B. 2007. *Strengthening America: The Civic and Political Integration of Muslim Americans. Report of the Task Force on Muslim American Civic and Political Engagement.* Chicago: Chicago Council on Global Affairs. www.thechicagocouncil.org/UserFiles/File/Task%20Force%20Reports/CCGA%20Muslim%20Task%20Force%20report.pdf

Wolfe, Alan. 2003. *The Transformation of American Religion: How We Actually Live Our Faith.* New York: Free Press.

Wuthnow, Robert. 2005. *America and the Challenges of Religious Diversity.* Princeton: Princeton University Press.

Yang, Fenngang, and Helen Rose Ebaugh. 2001. "Transformations in New Immigrant Religions and Their Global Implications." *American Sociological Review* 66 (2): 269–88.

Young, Donald. 1932. *American Minority Peoples.* New York: Harper and Row.

Younis, Adele L. 1995. *The Coming of the Arabic-Speaking People to the United States.* Edited by Philip M. Kayal. Staten Island, NY: Center for Migration Studies.

Zald, Mayer N., and John McCarthy. 1979. "Social Movement Industries: Competition and Cooperation among Movement Industries." *Research in Social Movements, Conflict, and Change* 3:1–20.

Zenner, Walter P. 1982. "Arabic-Speaking Immigrants in North America as Middleman Minorities." *Ethnic and Racial Studies* 5:457–77.

———. 1983. "Syrian Jews in New York City Twenty Years Ago." In *Fields of Offerings: Studies in Honor of Raphael Patai,* edited by Victor D. Sanua, 173–96. New York: Herzl Press.

———. 2000. *A Global Community: The Jews from Aleppo, Syria.* Detroit: Wayne State University Press.

———. 2002. "The Syrian Jews of Brooklyn." In *A Community of Many Worlds: Arab Americans in New York City,* edited by Kathleen Benson and Philip M. Kayal, 156–70. Syracuse: Syracuse University Press.

Zhou, Min, and Carl Bankston III. 1998. *Growing Up American: How Vietnamese Children Adapt to Life in the United States.* New York: Russell Sage Foundation.

Zolberg, Aristide. 2002. "Guarding the Gates." In *Understanding September 11,* edited by Craig J. Calhoun, Paul Price, and Ashley Timmer, 285–301. New York: Social Science Research Council.

———. 2006. *A Nation by Design: Immigration Policy in the Fashioning of America.* Cambridge, MA: Harvard University Press.

# Index

Abdo, Geneive, 7
Abdullah, Bilal, 271n30
Abou El Fadl, Khaled, 186
Abraham, Nabeel, 40
Abrahamic faiths, 2
absconder initiative, 54, 165–67, 246,
    255, 256, 276n45, 292n13
Abu Ghraib prison complex, 51–52
accommodation, challenges of, 227–29,
    302n5, 305n20
*Achille Lauro* (ship), 40, 273n15
Aciman, André, 279n11
Afghanistan, 66, 67, 138, 258; Al Qaeda
    in, 49–51; Soviet invasion of, 76;
    war in, 33, 51, 96, 149, 171, 172,
    244, 272n3, 276n46
Afghans, 67, 73, 76, 84, 87, 88, 91–93,
    95; in community-based organiza-
    tions, 103, 108, 115; economic
    discrimination against, 147, 148;
    hate crimes against, 129; political
    engagement of, 215; recent immi-
    gration of, 2
African Americans, 67, 68, 79, 146, 217,
    238, 288n28; Muslim, 8, 49, 94–96,
    154, 192, 220, 233; profiling of, 139
Agence France Press (AFP), 242
Ahmed, Ahmed, 197

Ahmed, Ismael, 235, 306n34
Ahmed, Kafeel, 271n30
airport profiling, 5, 42, 139–42, 287n19
Akram, Susan, 62
Alabama, 259
Alamo Car Rental, 147
Alawai, 281n25
Alba, Richard, 64
Albanians, 276n46
Alevi, 243, 281n25
Algeria, 67, 257
Algerians, 73, 84, 87–93, 108, 282n34
Aliens Act (1798), 34
*Aliens in America* (television series), 152
allegiance, demonstrations of, 31, 185,
    189–91, 217, 235, 250
Almansoop, Ali, 3
Almontaser, Debbie, 153
Alsultany, Evelyn, 81, 192, 295n17
Amen, Ron, 286n14
American Airlines, 5
*American Anthropologist*, 6
American Arab Anti-Discrimination
    Committee (ADC), 3, 89, 134, 199,
    244, 298n52; Action Alerts of, 44,
    214; airport profiling reported by,
    139; amicus brief against wiretap-
    ping filed by, 184, 294n4; coalition

Sedition Act (1918), 35, 61
Senate, U.S., 215, 260, 262; Judiciary
    Committee, 258; Subcommittee on
    the Constitution, 255
Sensenbrenner, James, 280
September 11 Digital Archive, 25, 29,
    121, 145, 271n33
Shafiʿi Islamic jurisprudence, 243
Shaheen, Jack C., 40, 152
Shain, Yossi, 278n62
Shamieh, Betty, 197, 297n37
Shata, Reta, 303n12
Shatara, Fuad, 101
Shehadeh, Michel Ibrahim, 42–43
*Sheik, The* (film), 40
Shiʿa, 86, 96, 225, 243, 249,
    273nn13,14, 281n25
Shryock, Andrew, 82
Siegel, Norman, 182
Sikh American Legal Defense and Educa-
    tion Fund (SALDEF), 182–83,
    194–95, 284n9, 288n29, 289n35,
    298n49, 305n20
Sikh Mediawatch and Resource Task
    Force (SMART), 200, 210, 267n6,
    298n49. *See also* Sikh American
    Legal Defense and Education Fund
Sikhs, 8, 73, 194, 231, 239, 279n14; bias
    incidents against, 144, 289n35; in
    coalition networks, 203–4; in com-
    munity-based organizations, 103,
    111; hate crimes against, 1, 2, 8,
    129–31, 203, 219, 246, 260, 261,
    265, 267n1, 286n8, 288n29; impact
    of PATRIOT Act on, 162; patriotism
    of, 191; political empowerment of,
    241; profiling of, 139, 142; work-
    place discrimination against, 147,
    228, 305n20
Sikh Society, 141
Simmel, George, 10
Sisters of St. Kashmir, 231
situational alliances, 203–5
Six-Day War (1967), 40, 101, 102
*60 Minutes*, 52
Small Business Administration, U.S., 69
Smelser, Neil, 6, 32
Smith, Timothy, 98, 221
Smith Act (1940), 57
Snow, David, 19, 21
socialization, 84, 224; political, 31,
    211–17, 250
social justice alliances, 205–8
Social Security, 98
Society of St. Vincent de Paul, 226
*Sociological Theory*, 6
Sodhi, Balbir Singh, 1, 2, 129

Somalia, 67, 258
Somalis, 108, 229
Sonenshein, Raphael, 201
South Asian American Leaders of Tomor-
    row (SAALT), 1, 113, 283n9, 286n9
Southern Poverty Law Center, 126
Soviet Union, 36, 47, 76, 280n23
Soyer, Daniel, 98
Spain, bombings in, 22, 149, 269n20
special registration, 6, 31, 58, 81, 97,
    135, 152, 168, 247, 264. *See also*
    National Security Entry-Exit Regis-
    tration System (NSEERS)
Sri Lanka, 278n2
Staeheli, Lynn, 28
State Department, U.S., 4–5, 119, 240,
    254, 256, 257
Steinberg, Stephen, 10
stereotyping, 1, 2, 13, 16, 24, 34, 39–42,
    96, 125, 127–28, 155, 220, 251–52;
    combatting, 8, 197, 216, 230, 233,
    236, 238; flag displays and, 191;
    framing mechanisms for, 187; in
    government initiatives, 44; in media,
    6, 16, 30, 150–52, 248; Orientalist,
    62; racialization and, 79. *See also*
    profiling
Stern, Howard, 185–86
Stockton, Ronald, 234, 273n10
Stroman, Mark Anthony, 3
Student and Exchange Visitor System
    (SEVIS), 257
Sudan, 67, 258
Sudanese, 259
Sufis, 225, 243
Suleiman, Michael, 40, 101–2, 301n81
Sultan, Sherien, 145, 289n32
Sunnis, 13, 95, 96, 225, 243, 249,
    281n25
Sununu, John, 260
Supreme Court, U.S., 37, 43, 50, 57
Sutherland, Dan, 295n20
Syria, 52, 66, 71, 72, 75, 101, 258,
    273n13, 278nn1,10, 280n23,
    281nn25,26; Ottoman province of,
    78, 278n9
Syrians, 68, 70–74, 83–88, 90, 91, 93,
    96, 280n22; Christian, 78–80, 86,
    144, 221, 248, 249, 269n15,
    280n24; in community-based orga-
    nizations, 100–102, 108; early-
    twentieth-century immigration of, 2,
    39; pan-Arabism and, 244; registra-
    tion with INS required for, 259

Taguba, General Antonio, 51–52
Tahir-Kheli, Shirin, 240

Taliban, 50, 51, 76, 153
Taxi Workers' Alliance, 203
Taylor, Anna Diggs, 262
Tehranian, John, 79
Terrorism Information and Prevention
System. *See* Operation TIPS
Texas, 86; hate crimes in, 232
Thanks-Giving Square Foundation,
305n27
Thomas, Saint, 280n24
Tides Foundation, 240
Tierney, Kathleen, 100, 268n12
Tilly, Charles, 20
Tiryakian, Edward, 272n3
Tocqueville, Alexis de, 98
Torpey, John, 54, 64
Totah, Khalil, 101
Transportation, U.S. Department of, 142
Transportation Security Administration
(TSA), 183, 194, 255
Traveler Redress Inquiry Program
(TRIP), 183, 262
Treasury Department, U.S., 103, 163–64,
262; Office of Foreign Asset Con-
trol, 284n10
Treasury Guidelines Working Group,
284n10
Tunisia, 67, 258
Tunisians, 84
Turkey, 66, 67, 72, 164, 276n46,
278nn1,9; Armenian genocide in,
10, 71, 280n23
Turks, 74, 76, 78, 79, 84, 85, 87, 88, 91,
93; cultural legacy of, 244; economic
discrimination against, 148; identifi-
cation with national origin of, 14;
recent immigration of, 245
Trans World Airlines (TWA), 273n14,
274n22

UCLA. *See* University of California, Los
Angeles
Uniform Code of Military Justice,
276n42
Union of Orthodox Jewish Congrega-
tions, 305n20
United Arab Emirates, 67, 72, 258
United Auto Workers (UAW), 134
United for Peace and Justice, 294n4
United Kingdom, 22–24, 286n13; colo-
nial territorial ambitions of, 101,
248; media in, 150; missionaries
from, 280n24; terrorism in, 22, 41,
149, 187, 271n30, 276n33, 289n40,
298n49. *See also* London
United Nations, 51–53, 67
United Religions Initiative, 305n27

*United States v. Cartozian* (1925), 80
United Syrian Society, 101
Unity Task Force (Brooklyn), 204,
298n52
University of California, Los Angeles
(UCLA), 271, 273n9
University of Connecticut, 291n6
University of Michigan, 108, 302n5
University of Notre Dame, 5, 263
University of South Florida, 264
U.S. Airways, 141, 288n25
USA PATRIOT Act (2001), 5, 6, 123,
125, 175, 177, 254, 263–65, 291n6;
coalitions for repeal or modification
of, 206–7; fear of "other" and pub-
lic support for, 81; government mon-
itoring and surveillance under, 15,
169, 259; noncitizens impacted by,
162–63, 246; passage of, 254; reauthorization of, 262; secret evidence
use under, 182
*USA Today*, 42, 180

Valentino, Rudolph, 40
Vera Institute, 137, 158, 287nn15,16
Vermeulen, Floris, 100
Vietnamese, 122
Villaraigosa, Antonio, 240
Violent Gang and Terrorist Organization
File, 261–62
Virginia, 256, 259
Volpp, Leti, 62
voluntary interviews, 54, 123, 135,
165–66, 168, 177, 254, 255
voting, 180–81, 232–36, 240, 242, 251,
299n60; political socialization in,
211–13, 217, 299n64

*Wall Street Journal*, 5
War on Terror, 23, 33, 81, 149
War Relocation Authority, 36
Washington, D.C., 85, 159, 191, 233,
240, 283n9; African American Mus-
lims in, 94; community-based orga-
nizations in, 102; Day of Action to
Restore Law and Justice in, 196;
Islamophobia in, 216; Million Man
March in, 229
Washington, Harold, 279n20
*Washington Post*, 65, 152
Watanabe, Teresa, 32
White House Commission of Aviation
Safety and Security, 141–42
Whitney Biennial, 197
Wiesenfeld, Jeffrey, 153
Wilgoren, Jodi, 89
Wilson, Joe, 261

| | |
|---|---|
| Text: | 10/13 Sabon |
| Display: | Akzidenz Grotesk |
| Compositor: | BookComp, Inc. |
| Indexer: | Ruth Elwell |
| Illustrator: | Bill Nelson |
| Printer and binder: | Sheridan Books, Inc. |